Recruiting, Interviewing, Selecting & Orienting New Employees

Fourth Edition

Other Books by Diane Arthur

The Employee Recruitment and Retention Handbook (2001)

Recruiting, Interviewing, Selecting & Orienting New Employees, Third Edition (1998; also published in the People's Republic of China in 2000)

The Complete Human Resources Writing Guide (1997)

Managing Human Resources in Small & Mid-Sized Companies, Second Edition (1995)

Workplace Testing: An Employer's Guide to Policies and Practices (1994)

Recruiting, Interviewing, Selecting & Orienting New Employees, Second Edition (1991)

Managing Human Resources in Small & Mid-Sized Companies (1987)

Recruiting, Interviewing, Selecting & Orienting New Employees (1986; also published in Colombia in 1987)

Self-Study Publications by Diane Arthur

Fundamentals of Human Resources Management, Fourth Edition (2004)

Successful Interviewing: Techniques for Hiring, Coaching, and Performance Meetings (2000)

Success Through Assertiveness (1980)

RECRUITING, INTERVIEWING, SELECTING & ORIENTING NEW EMPLOYEES

Fourth Edition

DIANE ARTHUR

AMACOM
American Management Association
New York • Atlanta • Brussels • Chicago • Mexico City • San Francisco
Shanghai • Tokyo • Toronto • Washington, D.C.

This publication is designed to provide accurate and authoritative information in regard to the subject matter covered. It is sold with the understanding that the publisher is not engaged in rendering legal, accounting, or other professional service. If legal advice or other expert assistance is required, the services of a competent professional person should be sought.

Library of Congress Cataloging-in-Publication Data

Arthur, Diane.
    Recruiting, interviewing, selecting & orienting new employees / Diane Arthur.— 4th ed.
       p. cm.
    Includes index.
    ISBN 0-8144-0861-3 (hardcover)
    1. Employees—Recruiting.   2. Employment interviewing.   3. Employee selection.   4. Employee orientation.   I. Title: Recruiting, interviewing, selecting, and orienting new employees.   II. Title.

HF5549.5.R44A75   2006
658.3'11—dc22

2005015775

Printing number

10   9   8   7   6   5   4   3   2   1

To My Top Selections
Warren, Valerie, and Vicki

Contents

Preface

The primary focus of *Recruiting, Interviewing, Selecting & Orienting New Employees*, published first in 1986, then in 1991, and most recently in 1998, remains unaltered: It is still a comprehensive guide through the four stages of the employment process identified in the book's title. The book's wide-based readership is also the same: HR specialists who need in-depth information about the entire employment process; non-HR professionals whose jobs encompass select employment-related responsibilities; and seasoned HR practitioners looking for a refresher in one or more recruiting, interviewing, selecting, or orientation subcategories. The methods and techniques described continue to be applicable to all work environments: corporate and non-profit, union and nonunion, technical and nontechnical, large and small. They also pertain to both professional and nonprofessional positions. And the book continues to be useful as a reference for training workshops in various aspects of the employment process, and as a text for college and other courses dealing with employment issues.

That said, as a reflection of today's evolving workforce, economy, and interviewing trends, several topics have been added, expanded upon, or otherwise revised in this fourth edition. For example, an entirely new first chapter explores why recruitment efforts often fail, how to attract and compete for applicants, and what workers expect from their employers. It also examines the unsettling trend of outsourcing jobs. A related chapter on recruitment sources provides an expanded look at traditional and innovative recruitment sources. And the chapter on electronic recruiting receives a makeover, including a long-awaited proposed definition of applicants and a look at electronic recruiting risks.

The book's coverage of the interviewing stage is expanded to encompass the right fit and important questions interviewers should ask themselves before job applicants ask them. A new chapter on types of employment interviews explores seven different configurations, including video, departmental, and peer interviews.

The portion of the book devoted to selection has a new look, beginning with the chapter on documentation, which has been expanded to include a comparison between taking notes and using forms. Readers will also find useful the chapter on background and reference checks, complete with valuable legal guidelines and reference and background checklists.

The section on orientation reflects evolving methods of organizational and departmental indoctrination as we take a look at online versus traditional orientation programs, a blended approach to learning, partner programs, and onboarding.

From an organizational standpoint, this fourth edition reflects feedback from readers who have suggested that the book would be easier to navigate if there were four sections that replicate the topics identified in the book's title. Some people have indicated that they may only want to focus on one or more segments at a given time and would like to be able to turn to specific topics with ease; others have said that they like to know absolutely when one stage of the process ends and another begins. Hence, the fourth edition takes a more compartmentalized approach, offering four distinct parts: recruitment, interviewing, selection, and orientation.

As with previous editions, readers are cautioned on two points: First, any reference made to specific publications, websites, services, or institutions is for informational purposes only and is not to be considered an endorsement. Second, this book is not intended to provide legal advice.

Recruiting, interviewing, selecting, and orienting new employees are tangible skills. How well you practice these skills will directly affect many common organizational problem areas, such as turnover, employee morale, and absenteeism. By diligently implementing the methods described in this book, your organization can greatly improve its employment efforts and levels of employee productivity.

D. A.

RECRUITING, INTERVIEWING, SELECTING & ORIENTING NEW EMPLOYEES

Fourth Edition

PART I

Recruiting

Recruitment Challenges

Anita Norris sits in Damien Lanyard's office, looking somewhat dejected. As the assistant vice president of human resources (HR) at Cromwell, Inc., a computer sales/service firm with approximately 2,000 employees, Anita is in charge of company-wide recruiting. Over the past six months Cromwell has experienced several major challenges with regard to recruitment, including an inability to attract quality applicants. Damien, the vice president of HR, rocks quietly in his chair for a moment before asking what Anita anticipates: "What's going on here? We've got jobs staying open for weeks before filling them. When we do fill them we're not getting the cream of the crop. I'm told we're not sufficiently responsive to workers' expectations, and word is that new hires are nervous about joining us because of increased overseas outsourcing. So, Anita, what's going on and how can we fix this?"

This fictitious scenario is playing out for real in numerous businesses nationwide. With a roller-coaster-like economy that continues to confound labor experts, employers hesitate to launch aggressive recruitment efforts, despite knowing that jobs will remain unfilled, existing workers will become overstressed and unmotivated, and productivity and quality of services or products could ultimately decline. Conflicting newspaper reports support a collective sense of confusion. For example, consider these headlines from two papers on the same day, January 8, 2005: *The New York Times* reported, "Jobs Picture Shows Some Signs of Life"; *Newsday* stated, "Job Growth Disappoints."[1]

An offshoot of an unstable economic recovery that impacts recruitment is the increasing number of employers that are requiring new hires to sign noncompete agreements in an attempt to keep what talent they have from leaving and working for the competition. These enforceable contracts, barring employees from working for competitors in the future or from working on projects for a competing product, often result in costly litigation when violated. They also increase hard feelings between competitors and limit future options for employees. Upon learning of a prospective employer's noncompete requirement, applicants may balk and opt to decline an offer of employment rather than sign.

In addition to the economy, there are other factors that inhibit recruitment efforts. For example, consider the alarming impact of illiteracy in this country. According to literacy experts, 20 percent of the population of the United States cannot read or write English proficiently.[2] That translates into a large group of people that are unemployable, underemployed, or concealing their illiteracy from their employers. The pool of available workers to hire from is affected; billions of dollars in profits are lost each year; problems of declining competitiveness, both nationally and internationally, result; and workers who cannot read instructions may endanger the lives of coworkers.

Age is another issue that hinders recruitment efforts as "baby boomers" continue to age and contemplate retirement. According to the Department of Labor Statistics, the number of adults in the "retirement" bracket of age 55 and older will grow by 18 million between 2002 and 2012. The number of adults ages 16–54, on the other hand, will have grown by only a third of that number: a mere 6 million. The news grows more sobering: Adults age 55 and over are expected to begin leaving the workforce "in droves" beginning in 2008, leaving a ". . . big demographic hole behind them."[3]

To echo our HR vice president Damien, "What's going on and how can we fix this?"

How to Make Recruitment Efforts Succeed

Every employer is dealing with the same fluctuating economy, an equivalent percentage of workforce illiteracy, an identically high number of retiring boomers, and the same disappointingly low number of incoming, younger workers; yet some employers are more successful than others in their recruitment efforts. While the resources successful recruiters use make a difference (see Chapter 2), there's more to it than that. To achieve the best possible results, proactive employers apply as many of the twenty-six "ABC Guidelines for Successful Recruitment" as possible every time they have a job opening.

ABC Guidelines for Successful Recruitment

As soon as you know there's going to be a job opening, either because of a vacancy or the creation of a new position, kick these twenty-six "ABC Guidelines for Successful Recruitment" into high gear.[4] This means being:

*   *Attractive.* Promote your organization as the kind of place employees will want to call their place of work. Highlight your most generous and unique benefits, have employees promote your attributes among friends, and publicly pat yourself on the back for accomplishments. In addition, convert failures or shortcomings into attributes. For example, try stating something like this: "Last year you read about our competition; now it's our turn! We've already surpassed Drexel's profits by 40 percent and we've just gotten started! Join a winning team—work for Hartman!"

- *Believable.* If what you're offering sounds too good to be true, repackage your wares. Skeptical applicants shouldn't have to cross-examine interviewers to determine if your hard-to-believe advertised benefits package is real.

- *Centered.* Identify and focus on anywhere from three to six critical, job-specific competencies; that is, qualities or traits that contribute to a person's ability to effectively perform the duties and responsibilities of a given job. Clearly communicate and adhere to them in your recruitment efforts. For example, here are key competencies that may be identified for a project manager: being able to apply technical expertise to solve business problems; ability to focus on key elements of a project; capable of motivating and working effectively with a wide range of people; and ability to negotiate in order to accomplish goals.

- *Diligent.* Effective recruiting requires a steady and energetic application of effort across the board.

- *Empathetic.* Try to understand and take into consideration an applicant's needs and interests in relation to organizational goals, in order to strike a balance and find common denominators between the two. For example, if an applicant expresses an interest in becoming an integral member of the management team within five years, but the job he's applying for is a support position with little likelihood of promotion, it's likely he'll grow disenchanted and leave.

- *Flexible.* If you've tried one recruitment source and it's not yielding the kind of results you need, move on to others. Do this even if it's a recruitment source you've relied heavily on in the past, with good results.

- *Greedy.* Tell yourself that your company is entitled to be staffed by the best possible workforce, and seek out those applicants that maximally meet your needs. Aim high, but be realistic.

- *Hip.* Stay informed and current when it comes to the latest developments in recruitment, as well as what sources and techniques your competitors are using.

- *Informative.* Anticipate what applicants are likely to want to know about a job and your company and be prepared to tell them, either verbally or in the form of some written material, a CD-ROM, or online.

- *Judicious.* Exercise sound judgment when matching applicants with jobs. Avoid decisions ruled by emotion.

- *Knowledgeable.* Be thoroughly familiar with the parameters of the job, how it interfaces with other positions, the department, and the company. Also, be aware of how other organizations view this job in terms of responsibility, status, and compensation.

- *Linear.* Think in terms of a series of straight lines connecting the applicant, the job, and the company. This practice helps keep you on track to accomplish your goal of filling staffing openings as quickly as possible with the most suitable employee.

- *More.* Review your current recruitment efforts and think of whether you could be doing more. In fact, take each of the keywords in these guidelines and ask yourself if you can be *more* attractive, *more* believable, *more* centered, *more* diligent, and so on.

- *Notorious.* Strive to become the brand-name organization everyone talks about. Your goal is to become the company that job applicants want to work for and other companies want to imitate.

- *Open-Minded.* Whether you're recruiting IT specialists, engineers, or secretaries, view the job from the applicant's perspective. Ask employees in the classifications you're trying to fill to identify key elements of the job so that you can emphasize those significant aspects to applicants.

- *Persistent.* Continue exploring various recruitment sources until you find the right employee. Resist pressure to settle or compromise your standards if you're unable to fill an opening right away. Rather, reexamine the sources you've chosen and adjust as needed.

- *Quick.* The moment you discover you're going to have an opening, act on it. Spread the word among employees, run an ad, do whatever you can to spread the word that you have a job to fill.

- *Realistic.* It's one thing to seek out the best possible applicant for a job and to be persistent about it, yet quite another to hold out for the ideal employee who may only exist on paper or in your mind. Adhering to job-specific competencies will enable you to remain realistic.

- *Sensible.* Carefully determine the best recruitment source based on a number of factors, including the nature of the job and the current job market.

- *Tireless.* If you relax your recruitment efforts, chances are another organization will grab the applicant you failed to pursue.

- *Unified.* Make certain everyone concerned with the recruiting effort is working toward the same goal—that is, that they're in agreement with regard to the qualities and skills being sought.

- *Vocal.* If there are agencies or other firms assisting your company with a job search, then openly and clearly express to them the qualities and skills you need in an applicant.

- *Watchful.* Look for signs that confirm the recruitment sources you're using are producing the kinds of results wanted, and that the applicants coming forth possess needed qualities.

- *"Xentigious."* I made this word up (the last two syllables rhyme with *litigious*) to mean "keep it legal." Regardless of how desperate you are to fill an opening, never, ever, step outside the boundaries of what's legal—it's not worth it.

- *Youthful.* Be youthful both in thinking and spirit in order to compete for top performers, especially the scarce but vitally important group of younger workers. Specifically, think in terms of what's important to younger workers in relation to working conditions, hours, perks, and the like.

- *Zealous.* Applicants are more likely to be interested in becoming part of a company if the recruiters are enthusiastic and appear to genuinely enjoy working there. Accordingly, consider briefly sharing some of your experiences with the company, offering vivid images of what it's like to work there.

Let's take a look at how these guidelines may be applied to an actual recruiting situation. Roger, a customer service representative, has just informed Anita (our assistant VP of HR at Cromwell, Inc.) of his intentions to resign, offering two weeks' notice. She knows there's no one else in the company who can do Roger's job; that means she has to find a replacement from the outside and bring that person on board, ideally before Roger leaves. It's going to be a challenge, and Anita needs to begin her search immediately (*quick*).

She begins by listing the primary qualities she needs in a customer service rep: excellent interpersonal skills, the ability to be empathetic, and good listening skills. She thinks for a moment and then adds "interested in improving departmental procedures" (*centered*). Now where could she go to find someone fast? Anita recalls a colleague from the last regional meeting of HR practitioners who commented that she'd had luck using a particular agency when replacing customer service reps (*hip* and *sensible*). Anita has successfully used this agency in the past, and decides to get in touch with them now. She e-mails the following message to Jim, her agency contact:

> Call me **ASAP** re: immed. open. for a **CS** rep. $ is so-so, but bene-fits are super, incl. health club member, 4 wks. vacation, and on-site med. services (*attractive*). In fact, I'm pretty sure we offer a better benefits package than anyone else in our business (*believable*), but you probably shouldn't say that. Instead, I'll give app's a copy of our benefits video when they come in for interviews (*informative*). Send app's to me since I know the job thoroughly (*knowledgeable*). Jim, we need someone who has great interpersonal skills, listens well, and is empathetic. Also, someone who's interested in getting involved (*vocal*). Ideally, I'd like to see applicants with experience in our industry (*greedy*), but I'll consider folks with **CS** exper. elsewhere. The important thing is that we get someone who can do the job and will work well in this environment (*linear*). As always, stress to anyone interested that we pride ourselves on being an **EOE** and won an award last year for our efforts in workplace diversity (*xentigious*).

As soon as she finishes e-mailing Jim, Anita calls her employee relations manager, June. "Would you please post Roger's opening? I don't think we've got anyone in-house for the job, but let's be sure. I also want to let our staff know so they have a chance to make referrals. Oh, and call Josh at the ad agency and see if we can make the deadline for the next issue of *All the News*. Come down to my office this afternoon and I'll give you the particulars (*flexible*)."

Anita sticks her head out of her office and calls out to one of her HR reps. "Sandy, got a minute? I need your help." Sandy gets up from his desk and approaches Anita's door. "What's going on?" "Roger is leaving and we need to fill his job fast. I'm going to need you to stay on top of the details for me; you know, screening applicants on the phone, lining up interviews, that sort of thing. We've got to be organized and focused—he's only given us two weeks' notice (*diligent*)."

Anita sits back in her chair and reflects on what she has done thus far with regard to the customer service opening. She's satisfied that she had started the recruitment search appropriately and had everyone working toward the same goal (*unified*).

The next morning Anita receives a call from Jim. "I've got two top-notch people for you to see; both with prior experience. One of them says he's heard good things about your company and was hoping something would open up so he could apply (*notorious*)." Anita schedules appointments with both applicants for later that day. Meanwhile, she learns from June that one of their employees has referred a friend of his for the job. Anita schedules him for an interview as well.

Before meeting the three applicants, Anita goes over a checklist of things to do: She reminds herself to try and understand the applicants' needs and interests in relation to company goals (*empathetic*), exercise sound judgment based on skills and abilities (*judicious*), and be practical in making a selection (*realistic*). She also knows applicants are more likely to be interested in joining the company if she comes across as enthusiastic, so she thinks of a few especially interesting experiences she's had with Cromwell since joining the company (*zealous*).

Anita interviews the three applicants and comes away unimpressed. She contacts Jim to ensure that he understands the qualities she's seeking. Then she talks to June to make certain employees understand the nature of the job before making referrals (*watchful*), and to confirm that an ad will run in the next edition of *All the News* (*persistent* and *tireless*). Anita leaves her office disappointed, but not disheartened. She knows she's applying the ABC Guidelines for Successful Recruitment, thereby improving her chances of finding a good replacement for Roger. She just has to persevere.

How to Attract and Compete for Qualified Applicants

Despite the economy's impact on employment—that is, regardless of who's in the "driver's seat" at any given point, applicants or employers—it's critical that recruiters continuously work hard to attract and compete for top performers. Applicants have their own personal lists of "must haves," even during times of high unemployment when people are likely to be less selective and more grateful for a job— sometimes any job. If forced to deviate from that list and take a job they really don't want, chances are when the market shifts (and it will), they'll act on harbored feelings of resentment and leave at their earliest opportunity. A workforce of disgruntled workers is guaranteed to hurt even the most successful business.

Here, then, is my advice with regard to attracting and competing for applicants: Go after applicants with no less vigor during your most productive, profitable times than you do during your worst. It will keep your skills sharpened and you'll earn a reputation for being fair, as opposed to self-serving. A reputation for fairness can earn you big points when the economy shifts to work against you.

That said, let's look at some specific ways of attracting applicants. Keep in mind that this discussion is not about recruitment sources—we'll discuss those in Chapter 2; rather, it is about determining what you have to offer that would make someone want to be your employee. Remember, while you're interviewing applicants and deciding if they're right for your company, they're interviewing you and deciding if you're the right fit for them.

All That Glitters . . .

Let's get the issue of miscellaneous "stuff" out of the way right up-front. Giveaways are great, but too much in the way of freebies and perks can come across as little more than an attempt to "buy" an applicant. In addition, employees quickly become accustomed to these perks, whether it's bringing pets to work, concierge services, or free catered lunches. If unmotivated by their jobs, employees will probably grow restless and simply require more stuff. To avoid earning the reputation of being long on talk and short on substance, as well as incurring high turnover costs, you need to put as much energy and thought into keeping employees motivated as you devote to your efforts to attract them.

If you're determined to offer tangible goods as a means of attracting applicants, follow these two simple rules:

1. *Find out what your competitors are giving away.* If you can match or top their perks, fine; just be careful not to get caught up in a game of who can "out-gift" whom.
2. *Offer these perks regardless of market conditions.* You'll be perceived as generous when the economy favors employers, and consistent when it favors applicants and employees.

Better yet, get personal. A shotgun approach to perks may find a few targets, but you're likely to be more successful if your giveaways suit the personal tastes of the recipients. Personalization also shows effort and interest on your part and is more likely to accomplish the desired results. While you certainly can't be expected to know what each individual likes, there are a few approaches that will more closely appeal to everyone's tastes. One is to offer would-be employees catalogs from which they can choose gift items. Another is to have generic categories, such as 'membership," and allow recipients the option of perhaps joining a health club rather than a country club. You might also have a list of a dozen or so comparably valued perks and allow applicants to chose three that appeal to them.

What You See . . .

Many years ago I went on a job interview with a publishing firm in New York City. I sat opposite the desk of my interviewer, with my back to the open doorway. Within minutes, I became uncomfortably aware that my interviewer's attention had been diverted by a conversation between two employees outside his door. They were speaking rather loudly, so I couldn't help but hear them discussing an applicant they had seen for the position I was there to interview for. If that wasn't awkward enough, my interviewer then called out, "Hey! Come and talk to me when I'm done here! I'd like to hear more about her!" The interview continued, but it was over as far as I was concerned. When they called me back for a second meeting, I declined.

Negative impressions can have a lasting effect, especially if they occur during the initial contact with a prospective employer. Consider these examples of poor first impressions, and imagine being on the receiving end:

- A recruiter for a top financial services firm schedules a recent graduate from a top school for a series of interviews, keeps her waiting, and then, without explanation or apology, has the receptionist announce that the interview needs to be rescheduled.

- An interviewer for an insurance company eats lunch during his meeting with a prospective employee, stating that he doesn't have time for both lunch and the interview.

- An applicant for a printing/graphics company has to compete with the radio as her interviewer explains that he wouldn't miss for anything an important announcement concerning his favorite team.

- A recruiter excuses herself to discuss fabric swatches with her interior decorator during the course of an interview.

Would you be interested in working for any of these companies?

While there's no excuse for behaving rudely at any stage of the employment process, exhibiting bad manners at the outset can be especially damaging. An applicant is not invested at this stage and thus is usually able to walk away with little more than a loss of time. The company, on the other hand, stands to lose a potentially valuable employee and earn a reputation for being an undesirable place to work. In addition, organizations need to bear in mind that applicants are far more than just potential employees: They are likely to be consumers of your product and could well end up working for your competition. Word about an employer's hiring practices spreads fast, and you can count on applicants sharing their job search experiences with others.

According to Tom Rath, global practice leader of the Gallup Organization in Washington, D.C., "One thing that we've found with prospective employees is that it is rare that someone walks away from a job application in a neutral state of mind. It is always either a positive or a negative point of view."[5]

That said, it's not difficult for businesses to earn a reputation as an attractive place in which to work by taking steps to ensure that they project a positive first impression. This can be accomplished in ten effortless ways:

1. Allot a sufficient amount of time so i
2. Apologize if you're running late.
3. Be courteous.
4. Be prepared.
5. Display a sense of pride in and invc
6. Exhibit enthusiasm and interest.
7. Keep appointments.
8. Promptly acknowledge and respor
9. Remain professional at all times.
10. Stay focused on the applicant dur

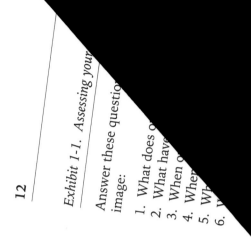

Exhibit 1-1. Assessing your

Answer these questio image:

1. What does o
2. What hav
3. When o
4. Wher
5. W
6.

12

Brand Image as a Competitive Edge

With a projected mass exodus of boomers from the workforce and a dearth of younger workers to replace them, and with 20 percent of the U.S. population unable to read or write English proficiently, an unstable economy, and increased outsourcing of jobs (discussed further below), competing for qualified applicants is growing more intense.

One of the most effective ways for businesses to compete for qualified applicants is to enhance their overall brand image.[6] But what if your company name isn't a household word? What if no one outside your immediate geographic area knows who you are? Given the current competitive nature of recruiting, is there time to become known?

On the surface, these seem like plausible and even insurmountable concerns. A company's brand is what differentiates its products or services from others. Recruiters from well-known businesses need not describe to applicants what it is that they make or do. Think about companies like Microsoft, Procter & Gamble, Sara Lee, Disney, and PepsiCo, and you will immediately conjure up an image of their product. Some companies are so well known that all you have to do is mention their initials, like IBM, HP, 3M, or AT&T. Yet others are quickly recognized simply by their logos, such as Nike and McDonald's. With recognition comes a sense of identity, or what their brands stand for. For example, Rolex stands for quality, Burger King means fast food, and Starbucks represents trendy coffee. But while it's certainly true that lesser-known and unknown organizations must work hard at cultivating their brand image, even those giants that are household names work at brand redevelopment. The bottom line is every organization needs to hone its brand image.

Brands involve public perception. Exhibit 1-1 is a simple yet revealing questionnaire you can use to start thinking about your organization's overall image and what you can do to enhance it.

Companies can't let down their guard even after they've hired employees. Top performers have been known to accept a job offer and then back out or just not show *organization's overall image.*

...ns to learn what you can do to enhance your organization's overall

...ur organization stand for?
...e our customers/clients come to expect from us?
...ur company's name is mentioned, what are people likely to envision?
...our name is mentioned, what would we like people to envision?
...at must we do to get people to change how they envision us?
...Which of the following words or terms are people likely to associate with our product or service?

Cleanliness	Innovative
Consistency	Integrity
Dependability	Quality
Fun	Quick service
Good service	Reliability
Good value	Safety
Other _____	

7. Which of the following words or terms do we *want* people to associate with our product or service?

Cleanliness	Innovative
Consistency	Integrity
Dependability	Quality
Fun	Quick service
Good service	Reliability
Good value	Safety
Other _____	

8. What must we do if we want to be perceived as more _____?

up. Recommendations for avoiding this result include shortening the amount of time between job offers and starting dates, negotiating offers quickly, and offering signing bonuses, especially for hard-to-fill openings.

Lightening Up

I was once asked to conduct a training program for an investment bank. As we began to discuss the contents of the workshop, the HR manager interrupted and said, "I'm less concerned with the 'what' than I am with the 'how.' How are you going to keep the managers interested in the subject matter?" That was a fair question, so I proceeded to describe some of the learning techniques I thought were appropriate. Once again, he interrupted, this time to ask, "What I mean is, do you have any games that they can play?" I was silent for a moment. As a matter of fact I did, but this was an investment bank—not exactly what comes to mind when you think of playing games. The HR manager anticipated my reaction and responded by saying, "I know what you're thinking: This is a serious environment where we keep our heads down and work, work, work. That's not far from the truth, and that's why we need a change. The managers need to loosen up a little; wouldn't you agree?" I was delighted to comply, and went on to talk about some of my favorite "fun" training tools.

Does fun belong in the workplace? A lot of people think so. In 2002, the Society for Human Resource Management (SHRM) surveyed its membership about this very subject.[7] More than 75 percent of the nearly 600 respondents replied affirmatively. While there is some disagreement as to whether the best sort of fun is planned (e.g., staging contests and competitions, holding theme days, providing "joy breaks" for workers to listen to comedy tapes or read cartoons, arranging entertainment, etc.) or should be encouraged to develop spontaneously, respondents agree overwhelmingly that there isn't nearly enough fun going on at work.

Everyone, to a lesser or greater extent, likes to laugh and have fun. Typically, "play" is reserved for off-hours, before coming to or after leaving work. But playing and having fun during working hours does not negate productivity; rather, productivity is actually enhanced by fun. SHRM's survey found that proponents of fun work environments are better able to attract applicants and experience an increase in degrees of employee enthusiasm, group cohesiveness, employee satisfaction, and employee creativity. Conversely, they see a decline in anxiety and stress, boredom, turnover, absenteeism, and interpersonal conflicts.

Opponents may express concern over the possible negative repercussions resulting from fun at work; they cite the risks of equipment damage, sexual harassment claims, and increased errors. In reality, SHRM reports, businesses that do not promote fun have higher incidence rates in each of these areas.

Southwest Airlines tops any list of companies that promote fun in the workplace. Indeed, its cofounder and CEO, Herb Kelleher, was once nicknamed "The High Priest of Ha-Ha" by *Fortune* magazine. He is quoted as saying:

> **If you feel real good about coming to work, if you feel real good about what you're doing, if you feel you are doing something for a meaningful cause and you're having fun while you're doing it, then you look forward to coming to work. You don't succumb to stress as easily and you cooperate with other people more quickly and more easily. If you have a sense of humor, it tends to not allow you to make mountains out of molehills.[8]**

Another company that encourages fun at work is PETsMART, Inc. in Phoenix, Arizona. Carol Cox, senior vice president of HR, has said, "We want to get across who and what we are, and what our culture and style are, so we can attract the right applicants. What we say to people is that it is a fun, warm, and very caring atmosphere."[9]

Yet another example of a business that recognizes the importance of fun in the workplace is Nextel Communications, where managers have been known to distribute toys in the call center, hold carnivals and festivals, and conduct game shows to positively encourage the workforce. Employees with perfect attendance can spin a wheel and earn "funny money," which they can use to purchase merchandise from the Nextel catalog.[10]

These and similar innovations will give you an edge when it comes to competing for qualified applicants.

Workers' Expectations

Here's my favorite illustration of workers' expectations: While waiting for a colleague to arrive for a breakfast meeting, I became increasingly aware of the group of four people seated at the table next to mine in the restaurant. Although the table was round, three members of the group were clustered so closely together that they actually appeared to be seated across from the fourth person, a young man around twenty-five years of age. The collective body language on the part of the trio seemed adversarial. Dressed in dark-colored, conservative business suits, they sat tall in their seats, arms folded across their chests, chins pointed slightly upward, eyes focused intently on the young man across the table. While all three were smiling, their smiles seemed forced and strained. I glanced at the recipient of this rather hostile display to see how he was reacting. I was surprised to observe that he was not only undisturbed, but he actually seemed to be enjoying himself. Wearing casual trousers and a short-sleeved shirt, he sat with his chair pushed back from the table, the ankle of his right leg crossed over his left knee, posture slightly slouched. He rocked gently in his chair as he lazily twiddled his thumbs and grinned widely at the trio across from him. The portion of the interview that I overheard went something like this:

Interviewer 1: As you know, we've put together an extremely generous package of pay, health benefits, and perks. Everything we discussed at our last meeting is included.

Interviewer 2: I've got to say, nobody ever offered me anything even close to this package when I started!

Interviewer 3: So now that you've had a chance to look everything over, I'm sure you'll agree that everything you could possibly want is included. All that's left is for you to say yes!

What followed was an uncomfortably long period of silence. The interviewers shifted nervously in their seats until the applicant finally spoke.

Applicant (speaking slowly): I just don't know if I'm ready to make a decision.

Interviewer 2 (leaning forward, hands clasped): Listen. I've been authorized to sweeten the pot a bit more. Say yes right now and we'll throw in a $5,000 signing bonus!

The applicant didn't say a word. Instead, he pushed his seat back further and focused his gaze downward.

Interviewer 3 (nervously): We're giving you everything you asked for. What else do you want?

At this point, the applicant pulled his chair in close to the table, cupped his face in his hands, and looked at each interviewer in turn.

Applicant (using a slow, deliberate tone): I want you to offer me something no other employee has. Then maybe I'll come to work for you.

The three interviewers were visibly shaken. After several uncomfortable moments the process continued.

Interviewer 1 (quietly): We believe we've offered you an exceedingly comprehensive package and the opportunity to work for a fine organization. We weren't prepared to go beyond that. However, if you could be more specific about what it is you want, perhaps we can work something out.

Applicant (smiling): I don't know. I guess I don't really want or need anything else. But I appreciate the fact that you'd consider offering me more. I think I've heard what I need to know. Let's say we have a deal.

Granted, this unnerving scene took place in the 1990s when the job market was bright and applicants clearly had the upper hand. But remember what I said earlier about continuously working hard to attract and compete for qualified applicants: Employers need to be ever vigilant about what workers want, regardless of who's driving the economy at any given time.

What Matters Most

No one should claim that money doesn't matter. Regardless of all the theories about motivation, money often weighs heavily in determining whether a person takes or stays with a job. Aside from meeting both real and perceived needs, money continues to be a key factor in how we rate one another. That is, our worth is determined, to a large extent, by how much we make today, in relation to what we were making, say, five years ago, as well as in comparison with what others in comparable positions earn.

But there are other factors that are just as motivating as money, and job applicants and employees continuously tell employers what these are, albeit sometimes indirectly. For example, when positions remain open for a long time, it could be due to ineffective recruitment sources, but it could also be because applicants aren't excited by what the company is offering. Quick resignations could be the result of employees getting better offers, or it could be because a recruiter painted an inaccurate picture of the job. High turnover figures could be attributable to many causes, including ineffective employer/employee relations; it could also be due to a lackluster work environment in which employees feel undervalued.

Sometimes applicants and employees clearly verbalize exactly what it is they expect from their employers. According to a survey conducted by CareerBuilder.com, 82 percent of some 1,200 full-time workers stated that a safe work environment was the most important element of a job. Other key "job satisfiers" included good relations with direct supervisors, career growth opportunities, and sociability with peers.[11]

In another survey conducted by TrueCareers, 40 percent of respondents expressed a keen interest in protecting their financial stability by negotiating severance agreements and outplacement assistance before committing to a job.[12] This sends employers a clear message that many applicants are evaluating career options based on what would happen in the event of a layoff.

Too often employers assume they know what's best for employees. This frequently happens with regard to benefits. Some employers are exceedingly generous in terms of their offerings; unfortunately, they fail to take into account individual needs and preferences. For example, a twentysomething single worker is more likely to favor free pet insurance over prepaid child-care services. On the other hand, older "sandwich generation" workers, responsible for children and their aging parents, might respond favorably to elder-care provisions. Assumptions concerning compensation can also backfire. Not everyone is interested in stock awards or a cookie-cutter 401(k) plan.

What this means is that employers would do well to 1) survey employees as to their expectations, and 2) wherever possible, offer comparably valued choices in benefits and compensation packages.

Technical applicants, for example, are most interested in jobs where they can work on exciting new products using state-of-the-art technologies. They want each new experience to make them more marketable in the future, so often they can be lured by subsidized education and training programs. Furthermore, they expect immediate rewards rather than promises of future benefits. Since technical workers are trending toward shorter and shorter stints with any given employer (eighteen months is the current average), they would prefer sign-on bonuses and stock options rather than pension plans and other benefits with longer vesting cycles. And, of course, depending on which way the economic winds are blowing, lifestyle can be a key discriminator. Factors such as flextime, flex-dress, and telecommuting often tip the scales when a technical applicant has multiple job offers.

Offshore Outsourcing Jobs

It's a growing trend: More and more businesses nationwide are offshoring jobs; that is, they are assigning work to individuals overseas, leaving U.S. workers—often long-term workers—unemployed. The U.S. Department of Labor, in conjunction with Forrester Research, forecasts an increase of jobs going offshore—from approximately

588,000 jobs in 2005, to more than 3.3 million in 2015.[13] The categories of jobs being outsourced offshore include: management, business, computer, architecture, life sciences, legal, art design, sales, and office. The group that is expected to be impacted the greatest is office workers, where 296,000 jobs outsourced offshore in 2005 will grow to 1.7 million jobs in 2015. Next comes computer jobs, increasing from 109,000 to 473,000; business, from 61,000 to 348,000; and management, from 37,000 to 288,000. The smallest changes are expected to affect art design, life sciences, and legal services. Falling somewhere in between is sales and architecture.

According to Graham S. Toft, a senior fellow and director of the Center for Economic Competitiveness at the Hudson Institute in Indianapolis, this dramatic increase in offshore outsourcing is attributable to three factors:

1. Education abroad has improved.
2. Investment capital diverted to China and India is more supportive of existing or new businesses.
3. Companies are facing pricing pressures as a result of an increasingly competitive global market.[14]

In some instances, soon-to-be displaced employees are forced to train their overseas replacements, adding to feelings of resentment among those being terminated and casting a sense of impending gloom over impacted workplaces. There is also concern that this movement is working against organizational gains made with regard to diversity: How can employees be expected to support a concept that nurtures individuality when their jobs are being taken from them and given to those from other cultures? In addition, in an unstable economy where employee loyalty is strained, at best, outsourcing is threatening to cause further erosion.

It's significant to note that many of the employees who are being displaced are valued workers with an appreciable set of skills; that they are being let go for reasons that have nothing whatsoever to do with their abilities only adds to a sense of bitterness. It also contrasts significantly with the long-standing concept that a person is fired for cause because of incompetence, insubordination, or dishonesty.

Offshore Outsourcing Drawbacks

Critics of offshore outsourcing point to the loss of high-paying jobs and technical knowledge to workers in foreign countries. In addition, there is concern over its negative impact on employee productivity and morale. In a SHRM Weekly Online Poll, conducted on March 23, 2004, nearly 400 survey participants were asked to respond to this question: "In general, how much of an impact do you think offshoring has had on U.S. employee productivity and morale?"[15] The responses with regard to employee productivity are shown in Exhibit 1-2, while the responses with regard to employee morale appear in Exhibit 1-3.

In another survey, this one a national study of information technology workers conducted by the Washington Alliance of Technology Workers, 93 percent of the

Exhibit 1-2. SHRM survey results: Impact of offshoring on U.S. worker productivity.

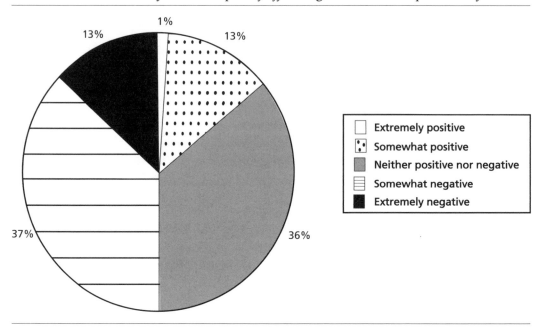

Exhibit 1-3. SHRM survey results: Impact of offshoring on U.S. worker morale.

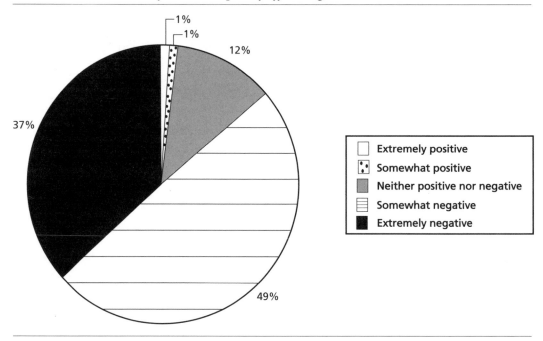

respondents reported that they are concerned about the impact of offshore outsourcing; one in four stated that their companies had resorted to this practice; and more than 50 percent said they were worried that this trend would negatively impact wages and benefits.[16]

Offshore Outsourcing Benefits

There are those who are able to cite benefits to outsourcing.[17] At the top of the plus list is cost savings, since exporting routine jobs can lower costs for businesses by as much as 60 percent. For example, in 2003, the average software engineer in India earned 267,000 rupees a year in combined salary and benefits. That's the equivalent of just under $6,000, as compared with the average U.S. software engineer who earned $78,800. Some corporations claim that they are able to capitalize on time zone differences, thereby speeding up production considerably. Other businesses, such as Computer Associates International Inc., maintain that they have invested in foreign locations because that's where their customers are. Some companies, like the investment banking division of JPMorgan Chase & Co., created junior analyst jobs in India to support its research departments in the United States and Great Britain and boost productivity.

Interestingly, while it was once considered a huge proponent of outsourcing, JPMorgan Chase announced in 2004 that it was ending a $5 billion outsourcing contract with IBM and would rehire nearly 4,000 employees and contractors, claiming that it can meet its technology needs more efficiently in-house.[18]

Other companies that have severed offshore outsourcing agreements, either because projected savings didn't materialize or because they were dissatisfied with services, include Lehman Brothers Inc. and Dell Inc.[19]

Many businesses fail to reveal to their clients that they outsource offshore.

Most jobs that are outsourced overseas go to India. But other countries are also throwing their hats into the ring. According to A. T. Kearney, a global consulting firm, the top-ten countries that are vying for India's number-one position are China, Malaysia, the Czech Republic, Singapore, the Philippines, Brazil, Canada, Chile, Poland, and Hungary.[20]

Summary

Today's employers are compelled to wrestle with numerous recruitment challenges, including an unstable economic recovery that has resulted in an unpopular rise in noncompete agreements; alarmingly high numbers of illiterate workers who are impacting profits and competitiveness; a growing number of baby boomers who are contemplating retirement; and relatively few adults age 16–54 to replace them.

To successfully deal with these challenges, readers are encouraged to apply as many of the ABC Guidelines for Successful Recruitment as possible every time there is an opening. For example, be *attractive* by promoting your organization as the kind of place employees will want to call their place of work.

It's also critical to continuously work hard to attract and compete for top performers, regardless of the state of the economy and who's in the "driver's seat"— applicants or employers. This will keep your recruitment skills sharpened and earn you a reputation for being fair as opposed to self-serving. While offering tangible goods as a means of attracting applicants has some merit, giving too much away can come across as little more than an attempt to "buy" an applicant. If you are going to offer perks, find out what your competitors are giving away. Better yet, strive to have your giveaways suit the personal tastes of the recipients, thereby showing effort and interest on your part. Also, avoid conveying negative impressions, especially those that occur during the initial contact with an applicant. In addition, as part of your initiative to compete for qualified applicants, work to enhance your overall brand image and strive to promote fun in the workplace.

In considering workers' expectations, factor in more than money. Surveys reveal that employees seek a safe work environment, good relations with supervisors, career growth opportunities, and sociability with peers. Money-related items, such as stock options and bonuses, don't rank as high.

Finally, despite growing concern over the negative impact of offshore outsourcing on employee productivity and morale, there are those who cite certain benefits, especially lower costs, that they believe offset the damaging effect on workers.

Notes

1. Edmund L. Andrews, "Jobs Picture Shows Some Signs of Life," *The New York Times* (January 8, 2005), p. C1; and Randi F. Marshall, "Job Growth Disappoints," *Newsday* (January 8, 2005), p. A14.

2. Leslie Kaufman, "Can't Read, Can't Write, Can Hide It," *The New York Times* (October 31, 2004), Section 10, p. 1.

3. Eduardo Porter, "Coming Soon: The Vanishing Work Force," *The New York Times* (August 29, 2004), Section 3, p. 1.

4. These guidelines are based on material from Diane Arthur, *The Employee Recruitment and Retention Handbook* (New York: AMACOM, 2001), pp. 117–122.

5. Gene J. Koprowski, "Rude Awakening," *HR Magazine*, Vol. 49, No. 9 (September 2004), pp. 50–55.

6. Arthur, *The Employee Recruitment and Retention Handbook*, pp. 50–52.

7. "Fun Work Environment Survey" (Alexandria, VA: Society for Human Resource Management, November 2002).

8. Arthur, *The Employee Recruitment and Retention Handbook*, p. 54.

9. Michelle Neely Martinez, "Breaking the Mold," *HR Magazine* Vol. 46, No. 6 (June 2001), pp. 82–90.

10. Laura Stack, "Employees Behaving Badly," *HR Magazine* Vol. 48, No. 10 (October 2003), pp. 111–116.

11. Rebecca Theim, "Gearing Up for Activity Ahead," *Employment Management Today* Vol. 7, No. 2 (Spring 2002).

12. Ibid.

13. "Jobs Going Offshore," U.S. Department of Labor and Forester Research, 2002, cited in Pamela Babcock, "America's Newest Export: White-Collar Jobs," *HR Magazine* Vol. 49, No. 4 (April 2004); available at http://www.shrm.org/hrmagazine/articles/0404/0404 covstory.asp.

14. Pamela Babcock, "America's Newest Export: White-Collar Jobs," *HR Magazine* Vol. 49, No. 4 (April 2004), pp. 50–57.

15. Society for Human Resource Management (SHRM) Weekly Online Poll: March 23, 2004, *QOTW—Offshoring #2* (Alexandria, VA: SHRM Research); available through http://www .shrm.org/hrresources/surveys_published.

16. Stephenie Overman, "Technology Industry Trends," High-Tech Net Forum Library, April 23, 2004 (Alexandria, VA: SHRM); available through http://www.shrm.org/technet/ library_published (SHRM member log-on required).

17. James T. Madore and Pradnya Joshi, "U.S. Loss, Foreign Gain," *Newsday* (March 28, 2004), pp. 36–38.

18. Pradnya Joshi, "Bank to Hire Back Workers," *Newsday* (September 16, 2004), pp. A32 and A36.

19. Babcock, "America's Newest Export: White-Collar Jobs."

20. Maureen Minehan, "Offshore Outsourcing: Not Just About India Anymore," SHRM Global Forum, January 6, 2005; available through http://www.shrm.org/technet/library. May require SHRM member log-on.

CHAPTER 2

Recruitment Sources

"I need a customer service rep—fast!" "I'm losing my public relations manager—do you know anyone who can replace her?" "The employment agency I've been using keeps sending me unqualified applicants; they just don't seem to get what I'm looking for!" "We're getting a ton of resumes in response to our ad for a warehouse supervisor, but no one is qualified!" "Our website is outdated; I'm still getting resumes for a job we filled two weeks ago!" "Our top competitor lost their best technical specialist the same time we did and they hired a dynamite replacement a week later; we still can't find anyone—what are we doing wrong?" "The labor pool keeps changing and I can't keep up. Are we in an economic upswing or downswing this week? Are we in charge or are the employees? Help!"

Can you relate to any of these comments? You're not alone if you can. These are common cries heard these days throughout business, nationwide. Filling a vacancy or a newly created position poses numerous challenges, but it all comes down to this: Where can you find qualified applicants in the least amount of time for the least amount of money? According to the Saratoga Institute, the average time to fill a requisition in 2004 was forty-eight days; the average cost per hire was $2,928. Depending on the job opening and the company's budget, that can be a long time and a lot of money.[1]

Some organizations ignore the multitude of recruitment options and use the same sources each time, albeit with mixed results. For example, a company that relies heavily on newspaper ads should consider the time of year (ads running just before Christmas, for instance, generally do not do well) and even the day of the week (certain jobs attract more applicants in the middle of the week than on weekends). Repeatedly using the same recruitment sources can also make you susceptible to charges of systemic discrimination—the denial of equal employment opportunity through an established business practice such as recruitment. Even though the discrimination may be inadvertent, the disparate effect it produces may develop into a prime area of vulnerability for employers. Relying on the same recruitment source each time a particular position becomes available could have an adverse impact on members of certain protected groups lacking the same access as others to that source. This, in turn, could translate into the inadvertent but no less illegal denial of equal employment opportunity.

Electronic recruitment will be reserved for separate discussion in Chapter 3.

Prerecruitment Considerations

Consider four factors before embarking on a recruitment campaign: how much money is available; how quickly the opening must be filled; whether a wide audience must be reached; and the exemption level of the available position.

Recruitment Budget

The amount of money allocated for recruitment can greatly affect your options. For example, display ads and search firms can cost several thousand dollars with no guarantee of attracting a substantial number of qualified applicants. On the other hand, some of the most effective recruitment sources, such as employee referrals, cost very little.

Mike Sweeny, of T. Williams Consulting, Inc., shares a three-step recruiting cost ratio formula to help organizations determine their recruitment budgets.[2] The process begins with determining total recruiting costs. This is accomplished by adding four cost areas:

1. Fixed overhead recruiting expenses
2. Sourcing expenses attached to specific resources (e.g., advertising)
3. Signing bonuses
4. Expenses associated with travel or relocation

The next step is to determine the total compensation involved; that is, the sum of the annual base starting compensation for all positions. The recruiting cost ratio is then determined by dividing the total recruiting costs by the total compensation figure.

Quick Results Recruitment Sources

Openings can occur suddenly and unexpectedly, usually when employees decide to leave with little or no notice. Being prepared is your best defense. Begin by ensuring that your employee data bank is up-to-date; this way, you can immediately turn to existing staff as an immediate resource, even if it is an interim replacement until you've hired someone permanently. In addition, have an employee referral program in place. Launch it as soon as you know there's an opening, spreading the word to as many employees as possible. Focus, too, on recruitment sources most likely to yield immediate results, such as going through your HR files for applicants who were previously interviewed and assessed. You might do well turning to your preemployment training pool, if you have one, or consider hiring contingency workers as a stopgap measure.

Broad-Based Recruiting

Some positions are highly specialized and more difficult to fill. To improve the chances of a job match, you'll want to reach as many applicants as possible. Also, if uncertain as to the type of individual being sought, you'll want to interview as many applicants as possible.

Employment agencies and search firms may be helpful in these instances, although they tend to recommend nearly everyone when the requirements are broad. Ads in newspapers and journals can be effective also. Consider advertising in out-of-town publications for hard-to-fill openings, being prepared to accommodate the travel needs of viable applicants.

Exemption Status

The Fair Labor Standards Act defines *exempt* employees as workers who are legally exempted from receiving overtime compensation; that is, employers do not have to pay professionals for overtime. The term *nonexempt* literally means "not exempt from overtime compensation," or, stated another way, entitled to receive overtime pay. The distinction is significant in that recruitment sources that produce qualified exempt or professional applicants may not work as well for nonexempt applicants. For example, direct mail recruitment, search firms, campus recruiting, job fairs, research firms, and professional associations could conceivably produce qualified exempt applicants, whereas high school guidance counselors, government agencies, advertising in the classified section of newspapers, and employment agencies will more than likely yield a choice group of nonexempt applicants.

Of the factors indicated—cost, immediacy, audience, and exemption level—a specific recruitment source may meet some criteria but not others. Employers are advised to explore the ramifications of utilizing each resource in relation to these four factors, deciding which are most important for a given job opening.

Newspaper ads provide a prime example. They are expensive, but more likely to yield immediate results. Assuming they appear in the most-likely-to-be-read section of an appropriate paper on the right day of the week at the right time of year and contain the necessary text, newspaper ads will reach a wide audience at the level you're trying to reach.

Proactive and Reactive Recruitment

After examining the four prerecruitment criteria, consider how aggressive you need to be in order to fill a particular opening. If immediacy is a primary factor, search out proactive recruitment sources that will make a concerted effort to find employees. This is the reverse of reactive recruitment, where you wait for applicants to apply, hoping that the right person is among them.

Some recruitment sources are inherently reactive, by their very nature prohibiting recruiters from aggressively pursuing applicants. Consider one of the most popular recruitment sources, employee referrals. HR provides employees with the job description and a list of requirements, then waits to see who applies. The onus for referring applicants is on the employees. This is cost-effective and could work if time is not a factor. For example, perhaps you have an employee who wants to retire but is willing to wait until a replacement is found, or maybe a department head is thinking about creating a new position but doesn't need to fill it immediately. More often than not, however, time is crucial. When an employee resigns, you usually need to move fast, and that means being proactive.

Proactive recruiters start looking for a replacement as soon as they learn of an opening. They expand their recruitment pool to encompass other than traditional recruiting sources and aggressively go after applicants, luring them with attractive employment packages. Such packages are not only offered by large, "money is no object" companies. Any organization can put together a tempting offer reflecting such items as shared decision making, child- and elder-care referrals, suggestion/ award programs, health club memberships, and company-sponsored social affairs. One small publishing firm provides each employee with a complete turkey dinner at Thanksgiving. An electronics company, located in snowy New Hampshire, gives each worker ten free skiing lessons. Once free of traditional thoughts when it comes to "perks," there's no limit to the cost-effective extras you can offer applicants.

Being proactive means more than avoiding a lengthy gap between the time an incumbent vacates a position and someone new is hired. When you're in control of who's being targeted you're more likely to find qualified applicants. With direct mail recruiting, for example, employers contact specific applicants known to have certain skills and knowledge. While the response rate is usually low, around 2 percent, at least you know that the people responding are viable applicants.

Another example of proactive recruitment is preemployment training that provides a supplemental workforce. These are employees recruited through conventional means and trained in job- and industry-specific matters. They are then placed in a standby pool. When there's an opening, employers can turn to this supplemental workforce and select a suitable applicant. Of course, there's no guarantee that the person who would make the best fit will remain in the pool, waiting to be offered a job.

Professional associations and inter-HR networking can also provide employers with an opportunity to proactively recruit. Direct contact with potential employees or communication with others in your field can often put you in touch with qualified applicants.

Targeting Special Interest Groups

Taking a shotgun approach to recruitment in terms of who will be drawn in by whatever source you're using may result in a qualified applicant pool; however, certain special interest groups may need to be targeted directly in order to minimize inadvertent violations of certain equal employment opportunity laws. This approach is also likely to produce a more diverse pool of applicants, thereby potentially enhancing productivity and profitability.

Begin targeting special interest groups by developing a keener insight into the characteristics of each group.

Older Workers

In 2003, the Society for Human Resource Management (SHRM), in conjunction with the National Older Worker Career Center (NOWCC), conducted an extensive study entitled "Older Workers Survey."[3] The survey identified workers over age 65 as "older," although the Age Discrimination in Employment Act of 1967 (ADEA) applies to individuals age 40 and over. The term encompasses baby boomers born between 1945 and 1964, and traditionalists born prior to 1945.

Overwhelmingly, respondents to SHRM's survey gave ten key reasons for hiring older workers. A greater willingness to work different schedules topped the list, followed by their effectiveness as mentors. Also considered key was the invaluable experience brought to a job by older workers, as well as their strong work ethic. Respondents also viewed older workers as more reliable with a greater diversity of thought/approach to tasks. In addition, they were considered more loyal and likely to take work more seriously, and valued for having established networks. Finally, older workers have a higher retention rate.

Only one percent felt there were no advantages to hiring older workers. In contrast, the only major disadvantage cited for hiring older workers was a failure to keep up with technology. Indeed, 19 percent said that there were no disadvantages whatsoever to hiring older workers.

The advantages of older workers in the workforce will only be relevant if there are enough of them to hire. According to the U.S. Bureau of Labor Statistics, more than 25 percent of the working population will reach retirement age by 2010, resulting in a potential worker shortage of nearly 10 million.[4] The U.S. Census Bureau reports that the number of people age 55 and older will increase to 73 percent by 2020, while the number of younger workers will grow only 5 percent.[5]

Despite these figures, most employers do not appear to be taking the anticipated labor shortage seriously. According to the 2003 SHRM/NOWCC/CED Older Workers Survey, ". . . few organizations are currently preparing for the loss of knowledge and experience when workers aged 55 and over retire. In addition, fewer than 50 percent of survey respondents attempt to capitalize on and incorporate the experience of older workers."[6]

Employers can take a proactive approach to hiring older workers by logging on to these and other similar websites:

- Wisconsin Job Centers (www.dwd.state.wi.us/dws/directory)
- Senior Community Service Employment Program
  (www.dhfs.state.wi.us/aging/Genage/SENCSEP.HTM)
- U.S. Department of Labor (www.doleta.gov/seniors)
- American Association of Retired Persons (www.aarp.org)
- Coalition of Wisconsin Aging Groups (www.cwag.org)
- Senior Job Bank (www.seniorjobbank.com)

Other recruitment sources for older workers include senior citizen community centers; social service agencies and organizations with large senior memberships;

Forty Plus, a national organization that helps those over age 40 to find employment; and the AARP free booklet entitled "How to Recruit Older Workers." Also, do not overlook the obvious resource of your company's own retirees. In addition, if you run advertisements, use language that encourages older workers to apply. For example, state that "This job is suitable for retired persons." In addition to qualifications, describe the qualities you're seeking. Since many older adults are not actively seeking employment, advertise in sections other than the classifieds—for example, try the television or sports sections. You might also want to have pictures of older workers in your ads. Consider, too, sponsoring open houses and second-career fairs specifically for older adults.

When hiring older workers, be prepared to answer questions about how the return to work will affect a retiree's income. Limitations on the amount Social Security recipients can earn without penalty have been reduced in recent years, but regular employment could still produce too high a level of income for some. Also, be familiar with the benefits full- and part-time workers may be entitled to, including medical and life insurance, sick leave, paid vacations, and holidays.

Once hired, assure older employees that their work is valued by offering the same opportunities for advancement and challenging work that are available to their younger colleagues. Develop training programs to help older workers redirect their skills and knowledge and, if needed, provide counseling to aid in the transition to their new status.

Youth

A shortage of younger workers is imminent. As stated earlier, their numbers are expected to grow only 5 percent by 2020. The contrast between the characteristics of this group, which includes Generation X (those born between 1965–1980) and "millenials" or Generation Y (those born between 1981–1993), and those of traditionalists and baby boomers is significant. According to the SHRM's 2004 "Generational Differences Survey Report," these distinctions can be made between the four workforce generations.

Traditionalists are reportedly respectful of an organization's hierarchy, accept authority figures, prefer structure, give maximum effort, and stay with a company for a long time. Baby boomers also accept authority figures, give maximum effort, and are inclined to stay with a company for the long term; in addition, they are results driven. Generation Xers are considered technologically savvy, like informal work environments, embrace diversity, learn quickly, and value work/life balance. Millenials are also technologically savvy, prefer informal work settings, value diversity, and learn quickly; they are also said to require greater supervision.[7]

In addition to the distinguishing traits cited in the "Generational Differences Survey Report," Generation Xers and millenials are also set apart by their preference for communicating electronically; they demand work that is both interesting and reflective of leading-edge technology. Not wedded to one job or even one field, younger workers are open to alternatives and look for exciting and entertaining opportunities that will expand their skills, knowledge, and interests.

Cam Marston, president of Marston Communications, tells us that younger workers are more detached from their jobs than prior generations. What they value most is a meaningful personal connection with their bosses. "The boss is the company," says Marston. Younger workers "rarely quit the job or the company; they quit their boss." Younger workers also think in terms of the impact their careers will have on their personal lives. According to Marston, millenials think of jobs as "gigs" between their days off.[8]

Methods for recruiting younger workers should take these characteristics into account. Suggestions include using interactive techniques, such as CD-ROMs, and revising company brochures to focus on new technology, promotional opportunities, geographic alternatives, and family leave policies.

One technique for attracting youthful workers is to provide funding for scholarships. Increasingly, businesses are offering scholarships to employees attending college or technical school. Other companies provide scholarship funding to local schools in the hope that graduates will seek employment with them. Some businesses go a step further, enticing top students from select colleges to commit to employment by granting 100 percent tuition aid from the second or third year of school through graduation. In return, students must commit to work for that organization for a minimum period of time, ranging from one summer to one year after graduation. Information regarding the management of scholarship programs is available to employers from the Council for Aid to Education (phone: 212-689-2400).

Women

Women make up more than 50 percent of the population, but are far from filling an equal percentage of top jobs in the United States. In 2003, a study conducted by Catalyst, Inc., a nonprofit research firm, reported that 7.9 percent of senior level jobs and 13.6 percent of board positions in Fortune 500 businesses were held by women. In some arenas, this represents an improvement over past numbers, but other reports indicate that women are actually losing ground. Peopleclick Research Institute released a study in 2004 revealing that, between 1990 and 2000, the percentage of women in executive positions (i.e., vice president and above) dropped from 31.9 percent to 18.8 percent.[9]

Many experts feel enough strides have not been made. Joyce Gioia, coauthor of *How to Become an Employer of Choice,* maintains, "Women will lead the corporations of the future, and if you don't have women leaders you might not be in business in the future." She goes on to say that women bring creativity and innovation to businesses and, thus, are assets. Catalyst supports the claim that women are assets with studies that reveal companies with the highest representation of women at the top have better financial performance than those with lower numbers: specifically, a 35.1 percent higher return on equity and a 34 percent higher total return to shareholders.[10]

The list of barriers to women advancing in business, as profiled by Catalyst, is topped by exclusion from informal networks and gender-based stereotypes, followed by lack of role models, lack of line experience, and a style that differs from the organizational norm. Additional barriers include lack of awareness of organizational politics, lack of mentoring, inhospitable corporate cultures, lack of opportunities for visibility, and a strong commitment to family. Least significant in terms of representing barriers, but reported nevertheless, is a lack of challenging assignments and sexual harassment.[11]

These reports should send a clear advisory to every company in this nation to examine its structure and environment for compatibility when it comes to hiring women at all levels, especially at the top.

Many of the women in the workforce are mothers requiring alternative work arrangements. Such alternatives might include flexible work schedules, job sharing, and at-home officer positions.

The National Organization for Women (NOW), National Institute for Women in Trades, Technology & Science, and Women in Technology International are examples of viable national resources for recruiting women.

Minorities

It is projected that the term *minority*—here intended to encompass a broad spectrum of ethnic groups including, but not limited to, African-Americans, Hispanics (e.g., Puerto Ricans, Cuban-Americans, Mexican-Americans, as well as people originally from more than twenty additional Central and South American nations, and Spain), Asian-Americans (e.g., Korean, Japanese, Chinese, and Filipino), and Native Americans—will soon disappear from our employment vocabulary. How can we continue to call "minority" a collective group of people that's projected to represent 37 percent of the labor market in 2020 and more than 50 percent in 2060?

Although these groups may represent a large percentage of tomorrow's workforce, few will be targeted for professional positions. Those qualified will be drawn to employers offering not only the usual growth opportunities and benefits, but also a multicultural or diverse environment.

Data shows that the Hispanic community is the fastest-growing group in the country, representing the largest minority in the nation: By 2050, they will constitute 25 percent of the population.[12] The Hispanic community is diverse, encompassing various subgroups, including Mexican-Americans and Cuban-Americans. Organizations such as the Hispanic Alliance for Career Enhancement (HACE) help educate businesses about the Hispanic community as well as link companies with potential employees. Taking a long-term, proactive approach of partnering with schools will also help cultivate the future Hispanic talent pool.

Businesses are encouraged to develop and maintain an ongoing relationship with various minority professional associations to aid in recruitment efforts. Numerous national associations with local chapters, such as the National Black MBA Association, National Association of Asian-American Professionals, and the American Indian Science and Engineering Society, are all viable sources of job applicants.

One minority recruitment source that is often overlooked is a company's own employees. Training existing staff for higher-level jobs may help resolve recruitment woes while at the same time demonstrating that management is committed to minority development and placement.

Applicants with Disabilities

According to the 2000 National Organization on Disabilities (N.O.D.), people with disabilities represent the single most underutilized labor resource. Approximately two-thirds of those with disabilities in the United States are unemployed; most of them reportedly want to work.[13] But only three in ten working-age adults with disabilities are employed full- or part-time as compared with eight in ten adults without disabilities. N.O.D. reports that adults with disabilities are no more likely to be employed today than they were a decade ago.

One of the primary reasons has to do with how we perceive people with disabilities. Many of us are locked into an image of someone in a wheelchair. In reality, the term *disabled* encompasses a broad spectrum of impairments. Categories include visual, hearing, and speech impairments; heart disease; developmental disabilities such as cerebral palsy; mental illness; acquired immunodeficiency syndrome (AIDS) or human immunodeficiency virus (HIV)-positive status; and limitations resulting from accidents. Experts say that each of us has a 20 percent chance of becoming disabled over our work lives.

Another reason commonly cited for failing to actively pursue applicants with disabilities is cost. Laws require that employers make reasonable accommodations for applicants with disabilities, without creating "undue hardship" for the employer. In determining whether a given accommodation would result in undue hardship, the law assesses employers on the basis of the overall size of the business, the nature of the business, and the nature and cost of the required accommodation. If a job should require the modification of certain equipment or procedures to accommodate a worker, employers are advised to seek advice and assistance from organizations such as the Job Accommodation Network (1-800-JAN-PCEH), established by the Office of Disability Employment Policy within the Labor Department (formerly known as the President's Committee on Employment of People with Disabilities), or the National Support Center for Persons with Disabilities (1-800-IBM-2133), established by IBM.

Recruiting people with disabilities requires a proactive approach, beginning with establishing relationships with agencies that represent or train people with disabilities before openings occur. Once a position is available, contact these organizations; in addition, make clear to search firms or employment agencies that you expect them to refer qualified people with disabilities.

Here are some specific resources that may be helpful in your efforts to recruit applicants with disabilities:

- National Association of Rehabilitation Facilities (703-648-9300)
- National Center for Disability Services (516-747-5400)
- Project Employ (202-376-6200) and the Workforce Recruitment Program (724-891-0275), both of which are part of the Office of Disability Employment Policy
- Rehabilitation Services Administration (202-205-8719; http://www.ed.gov/offices/OSERS/RSA/)
- Department of Veterans Affairs (800-827-1000)
- Career and Employment Institute (516-465-3737)
- Association of Higher Education and Disability, or AHEAD (614-488-4972)

Immigrants

A 2004 survey conducted by National Public Radio, Kaiser Family Foundation, and Harvard University's Kennedy School of Government reveals that the public view on immigration has improved since the terrorist attacks of September 11, 2001, although many negative attitudes continue to prevail.[14] Native-born U.S. residents who know immigrants as neighbors or coworkers are reported as having a greater comfort level with legal immigrants. Between 2003 and 2004, non-U.S. citizens filled nearly three out of every ten new jobs in the United States.

The influx of immigrants into this country is expected to continue and will undoubtedly have two key effects on U.S. employers. First, employers must be certain to hire only those who have the legal right to work in this country. That means carefully checking documents and dealing with periodic government intervention. Second, with more immigrants arriving in the United States, the issue of speaking only English at work will continue to be an important human resources issue. Employers are also advised to note that birth rates are declining for all groups in the United States as well as in almost all Western countries and Japan. This means U.S. businesses will have to be more accepting of widespread legal immigration as a matter of economic necessity.

Gays, Lesbians, and Bisexuals

An increasing number of businesses are advertising in gay publications, participating in job fairs run by gay professional and student groups, and using online services such as Gay.com and GayWork.com. Companies that are involved in these recruitment campaigns are not so much seeking to hire gays, lesbians, and bisexuals; rather, they don't want to overlook qualified applicants who just happen not to be heterosexual. In other words, sexual orientation is not the issue; qualifications are what matters.

Some recruiting firms, such as McCormack & Associates, specialize in helping companies find applicants of diverse backgrounds, including sexual orientation. Businesses also find that employee referrals are a viable recruitment resource.

With only an estimated 10 percent of the population reported to be homosexual or bisexual, one may wonder if the effort is practical. It is, if you consider that this percentage contains a disproportionately high number of desirable applicants. Studies report that gays tend to be better educated and more successful professionally than the population as a whole.[15]

Some recruiters are stymied by how to reach a group whose members may prefer not to be identified by their sexual orientation. It appears, however, that Generation Xers and, to a larger extent, millenials, are more forthcoming about their orientation and may ask recruiters about a company's partner benefits.

Some companies that have participated in gay job fairs and/or otherwise actively recruited gay, lesbian, and bisexual applicants include IBM, Ford, Sun Microsystems, Citigroup, Morgan Stanley, NCR, Microsoft, and Capital One Financial Corp.[16]

Unemployed Workers

Being laid-off, downsized, or excessed no longer has the stigma attached to it that it once did. The economy is in turmoil, as more businesses buy one another out, merge, or dissolve. When any of these events take place, all employees are vulnerable.

Recruiters are starting to see this group of unemployed workers as a viable recruitment source. By partnering with similar businesses that are undergoing a major reorganization, a growing number of employers are creating win-win scenarios: Downsized workers find new employment, and recruiters fill their openings with experienced people ready to begin work right away, often without requiring more than a minimum amount of training.

Hiring downsized employees is an especially viable recruitment resource in large and midsize cities. For example, in Grand Rapids, Michigan (population 197,800), major companies like Steelcase have provided an excellent applicant pool for neighboring businesses, such as Kawasaki Motor Corp. USA.

Recruiting unemployed applicants requires proactive thinking. Businesses need to establish ties with companies with similar employee pools well before there are signs of trouble, agreeing on how a shift in employers could take place. Having a formal transition program in place at both locations is ideal, complete with counseling services available for displaced workers.

Interns

Interns are often viewed as contingency or temporary workers, retained for a limited period of time or specific assignment, instead of as members of a special interest group available for full-time hire. If you're inclined to view interns this way, you could be robbing your organization of valuable, future talent. Hiring interns has many advantages: They know your organization and what's expected of them; you, in turn, know their style of work, strengths, work ethics, interpersonal skills, and areas requiring improvement. One could say that you've had a chance to try one another out before making a commitment. The primary disadvantage of hiring interns is timeliness. Interns are often students who work for businesses during the summer, performing tasks that relate to their major course of study. If they first come to you as freshmen or sophomores, you'll have to be patient and wait two or more years until they graduate before you can bring them on board as full-time employees.

Many interns qualify as employees and as such are subject to minimum wage and overtime laws, workers compensation coverage, and possibly unemployment compensation.

Former Employees

Employers used to adhere to strict "no rehire" policies; however, in an erratic economy, former employees are rapidly becoming a viable recruitment source as employers increasingly strive to convert former hires into new hires.

In many instances, rehires are brought in at a higher level and earn more in the way of salary and benefits than they did the first time around. This can send a negative message to a company's current workforce—that is, the best way to get ahead in an organization is to leave it and then come back.

If your organization wants to recruit former employees for rehire, carefully review their work history before making contact. Delve deeply into the reasons for termination, whether voluntary or forced; look at their past performance reviews, identifying any problem areas; and talk with their former supervisors to review their skills.

Traditional Recruitment Sources

Traditional recruitment sources are methods for finding employees that are easily recognized, conventional in nature, acceptable to most types of organizations, and appropriate for filling a wide range of positions. Before embarking on a traditional recruitment campaign, remember to consider the four factors discussed earlier in this chapter: how much money is available; how quickly the opening must be filled; whether a wide audience must be reached; and the exemption level of the available position. In addition, carefully weigh the advantages and disadvantages of each source before proceeding.

Here, then, are some of the most commonly used traditional recruitment sources. Exhibit 2-1 summarizes the key advantages and disadvantages for each source.

Advertising

Advertising, whether in newspapers or professional publications, remains one of the most popular and effective means for soliciting applications. Careful planning in terms of content, timing, and location is likely to generate a large response and often results in hiring.

Exhibit 2-1. Key advantages and disadvantages for traditional recruitment sources.

Traditional Recruitment Source	Advantages	Disadvantages
Advertising	Reaches a wide audience	Costly
Campus Recruiting	Can select top students Opportunity to groom future management	Hard to assess potential
Contingency Workers	Can fill jobs in a hurry	Possible legal ramifications
Direct Mail	Personalized Selective	Time-intensive Risk that mail may not be opened
Employee Referrals	Employee morale booster if referrals are hired Expeditious Inexpensive	Employee demotivator if referrals are not hired
Employment Agencies and Search Firms	Access to large labor pool	Costly
Former Applicants	Good public relations	Outdated records
Government Agencies	Cost-effective	Nonexempt only
Job Fairs	May fill several openings in a short period of time	May not be able to hire anyone
Job Posting	Creates openings at lower levels Morale booster Reveals hidden skills	Managers feel lack of control Time lost waiting for replacement
Military	Can find applicants with hands-on experience Strong work ethic Experience in teaming and managing	Applicants may lack general business skills
Newspaper Inserts	Ad may stand out and can be easily removed	Easily lost Easily overlooked
Open Houses	Good public relations May fill several openings at once	Costly Time-consuming
Outplacement Firms	Large numbers of applicants	Incomplete picture of applicants' intangible qualities
Professional Associations	Personal referrals	Someone else's rejected applicants

Radio and Television	Reaches a wide audience Reaches prospects not actively looking for a job Can be cost-effective	Can be costly

Research Firms	Allows for greater
	  involvement in the
	  interviewing process
		Services end upon
		  contacting applicants

Voice Ads (Prerecorded Phone Messages)	Easy to produce	Time-consuming

To increase your chances of finding top-notch applicants via advertising, apply these ad placement strategies:

- *Capture the job hunter's attention.* Consider carefully the location of the ad, an appropriate job title, graphics, use of white space, and the placement of a logo.
- *Hold the job hunter's attention.* Provide just enough information to pique readers' interest so that they establish a connection between your needs and their skills.
- *Design your ad to be the last one a job hunter wants to read.* Use language that creates an image of how great employment with your company would be.

When designing the contents of an ad, define the audience you want to reach. If looking for individuals with very specialized skills, your ad should clearly enumerate those skills. If, on the other hand, you are scouting for talent, the wording should be less specific. The same holds true for the extent to which the job's duties and responsibilities are spelled out. Some employers want applicants to know virtually everything about a job before they apply. Others prefer to learn about the applicants and establish mutual interest before describing the details of the job. When advertising, make certain that enough information is provided for job seekers to determine whether it is worth their while to apply. Also be sure to include the method of contact.

Design your ad so that it will stand out. Use of creative graphics, color, clever job-related language, and tasteful humor can accomplish this objective and still project an appropriate image. Keep in mind that the contents and appearance of your ad is a reflection of your organization. Consider the image you wish to project and convey your message clearly and concisely.

Make certain the language in your ads doesn't violate equal employment opportunity (EEO) laws and regulations. Examples include stating an age preference (e.g., terminology such as "young man" or "mature woman"), a preference for either gender, or certain other subjective terms, such as "attractive." With regard to gender, it is significant to note that masculine or feminine terms do not automatically constitute an EEO violation. The Equal Employment Opportunity Commission (EEOC) has issued a policy statement regarding sex-referent language in employment advertising, noting that terms such as *patrolman* or *meter maid* have become "colloquial ways of denoting particular jobs rather than the sex of the individuals who perform those jobs." Furthermore, the statement continues, " . . . the use of sex-referent language in employment opportunity advertisements and other recruitment practices is suspect but is not a per se violation of Title VII." The EEOC goes on to urge employers to clearly indicate their intent to consider applicants of both genders whenever sex-referent language is used. Your recruitment ad should include a statement confirming nondiscriminatory intent, such as "equal employment opportunity employer, male/female."

Campus Recruiting

In general, students are attracted to companies that enjoy a good reputation, are successful, will look impressive on their resumes, have shown an interest in their school over a long period of time, and keep up with technological change. To gain students' attention, many employers are replacing traditional company recruitment brochures with technological tools that provide more than the standard company history and answers to typical questions about products, services, customers, work environment, and culture. Students today are looking for more concrete information; they want to know what life is like in the company, how people treat each other, and what (if any) bad publicity the company has received recently. This offers students a comprehensive sense of what working for the company would be like.

Some organizations are conducting online, interactive chat sessions, or webinars, with students who are majoring in subjects that are of particular interest to the hiring company. This approach allows businesses to reach out to students without leaving their offices; it also lets students know that the business is technologically savvy. Webinars reportedly cost from $10,000 to $40,000 to produce, depending on the number of users in various locations. The cost is offset by the time saved not having to recruit on-site.

Professor programs are another method of school recruitment. Professors identify students who are high-potential applicants and take information about a company back to their students after meeting with company management and observing employees at work. A variation of the professor program occurs when company executives teach courses at selected schools, giving them direct access to students with demonstrated potential.

Gerry Crispin of CareerXroads estimates that the average cost per college hire is around $4,100. With about 500,000 students getting jobs each year as a result of campus recruiting, that's more than a $2 billion tab.[17] With that kind of expenditure, more businesses are limiting themselves to a handful of target schools, developing relationships with these schools, and often identifying future employees as early as a student's sophomore year. These target schools are generally selected based on the quality of their academic programs, the school's reputation, and the diversity of the student population.

Employers unable to compete for top students from prestigious colleges are urged to recruit from lesser-known schools. For many jobs, even at a management level, a person's educational credentials may take a back seat to other skills and job-related knowledge not necessarily acquired through formal education.

Contingency Workers

Contingency workers are individuals working less than a full forty-hour week without comprehensive benefits, carrying portable skills from job-to-job. Their work is literally contingent on an employer's need for them. Most hold one or two assignments within a six-month period. Contingency assignments are available in virtually every field and profession. Part-timers, temps, freelancers, contract employees, and consultants all fall under the "contingency" umbrella.

People accept contingency jobs for a variety of reasons. Teachers during summer school vacations; peripheral workers, such as retirees who no longer want to work full-time; women with child- or elder-care responsibilities; and college students—all may seek out contingency assignments for additional income. Others look to contingency work as a path to long-term employment. Some others take temporary assignments to improve skills or gain exposure to a particular work environment. Many enjoy the flexible work schedules that can accompany contingency assignments. Still others accept contingency work as a stopgap between full-time jobs.

Companies generally hire contingency workers when they're pressed to fill an opening in a hurry or need to provide a service for a specified period of time.

Increasingly, the courts are examining the relationship between companies and their contingent workers. *Enforcement Guidance: Application of EEO Laws to Contingent Workers Placed by Temporary Employment Agencies and Other Staffing Firms,* a document prepared by the EEOC, helps employers address the application of federal employment antidiscrimination statutes to individuals placed in job assignments on a contingent basis. The Internal Revenue Service (IRS) is also interested in your relationship with contingency workers. As such, employers are urged to review the IRS's "twenty-factor test" to determine if individuals are properly classified as contingency workers.

Direct Mail

Companies use direct mail campaigns to target specific individuals. The first step is determining whom to contact. Since the expected response rate is low—between 0.5 percent and 2 percent—you will need several different mailing lists. These lists and list information may be obtained through professional associations, business directories, trade groups, and magazine subscription lists. *Direct Mail List Rates and Data,* published by Standard Rate and Data Service, Inc., in Skokie, Illinois, can offer additional assistance. You may also opt to hire the services of direct mail specialists or consultants to help plan and implement your mail campaign. Obtain a copy of the *Mailer's Guide* from the local post office for guidance on most efficiently sending your materials.

Direct mail campaigns often fail because recipients throw away the envelope without opening it. Sometimes putting an attention-getter on the envelope can mitigate this problem, although these are often little more than unprofessional teasers. For example, "We want to give you $150,000!" is unprofessional, not to mention untrue. Try printing "personal" or "confidential" on the outside, instead.

The letter should contain a clear, brief, easy-to-read message. The first sentence should inform the reader of your purpose and interest. Include information about the requirements of the job, its duties and responsibilities, and its benefits. Try to anticipate any relevant questions an applicant might ask and provide appropriate answers. Enclose a response card or ask to be contacted by telephone.

One final suggestion: Ask for a referral. In the event that your initial prospect is not interested in the position, she may know of someone who is.

Employee Referrals

One of the most expeditious, cost-effective, and morale-boosting recruitment sources is a company's own employee referral program. This method entails "spreading the word" as soon as a position becomes available. The department head in charge of the area with the opening tells other department heads; employees talk to one another; word of the job opening may be carried outside the organization to family, friends, and acquaintances. Employees, especially those known to be valuable and reliable human resources, can often lead their company to prime applicants.

To make this method more effective, employers offer incentives of varying worth if employees refer qualified applicants who are ultimately hired and satisfactorily complete a predetermined period of employment and a minimum level evaluation. These are usually cash awards, generally ranging from twenty-five dollars for a nonexempt hire to several thousand dollars for a top-level executive. In addition to cash bonuses, some employers offer savings bonds, gift certificates, and merchandise. For especially hard-to-fill openings, employers have been known to grant trips and cars, with taxes and the first year's insurance paid.

Employee referral programs generally work well for all concerned. Employees respond favorably to the incentives offered, and employers usually spend considerably less time and money than they would for other recruitment sources, such as advertising or search firms and employment agencies.

Employment Agencies and Search Firms

Employment agencies generally recruit for nonexempt and some exempt jobs, while search firms typically handle only professional openings, based on a minimum dollar figure.

Employment agencies and search firms are popular with employers primarily for two reasons. First, these recruitment sources have access to a large labor pool and can readily scout the market for qualified applicants—which includes seeking out people who are seemingly content with their current jobs. Second, they can often fill a position more quickly than a company could on its own.

The most significant reason for not retaining the services of an agency or search firm is the cost. While the fee structure of each employment service varies somewhat, most work on a contingency basis; that is, they do not collect the fee until a referred applicant is hired. The fee for an employment agency is usually a percentage of the first year's salary, ranging anywhere from 10 percent to 25 percent. Executive search firms may charge more, from 25 percent to 30 percent of the new hire's salary for the first year. For example, at 30 percent, an executive earning $125,000 would cost a company $37,500 in fees. There may be additional charges for incentives, bonus compensation, and related out-of-pocket expenses.

Before agreeing to register an opening with either an employment agency or a search firm, consider these five guidelines:

1. *Be certain that the agency will evaluate applicants and refer only those who meet the standards stipulated.* Too often, agencies merely forward resumes to a client, expecting the company's interviewer to do the screening.

2. *Be firm about the job's requirements and refuse to consider anyone who doesn't meet them.* In this regard, it's prudent to forward a copy of the job description for available positions.

3. *Ask for a written agreement detailing the fee arrangement.* These details include how much, when it is to be paid, and any other stipulations. For instance, some search firms will refund a percentage of the fee paid if employees placed as a result of their efforts are terminated within the first three to six months of work.

4. *Be selective in determining which agencies and search firms will receive your business.* Meet with and interview representatives in advance to make certain that they clearly understand your objectives. Establish their degree of knowledge in the specific field for which they will be recruiting, and make certain that you feel comfortable working with them. Ask for information regarding their methodology, experience, and track record. Don't hesitate to ask for references and gauge their reputation in the field. Also be sure that the person with whom you meet is the person actually handling your company's account.

5. *Formally notify all agencies and search firms with whom you will be working that you are an equal opportunity employer.* Also, share information regarding your organization's affirmative action and diversity programs. Clearly stipulate that you expect them to comply fully with all employment laws and that you will terminate your relationship if they should violate these laws at any time.

Once you have decided to work with a particular employment agency or search firm, encourage their representatives to learn as much as possible about both your organization and the specific job opening. The more information they have, the better able they will be to meet your needs effectively and expeditiously.

Employers should note that state and federal laws might regulate private employment services. Coverage varies among the states and may impact annual licensing, fees, and certain practices, such as misrepresenting a job or advertising without identifying the source as an employment service.

With more than 20,000 placement agencies in the United States, employers can afford to be selective when choosing an employment service. Recommendations from satisfied clients can assist you in the process, as can publications such as *The Directory of Executive Recruiters,* published by Consultants News.

You can also search for executive recruiters on the Internet at such websites as Recruiters Online Network or the Association of Executive Search Consultants.

Former Applicants

Previously rejected applicants may very well become excellent future employees. Often, there are several qualified applicants for one opening; choosing one does not render the others unqualified. If a similar position becomes available down the road, checking back with them could lead to hiring.

A simple database on your computer can help you log and keep track of all applications received. Retrieve applicants according to the job for which they originally applied, areas of expertise, formal education, or areas of interest.

When scanning HR records for existing applications, review notes taken by the previous interviewers. They may recall the applicants well enough to provide you with valuable, unrecorded insights.

Upon contacting former applicants, be sure to update their records. What have they done since applying for work with your company? Have they added to their bank of marketable skills? Do they have any additional, applicable educational credentials? Whom can you contact for an update on their work? A new round of interviews will be necessary, even if you were part of the initial interviewing process.

Consider being proactive by keeping in touch with viable former applicants, even when you don't have suitable openings. Periodically follow up with them so that when a suitable opening comes along, you don't have to take the time to reestablish contact and update your records.

Government Agencies

Government agencies are valuable recruitment sources for entry-level and other non-exempt openings. Welfare-to-work agencies and local nonprofits, such as those serving individuals with disabilities, provide basic life skills and job training to their clients. In addition, they often offer English as a second language (ESL) training and help high school dropouts acquire their general equivalency diplomas (GEDs). Some nonprofit agencies also provide short-term mentors to new workers to help them as they settle into their jobs with your company.

There is no cost to employers for any of these services. Additionally, businesses may be entitled to additional savings. If, for instance, a company hires someone transitioning from welfare to work, it could save between 25 percent and 40 percent in federal income tax per employee. Contact the IRS for qualifying conditions and required forms.

As an additional benefit to recruiting through government agencies, clients are usually unemployed and therefore eligible to begin work immediately.

Job Fairs

Job fairs allow recruiters to interview several applicants over a short period of time, usually one to two days. The fairs are often for a specialized field (e.g., engineering) or may focus on placing members of specific groups, like women, minorities, or people with disabilities.

Generally, recruiters who are interested in participating in job fairs contact the fairs' hosts through online or newspaper ads that announce the location and date of the next event. For a flat fee, they can review the resumes of prescreened, qualified applicants, identify those they wish to interview, and set up appointments. Recruiters are usually permitted to hire an unlimited number of qualified people. As such, most conduct brief interviews during the fair so they can maximize the number of applicants they see. Once they've established mutual interest, recruiters can arrange for the applicants to come to their place of business for in-depth interviews.

If all goes well, you may hire several people for what it would cost to hire one employee using a search firm. It's also possible that no one suitable will be found. Even then, your efforts are not wasted. Job fairs usually include social functions in the evenings; these events are wonderful opportunities to meet and exchange information with recruiters from other organizations. This type of networking among recruiters often results in a sharing of resumes and leads, especially for hard-to-fill positions.

Job Posting

Job posting is a process of internal recruitment whereby available positions are offered to existing staff before exploring outside sources. A simplified job description, citing the department, location, exemption status, salary grade and range, work schedule, requirements, primary duties and responsibilities, and working conditions, is posted on the company intranet and in central locations. A closing date for submitting all applications should also be listed. The standard deadline generally ranges from one to two weeks. Some employers require interested employees to receive permission from their existing supervisors before applying; others request supervisor notification. Still others respect the confidentiality of the process until a decision has been reached. A sample job posting form appears in Appendix A, and a sample job posting application form is shown in Appendix B.

Employees who apply for jobs via job posting are treated the same way as any outside applicant. If a qualified applicant is found, arrangements for a starting date in the new position are made between the existing department head, human resources, and the new department head. Two weeks is usually allowed for finding a replacement to fill the position being vacated.

Some organizations have a policy of posting all openings; others post only nonexempt positions. Some businesses steer clear of internal job postings altogether for several reasons, including the following:

- Managers may want to promote someone they've been grooming, and thus don't want to consider anyone else.

- Managers may resent employees who apply for jobs outside their department, tending to take such a move personally.

- Losing an employee to job posting may mean waiting a long time for a replacement who may not be as qualified.

- Some companies prefer to bring in "new blood" rather than recycling existing employees.

Promoting or transferring employees from within offers several advantages:

- It usually creates an opening at a lower, easier-to-fill level.

- The company saves considerable time and money by transferring someone already familiar with the organizational structure and methodology.

- The process boosts employee morale.

- Hidden talent may be uncovered.

The success of a job posting system depends largely on how well it is designed and monitored. For example, an organization may stipulate that employees must be with a company for at least one year, and in their current position for at least six months, before using the job posting system. The number of jobs for which an individual may apply within one year may also be limited, generally to three. In addition, a rating of satisfactory or better on their most recent performance appraisal may be required for an employee to use the job posting system. These guidelines may mitigate the problem of the "revolving door" employee who opts to apply for virtually every job posted.

Military

Military personnel frequently have a great deal of hands-on experience in a variety of tasks. They tend to have a strong work ethic and understand organizational structure. Other advantages include a background of providing support (both up and down the chain of command) and prior training in teaming and managing activities. In addition, because of the physical fitness requirements of military service, veterans tend to be healthy employees—a factor that can translate into reduced costs for health care claims and fewer workdays lost to illness.

There are several programs that can facilitate your company's publication of job openings and recruitment from the ranks, including the Retired Officers Association

(703-838-0537), the Army Career and Alumni Program (www.acap.army.mil), the Non-Commissioned Officers Association (www.ncoausa.org), and Transition Assistance Online (www.taonline.com).

Newspaper Inserts

Unlike ads that must be cut or torn out, insert ads can easily be slipped out of newspapers. The higher quality of the paper used for inserts (not to mention the absence of newsprint on one's clothing and hands) might appeal to job seekers. In addition, newspaper inserts may use multiple colors and are generally larger than standard newspaper or magazine ads, making them stand out visually.

Arguments against the use of newspaper inserts include the possibility that they will fall out of the paper and be lost, or they may be overlooked as job hunters head straight for the classified or special employment sections. Other detractors of this approach feel that inserts will not be taken seriously.

Open Houses

Organizations hosting an open house generally run ads across numerous geographic markets, as well as post notices on their company websites. These ads announce a recruitment drive for specific dates. Unless the company is well known, a detailed description of the company's product and reputation are included, along with details of the benefits package. All available jobs, with starting salaries or salary ranges, are listed as well. On the date advertised for the open house, company recruiters gather to greet and interview interested applicants. Hiring decisions are either made during the open house or arrangements are made for more in-depth interviews on company premises.

An open house can be a risky proposition in terms of cost and time. It is difficult to predict whether there will be a large turnout of qualified applicants or if these applicants will ultimately be hired. Prescreening applicants by telephone or asking them to submit resumes in advance are two ways of safeguarding against disappointing results.

On the other hand, you could end up filling several openings at one time.

Outplacement Firms

Outplacement firms are generally retained by companies to help higher-level managers and executives find new employment following termination. Lower-level management and nonexempt workers who have lost their jobs through plant closings or other major workforce reductions may be provided with partial or group outplacement services. While outplacement firms can be very effective for those seeking guidance in finding new employment, they can also be a valuable recruitment source. Most of these firms are staffed with generalists who do not specialize in placing people in particular occupations or fields. Therefore, they may know of a number of applicants meeting various job specifications. In addition, the immediate availability of job seekers referred by outplacement firms can be a big plus.

One significant disadvantage of interviewing outplacement firm referrals is that these applicants have just been through the traumatic experience of losing a job. Consequently, the stress of having to market oneself, added to the pressure of finding new employment, can greatly impact an applicant's self-image. This, in turn, affects how the applicant comes across and is perceived by the interviewer, which may obscure the applicant's intangible qualities (e.g., problem-solving and decision-making abilities).

Professional Associations

Most employers agree that a primary benefit of joining a professional association is the opportunity to network with colleagues from other organizations. For HR specialists, this can mean exchanging information about the market in general and specific job openings in particular. If you have either interviewed or reviewed the resume/application of some viable applicants, you can share this information with your professional colleagues, assuming you have the applicants' permission to do so. Hopefully, your colleagues will do the same for you.

In addition to the cost-effectiveness of these exchanges, you may benefit from a professional recommendation of specific applicants.

A variation on this technique is to join professional associations in those fields related to your recruitment responsibilities. The association's membership directory, mailing list, placement service, and publications could provide the names of your company's future employees.

Radio and Television

There are two main advantages to using radio or television advertising to fill an opening. First, you will appeal to a large audience in a short period of time. Second, you can reach and tempt prospects not actually looking for a job. This can be a real plus when you have hard-to-fill positions.

In the past, employers have tended to shy away from radio and TV advertising primarily because of the cost. But while still ranked among the more expensive recruitment sources, mass media, especially radio, has become more financially accessible. The growth of independent radio stations and cable television has created greater opportunities for employers with limited budgets.

Proponents of radio advertising emphasize that radio often reaches people when "their guard is down"—that is, when they are not necessarily thinking about job hunting. For example, they may have the radio on while getting ready for work in the morning or sitting in traffic, commuting to and from work. Companies looking for applicants in particular fields, including technology, should determine which music stations these individuals are likely to prefer and run ads on those stations. Radio is considered a valuable resource for technicians since many technical people are also musicians, and music and technology are said to use the same side of the brain.

Television advertising receives high marks from supporters because aspects of the job can be demonstrated as well as described. Done well, TV advertising can encourage job seekers to respond.

Research Firms

Research firms may be described as abbreviated versions of full-service executive search firms, providing essentially one-half the services. Their primary function is to provide organizations with information about potential high-level professional employees; the interview and evaluation is then up to the employer. Research firms generally charge by the hour, as opposed to a percentage, although some offer flat-rate fees.

Most research firms begin by ascertaining the specifications of available positions. Then target companies—that is, those likely to have employees meeting the job's specifications—are identified. Specific employees within the target companies are researched next, with any relevant information being turned over to the client company in written form. Contacting well-established persons within a given industry to request personal recommendations of potential employees is a variation on this procedure.

At this point, most research firms terminate their services, although the client company may ask the firm to make the initial contact with the targeted applicants. This phase is intended to clarify qualifications and to determine mutual interest.

Research firms are most useful when a company is looking for a cost-effective way to recruit top-level professionals or when more hands-on involvement in the interviewing process is desired.

When evaluating the services of a research firm, consider whether the company services a wide range of industries or specializes in one particular field. Also, determine its "success rate" and reputation. Ask for references from satisfied clients to determine the extent to which the research firm provided its client companies with applicants whose qualifications reflected the job's specifications. In addition, find out how long it took for a firm to produce the applicants. Finally, ask how many job offers were extended to applicants as a result of the research firm's efforts.

Voice Ads

Employers can prerecord a weekly message listing all available openings and include it on the company's automated phone system. Interested applicants leave their names and phone numbers, and the employer takes it from there. Some messages include a request for a resume by a certain date. Others ask only for a phone number so they may call back and conduct a screening interview over the phone. Companies that have volume openings with tight production schedules may encourage callers to either leave specific job-related information, such as length and type of experience, or to come by for an interview. This recruitment technique requires a minimum amount of effort, no cost, and could produce the desired results.

Innovative Recruitment Sources

Innovative recruitment sources are less conventional than traditional sources. Some may be considered quirky or unusual, appealing only to certain work environments during specific market conditions, while others are gradually making their way over to the traditional side of the ledger. Often, they're used when traditional recruitment sources don't yield the results needed in terms of quality applicants or timelines. As with traditional sources, it's advisable to review the four prerecruitment factors discussed earlier: how much money is available; how quickly the opening must be filled; whether a wide audience must be reached; and the exemption level of the available position. Also, consider the advantages and disadvantages of each source before making a selection.[18]

Following are some of the more popular innovative recruitment sources. Exhibit 2-2 summarizes the key advantages and disadvantages for each source.

Airplane Banners

Imagine a picturesque summer day; you're at the beach, enjoying the sun and surf. The furthest thing from your mind is work, current or future. Then you hear the sound of an engine; you follow the sound upward and see a banner lazily trailing behind a plane, advertising jobs.

The scene could just as easily be a sporting event or a rock concert; anywhere tens of thousands of would-be employees might congregate. Companies such as Ads ThatFly.Com and AirSign.Com will fly your ads with letters that are seven feet tall and messages that are generally up to fifty characters in length. Not grand enough? Try Heli-Banner (www.aerial-media.com), a company that offers to place your message on an 80-foot by 250-foot, helicopter-drawn banner, guaranteed for up to 200 hours of flight. Heli-Banner suggests planning multimarket campaigns simultaneously over sporting events, festivals, concerts, morning and evening drive-time traffic, and beaches.

While airplane banners certainly are attention-getters, many people object to them being overly intrusive and unprofessional.

Other Banners and Signs

Your business can use banners and signs as successful recruitment tools if it occupies a separate building that's located on a main street. Drape a banner across the front of your building or post a sign, inviting customers, clients, and passersby to stop in to inquire about employment opportunities. The banner or sign can simply state that there are jobs available. Or it can list the openings, which requires that you prepare

Exhibit 2-2. Key advantages and disadvantages for innovative recruitment sources.

Traditional Recruitment Source	Advantages	Disadvantages
Airplane Banners	Attention-getters	Intrusive Unprofessional
Banners and Signs	Cost-effective	Require busy location Unprofessional
Billboard Advertising	High-volume attention-grabber	Conveys limited amount of information
Bumper Stickers	Incentive for employees as part of employee referral program	Not taken seriously
Company-Sponsored Social Events	Cost-effective	Reaches a limited number of people
Competitions	Opportunity to evaluate skills before extending a job offer	Time-consuming
Customers, Clients, and Guests	Potential employee has in-depth knowledge of what it's like to work for you	Rejection or termination could sever relationship
Fast-Track Training	Provides marketable skills	Fails to support long-term advancement
Kiosks	Make it easy for a person to apply	Unmonitored applicant flow
Medical Offices	Cost-effective	Low volume of applications
Movie Ads	Can attract people who are not actively looking for a job	Intrusive
On-Site Recruitment	Can reach a wide audience Time-saver Good public relations	Lots of unqualified applicants
Preemployment Training	Creates trained workforce	No guarantee trained workers won't apply skills elsewhere
Response Cards	Personalized Selective	Time-consuming
Retirees	Experienced workers who can serve as mentors	Inflexibility

a new banner or sign each time a different job needs to be filled. Companies using this technique may also list their main benefits to lure potential employees. Also, unless the nature of your business is well known or has brand-name recognition, identify your product in a few words. Be sure to specify how interested applicants should contact you.

Banners and signs are real "you never know" recruitment sources. The investment is minimal and the payoff could be substantial. On the other hand, they can look carnival-like, leaving would-be employees to wonder if they should take such come-ons seriously.

Billboard Advertising

Most people view billboards while driving, often at high speeds, so they will not have much time to take in the details—unless, of course, they're stuck in traffic. Accordingly, an effective billboard ad must catch one's eye immediately, offering a limited amount of information that the average driver can both understand and remember, since it's unlikely that pad and pen will be handy. Billboard ads are usually limited to an enlarged logo with company name, a statement about employment advantages and available jobs, and a phone number in an easy-to-recall format. Since so many drivers use car phones, encouraging calls at all hours can increase the number of applicants who respond.

Billboard ads seem to work most effectively for hotel/motel chains, restaurants, and airlines, and generally target nonexempt-level workers.

Bumper Stickers

Bumper sticker ads offer little space for your message and there isn't much one can do to make the stickers visually outstanding. Also, unless someone is stuck in traffic directly behind a car sporting a bumper sticker advertisement, there's very little time or chance to read it. For these reasons, companies that advertise on bumper stickers usually include little more than a generic statement about employment opportunities and note, in large letters, their easy-to-remember phone number.

If company employees are willing to place this inexpensive form of advertisement on their cars' bumpers, employers may get some viable nonexempt applicants. Consider this a variation on employee referrals and offer bonuses when bumper stickers result in new hires.

Bumper sticker ads may be viewed as an act of desperation by job seekers and, as such, not be taken seriously.

Company-Sponsored Social Events

If your organization goes in for huge social events to celebrate special occasions, such as picnics on Independence Day, encourage employees to bring along family and friends. Then set up a "job opportunities" table with a list of openings and informational brochures. This form of recruitment requires an investment of only additional food and one or two employees willing to answer questions from interested applicants.

Competitions

Donald Trump's *The Apprentice* is one long job interview. Sixteen people are competing toward one goal—the chance to work for him. Over a period of weeks we watch as he fires one contestant after another, narrowing the field for those remaining until he makes his final selection. Not surprisingly, some companies have patterned a new recruitment technique after Trump's TV show. While the specifics may vary, the process is essentially the same. A selected number of interested applicants—usually unemployed—spend anywhere from a couple of weeks to several months competing for a job. Sometimes the job is an executive position, but it could also be a low-end professional or, in some instances, an entry-level opening. During the competition, applicants learn new skills and then apply them to simulated job-related tasks under the scrutiny of selected company human resources and departmental representatives. In addition to their ability to learn and perform specific tasks, contestants are evaluated on relevant intangible skills, such as problem solving, ability to interact with others, decision making, and communication. Applicants may drop out at any time; evaluators may eliminate contestants at any point in the process. At the end, one person is awarded the coveted prize: a job.

While competitions per se are new, they bear a resemblance to job tryouts, a process used by some businesses to see whether a person will fit into a corporate culture before extending a job offer. Even though applicants enter into job tryouts or competition arrangements voluntarily, companies need to be careful about the matter of salary. Can you have people working for you for a month without paying them? With regard to Trump-like competitions, as long as the contestants are learning new skills, employers are not required to pay them, because it is considered education. Compensation is required, however, with regard to the job tryouts.

Customers, Clients, and Guests

One innovative recruitment technique that is growing in popularity is encouraging customers, clients, and guests to become employees. This is especially helpful for small businesses that, over time, develop relationships with their clientele and get to know a great deal about them. These regulars, through interaction with company employees, learn the product, understand the culture, have an understanding of what it's like to work there, and are thus able to make informed decisions about applying for work.

According to John J. Sullivan, a human resources consultant and professor of management at San Francisco University, former customers reportedly sell three times or more as much as other employees.[19] This impressive correlation between former customers and productivity is supported by a survey of national retail sales associates conducted by Unicru, a company that automates hiring and employment processes: The more a person shopped at a store before working there, the more products they sold as employees.[20] And research conducted by Kenexa, a workforce automation company, reveals that customers that become employees are less apt to steal.[21]

The one real negative to hiring customers, clients, or guests could come about if the customer-turned-employee applies for a job and is either rejected or doesn't do well once hired. In that event, it's unlikely they'll continue to frequent your business.

Fast-Track Training

Fast-track training, often offered by community colleges and completed over one to six months, enables individuals to acquire specific skills, thereby making them more marketable. Attendees of these training programs include students, unemployed individuals seeking training for new jobs, employees wanting to improve existing skills, and those with minimal work experience seeking specialized abilities.

Proponents say that these practical, accelerated training programs meet the needs of both businesses and job seekers. Critics argue that these crash courses offer little to support long-term advancement; additionally, they can't help people acquire critical thinking, writing, or math skills. Naysayers do concede, however, that fast-track training may be better than nothing.

Kiosks

You see them at airports, shopping malls, or in large stores like Kmart, Target, and Circuit City: kiosks where customers can momentarily interrupt shopping to apply for a job. These businesses view all customers as potential employees, so they want to make it as easy as possible for them to fill out job applications. Most kiosks are already linked to the Internet, making the process quick and easy.

A variation on the Web-enabled kiosk is to have company representatives stationed throughout or in front of their stores, clipboard and applications in hand, ready to approach would-be employees. Sometimes sales personnel actually put a job application in your bag along with your purchase and receipt. Their attitude is, "It couldn't hurt."

This approach may generate many applications, but companies have no way of monitoring their quality.

Medical Offices

Some employers focus on attracting members of specific groups into their workplace by posting job openings in medical offices. Offices of gynecologists, obstetricians, and pediatricians can attract women applicants; doctors specializing in geriatrics can draw older workers; and physical therapists can entice those with physical disabilities. Fliers are usually left with the receptionist so that anyone interested can contact the employer.

This is a cost-effective, easy way to reach out to targeted populations; however, the approach is unlikely to generate a high volume of applications.

Movie Ads

You get to the movies in plenty of time to grab a tub of popcorn and a drink. You find a seat and settle in, ready for the show to begin. If you're lucky, instead of listening to music, there will previews of coming attractions. Imagine, now, in addition to clips of upcoming movie releases, your company's name comes on the screen, advertising job opportunities! This technique is gaining in popularity, although it may be more challenging in the future since there are those who want movie theaters to publish the "real" start times for movies so they aren't forced to sit through a series of ads and promotions. Businesses that opt for this proactive form of recruiting limit the amount of information to a minimum by usually offering just the company name, an easy-to-remember phone number (few moviegoers are prepared to write in a dark theater), and either a list of openings or a statement about job opportunities. Some employers try to link their promotions to specific movies and anticipated types of viewers; others go for the shotgun approach and just run their ads, regardless of what's showing.

On-Site Recruitment

On-site recruitment is limited to the types of businesses that attract large numbers of people to their locations each day. It can be quite effective especially for nonexempt-level positions. For example, railroad companies may place pamphlets that describe employment opportunities on car seats; airlines might do the same with seats on planes; department stores might attach fliers to packages at cashier stations; and fast-food chains or family restaurants might describe job openings on tray liners and table tents.

The brief message, which usually describes the benefits of working for the company, is often framed in bright, eye-catching colors and graphics. Pictured, too, may be people reflecting diverse traits and characteristics. Interested applicants are invited to visit or call the employment manager or equivalent to obtain an application form. In some instances, postage-paid applications are attached to the message so that those who wish to apply can complete the form for submission.

Preemployment Training

Preemployment training ensures the hiring of those applicants "guaranteed" to possess the basic knowledge and skills needed to perform a given job. It is typically accomplished through the promotion of a program that offers various skills training, free of cost to participants. Such prospects are not necessarily being trained for specific jobs; nor are they being offered employment. The emphasis is on preparation, so that when jobs do become available, the trained individuals will be considered first. Employers benefit by having an available workforce of skilled individuals from which to choose, without wasting time screening a group of untested applicants. In addition, once hired, program graduates need not devote the first several days, or in some cases weeks, to learning their jobs. Program participants benefit by acquiring marketable skills and being first in line for employment opportunities. Of course, there is no guarantee the acquired skills will not, ultimately, benefit another company.

Many businesses are extending preemployment training beyond primary job functions. By tapping into unconventional markets, such as the homeless and ex-convicts, prospective employers also provide training in social skills and office etiquette. Since businesses seldom have the time, resources, or know-how to teach these "softer skills," they enter partnerships with nonprofit organizations that specialize in helping the disadvantaged. Together, the two prepare would-be employees for various situations likely to arise in the world of work.

Response Cards

Response cards are a takeoff on direct mail recruitment, since the cards are mailed to the homes of targeted applicants. The language on the response card is designed to pique the interest of even those who are not looking for new employment. After a brief description of the job opportunities available, potential applicants are invited to complete a brief questionnaire that is easily detached from the informative portion of the card to be mailed, postage-paid, to the employer.

Response cards may also be attached to ads appearing in magazines. General information about the company and available jobs is provided; those interested are invited to complete the card and mail it in.

Companies report that they continue to receive responses up to a year after ads with detachable cards have run. While the return rate is not especially high (under 5 percent), many employers report a high ratio of hires as a result.

Employers can also add a twist to using response cards. Try sending out letters inviting people to return an accompanying coupon that entitles them to a free poster or calendar. Ask them to provide basic information about their skills and knowledge. They get a free gift, you get names for your data bank.

Retirees

At a time when more retirees want to return to work, employers are looking at this group as a fertile source of applicants. Some retirees want to return to the same type of work with the same level of intensity; others are looking for less demanding tasks; many prefer part-time work.

Employers are advised to contact the AARP as a starting point for recruiting retirees. Medical offices and senior citizen centers are additional viable resources.

Summary

Before embarking on a recruitment campaign, consider four factors: how much money is available; how quickly the opening must be filled; whether a wide audience must be reached; and the exemption level of the available position.

Next, determine how aggressive you must be in order to fill a particular opening. If immediacy is a primary factor, search out proactive recruitment sources; otherwise, explore some excellent reactive sources.

Taking a shotgun approach to recruitment in terms of who will be drawn in by whatever source you're using may result in a qualified applicant pool; however, certain special interest groups may need to be targeted directly in order to minimize inadvertent violations of certain equal employment opportunity laws. This approach is also likely to produce a more diverse pool of applicants, thereby potentially enhancing productivity and profitability.

There are numerous recruitment sources that will yield excellent applicants. Some are traditional, like advertising and search firms. Others, like company-sponsored social events and fast-track training, are more innovative, but can be equally effective.

Notes

1. Saratoga Institute, *2004 Workforce Diagnostic System*, "Executive Summary" (PricewaterhouseCoopers LLP, 2004); available at http://www.pwc.com/us/eng/tax/hrs/wds-exec-summary.pdf.

2. Mike Sweeny, T. Williams Consulting, Inc., Collegeville, Pennsylvania, August 14, 2002; available at http://www.workforce.com/archive.

3. Jessica Collison, "2003 SHRM/NOWCC/CED Older Workers Survey" (Alexandria, VA: SHRM Research), June 2003.

4. Nancy R. Lockwood, "The Aging Workforce: The Reality of the Impact of Older Workers and Eldercare in the Workplace," *SHRM Research Quarterly* (December 2003); available at http://www.shrm.org/research/quarterly/0304aging_essay.asp.

5. Ibid.

6. Collison, "2003 SHRM/NOWCC/CED Older Workers Survey."

7. Nancy R. Lockwood, "Leadership Styles: Generational Differences," in SHRM's "Briefly Stated" series; available at http://www.shrm.org/research/briefly_published.

8. David P. Marino-Nachison, "HR Must Reach Out to Younger Employees," SHRM Global News (Alexandria, VA: SHRM); available through www.shrm.org/global/news_published/CMS_008845.asp.

9. Eve Tahmincioglu, "When Women Rise," *Workforce Management* (September 2004), pp. 26–32.

10. Ibid.

11. Ibid.

12. Robert Rodriguez, "Tapping the Hispanic Labor Pool," *HR Magazine* Vol. 49, No. 4 (April 2004), pp. 73–79.

13. SHRMOnline, "SHRM Disabilities Toolkit" (Alexandria, VA: Society for Human Resource Management); available through http://www.shrm.org/hrtools/toolkits_published/.

14. Kathy Gurchiek, SHRMOnline, (Alexandria, VA: Society for Human Resource Management); available at www.shrm.org/hrnews_published/archives/CMS_010270.asp.

15. Patrick J. Kiger, "Diversity Aside, Does It Pay to Search for Gays?" *Workforce Management* (March 2004); available to registered members at http://www.workforce.com/archive/feature/23/65/32/index.php.

16. Ibid.

17. Joe Mullich, "College Recruiting Goes for Niches," *Workforce Management* (February 2004).

18. Portions of the section on "Innovative Recruitment Sources" are excerpted from: Diane Arthur, *The Employee Recruitment and Retention Handbook* (New York: AMACOM, 2001), pp. 110–117.

19. Eilene Zimmerman, "Stores Find Good Workers Among Devoted Customers," *The New York Times* (January 2, 2005), Section 10, Job Market, p. 1.

20. Ibid.

21. Ibid.

CHAPTER 3

Electronic Recruiting

Long-time HR specialists undoubtedly remember receiving stacks of resumes sent either by search firms, in response to newspaper ads, or through one of the other more traditional recruitment resources described in Chapter 2. Too busy to do them justice during a typical workday, you probably loaded these resumes into your briefcase and dutifully reviewed them during the commute home or after dinner in front of the TV (muted, of course). As the evening grew later and you came across a resume longer than one or two pages, you groaned, fighting the temptation to "file" it for violating the unwritten law against submitting a resume that is too long for a tired HR professional to review at the end of a busy day.

The process of receiving and reviewing resumes and employment applications has changed dramatically over the past decade. Increasingly, employers are using the Internet to recruit, either by developing an online presence of their own or by linking up with Web-based job search services. Applicants, too, are preparing and transmitting many more resumes electronically, thereby relieving recruiters from being inundated with thousands of paper resumes. The Internet, then, is rapidly moving up in the ranks of recruitment, as many more applicants and employers communicate with one another, computer to computer.

Definition of an Applicant

As a result of the onslaught of resumes and applications transmitted electronically, the Equal Employment Opportunity Commission (EEOC) has proposed guidelines to define when a person who applies for a job over the Internet is considered an applicant. This is important since employers are required to keep records for applicants on the basis of race, gender, or ethnicity, to preclude charges of discrimination. Until recently, the definition of an applicant applied to anyone who expressed an interest in a given job. Matters became complicated, however, when people started sending out dozens of electronic resumes without a particular job in mind. It's not uncommon for individuals to be unaware of which organizations receive their resumes.

The guidelines, formulated over a period of more than three years, are the result of the combined efforts of the EEOC, the Department of Labor's Office of Federal

Contract Compliance Programs (DOL OFCCP), the Department of Justice (DOJ), and the Office of Personnel Management (OPM).

The proposed guidelines stipulate that "the core of being an 'applicant' is asking to be hired to do a particular job for a specific employer."[1] Specifically, three conditions must be met for an individual to be considered an electronic applicant:

1. An employer must take steps to fill a given job opening.
2. An individual must follow the employer's standard application procedure.
3. The individual must express interest in the opening. (In other words, casual browsers are not considered applicants.)

If someone completes a profile and forwards a resume in response to an ad posted by an organization, he would be considered an applicant. Also, if a person posts a resume on an Internet resume bank without expressing an interest in a specific job with a particular employer, she would become an applicant if the employer contacts him about a specific job and the person expresses interest.

Applicant status is not impacted by level of qualification. That is, even if someone does not meet the minimum requirements of a job, they are still considered applicants if they meet the applicant-criteria.

Here are some examples of instances whereby individuals would not be considered applicants under the proposed guidelines:

- Transmitting a resume to the "jobs" e-mail address on a company's website, without indicating interest in a specific job
- Posting a resume on any major job board
- Having a resume "passed on" by one company to another company, without first ascertaining the applicant's interest in a particular job

These proposed guidelines apply exclusively to the Internet and related technologies, including resume banks, job boards, organizational websites, resume databases, and online job listings. The old guiding principle stemming from the 1978 Uniform Guidelines on Employee Selection Procedures (and subsequent rulings issued in 1979 and 1980) continue to apply to those who submit paper resumes; that is, an applicant is "a person who has indicated an interest in being considered for hiring, promotion, or other employment opportunities."[2]

The Society for Human Resource Management (SHRM) responded to the interagency proposed guidelines by expressing concern over three key aspects:

1. The resulting dual record-keeping requirements for electronic and paper applications.
2. Treatment of persons who fail to meet the minimum qualifications for a job (According to Wendy Wursh, SHRM manager of employment regulations, "Omitting any guidelines on the minimum qualifications for an employee will present problems to employers because it could expand the definition of applicant to anyone who shows interest in the job whether or not they are even qualified.")[3]

This concern is shared by the OFCCP, which issued a separate proposal stating that an individual expressing interest in a specific job must meet the minimum requirements.

3. Lack of guidance on how employers should obtain demographic information from people who apply for jobs electronically.

As of this writing, the EEOC is reportedly reviewing input from various businesses and civil rights organizations. It will then issue a final version of the guidelines.

Electronic Resumes

Up until the late 1980s and early 1990s, all resumes were printed and delivered on paper. Today, many companies report receiving a 50/50 ratio of paper and electronic resumes, while others boast of having a "no paper" policy.

Proponents of the electronic format offer the following reasons for discouraging paper resumes:

- Paper costs considerably more than the average electronic file of six kilobytes.

- Processing paper into an electronic format takes longer than processing an originally electronic file.

- Mail delivery is slow: The average U.S.-based letter takes three days to reach its destination; the average electronic transmission takes three seconds.

- Electronic files can be formatted, extracted, and otherwise manipulated countless ways; they can also be incorporated with other data or stored in various applications or systems.

Paper resume supporters argue that electronic resumes are often difficult to read and lack a professional look. In addition, they argue, some applicants express concerns about confidentiality and privacy, as well as fear that their resumes will get lost in a mile-high cyber pile, so they continue to favor a mailed paper resume. Accordingly, if businesses don't offer a paper resume option, these applicants may bypass them entirely and ultimately become someone else's employees.

Whatever your personal preference, everyone agrees on one thing: Reading electronic resumes is unlike reading paper resumes. While the focus remains the same—searching for information that reflect a person's ability to perform a job—the presentation and format of that information is dramatically different. As one recruiter puts it, "What pleases a computer is likely to bore a person."

Scannable/Text-Based Resumes

Scannable/text-based resumes are basically devoid of all formatting: no bold type, italics, underlining, bullets, fancy fonts, tabs, columns, or rule lines. Scannable resumes, then, are text-focused as opposed to design-focused. Typically, they are created and/or saved in a text (.txt) file format. The most scannable documents are those that have high-quality letter forms, high contrast, and no columnar structure that will turn well-written phrases into gibberish after the document is scanned.

If electronic-oriented employers receive an applicant's printed scannable resume as hard copy, they will scan it electronically, converting it into a digitized format so they can then search for keywords to establish a preliminary match between an applicant and a job. The scanning process benefits applicants with the most measurable, tangible skills; applicants who exclude key relevant terms and familiar industry acronyms are likely to be bypassed. Action words, indicating the nature and level of work accomplished, are less important than industry-specific language in electronic resumes. Some programs limit the number of items they will scan for and usually start at the top of the document. Savvy applicants know this and therefore place their most important keywords at the beginning. The process can also search for years of experience, education, and other desired specifications. Employers can even assign weighted values to the various criteria.

Because the automated system transferring information from resumes into an applicant database stresses keywords and phrases that describe the skills and core work required for each job, applicants tend to focus on nouns, not verbs. For example, if an applicant were to write, "Managed five operators," the word *managed* might be bypassed; however, if the applicant were to write, "Manager of five operators" the word *manager* would stand out.

Instead of scanning mailed or faxed print versions of resumes, many employers are asking applicants to e-mail their resumes, either as an attachment or in the body of an e-mail message, or to paste their resumes into a Web-based form. Text-based resumes work best for posting on websites that use built-in forms. Employers can then immediately search for keywords since the resume is already in digitized form. Note that some businesses discourage resumes sent as attachments to e-mails and won't open these attachments because of concerns about computer viruses and incompatibilities among word-processing programs.

All of these scannable/text-based resumes are in contrast with those in portable document format (PDF). PDF documents can also be sent as e-mail attachments, but special software, usually Adobe Acrobat Reader, is required to open and read the file on the receiving end. Without the right software, words may not all appear on the same line and pages may not align properly. Employers cannot load PDF resumes into databases without first printing them and scanning them.

Clearly stipulate the form in which you prefer to receive resumes when posting jobs. For example, do you want a formatted "print" resume sent as an attachment to an e-mail message? Or do you favor a text-based resume stripped of formatting and pasted directly into the e-mail message (with the applicant's print resume also attached)?

Cover Letters

Resume-writing guides recommend including cover letters regardless of the format in which the resume is submitted. Indeed, few employers seriously consider a resume without an accompanying letter that identifies the specific job or type of job sought, as well as highlights of the submitter's qualifications. Cover letters can grab a recruiter's attention by suggesting a preliminary job/applicant fit, so wise applicants take care to word theirs carefully.

Here are some of the critical components of a cover letter:

- *Cover letters should be addressed to a specific person.* Salutations such as "Dear Hiring Manager," "Dear Sir or Madam," or "To Whom It May Concern" could be interpreted to mean that the applicant has not done her homework or has an insufficient degree of interest. It's a given that the person's name should be spelled correctly.

- *Most cover letters are in response to a specific posting or ad; accordingly, the job should be identified in the first paragraph.* Even if an applicant is taking an exploratory approach with no specific opening in mind, he should narrow his focus and identify suitable, albeit generic, job titles. Recruiters should not have to work at matching the person with a job.

- *The most effective cover letters reveal exactly how the sender qualifies for a particular job.* The applicant should stress keywords and phrases, even if it means that some information is extracted from the resume itself; some form of duplication is acceptable if it serves to reinforce key skills. The most desirable letters are those that identify concrete examples demonstrating relevant job-related accomplishments.

- *Effective cover letters restate specific job requirements identified in the ad followed by a brief statement reflecting the applicant's qualities.* When an applicant is responding to an ad that he qualifies for in every way, the end result can be impressive: Here's the job—here's the person; it's a match.

- *Cover letters that demonstrate knowledge of the employer are a nice touch, if not overdone.* For example, an applicant might write, "Now that Bixby Industries has expanded its product base as a result of its acquisition of Triad Inc., I would like to offer my extensive expertise in marketing and become a part of your exciting, new work environment." This shows that the applicant has taken the time to do some research and has bothered to incorporate that research into a personalized letter.

- *Well-written cover letters stress how the applicant's skills or prior experience can benefit the employer in terms of meeting its needs, solving its problems, or increasing its revenues.* A brief example or two of how the applicant has met an employer's needs in the past is ideal.

- *Good cover letters shouldn't overplay the applicants' hand.* Many applicants submit cover letters that are effective right up until the end. Then they come across as too pushy by saying something like, "After reading my resume, I'm sure you'll agree there's no point in looking any further: there's no doubt that I'm the right person for this job! I'll call you on Thursday and arrange to come in so we can talk face-to-face." Regardless of how qualified a person may appear to be, this approach can be perceived as too intense. You're forced to ask yourself a series of questions: Can I overlook this extreme proactive approach? Is it reflective of how this individual approaches tasks? If so, it is a desirable approach? Will that approach fit in with our corporate culture?

Chronological and Functional Resume Formats

As with paper resumes, electronic resumes may either be in a chronological or functional format. The chronological resume is organized by job title with the most recent position listed first. Applicants who submit chronological resumes generally have a history of experience in one traditional field, plan on pursuing a job in that same field, have no discernable gaps in time between jobs, and have been with most of their employers for a minimum of one to two years. Anyone looking at their resumes would be able to determine in a matter of seconds exactly when and where they've worked and what they've done at each job. Employers tend to prefer the chronological resume because the format lists prior positions beginning with the most current. Chronological resumes are generally perceived as fact-based and easier to scan.

Functional resumes are arranged according to areas of skill and accomplishment. They are typically submitted by applicants with diverse experiences in nontraditional fields that don't add up to a definable direction. For example, functional resumes may be preferred by college students with minimal or unrelated job, intern, or volunteer experience, and by individuals hoping to move into a field different from what they've been involved in to date. People with significant gaps in employment also tend to favor functional resumes, hoping to draw attention away from periods of unemployment. Some employers dislike this arrangement, finding it difficult to match the skills identified with actual job titles, levels or areas of responsibility, and dates.

Career Websites

Companies that put up their own career websites are recruiting proactively, thereby increasing their chances of finding suitable employees. In an iLogos survey of Fortune 500 companies, 83 percent of respondents reported posting jobs either to their career website or a job opportunity section on their corporate site, representing an increase of almost 11 percent from two years prior.[4]

Career Website Objectives

Before spending a lot of money and effort loading up your website with attractive graphics and inviting verbiage, be clear as to your primary objective. Think twice if you're tempted to say you want "to lure applicants." Any recruiter who has ever used a recruitment source that did not carefully target applicants with the required credentials or skills knows that this answer is not really accurate. It's awful to run an ad and only get a handful of responses; it's far worse to get inundated with responses from unqualified applicants—which is what can readily happen if your job postings fail to clearly identify the parameters of the position.

Rather than taking a hit-or-miss approach targeting no one in particular, plan your postings with a specific objective in mind: that is, attracting qualified applicants whose backgrounds and interests are compatible with the environment and offerings of your organization. This statement identifies your company as unique and immediately sets it apart.

What Applicants Are Looking For

Many job hunters report that they can learn a great deal about a potential employer from its website. As one second-year MBA student at the University of Texas at Austin noted: "A lot of what I'm looking for is a good fit. I can tell a lot about how a company regards its employees from its Web presence, particularly the parts designed to attract applicants. But so many [corporate] recruiting sites don't seem to understand that the applicant is the customer in the relationship."[5]

According to Steve Pollock, president of WebFeet Inc., a California recruitment technology provider, the best websites provide helpful information about the company and make it easy to apply for a job. In particular, businesses need to focus on four areas: content, navigation, branding, and functionality. Research conducted by Pollock reveals that about half of job hunters became more interested in working for a company after visiting its website, while one in four lost interest in a company based on their website.[6]

Enhancing your company's website to make it more applicant-friendly is not difficult. Here are some factors to incorporate:

- Make job listings easily accessible.
- Keep postings current.
- Avoid slow-to-load images.
- Don't get carried away with the latest bells and whistles unless they serve a purpose and are consistent with your corporate image.
- Keep screening questions simple and to a minimum.
- Allow submission options (e.g., online applications, e-mail, or fax).
- Offer a "resume builder" tool.
- Offer "cut and paste" capability so applicants can edit an existing resume.
- Provide detailed information about the history of your organization, its products or services, the culture, and benefits of working there.
- Provide information about the geographic area, including housing, taxes, schools, and recreational and cultural activities.
- Enable applicants to register to receive updates about new jobs.
- Ensure that the contents of your job postings are in full compliance with employment laws.

- Provide a calendar of career-related events.
- Periodically review visits to your website to identify patterns.
- Test out your website numerous times before launching it.

In addition, talk with colleagues and competitors to determine who uses their sites and the kind of feedback they're receiving. Consult with your technical staff, other employees, and even external applicants about what they expect to find on a webpage and what turns them off. Information from these sources can supplement advice from outside Web experts.

Getting Started

Career websites are generally organized according to job function, geographic location, or business unit. A statement as to the organization's mission is offered, as is generic information about the work environment and benefits of working there. A table of contents allows job seekers to browse topics of interest, including specific job offerings. Experiment and ask for feedback—from staff, consultants, and applicants—about which format is likely to draw the greatest number of qualified job hunters.

The overall appearance and visual design of a website creates an important first impression for applicants that either keeps them interested in continuing or turns them away. For example, too much text can cause readers to glaze over, and huge graphics that slow downloads to a crawl are likely to make viewers impatient. Strike a balance between smaller graphics that load quickly and meaningful text to capture and retain the interest of job hunters.

Companies generally start with a bare-bones online presence: a home page that provides the company name; geographic locations; phone, fax, and e-mail numbers; and basic information about the company in terms of its history, primary product areas, and who to contact. The site's text, tone, and look should be reflective of the company's corporate culture. These pages are later upgraded, depending on requests received for more information, as well as the company's own observations and advice from consultants. On average, start-up pages are redesigned two to three times in the first six to eighteen months.

Soliciting Professional Help

Many organizations solicit professional help in setting up their career websites. Before making a commitment to outside consultants, however, verify their effectiveness by talking with businesses, preferably ones similar to yours, that have used their services. Here are some questions to ask previous clients of potential consultants:

- Do they have both technical expertise and design experience?
- How helpful were they in a set-up situation?
- How patient were they in explaining terms and processes to nontechnical HR people?

- Did they bother to find out what your company was all about, in terms of its products, market, and direction?
- Did they acknowledge that you know your business best and therefore, should either write the text for your site or at least contribute to it?
- Did they make suggestions as to the best format and design of your website?
- Did they advise you about appropriate equipment for high-speed access?
- Did they try to start you off with more than you needed?
- Did they continue to offer support services after building your website?
- Did they recommend upgrades to your site after a probationary test run?

Website Upkeep

Once established, maintaining a career website is crucial. Job listings should be current. Few things prove more irritating for applicants than sorting through old listings and dated information. Also, keep up-to-date with regard to new design elements, including colors and backgrounds, and effects, such as flash demos. And to keep from appearing complacent, give the site a face-lift every six months or so.

The issue of exposure is also essential. Even an inexpensive website is ineffective if it is not seen or accessed. While employers need to display their Internet address, or Uniform Resource Locator (URL), on business cards, brochures, advertisements, and letterhead, that alone may not ensure sufficient exposure. Many companies additionally purchase hypertext links or hotlinks that lead directly into their servers from popular employment service sites. Web surfers are thus able to jump from one site to another, ensuring easier access and greater exposure.

It's also a good idea to track how often the career site is being accessed and what pages are the most popular. Tracking the number of hits on each page and capturing information about visitors can offer insight into how the website should be redesigned and what features should be revised, included, or eliminated down the road.

Hypertext Markup Language

As long as you have a computer connected to the Internet and the software to manage a website, job seekers browsing the Web can view whatever you post. The actual documents are ordinary text and graphics converted into a special programming language called hypertext markup language (HTML). New software makes HTML easier to use and eliminates the need for special coding. Once a webpage is created, you can view it using any one of a number of browsers, like Microsoft Internet Explorer, regardless of the kind of computer or operating system you have. It is the HTML that allows an organization to get its message across.

However, just as an effective newspaper ad cannot write itself, HTML cannot transform poorly organized data and unattractive graphics into an outstanding website. That requires expertise derived from understanding how HTML works in relation to the desired result. Accordingly, you need to choose between learning HTML and locating a program that creates HTML files for you. Employers and HR professionals generally choose the latter.

There are numerous HTML programs available, ranging in capabilities. Some offer excellent editing capabilities, allowing you to build an entire website from scratch. Many programs can also import from virtually any word-processing program and provide customized templates, but may require a good deal of HTML expertise; others are easier to use but offer less in the way of services. There are also tools that can simply convert word-processing documents into HTML.

Keep in mind that even the most sophisticated HTML program cannot create visually dazzling pages. That task falls to you or a design specialist to accomplish.

Online Recruitment Guidelines

Here are some additional guidelines to make your career website a success:

1. *Make searching for job openings easy.* A user-friendly site should have an "employment" button in a prominent place on the home page and offer a resume builder service or forms that route the data into your e-mail or database.

2. *Make the site navigable.* Broad appeal is an important ingredient to website success. For people who know exactly what they want, speed and easy access are crucial. More casual browsers, on the other hand, will want to explore, interacting with stimulating graphics and interesting text.

3. *Be prepared to respond to applicants quickly.* In describing the recruitment capabilities of the Internet, a frequent user accurately notes that it "offers incredible new opportunities to disappoint." After applying for a position, within only minutes applicants expect a quick response. If they don't get it, chances are they'll lose interest and move on.

4. *Maintain an up-to-date employment opportunity database.* The importance of keeping a website current cannot be overemphasized. If you cannot manage this task internally, hire the services of a company that can.

5. *Screen out unqualified applicants.* Does this sound impossible? Maybe, but there is a technique that Texas Instruments Inc. (TI) has reportedly used for years with success: an applicant profiler (www.ti.com/recruit/docs/fitcheck.shtml). Before applicants apply for a job opening, they complete a "Fit Check" by answering a series of questions designed to determine their qualifications and compatibility with TI's corporate culture. After reviewing the results of the Fit Check, they can decide whether to proceed with an application. The result: a prescreened, interested, and qualified applicant pool.

6. *Balance content with design.* Maybe appearances shouldn't matter to job seekers, but they do. As with display newspaper ads, visual appeal will draw applicants to your page and the content will pique their interest.

7. *Keep it organized.* Job seekers want to focus on the relevant data right away. While some people may want to browse the entire site, taking it all in, others will zero

in on what you have to offer, decide if they're interested, and apply. If this can't be done with ease, chances are they'll move on to another site.

8. *Take advantage of all the information you can learn about your Web visitors.* You will not hire every applicant expressing an interest in your company, but you can collect data about them that may prove useful to recruitment strategies later on. One of the pluses of electronic recruiting is that everything is measurable. Decide what you want to know—there's bound to be an Internet service that can provide it. For example, it may be helpful to determine which schools or organizations the people visiting your website have attended. Or perhaps you're interested in what other pages visitors look at. This kind of information can be valuable to the ongoing reevaluation of your career website.

9. *Make your address easy to remember.* Vanity license plates have been popular for years; it is therefore no surprise that companies are custom-designing their website addresses. For a nominal fee, you can register a unique, easy-to-remember URL.

10. *Don't say too much.* Many companies believe that applicants can make more informed decisions if they have access to a maximum amount of information. In fact, it's more effective to provide just enough information to create a level of interest on the part of job hunters, encouraging them to apply. Think in terms of supplying answers to these questions: What are the primary duties and responsibilities of the job? What are the qualifications required to perform the job? Why would someone want to work for you—and how can they apply?

International Electronic Recruiting

Websites offer a global presence as an increasing number of companies are posting their job openings online in more than 100 countries. Not surprisingly, most of these sites are produced in English. Since English is the most widely spoken language in the world, this may seem advantageous. However, for most people, English is a second language. They may be familiar with the basic structure of the language and able to converse in or read it. This does not mean, though, that they are aware of the nuances we so often use without regard to whether they constitute "proper English."

It's impractical, costly, and excessively time-consuming to prepare variations of each webpage in several different languages. You can, however, develop one site in one language that most people will be able to understand. This requires a focus on how you speak and read the English language. Here are some guidelines:

1. *Avoid jargon.* Made-up words can interfere with a clear, precise message. The meaning may confuse readers, thereby slowing them down. Clearly, industry-unique buzzwords or acronyms are appropriate, but only if you're fairly certain that at least 90 percent of your readers will understand their precise meaning.

    With terms that are ambiguous, provide a definition the first time the word or term appears in the text. It's also a good idea to review the document from the perspective of someone outside the culture of an American organization. If you have the least suspicion that readers will not share the meaning that is intended, either spell it out or make a clearer choice.

2. *Select proper word usage.* The English language is full of words that are confused with one another. For example, do you know the difference between *assure, ensure,* and *insure; affect* and *effect; adapt* and *adopt; advise* and *inform;* or *accept* and *except?* We all probably learned the meanings to these words at some point in our education, but when it comes time to use these words in a sentence, we often play a guessing game as to which one is correct. Americans can sometimes be casual about language. But to people for whom English is a second language, correct word usage is very important and they tend to be very precise. They probably know the difference between *continual* and *continuous,* so don't confuse the two in your text.

3. *Use proper grammar, punctuation, and spelling.* Web writing is unique; spaces between many words are eliminated and "periods" appear in the middle of sentences. In spite of this, the actual text of your job offerings should consist of proper grammar, punctuation, and spelling. Again, people for whom English is a second language are more likely to be aware of rules of grammar and will be able to pick out errors. These errors could be viewed as a carelessness that is representative of your organization, influencing an applicant's decision to submit an application.

4. *Do not avoid clichés.* If the subject were business writing, I would say the opposite; however, in writing Internet text for a population consisting largely of people for whom English is a second language, clichés can actually be helpful. Certain overused, stock phrases, such as "We need someone who can hit the ground running" are probably familiar and therefore more likely to accurately convey your meaning.

5. *Be careful about how you use numbers.* Something as simple as noting a resume filing date can be incorrectly interpreted by someone from another country. For example, in Europe, the numbers are reversed; hence a filing date of 8/12/07 would be interpreted as meaning December 8, 2007.

6. *Be careful about the colors you select for graphics.* In many countries, colors have very distinct, important, and sometimes religious meanings. Hence, misusing a color on your website can result in lost applicants. For example, in some cultures, purple is the color of royalty, while in Brazil it is associated with death.

You may choose to have your current website translated, graphics included, into another language. Many translation companies will do this for a nominal per-page fee, priced according to the content and the number and complexity of graphics involved. While this effort may appear to solve any potential problems associated with presenting your webpage in English, there is a wrinkle that comes with translation. The alphabet of other languages may have characters not found in English; therefore, you may need a separate product that can create websites in multiple languages. Likewise, if you decide to browse foreign-language sites, enlist the services of companies that will translate pages into English for a small sum.

Internet Job Boards

In addition to advertising jobs on your company's career website, you can post openings on a variety of Internet job boards. Here are some of the most popular types of job boards:

- *General Job Boards.* These are the most commonly used means of online recruiting. Companies post jobs and applicants respond, either to the system, which sends the application on to the company, or directly to an e-mail address. Some of the larger job boards can run up a tab of thousands of dollars a year. That's a lot of money considering that you're sharing advertising space with numerous other employers, including recruitment firms. To keep costs to a minimum, experts recommend first visiting several local job boards as well as those frequented by your applicants. See if they're suitable for the types of jobs you're likely to post; it may be that you'll need to use several sites. Ask for a trial run and resist signing any contracts until you've had success in terms of a response rate.

  Resume banks are extensions of general job boards, providing employers with the option of previewing resumes and paying for the contact information.

- *Industry-Specific Boards.* These boards target applicants with experience or interest in your particular type of business. It's not uncommon for these boards to offer free trials and rock-bottom sign-on prices. As with general job boards, don't sign a contract until you're fairly certain of success in finding suitable applicants.

- *Professional Associations.* Like industry-specific boards, professional associations target applicants with experience or interest in your field. Most professional associations offer either free posting as a benefit to their members, or they will post and review resumes for a nominal fee.

- *Resume Blasters.* Resume blasters are free for employers; applicants pay to "blast" a resume to recruiters who have identified desirable skills and competencies.

- *Recruitment Sourcing.* This invasive form of Internet recruiting targets passive applicants. Techniques used include x-raying (a process enabling the user to find employee home pages, staff directories, and biographies hidden inside a site); peeling (a technique that reveals additional unknown resources and applicants, made possible because personal documents are usually contained within a larger folder that holds many people-related documents); and flipping (a method allowing users to find people who create links from their home pages, simply by using the button on their search engine that reads, "Identify links to this URL").

- *Government Sites.* Government sites are often thought of as a wasteland of resumes, making it difficult to navigate and find anyone whose skills match your needs. You can narrow your focus, however, by posting jobs on state sites and clearly identifying the skills you're seeking.

- *Diversity Sites.* Targeting diversity sites for various ethnicities, people with disabilities, and the like, can produce qualified applicants and help you meet affirmative action goals as well. A word of caution: Some diversity sites claim to focus on placing specific groups (e.g., minorities); in reality, they're little more than links to larger, generic job boards.

- *Targeted Applicants.* If there's a way to personalize a rather impersonal recruitment source, this is it. A project manager works one-on-one with you to prepare a virtual profile of your business and then helps you with specific job postings. These postings are then e-mailed to a specific group of registered applicants who have been targeted based on their skills. After reviewing your profile, these applicants can contact your company to discuss job opportunities.

- *Streamline Services.* These services automate your recruitment efforts and applicant tracking, thereby saving you time. They usually link a job-posting page to your main website and allow you to post your openings on several job boards. One of the benefits to these streamline services is that they are flexible and customize according to your needs. Most charge a monthly fee.

- *School Job Boards.* Most colleges and universities, as well as high schools, offer job boards. These sites are similar to traditional job boards, generally targeting seniors and graduates. Look, too, for national sites that link schools.

- *Outplacement Services.* Outplacement firms will often post your jobs for free on their job boards. You can also keep in touch with companies issuing layoffs or experiencing mergers; they will usually allow you to post your job openings on their job boards.

Electronic Recruiting Risks

Joseph Beachboard, a partner in the law firm of Ogletree, Deakins, Nask, Smoak & Stewart, alerts employers to some of the risks associated with electronic recruiting.[7] His first concern has to do with resume-screening software. While screening software is intended to, and often does, help recruiters select the best applicants by searching for keywords or phrases, Beachboard suggests that there is significant legal risk if one selects software that categorically excludes members of certain protected groups. For example, if the software isolates words and terms that people in various protected categories do not typically use, then they could not be selected for consideration. Stated another way, if the software identifies words that are most commonly used by Caucasians and not by members of other ethnic groups, then only Caucasian applicants would be contacted, considered, and ultimately hired. This practice creates a disparate impact and could result in charges of systemic discrimination: the denial of equal employment opportunity through an established business practice—in this instance, recruitment.

Another risk associated with electronic recruiting has to do with Internet access. For instance, as a population, older workers are reportedly less comfortable with searching for jobs online than younger workers. Therefore, if employers rely heavily on electronic recruitment, they are potentially excluding many qualified older applicants, again potentially supporting claims of disparate impact and systemic discrimination.

People with disabilities are also reported to have limited access to the Internet. According to a report by the U.S. Department of Commerce, 63.1 percent of people age 25–60 without disabilities had used the Internet, while only 30.3 percent of people with multiple disabilities in that age range had access to the Internet.[8] In addition, a Cornell University analysis of electronic recruiting sites determined that only approximately 33 percent of all job boards and 25 percent of corporate career websites were accessible to people with vision or hearing impairments and those with limited dexterity.[9]

Applicant tracking is another electronic recruiting risk. With employers receiving thousands of resumes electronically, it can be an overwhelming task to maintain applicant flow data; that is, maintaining information about who's applying. The newly proposed multiagency guidelines defining an applicant (as described earlier in this chapter) may actually complicate matters further.

Because it's so easy for individuals to submit resumes electronically, many do so without much thought as to where the jobs are; they just send out their resumes to as many sites as possible. Hence, someone in Texas could apply for an opening in California and not even realize it. This creates a potential electronic recruiting risk for employers: Which states' laws govern the collection of data? Texas laws are more liberal than those in California when it comes to the amount of information employers can collect. So, if you're collecting information from someone in California and the job is in Texas, you have to carefully determine which laws govern. Matters such as these are best reviewed and determined by legal counsel.

Beachboard also cautions recruiters against saying too much on a site. His concern is that, with an unlimited amount of space on a website, employers have a tendency to volunteer more than they should about who would make the best applicant. A misstep in the statements you make on the site in and of itself could result in charges of discrimination. This concern extends to e-mail communications between employers and applicants. By their very nature, e-mails are informal; accordingly, inappropriate statements or non-job-related questions could be posed, resulting in charges of discrimination.

Many of these risks can be reduced if employers vary the recruitment sources they use. Despite the many advantages of electronic recruiting, employers must remember that there are many other effective means for finding qualified applicants, as identified in Chapter 2. Constantly ask yourself, "Am I reaching a wide range of people, thereby sidestepping legitimate charges of disparate impact and systemic discrimination?"

Electronic Web Sources

This list of specific publications, services, or institutions is for informational purposes only and is not to be considered an endorsement. That said, here are some electronic Web sources and sites, viable as of the date of this publication.[10]

Books

- *Weddle's Directory of Employment-Related Internet Sites: For Recruiters and Job Seekers 2005/6* and *Weddle's 2005/6 Guide to Employment Web Sites* (available at www.weddles.com), both by Peter D. Weddle

Internet Addresses—Recruiting Online

- All-Biz.com Network (www.all-biz.com), a resource for business professionals.
- America's Job Bank (www.ajb.dni.us), which links to nearly 2,000 state employment offices.
- BrassRing (www.brassring.com), a specialist in talent relationship management (TRM).
- Career Shop (www.careershop.com), with job posting and resume search features.
- Careerjournal.com (www.careerjournal.com), the executive career site of *The Wall Street Journal*.
- Dice (www.dice.com), technology job board.
- ExecuNet (www.execunet.com), a networking organization for senior managers earning at least $100,000 annually. Employers are allowed to recruit from its membership.
- EWork Exchange (www.ework.com), an international marketplace for employers with contingent work projects and applicants.
- Futurestep (www.futurestep.com), an executive search service for management professionals. Applicants complete online questionnaires to determine experience and skill level.
- HispanicOnline.com (www.hispaniconline.com), a career center where job listings can be posted.
- HR.com (www.hr.com), job board.
- Imdiversity Minorities' Job Bank (www.imdiversity.com), career and self-development information, targeting all ethnic minorities, and site for finding or posting job openings.
- Job Web (www.jobWeb.com), an online career fair for new college graduates.
- Monster Jobs (www.monster.com), a popular site with links to hundreds of companies with job listings.
- MonsterTrak.com (www.monstertrak.com), caters to college graduates.
- National Business and Disability Council (www.business-disability.com), for employers wanting to reach people with disabilities.
- National Resume Database (www.business-disability.com/Services/resume_database.asp) helps qualified college graduates with disabilities find jobs.
- Newslink (www.newslink.org/joblink/) posts classified ads from nearly 5,000 newspapers, magazines, and radio.

- Recruiters Online Network (www.recruitersonline.com) contains a job bank and recruiting tools.
- Step Stone (www.stepstone.com), an international recruiting site.

Summary

The process of receiving and reviewing resumes and employment applications has changed dramatically over the past decade. Increasingly, employers are using the Internet to recruit, either by developing webpages of their own or by linking up with Web-based job search services. Applicants, too, are preparing and transmitting many more resumes electronically.

One of the most dramatic changes that has come about as a result of the influx of electronic resumes is the newly proposed set of EEOC guidelines defining an applicant. This is significant since employers are required to keep records for applicants on the basis of race, gender, or ethnicity, to preclude charges of discrimination. These guidelines apply exclusively to the Internet and related technologies.

While electronic resumes currently dominate the marketplace, paper resumes still have their supporters. Regardless of your personal preference, everyone agrees that the two are vastly different.

Scannable resumes are basically devoid of all formatting and are text-focused as opposed to design-focused. Typically, they are created and/or saved in a .txt file format. If employers receive an applicant's printed scannable resume as hard copy they will scan it electronically, converting it into digitized format so they can then search for keywords to establish a preliminary match between an applicant and a job.

Many employers are bypassing the scanning step altogether and asking applicants to submit their resumes as an e-mail attachment, in the body of an e-mail message, or via a Web-based form built into their websites. Employers can then immediately search for keywords.

PDF documents require special software to open and read. Employers can print out PDF resumes but cannot load them into databases without first scanning the printouts.

The Internet may have changed the look of resumes, but cover letters remain fairly unchanged. They are still expected as an accompaniment to resumes, paper or electronic. Good cover letters identify the specific job or type of job sought, as well as highlight the submitter's qualifications.

As with paper resumes, electronic resumes may either be in a chronological or functional format. The chronological resume is organized by job title with the most recent position listed first. Functional resumes are arranged according to areas of skill and accomplishment. Employers tend to favor the chronological resume.

Companies that put up their own career sites online increase their chances of finding suitable employees. The primary objective of a career website is to attract qualified applicants whose backgrounds and interests are compatible with the environment and offerings of an organization. Applicants reportedly learn a great deal about a potential employer from the look and content of their site. Once an organization establishes an initial Web presence, it needs to focus on site upkeep. That means keeping job listings current and the site itself up-to-date with regard to new capabilities.

Websites offer a global presence as an increasing number of companies are posting their job openings online in more than 100 countries. While most of these sites are produced in English, for most people English is a second language. Accordingly, while they may be familiar with the basic structure of the language, they may be unaware of the many nuances we so often use. Easy-to-follow guidelines will help employers avoid international website snafus.

In addition to advertising on your company's career website, you can post openings on a variety of Internet job boards. Some of the most popular types include general job boards, industry-specific boards, government sites, diversity sites, and school job boards.

Increased Internet exposure brings with it a host of electronic recruiting risks. For example, employers need to be concerned about the legal risks of selecting resume-screening software that may categorically exclude members of certain protected groups. Another legal risk relates to the fact that some populations, such as older workers and people with disabilities, may have limited Internet access. Applicant tracking is yet another electronic recruiting risk, and maintaining applicant flow data in keeping with the newly proposed EEOC guidelines defining an applicant can complicate matters further. Many of these risks can be reduced if employers vary the recruitment sources they use.

Notes

1. Douglas P. Shuit, "The Insider," *Workforce Management* (April 2004), p. 54.
2. Margaret M. Clark, "EEOC Issues Much-Delayed Definition of Applicant," *HR Magazine* Vol. 49, No. 1 (April 2004), p. 29.
3. Bill Leonard, "Definition of Job Applicant Needs Work, SHRM Says," SHRM Online (June 15, 2004); available at www.shrm.org/hrnews_published/archives/CMS_008725.asp.
4. Yves Lermusiaux, "Finding Talent on the Web," *New York State HR Review* (Fall/Winter 2003), pp. 30–32.
5. Martha Frase-Blunt, "Make a Good First Impression," *HR Magazine* Vol. 49, No. 4 (April 2004), pp. 81–86.
6. Ibid.
7. Gillian Flynn, "E-Recruiting Ushers in Legal Dangers," Workforce Management Research Center; available at http://www.workforce.com/archive/article/23/10/03.php (registration required).
8. SHRM Online, "A Growing Digital Divide for Workers with Disabilities," *Workplace Visions*; available at http://www.shrm.org/trends/visions/5issue2003/1003a.asp with SHRM member log-in.
9. Ibid.
10. The online recruiting resources and Internet addresses listed are derived from the *2005 HR Yellow Pages: The Professional Sourcebook for HR Managers,* Supplement to the "HR Manager's Legal Reporter" (Old Saybrook, CT: Business & Legal Reports, Inc.), 2005.

PART II

Interviewing

CHAPTER 4

Interview Preparation

A commonly held but erroneous belief is that interviewing does not require any real preparation. The perception is that an interview is little more than two people sitting down together, having a conversation. As they talk, one person—the interviewer—asks questions, while the other—the applicant—answers the questions. Whether a job offer is extended depends on just how well the applicant answers the questions.

Such an impression is largely based on observations of interviews being conducted by seasoned interviewers who certainly can make employment interviews seem like effortless conversation. It is, however, an inaccurate observation because these interviewers have actually put a great deal of work behind this casual front by completing a number of preparatory steps before meeting the applicants.

Job Analysis

The process of interview preparation begins with a thorough job analysis. This includes a review of the position's responsibilities, requirements, reporting relationships, environmental factors, exemption and union status, salary, benefits, and growth opportunities. This important task provides necessary answers to four key questions:

1. Am I thoroughly familiar with the qualities being sought in an applicant?
2. Are these qualities both job-related and realistic?
3. Can I clearly communicate the duties and responsibilities of this position to applicants?
4. Am I prepared to provide additional relevant information about the job and the company to applicants?

Duties and Responsibilities

Job analysts (typically HR specialists) should make it a point to spend time in the department where openings exist, observing and conversing with incumbents as they perform various aspects of the job, as well as talking with supervisors in charge about their perspective of the scope of work involved. If possible, they should also seek out people who previously held the position to shed light on how the job may have evolved. Visiting on more than one occasion allows the job analyst to observe a typical day. If personal visits aren't feasible, lengthy conversations with several departmental representatives will suffice.

In reviewing the duties and responsibilities of an opening, job analysts will want to determine if they are realistic in relation to other factors, such as previous experience and education. Equally important is determining if they're relevant to the overall job function, and if they overlap with the responsibilities of other jobs.

Job analysts should review the duties and responsibilities of a job each time a position becomes available. Even if an opening was filled six months ago and is now vacant again, assessing its current status will ensure that no major changes have occurred in the interim. This, in turn, will guarantee up-to-date job information and accuracy when discussing the position with potential employees.

Education and Prior Experience

The process of job analysis continues with identifying appropriate educational and prior experience prerequisites. This can best be accomplished when managers and HR representatives join together to ask these key questions:

- What skills and knowledge are needed to successfully perform the primary duties and responsibilities of this job?
- Why are these skills and knowledge necessary?
- Why couldn't someone without these skills and knowledge perform the primary duties of this job?
- Are the requirements consistent with the job duties and responsibilities?
- Is the background of the present or last incumbent influencing us?
- Are we subjectively considering our own personal expectations of the job?
- Are we compromising because we're in a hurry to fill the job?
- Are we unrealistically searching for the ideal applicant?
- Are we succumbing to pressure from others, such as senior management, with regard to what are appropriate job requirements?
- Are the requirements in accordance with all applicable equal employment opportunity laws and regulations?

Arbitrarily setting high minimum standards in the hope of filling a position with the most qualified person can backfire. For example, suppose you're trying to fill a first-line supervisor's spot and you decide on someone who not only has a great deal of hands-on experience, but is also well-rounded. To you, this translates into someone with at least five years of supervisory experience and a four-year college degree. If asked some of the questions just suggested, you would probably conclude that these requirements are too high for a first-line supervisory position. Also, for reasons of possible discrimination, you would have to modify them. But even if there were no applicable employment laws, there is a good reason for setting more flexible standards: If you came across an applicant who fell short of this experience and educational profile but who met other intangible requirements and came highly recommended, you would not be able to hire her. It would be difficult to justify hiring someone not meeting the minimum requirements of the job, especially if you also rejected applicants who exceeded them.

In addition to asking yourself these basic questions regarding experience and education, there is a way of setting requirements that doesn't paint you into a corner but still allows you to be highly selective. By using carefully worded terminology you can choose the applicant who best combines concrete and intangible requirements. Suggested phrases include the following:

- Demonstrated ability to _____ required.
- In-depth knowledge of _____ required.
- Extensive experience in _____ required.
- Knowledge of _____ would be an advantage.
- Proven ability to _____ required.
- We are looking for an effective _____.
- Proven track record of _____ needed.
- Substantial experience in _____ essential.
- Familiarity with _____ would be ideal.
- Degree relevant to _____ preferred.
- Degree in _____ preferred.
- Advanced degree a plus.
- College degree in _____ highly desirable.
- An equivalent combination of education and experience.

These sample phrases all provide the latitude to select someone who may be lacking in one area, such as education, but compensates with additional experience. The use of such statements does not mean you're compromising hiring standards; rather, it means you're taking care to avoid setting requirements that cannot be justified by the specific duties of the job, while at the same time offering the widest range of choice among applicants.

Intangible Requirements

To lend balance to a lack of specific educational or experiential requirements, or to "round out" the concrete requirements of a job, intangible criteria can be helpful— for example:

- Ability to get along with coworkers, management, employees, clients, and customers

- Appearance
- Assertiveness
- Attitude
- Creativity and imagination
- Initiative
- Management style
- Maturity
- Personality
- Responsiveness
- Self-confidence
- Temperament

These factors can be significant, but only when examined in relation to the requirements of the opening. That is, in addition to determining any relevant education and experience prerequisites and examining the scope and degree of responsibilities, you should explore the question of what type of individual would be most compatible with the position. This may best be determined by learning as much as possible about such job factors as the amount of stress involved, the amount of independent work (as opposed to closely supervised work), and the overall management style of the department. The combined information should translate into a profile of the ideal employee.

Keeping this profile in mind as job seekers are considered can be helpful, particularly if two or more applicants meet the concrete requirements of the job. You can then compare intangible job-related criteria to help make the final decision. Intangibles can also be helpful in evaluating applicants for entry-level jobs for which there are few, if any, tangible educational and experience prerequisites.

Be careful when making comparisons based on intangibles, since the meaning of certain terms can be highly subjective. For example, some of the more popular applicant evaluation phrases—saying that an applicant has a bad attitude, a winning personality, a nice appearance, or a mature approach to work—may not translate the same way for everyone. Furthermore, such descriptions really do not tell anything substantive about what the person can contribute to a given job. Hence, be careful not to weigh intangible elements too heavily or select someone solely on the basis of any of these factors. If considered at all, such factors must be job-related, not based on personal bias.

Reporting Relationships

Another facet of job analysis has to do with reporting relationships. In this regard, ask yourself the following questions:

- What position will this job report to, both directly and indirectly?
- Where does this job appear on the department's organizational chart?
- What positions, if any, report directly and/or indirectly to this job?
- What is the relationship between this job and other jobs in the department, in terms of level and scope of responsibility?
- What is the relationship between this job and other jobs in the organization?

These questions all pertain to positions, as opposed to specific individuals. Once you've determined the nature and level of a reporting relationship, you can factor in any relevant personality traits of the person to whom the opening reports. For example, if the department head with an opening for an assistant is known to have a short fuse, you would be wise to seek out someone who has demonstrated in past jobs the ability to effectively deal with such outbursts.

Work Environment

A job's work environment consists of four distinct considerations: physical working conditions, geographic location, travel requirements, and work schedule. A work environment checklist appears in Appendix C.

Physical Working Conditions

Examples are working in areas that may not be well ventilated, exposure to chemicals or toxic fumes, working in cramped quarters, working in a very noisy location, working extensively with video display terminals, and sitting or standing for long periods of time. With regard to the last two points, employers are increasingly consulting with ergonomists for help with carpal tunnel syndrome problems and defining postures that minimize unnecessary static work and reduce the forces acting on the body.

If working conditions are ideal, few interviewers will hesitate to inform prospective employees. After all, this helps sell the company and the job, perhaps even compensating for areas that fall short—perhaps the starting salary is not up to par with that of a competitor or the benefits package is not as comprehensive. However, if the working conditions leave something to be desired, the tendency is to omit reference to them when discussing the job, in the hope that once employees begin work and discover the flaw in the work environment they will adjust rather than leave. Unfortunately, what frequently occurs is that new employees resent the deception and either quit, develop poor work habits, or harbor feelings of resentment over being had.

The problems of high turnover and poor morale as they relate to unsatisfactory working conditions can easily be prevented. First, accurately describe existing working conditions to prospective employees. If an unpleasant condition is temporary, by all means say so, but don't make anything up. Be sure to ask applicants whether they've ever worked under similar conditions before and for how long. When they respond, watch as well as listen to their answers. Often there is a contradiction between an applicant's verbal and nonverbal responses; skilled interviewers are able to incorporate and evaluate both types of response. Issues of actively listening and nonverbal communication will be developed in subsequent chapters; for now, suffice it to say that if an applicant verbally states that she doesn't mind standing seven hours a day, but you sense hesitancy in her body language, pursue the subject until you're more certain of her true response.

Another way of assessing potential employees' reactions to less-than-ideal working conditions is to show them where they would be working. Unless it's logistically impossible, a quick trip to the job site should be part of the interview. This way there will be no surprises and a new employee knows exactly what to expect.

Geographic Location

As stated, if at all possible show potential employees where they would be working. If recruiting from a central office for positions in satellite branches, be specific in the description of the job site and offer videos, CD-ROMs, or brochures realistically illustrating the location where an opening exists.

Sometimes a position will call for rotation from one location to another. If this is the case, be prepared to describe the working conditions of each location and how long each assignment is likely to last. Be sure to solicit a reaction to the idea of job rotation. Many employees prefer to settle into a work routine where they're familiar with the environment, the commute, and the other workers. On the other hand, some people like the variety offered by a rotational position.

Travel

Discuss the geographic span and the expected frequency of job-related travel. Tell applicants, too, how much advance notice they can generally expect to receive before having to leave. In the case of local travel, applicants will want to know whether they will be expected to provide their own transportation. They will also want to know how reimbursement for job-related travel expenses is handled.

Schedule

Employees, especially at the nonexempt level, need to know what days of the week they're expected to work, how many hours they're being paid for, when to report to work each day, and when they may leave. If alternative work arrangements are available, applicants need to know their options. Also important is how much time is allotted for meals and other scheduled breaks throughout the day. It's also a good idea to identify the number of vacation days, paid holidays, and any other days they may take off, such as personal days. Conveying this information to applicants can avoid disciplinary problems after they become employees.

Exemption Status

As noted in Chapter 2, the Fair Labor Standards Act (FLSA), defines the term *exempt* literally to mean "exempt from overtime compensation"—that is, an employer is not required to pay exempt employees for time worked beyond their regularly scheduled workweek. This generally pertains to executives, managers, and some supervisors. The term *nonexempt* literally means "not exempt from overtime compensation." Full-time nonexempt employees, such as clerical workers, must be paid for any time worked beyond their regularly scheduled workweek.

To assist with exemption classification, the Department of Labor offers a series of requirements that must be met before classifying someone as exempt. These requirements appear in test form: one for duties and another for salary. Together, they help employers determine the exemption status of their workforce.

The actual work or duties performed by employees, not their job titles, determines exemption status. With most positions there is no question as to whether they are exempt or nonexempt. However, some jobs fall into a gray area and are not as easily categorized.

In 2004, the Department of Labor released revisions to the rules governing overtime eligibility for white-collar workers under the FLSA. While the duties test has remained virtually the same, the salary test—that is, the salary level below which employees are automatically nonexempt and due overtime—has changed dramatically. Under the old rules, this figure was set at between $155 and $250 per week. The new rules raise the salary test to $455 per week. Employees making less than that amount are automatically entitled to nonexempt status and overtime. Employees classified as exempt who make between $155 and $455 per week are affected by the new overtime regulations. Fact sheets are available at www.dol.gov.

Union Status

The National Labor Relations Act (also known as the Wagner Act) clearly states:

> **Employees shall have the right to self-organization, to form, join, or assist labor organizations, to bargain collectively, through representatives of their own choosing, and to engage in other concerted activities, for the purpose of collective bargaining or other mutual aid or protection.**

According to a study conducted by the University of Maryland based on data from the *Union Membership and Earnings Data Book,* union membership has been steadily declining in manufacturing and the private sector, but rising in the public sector.[1] Over the past thirty years, union membership has gone from a high of nearly 40 percent of the total labor force to a current low of 16 percent. In the private, or nonmanufacturing, sector the numbers have dropped from 17 percent to 8 percent. However, the public sector shows an increase—from 23 percent to its current high of 37 percent. Much of this rise occurred prior to 1980; since that time, the percentage of the total labor force in the public sector has pretty much leveled off.

If applicants are interviewing for union positions, interviewers should be prepared to tell them if they are required to join. Interviewers should also share information relative to initiation fees or required dues and, essentially, what being a union member entails. Do not express your personal opinions regarding unions or try to influence applicants, either for or against unions. Also, avoid inquiries regarding the applicant's present views toward unions or questions about past union involvement. Your job is to be informative and descriptive only.

Salary Ranges

Whether this information is disclosed to an applicant at the initial interview is a matter of company policy, but interviewers should certainly know what a job pays so they can determine if an applicant warrants further consideration. If, for example, there is an opening for an administrative assistant offering an annual salary of from $50,000 to $62,500, and an applicant is currently earning $55,750 a year, there's no problem. On the other hand, if a managerial position becomes available with a salary range of from $65,000 to $78,000 and an applicant is currently earning an annual salary of $77,000, there is cause for concern. What is your company's policy regarding starting a new employee so close to the maximum of the salary range? If you offer the maximum, will this person accept an increase of just $1,000? What about subsequent salary increases? Does your company "red circle" employees who are at the ceiling of their ranges so that they remain frozen until either the salary structure is reevaluated or the position is reclassified?

Other types of salary-related issues may arise. Applicants may presently be earning considerably less than the minimum salary you're offering for what may be considered comparable work. It could be that they're currently underpaid, or not being altogether forthright about the actual duties and responsibilities they perform. This calls for a more thorough line of questioning during the interview regarding the level and scope of tasks they presently perform and are capable of performing.

Applicants sometimes indicate that they are currently earning considerably more than the maximum for an available position, but are receptive to taking a pay cut. This doesn't automatically mean they are overqualified or, if hired, that they'll get restless and leave the job. There are a number of explanations as to why someone would be willing to take a reduction in pay, including the opportunity to work for a specific company, the desire to learn new skills or enter a new field, or an inability to find suitable work in one's own profession.

Related to the issue of salary is the "sign on" or "hiring" bonus. Previously reserved for executive-level applicants and highly specialized, hard-to-fill positions, the bonus is now becoming an increasingly popular means for attracting top college graduates. It generally amounts to up to 10 percent of salary not surpassing $100,000, and between 15 percent and 20 percent for salaries over $100,000. Depending on how difficult it may be to fill a job or how desirable it is to attract a particular individual, the bonus may reach as high as 25 percent.

The sign-on bonus enables employers to attract top-quality employees without disturbing the company's salary structure. Problems relating to salary increases in subsequent years may arise if the person's new salary is the same or only slightly greater than the combined starting salary and bonus.

Benefits

Describing your company's benefits package can be an excellent selling point, especially for hard-to-fill positions. Recruiters are advised to prepare a forty-five to sixty second summary of company benefits, such as medical and disability insurance, dental coverage, life insurance, profit-sharing plans, stock bonus programs, vacation days, personal days, leaves of absence, holidays, and tuition reimbursement.

Be careful not to give the impression that a discussion of your company's benefits means an applicant is being seriously considered for a job. Make it clear that providing this information is part of the interview process, and that the selected applicant will receive more comprehensive benefits information at the time of hire.

Growth Opportunities

Generally, applicants are interested in whether they will be able to move up in an organization. It is therefore helpful to know about the frequency of performance appraisals, salary reviews, and increases; policies regarding promotions; relationship of a position's level and scope of responsibilities to that of others within a job family; policies governing internal job posting; likelihood of advancement; tuition reimbursement plans; and training.

It's important to provide an accurate account of growth opportunities to preclude the possibility of morale problems developing later on. For example, if an applicant is applying for a position that is one step removed from the top position in a given job family and that position has been occupied by the same person for the past ten years, the opportunity for growth by way of promotion is unlikely. There are, however, other ways to grow, such as an expansion of responsibilities that could, in turn, lead to the creation of a new job classification.

Job Descriptions

The primary purpose of a job description is to identify the essential function of a job; that is, those tasks that are fundamental to the position. It clarifies what the role of the job is and what the incumbent is expected to accomplish. Essentially, a job description forms the groundwork for an agreement between an employer and the incumbent as to expected job performance results. Accordingly, the language should be concise, straightforward, uncomplicated, and easily interpreted.

Every position in an organization should have a job description, whether it's generic or specific. Generic job descriptions are written in broad, general terms and may be used for several similar positions in different departments of the same company. For example, there may be one generic job description for the position "administrative assistant" rather than a separate administrative assistant job description for each department. Specific job descriptions define the duties and tasks of one particular position, such as "vice president of human resources." They are written when a position has unique responsibilities that distinguish it from other, similarly entitled jobs.

Job descriptions are multipurpose tools that can be used in virtually every aspect of the employment process:

Clarifying relationships between jobs	Demotions	Disciplinary actions
Employee orientations	Exit interviews	Grieving proceedings
Interviewing	Job posting	Outplacement
Performance appraisals	Promotions	Recruitment
Salary structuring	Selection	Training
Transfers	Workflow analyses	

Since job descriptions can be used for many different purposes, employers should take care to write them as comprehensively as possible. Initially, this will require a fair amount of time, but it will prove well worth the effort. Here are fifteen guidelines for writing job descriptions:

1. *Arrange duties and responsibilities in a logical, sequential order.* Begin with the task requiring the greatest amount of time or carrying the greatest responsibility.

2. *State separate duties clearly and concisely.* This way anyone can glance at the description and easily identify each duty. Consider also further identifying each task as "essential" or "nonessential."

3. *Try to avoid generalizations or ambiguous words.* Use specific language and be exact in your meaning. To illustrate: "Handles mail" might be better expressed as "sorts mail" or "distributes mail."

4. *Do not try to list every task.* Use the phrase "Primary duties and responsibilities include . . ." at the beginning of your job description and proceed from there. You may also choose to close with the phrase "Performs other related duties and responsibilities, as required."

5. *Include specific examples of duties wherever possible.* This will enable the person reading the job description to more fully understand the scope of responsibility involved.

6. *Use nontechnical language.* A good job description explains the responsibilities of a job in terms that are understandable to everyone using it.

7. *Indicate the frequency of occurrence of each duty.* One popular method is to have a column on the left of the list of tasks with corresponding percentages that represent the estimated amount of time devoted to each primary duty.

8. *List duties individually and concisely rather than using narrative paragraph form.* Remember, a job description is not an English composition.

9. *Do not refer to specific people.* Instead, refer to titles and positions. Incumbents are likely to change positions long before the positions themselves are revamped or eliminated.

10. *Use the present tense.* It reads more smoothly.

11. *Be objective and accurate in describing the job.* Be careful not to describe the present incumbent, someone who may have just been fired for poor performance, or someone who was recently promoted for outstanding job performance. Also, if you held that particular job, don't talk about yourself and how you handled it. Describe the job as it should be performed—not as you would like to see it performed.

12. *Stress what the incumbent does, instead of explaining a procedure that is used.* To illustrate: it is better to say the person in the job "records appointments," rather than saying "a record of appointments must be kept."

13. *Be certain that all requirements are job-related and are in accordance with equal employment opportunity laws and regulations.* This will preclude the likelihood of legal problems developing later on.

14. *Eliminate unnecessary articles such as "a" and "the" in the job description.* Do not make the description too wordy. Most job descriptions can be completed in one or two pages. The length of a job description does not increase the importance of the job.

15. *Use action words.* This means any word that describes a specific function, such as "organizes." Within a sentence, one word should stand out as most descriptive, a word that could readily stand alone. This action word will also convey to the reader a degree of responsibility. For example, compare "directs" to "under the direction of." Try to begin each sentence with an action word; the first word used should introduce the function being described. Here is a list of 125 sample action words that employers can refer to when writing job descriptions:

accepts	acts	administers	advises	allocates
analyzes	anticipates	approves	arranges	ascertains
assigns	assists	audits	authorizes	balances
batches	calculates	circulates	classifies	codes
collects	compiles	conducts	consolidates	constructs
consults	coordinates	corrects	correlates	counsels
creates	delegates	deletes	designs	determines
develops	devises	directs	disseminates	documents
drafts	edits	ensures	establishes	evaluates
examines	facilitates	figures	files	fills in
fines	follows up	formulates	furnishes	generates
guides	identifies	implements	informs	initiates
inputs	inspects	instructs	interprets	interviews
investigates	issues	itemizes	lists	locates
maintains	manages	measures	modifies	monitors

negotiates	notifies	observes	obtains	operates
organizes	originates	outlines	oversees	participates
performs	plans	prepares	processes	proposes
provides	pursues	rates	receives	recommends
records	refers	renders	reports	represents
requests	researches	reviews	revises	routes
schedules	screens	selects	signs	specifies
studies	submits	summarizes	supervises	tabulates
trains	transcribes	transposes	troubleshoots	types
utilizes	verifies	writes		

After writing a job description, ask yourself a series of questions to confirm its contents:

- What is the purpose of the job?
- Will the jobholder supervise the work of others? If so, can I provide job titles and a brief description of the responsibilities of those supervised?
- What duties will the jobholder perform regularly, periodically, and infrequently? Can I list these duties in order of importance?
- What degree of supervision will be exercised over the jobholder?
- To what extent will instructions be necessary when assigning work to the jobholder?
- How much decision-making authority or judgment will the jobholder have in the performance of required duties?
- What are the working conditions?
- What skills are necessary for the successful performance of the essential functions of the job?
- What authority will the jobholder have in directing the work of others?
- At what stage will the manager in charge review the jobholder's work?
- What equipment will the jobholder be responsible for operating? Am I able to adequately describe the equipment's complexity?
- What would be the cost to management of serious errors that the jobholder might make in the regular performance of required duties?
- What employees within the organization, and customers or clients outside the organization, will the jobholder interact with on a regular basis?

The exact contents of a job description will be dictated by the specific environment and needs of an organization. The basic categories of job information required for most positions are listed here:

Date

Job analyst

Job title

Department

Reporting relationship

Location of the job

Exemption status

Salary grade and range

Work schedule

Job summary

Duties and responsibilities, including extent of authority and degree of independent judgment required

Job requirements, including education, prior work experience, and specialized skill and knowledge

Physical environment and working conditions

Equipment and machinery to be used

Other relevant factors, such as degree of contact with the public or customers and access to confidential information

A job description form containing these categories appears in Appendix D.

A database of well-written job descriptions provides an organization with an understanding of how the job contributes to the achievement of companywide goals; it also offers a solid legal base with respect to employment-related decisions made relative to that job. Once a job description is written, review it on a semiannual or annual basis to make certain the content or requirements of the job have not changed.

The Right Fit

Jack had just interviewed three applicants for the customer service representative opening at the large retail store where he works. All three met the basic requirements of the job and appeared capable of performing the essential functions of the job as identified in the job description, but something bothered Jack about each of them:

- The first applicant had a great deal of relevant experience and demonstrated a thorough understanding of the job duties. There was no doubt in Jack's mind that she could do the job. What bothered him was a nagging sensation that she would resist adjusting to a new environment and would fail to work in concert with the other representatives.

- The second applicant was the least experienced but indicated a great willingness to learn and work hard. He was pleasant enough, but Jack had a troublesome image of him reporting to Eliza, the manager in charge of the department. During the interview, the applicant had indicated that, at his former job, there had been a slight verbal altercation between himself and another employee—a woman—

and his boss, also a woman, had "taken sides" against him. He felt there had been some gender bias involved.

- The third applicant had a sufficient degree of experience. Jack had no trouble picturing her working alongside the other representatives and taking direction from Eliza. What troubled him was that she didn't seem interested in doing anything beyond what was expected. There was no willingness to pitch in and help the other representatives, which is often required during the company's peak holiday season.

What should Jack do? He knows that there is no ideal employee, but each of these applicants fell short in areas that are critical to the successful performance of the job. Should he keep looking?

The answer is yes, Jack should keep looking, but not before he clarifies what he's looking for. The requirements and areas of responsibility identified in a job description are excellent indicators of the skills connected to a job; however, they cannot unveil what a person is willing to do once on the job, or how well his bank of intangible skills will allow him to fit within a new organizational culture. It's these elements together that produce the best possible employee; that is, the right fit.

The right fit begins with identifying what someone has accomplished, either at past jobs or through the performance of relevant non-job-specific tasks. By asking questions that will yield specific measurable and verifiable responses (see Chapters 6 and 7), and comparing the answers with the particulars identified in the job description, recruiters can largely determine what a person is capable of doing. In other words, they can isolate someone's tangible skills and abilities.

The next stage of determining the right fit has to do with what a person is willing to do with these tangible skills and abilities. Recruiters can relate past performance to the future by asking competency-based questions (Chapter 6). Always bear in mind, though, this important observation: Since we are all essentially creatures of habit, it's likely that job applicants will approach a problem, make a decision, or communicate in their new work environment in essentially the same way as they did in their former job. As such, it's important to ask for specific examples of how past performance relates to the performance of specific job-related tasks for the available position.

The final stage of identifying whether a person will be the right fit concerns a host of intangible qualities. Depending on the job and the work environment, these intangibles could include:

- Willingness to accept criticism
- Ability to function effectively in a different work environment
- Disposition toward working with others whose approach to problem solving may differ from their own
- Interest in learning from those whose work style differs from their own
- Outlook on accepting direction from someone whose communication style differs from what they're accustomed to

- Ability to work as an integral member of a diverse team
- Degree of flexibility
- Ability to adjust to sudden changes in direction
- Knack for multitasking
- Tolerance for working with individuals of varying degrees of effectiveness

In addition to identifying tangible requirements and tasks, then, recruiters need to clearly identify what a job requires in terms of willingness on the part of the employee, as well as relevant intangible qualities. Together, these three ingredients will result in the right fit.

Reviewing the Application and Resume

Never conduct an interview without first reviewing the applicant's completed application and/or resume, for two main reasons: First, you will begin to become familiar with the person's credentials, background, and qualifications as they relate to the requirements and responsibilities of the job; second, you can identify areas for discussion during the interview.

Each organization should have an application form, whether paper or electronic, that reflects its own environment. For example, the application form for a highly technical company will differ from one used by a nonprofit organization. Some companies have more than one form: one for professional or exempt positions, another for nonexempt positions. Appendix E contains a generic sample employment application form with categories that are applicable to many positions in most work environments.

When designing an application form, it's important to remember that all categories must be relevant and job-related. This is critical from the standpoint of compliance with equal employment opportunity (EEO) laws and regulations. In this regard, familiarity with federal laws is not sufficient, since many state laws are more stringent: Compliance with federal regulations could still mean violation of state regulations. Where there is a difference, the stricter law prevails. Oversight or ignorance of the law does not provide immunity.

Resumes differ from applications in that people start with a blank piece of paper or a blank screen, as opposed to a form with specific questions. Consequently, applicants can offer whatever data they choose on a resume. Generally, the same basic information should appear on a resume as appears on an application form, including work history (employer, location, duration, duties, and special accomplishments), educational degrees or certificates, and scholastic achievements. Career objectives may also be cited.

There are ten key areas to focus on when reviewing an application or resume. Remember these are guidelines only. Deviation from any one of the standards should not, in and of itself, result in the rejection of an applicant. Nor should a specific standard in this list be considered at all if it's not relevant to the responsibilities of the position in question:

1. *Scan the overall appearance of the application or resume.* Check to see that it's neat and easy to read. The handwriting on applications should be legible; and whether the resume is typed and printed or is submitted electronically, it should reflect resume-writing guidelines in terms of organizing the information and highlighting key accomplishments. The contents of applications and resumes should be grammatically correct and the language easy to understand. Paper resumes are generally one to two pages in length and should be professional in appearance. Cover letters usually accompany paper and electronic resumes, demonstrating added interest on the part of the applicant.

2. *Look for any blanks or omissions.* This is easy with an application form; with a resume, check to see that basic information relating to work and education has not been excluded. Make note of any missing data so you can ask the applicant about it during the face-to-face interview. Some employment application forms are poorly designed, as are some electronic resume formats. This can cause applicants to inadvertently overlook certain questions or categories. Or it may be that an applicant purposely omitted certain information. If this is the case, it's up to you to find out why and to determine the importance of the missing data during the interview.

3. *Review the applicant's work history and make a note of any time gaps between jobs.* If an applicant indicates that he took some time off between jobs to travel throughout Europe, make a note of it. Be careful not to pass judgment, deciding that this was a frivolous and irresponsible pursuit. Fill in the gaps and worry about drawing conclusions after the interview process is completed.

4. *Consider any overlaps in time.* For example, the dates on an application may show that the applicant was attending school and working at the same time. Of course, this is possible, but not if the school happens to be in California and the job was in New York (unless it was a correspondence school). Even if the locations are consistent, you need to verify the accuracy of the dates.

5. *Make a note of any other inconsistencies.* To illustrate, say there is an applicant with an extensive educational background who has been employed in a series of non-exempt jobs. This may be because she has degrees in a highly specialized field and cannot find suitable work, or it may be that her educational credentials are misrepresented. It's up to you to find out.

6. *Consider the frequency of job changes.* People voluntarily leave jobs for many reasons, including an inaccurate description of the work at the time of hire, an improper job match, personality conflicts on the job, inadequate salary increases, limited growth opportunities, and unkept promises. Some employees, knowing that they're doing poorly, voluntarily terminate their employment just prior to a scheduled performance evaluation. Then there are instances when employees are let go for reasons unrelated to performance: A company shuts down for economic

reasons, major organizational changes result in the deletion of positions, or a contingency assignment is completed and there is no additional work to be done. Of course, employees are also terminated for poor performance.

When reviewing an applicant's employment record, do not draw premature, negative conclusions regarding the frequency of job changes. Determining what constitutes a frequent change is highly subjective and often driven by the economy. Too often interviewers set arbitrary guidelines, sometimes patterned after their own work history. You may decide that changing jobs more often than once every two years is too frequent and indicates unreliability. However, at this stage of the interview process, you simply do not have enough information to make such a decision. After all, you haven't even met the applicant yet. Make a note that you want to discuss the pattern of job changes, and move on to the next category.

7. *Be objective when evaluating a person's salary requirements.* In our society it's assumed that everyone wants and needs to make more money. While money is one of the most commonly cited reasons for changing jobs, you will undoubtedly come across applicants who are willing to take a job at a lower salary than they were previously or are presently earning. The reasons vary. Sometimes an individual wants to move from one area of specialization to another and recognizes that a lack of expertise in the field will mean less money. Then there are those who want to work for a particular company and are willing to earn less in order to do so. Some people view job satisfaction as being of paramount importance. For those who have been unemployed for a long time and cannot find work at their old rate of pay, any job is seen as an opportunity. The message, then, is not to draw premature conclusions.

It is significant to note that factoring in information relevant to salaries earned in past positions may be a violation of the Equal Pay Act of 1963, which prohibits paying women less than men for performing substantially equal work (see Chapter 5). This could occur where an employer learns that a woman has been earning considerably less in previous jobs than a man with a comparable background of skills and experience. If both are hired for the same type of job to perform substantially equal work and are offered starting salaries that are, say, $5,000 above their previous salaries, and perform at comparable levels of effectiveness during their respective terms of employment, the pay differential between the two will widen that much more.

Consider, for example, a male applicant hired at a starting annual salary of $65,000 and a woman who is hired to perform comparable work at a salary of $59,000. Both receive an "excellent" evaluation at the time of their first performance evaluation, resulting in a 5 percent increase. The original $6,000 gap between their respective salaries has just increased to $6,300, as the male employee's annual earnings rise to $68,250 and the woman employee's salary increases to only $61,950. If their performance levels remain comparable at the time of their next review, warranting another 5 percent raise, the gap will increase to $6,615, since the man will now be earning $71,662.50 and the woman will only be making $65,047.50 (essentially what the man was offered at the time of hire). Over time, presuming continued comparable performance, this pay gap will continue to widen. Such a pay difference that is based on past earnings could be a violation of the Equal Pay Act if it is perceived to be a differential based on sex.

8. *Carefully review the applicant's reasons for leaving previous jobs.* Look for a pattern. For example, if the reason given for leaving several jobs in a row is "no room for growth," it may be that this person's job expectations are unrealistic. While this explanation could be perfectly legitimate, it could also be a cover-up for other, less acceptable reasons. This is a key area to explore in the face-to-face interview.

9. *Make a note to ask for elaboration of duties that are not clearly described on the application or resume.* Job titles may also require explanation. Some titles are not functional or descriptive and therefore fail to reveal their scope of responsibility. Examples of such titles include "administrative assistant" and "vice president." Sometimes titles sound quite grand, but upon probing, you discover that they carry few substantive responsibilities.

10. *Review the application or resume for "red flags."* Look for any information that doesn't seem to make sense or leaves you with an uneasy feeling. A classic example: The application asks for the "Reason for Leaving Last Job." The popular answer "Personal" should alert you to a possible problem. Many interviewers assume that they have no right to pursue this issue further—that to do so would be an invasion of the person's privacy. This is not true. You have an obligation to ask the applicant to be more specific. If people begin to volunteer information about their home life and personal relationships, then you must interrupt and ask them to focus on job-related incidents that may have contributed to their decision to leave. Also note that "personal" is frequently a cover-up for "fired."

Setting the Stage

If you've ever watched a video or DVD about employment interviewing, it probably didn't reference the significance of setting the stage; that is, the importance of allowing sufficient time for meeting with an applicant and conducting that meeting in an appropriate environment. And yet, these are two critical components to successful interviewing.

Allowing Sufficient Time for the Interview

When determining how much time to allot for each interview, think about the entire process, not just the portion devoted to the face-to-face meeting. Time is needed before the interview to review the application and/or resume; during the interview for both you and the applicant to ask questions and for you to provide information about the job and company; and after the interview to write up your notes, reflect on what took place, set up additional appointments, and check references. Additional time may also be required before or after the interview for testing.

Considering all that must be done, just how much time should be set aside for each interview? Much depends on the nature of the job—namely, whether it is non-exempt or exempt. Generally speaking, more time is needed for interviewing professionals: usually a total of one and a half to two hours, with sixty to ninety minutes for the face-to-face meeting and approximately thirty minutes to be divided between the pre- and post-interview activities. This amount of time should be sufficient for you to ascertain the necessary information about an applicant's qualifications and to get a good idea of job suitability and applicant interest. If the actual face-to-face interview runs much beyond 90 minutes, it becomes tiresome for both the applicant and the interviewer.

In the case of interviews for nonexempt positions, approximately forty-five to seventy-five minutes should be allotted, with thirty to forty-five minutes for the face-to-face meeting. More concrete subjects—such as specific job duties, attendance records, and the like—are usually probed at this level. These issues take less time to explore than do the numerous intangible areas examined at the exempt level, such as management style, level of creativity, and initiative.

The time frames discussed here should be used as guidelines only. Be flexible in the amount of time allotted, but also be aware that these general parameters can help you ascertain sufficient information and avoid discussing irrelevant factors. For example, if you find that your interviews are over within fifteen minutes, you may not be phrasing your questions properly; that is, you could be asking close-ended questions as opposed to competency or open-ended questions (see Chapters 6 and 7). It may also be that you're not adequately probing suspicious areas, or perhaps simply don't know what questions to ask.

If, on the other hand, your interviews last much beyond forty-five minutes for a nonexempt position or ninety minutes for an exempt position, it's likely that the applicant has taken control of the interview. When this occurs, interviewers often find themselves describing their own career with the company at some length, discussing the contents of books on their shelves, or explaining photos on their desks. It's not unusual for applicants lacking sufficient job-related experience to steer interviewers away from questions regarding their job suitability. By diverting the interviewer's attention and talking a blue streak about irrelevant matters, applicants hope to cloud the real issue of whether they're qualified for the job. Of course, some people simply like to talk a lot and don't intend to be devious. Regardless of the motive, however, interviewers are cautioned against allowing applicants to take control of the interview. This is less likely to happen if you're aware of the appropriate time frame for an interview.

To help maximize the time set aside for meeting applicants, consider the three scheduling guidelines that follow:

1. *Ideally, interview only during the time of day when your "biological clock" is at its peak— that is, when you're most alert.* If you tend to slow down around mid-morning, but

then pick up again around 1 p.m., it would be best to schedule interviews during the afternoon hours. Likewise, if you're at your best first thing in the morning, late-afternoon appointments would be unwise.

2. *When you have a number of positions to fill and several applicants remain to be seen, try to take a five-minute break between interviews.* The time can be used for just about anything, including taking a short walk, getting a drink of water, stretching, making a few short phone calls, or doing other work. The break will help you feel more in control of your interview schedule and also allow you to focus more clearly on your next applicant.

3. *Try not to conduct more than four or five interviews in one workday.* Obviously, this may not always be possible, particularly when you have a number of openings to fill. But if you can space your interviews with other work, you'll find that your attention level during the interviews, as well as during the other work, is likely to improve.

Planning an Appropriate Environment

If applicants are expected to talk freely, they must be assured that others can't overhear what they're saying. This is particularly important when discussing sensitive matters, such as why they are being asked to leave their present jobs. Hence, interviewers must ensure privacy. Not everyone has a private office, but everyone has access to privacy. This may mean borrowing someone else's office when it's not being used, using the company cafeteria or dining room during off-hours, or sitting in a portion of the lobby that is set apart from those areas receiving the most traffic. Such options may be preferable if your own office has partial partitions instead of full floor-to-ceiling walls. Sounds can easily carry over and around partitions; depending on their height, people can also easily peer over the top.

Interviewers should ensure a minimum number of distractions. More obvious distractions include your phone ringing without voice mail or someone answering it for you, people walking into your office during the interview, or papers requiring attention left exposed on top of your desk. Some interviewers claim that such distractions are actually beneficial in that they allow for an assessment of how the applicant handles interruptions. This is unlikely. Distractions and interruptions waste valuable time for both the applicant and the interviewer. Moreover, the applicant may be left with an unfavorable impression of the interviewer in particular, and possibly the organization overall.

A more subtle distraction, but one that can interfere as much as a phone ringing or someone barging in during the interview, is the interviewer's own thoughts. Thinking about all the work that needs to be done may not only prevent you from focusing fully on the applicant, but may even produce a feeling of resentment toward this person for keeping you from it. To guard against this tendency, remind yourself just before meeting an applicant that the sooner you fill the opening, the sooner you can move on to other tasks. It might also help if you cleared off your desk before the job applicant sits down for the interview.

Interviewers should also ensure that the applicant is comfortable. It's a simple fact that if the applicant feels comfortable, you'll be assured of a more productive meeting. Comfort level is not determined by how much furniture there is in your office, whether you have rugs on the floor, or if your office overlooks a scenic view. It's your behavior and general approach to the interview that will largely determine the comfort level of the applicant. If you come across as friendly, appear genuinely interested in what the applicant has to say, and have made an effort to ensure privacy and prevent interruptions, then the interview surroundings are not going to matter a great deal. Ideally, offer the applicant a choice of seats. If space is limited, however, and there's only one chair in addition to yours, that's all right, too. What matters is that the applicant feels welcome.

The most common office seating arrangements between an interviewer and an applicant are as follows:

- The applicant and interviewer seated on either side of a desk
- The applicant's chair on the side of the desk
- The applicant and the interviewer sitting on chairs across from one another, away from the desk
- The applicant and the interviewer seated at a table, either next to each other or across from each other

There is no one proper relationship between your seat and the applicant's seat. Some interviewers feel that desks create barriers between themselves and the applicant. If this is how you feel, then desks do indeed become barriers. Also, some interviewers want to see as much of the person they are interviewing as possible so they can better assess nonverbal communication. However, if you're comfortable seated behind your desk, then by all means sit there.

Planning Basic Questions

Plan a handful of questions that will serve as the foundation for your interview. The job description is an excellent starting point. By reviewing the job description, you can easily identify what skills are required and then proceed to formulate the questions you'll need to ask in order to determine whether the applicants possess these skills and are capable of performing the required duties and responsibilities. Hypothetical situations can also be developed and presented to applicants, which gives them a chance to demonstrate their potential.

Be careful not to list too many questions or become very specific during this stage of preparation. If you have an extensive list of detailed questions, the tendency will be to read from that list during the interview. This will result in a stiff, formalized session, which could conceivably make the applicant feel ill at ease. In addition, with a lengthy list of questions, interviewers are likely to feel compelled to cover the entire list and often end up being redundant. Again, this can result in the applicant feeling uncomfortable and wondering whether you are really listening to her responses.

Limit yourself to about a half-dozen general questions. Once you get into the interview, the other questions that need to be asked will follow as offshoots of the applicant's answers. In fact, if your first question is a good, open-ended question, the applicant's response should provide additional questions to ask. An example of an effective first question might be, "Would you please describe your activities during a typical day at your current (or most recent) job?" As you listen to the applicant's response, note any areas that you want to pursue further during the interview.

This one question alone will yield enough information to fill an entire interview if you listen closely to the applicant's answer and use portions of it as the basis for additional questions. Consider, for example, the applicant who is currently working as a customer service representative. Upon asking her the question "Would you please describe your activities during a typical day at your present job?" the applicant provides a rather scant response: "Well, let's see. Each day is really kind of different since I deal with customers and you never know what they're going to call about; but basically, my job is to handle the customer hot line, research any questions, and process complaints."

If you were to leave this answer and go on to another question, you would be overlooking a wealth of information. The applicant has handed you four valuable pieces of information worthy of exploration:

1. Her job requires dealing with a variety of people and situations.
2. She "handles" a customer hot line.
3. She "researches" questions.
4. She "processes" complaints.

Here are some additional questions you can ask, based on the applicant's own comments:

"What is the nature of some of the situations with which you are asked to deal?"

"Who are the people who call you?"

"What is the process that someone with a complaint is supposed to follow?"

"What is your role in this process?"

"Exactly what is the customer hot line?"

"When you say that you 'handle' the hot line, exactly what do you mean?"

"What do you say to a customer who calls on the hot line?"

"What do you say to a customer who calls with a specific question?"

"Has there ever been a time when you did not have the answer being sought by a customer? What did you do?"

"What do you do when a customer isn't satisfied with the answer you've given him? Give me a specific example of when this has happened."

"Tell me about a time when a customer was extremely angry. What happened?"

"Tell me about a time when a customer demanded to speak to someone else."

"Describe a time when you had to handle several demanding customers at the same time."

"Describe a situation in which a customer repeatedly called, claiming his problem had still not been resolved. How did you handle it?"

"How much of your time is devoted to researching questions?"

"Describe the research process, including the resources you use."

"How do you prepare for each day, knowing that you will probably have to listen to several people complaining about a variety of problems?"

These are just some of the questions triggered by the applicant's response to one broad, open-ended question. The answers to each of these questions is also likely to result in further inquiries that will ultimately provide you with a clear picture of the level and scope of this individual's current bank of responsibilities.

This single, open-ended question is so comprehensive that it, alone, could suffice as the only prepared question you have before beginning the interview. However, most interviewers feel better prepared if they have additional questions planned; furthermore, applicants lacking prior work experience cannot provide information about a typical workday. Here, then, are some additional questions that may be prepared before the interview. Note that all are broad enough so that the answers will result in additional questions.

For Applicants with Prior Work Experience

"What do/did you like most and least about your current/most recent job?"

"Describe a situation in your current/most recent job involving _____. How did you handle it?"

"What are/were some of the duties in your current/most recent job that you find/found to be difficult and easy? Why?"

"Why do/did you want to leave your current/most recent job?"

"How do you generally approach tasks you dislike? Please give me a specific example relative to your current/most recent job."

For Applicants with Formal Education but No Prior Work Experience

"What were your favorite and least favorite subjects in high school/college/other? Why?"

"Describe your study habits."

"Why did you major in _____?"

"How do you feel your studies in _____ prepared you for this job?"

For Applicants Without Formal Education or Work Experience

"Here are a series of hypothetical situations that are likely to occur on the job. How would you handle them?"

"What has prepared you for this job?"

Questions Interviewers Should Ask Themselves

When interviewers prepare to meet an applicant, they need to do more than plan questions to ask. They need, also, to be prepared to answer questions. Today's savvy applicants do their homework before meeting with company representatives; they want to ensure that the job is a proper match for their skills and interests, and therefore they come armed with both information and questions.

Whether an applicant actually asks you any or, heaven forbid, all of the following questions is irrelevant; asking yourself these questions and exploring the answers before meeting applicants will better prepare you for any interview. Here, then, are sixty-five questions interviewers should ask themselves and answer in advance of the interview.

Questions About the Organization

"Can you describe the work environment?"

"What is the overall philosophy of the company?"

"What is the company's greatest strength?"

"What is the company's most glaring weakness?"

"What does the organization expect from its employees?"

"What is the organization's commitment to equal employment opportunities and diversity?"

"How would you compare this company with its number-one competitor, in terms of profits, branding, and growth?"

"How accessible are members of senior management to employees at my level?"

"How are members of senior management addressed by those in lesser positions?"

"What is the prevailing management style?"

"What is the organization's mission statement?"

"What are the organization's short- and long-term goals?"

"How does this job fit in with those goals?"

"Are there plans for expansion in the near future?"

"What does the company's organizational chart look like?"

"How important is the department with this job opening in relation to other departments?"

"What would an employee do that would be considered a violation of corporate culture?"

"Are there any misconceptions about this company by the public?"

"How does the company view the issue of work/life balance?"

"What is the company's view with regard to the role of technology?"

"What are this company's greatest technological challenges?"

"What would this company's 'typical' employee say as he left work everyday?"

"How does this organization view fun in the workplace?"

Questions About the Job

"Can you describe a typical day in this job?"

"On average, how many hours a week did this job's previous incumbent work?"

"What is the most important aspect of this job?"

"What were some of the problems the last incumbent had to face in this job?"

"Why did the last incumbent leave this job?"

"Can you tell me about the person to whom I would be reporting?"

"Can you describe my coworkers?"

"Can you describe the people that would report to me?"

"Can you describe the ideal employee for this job?"

"What is it about this job that would scare away applicants with less fortitude?"

"What's the first task I would tackle if hired?"

"Who evaluates my job performance?"

"How does this position contribute to organizational goals?

"What are the greatest challenges I would face in this position as they relate to furthering the goals of the organization?"

"What makes this job an opportunity for me?"

"What benefits does this organization offer that your competitors do not?"

"Would I be required to sign a noncompete agreement?"

Questions About Growth Opportunities

"What are the characteristics of employees who advance in this company?"

"Is there a structured career path for this job?"

"What are my chances for advancement, assuming I do a good job?"

"What additional opportunities will this job likely lead to?"

"What departments generate the most successful employees?"

"How does the organization reward exceptional performance?"

"Does the company's salary program include team-based compensation?"

"What is the learning plan for this position?"

"If I didn't feel I was advancing quickly enough, what would the company do for me?"

"Why would a top performer leave this organization?"

Questions About the Applicant's Chances

"How would you compare my skills with those of other applicants?"

"What else can I say that will encourage you to select me?"

"What are the success factors that would convince you that hiring me is the right move to make?"

"Do you have any concerns about my skills, experience, or education that I can address for you?"

"How do I compare with the 'ideal applicant'?"

"How would you summarize my greatest asset?"

"How would you recommend I convert any areas requiring improvement into assets?"

Questions About the Interviewer

"How long have you worked here?"

"What position did you start out in?"

"How long did it take you to get to the position you're in now?"

"Why did you want to work here?"

"Were your expectations met?"

"What do you like most about working here?"

"What do you like least about working here?"

"What advice do you wish someone gave you before you started working here?"

Summary

Even the most seasoned interviewer prepares before meeting with an applicant. The process begins with a thorough job analysis, including a review of the position's responsibilities, requirements, reporting relationships, environmental factors, exemption and union status, salary, benefits, and growth opportunities. Job descriptions aid in this process by identifying the essential functions of a job; that is, those tasks that are fundamental to the position. A database of well-written job descriptions has two functions: It provides organizations with an understanding of how the job contributes to the achievement of companywide goals, and it offers a solid legal base with respect to decisions made relative to that job.

In addition to reviewing the particulars of a job, employers seeking a match between a job and an applicant need to determine the right fit; that is, what a person has demonstrated he can do in terms of tangible skills, whether he's willing to apply those skills and knowledge to your organization, and what intangible skills and attributes he has that will benefit the job.

Interviewers should always review the applicant's completed application and/or resume before the actual meeting. This will ensure familiarity with the person's credentials, background, and qualifications as they relate to the job so that the interviewer can identify areas for discussion during the interview.

Interviewers are advised to allow a total of about sixty to ninety minutes for the actual face-to-face meeting with exempt applicants, and approximately thirty to forty-five for interviewing nonexempt applicants. Additional time should be allocated for reviewing the application and/or resume, testing, writing up notes, reflecting on what took place, setting up additional appointments, and checking references.

Employers should provide a private and comfortable environment for interviews. They should also prepare a half-dozen or so questions in advance, to serve as the foundation for the interview.

Finally, interviewers should be prepared to answer questions applicants are likely to ask of them.

Note

1. The University of Maryland's survey of union trends is available at http://www.bsos.umd.edu/socy/vanneman/socy441/trends/unionsct.html.

CHAPTER 5

Interviewing and Legal Considerations

Pick up a newspaper on any given day and you're likely to read about the most recent in an ongoing series of employment discrimination settlements. For example, over a five-month period in 2004, papers across the country had headlines about two well-known companies and another about recent statistics concerning same-sex harassment[1]:

> **Wal-Mart Sex-Bias Suit Given Class-Action Status (subhead: ''1.6 Million Employees, Current and Former, Are Represented'')**
>
> **Morgan Stanley Settles Bias Suit with $54 Million (subhead: ''Firm Denies Wrongdoing; 340 Women May Qualify for a Share, but One Is Granted $12 Million'')**
>
> **Same-sex harass claims rising (subhead: ''In era of high-profile accusations, more cases are being filed, mostly by men, as the stigma eases'')**

That's just a sampling of sex discrimination cases. There are many more settlements concerning other forms of employment discrimination, including race, religion, and age. What does any of this have to do with you, personally, when you make a concerted effort not to discriminate? The answer is easy, albeit disconcerting: If you're in human resources and anyone in the organization is charged with discrimination, you are certain to be involved in what is often a lengthy legal process. If you're personally accused with employment discrimination, justly or not, you will find yourself embroiled in each step of the lawsuit. You may even be called upon to provide input if you're not in HR or personally involved with a particular employment discrimination charge. In other words, anyone having anything to do with any aspect of the employment process is expected to have a basic knowledge of equal employment opportunity (EEO). Unintentional violations caused by ignorance of the law are not excusable.

(Note: The information contained in this chapter is not intended to represent legal advice and is current as of this writing.)

Employment Legislation

EEO laws exist to ensure that individuals have the right to compete for all work opportunities without bias because of their race, color, religion, sex, national origin, age, or disability. Certain aspects of key employment legislation may not appear, on the surface, to relate directly to interviewing; however, closer examination reveals a correlation with the interviewing process. For example, the Equal Pay Act of 1963 requires equal pay for men and women performing substantially equal work. While this law does not relate specifically to determining job suitability, interviewers need to understand the parameters and ramifications of the law to ensure that they are not in violation. This could occur if women are offered lower starting salaries than men based on their respective current rates of pay rather than the scope of work to be performed. Likewise, the Drug-Free Workplace Act of 1988 stipulates that certain employers must develop policies prohibiting the use of controlled substances in the workplace. Familiarization with this law allows interviewers to explore the benefits and potential ramifications of applicant drug testing.

Note, too, that these laws pertain to employees being interviewed for internal promotions or transfers.

The following employment laws and categories of discrimination represent major federal statutes, rules, and regulations. The list is not all-inclusive. Employers are urged to obtain a copy of each of these and other laws relevant to their places of business. Unless otherwise noted, copies of the laws may be obtained from:

Equal Employment Opportunity Commission (EEOC)
Department of Labor
1801 L Street, NW
Washington, D.C. 20507
Phone: 202-663-4900
http://www.eeoc.gov/

State and local laws may differ and should also be considered. Failure to comply with any of these laws could result in costly litigation. Readers are urged to consult with counsel in all equal employment matters.

Civil Rights Act of 1866

Many people are surprised to learn that employment-related laws have been around for nearly 140 years. One of the earliest and most significant pieces of legislation was the Civil Rights Act of 1866. The most relevant portion for today's employers is Section 1981, Title 42, which ensures all people the same "equal rights under the law . . . as is enjoyed by white citizens . . . to . . . make and enforce" contracts.

Essentially, this law has been interpreted to mean that discrimination against nonwhites in the making of written or implied contracts relevant to hiring and promotions is illegal. This law was originally intended to support charges of race discrimination and was expanded in 1982 to include national origin discrimination. It applies to all employers regardless of the number of employees.

Over the years, this early civil rights act has been a significant weapon against employers because it permits the person suing to seek punitive damages in addition to compensatory damages such as back pay. Moreover, it provides for a jury trial.

While the awards for violation of this act can be substantial, the claimant must establish *intent* to discriminate on the part of the employer. That is to say, it is necessary to prove that the employer deliberately denied an individual an opportunity for employment or promotion on the basis of his race or national origin. This is to be distinguished from establishing *effect,* which means that while one or more representatives of an organization did not intend to deny someone equal employment opportunity on the basis of his race or national origin, the effect of a certain employment practice, such as exclusively using employee referrals as a recruitment source, was discriminatory. It is usually more difficult to establish intent to discriminate than it is to show effect.

Civil Rights Act of 1964

This is probably the best-known piece of civil rights legislation and the most widely used, because it protects several classes of people and pertains to so many employment situations, including interviewing. Title VII of this act prohibits discrimination on the basis of race, color, religion, sex, or national origin in all matters of employment, from recruitment through discharge. Criteria for coverage under Title VII include any company doing business in the United States that has fifteen or more employees. Title VII does not regulate the employment practices of U.S. companies employing American citizens outside of the United States. Violations are monitored by the EEOC.

Violators of Title VII are generally required to "make whole." This may include providing reinstatement, if relevant, and back pay. Jury trials are not allowed.

Plaintiffs in Title VII suits generally need not prove intent; rather, they may challenge apparently neutral employment policies having a discriminatory effect.

Many claimants sue for violations of both Section 1981 of the Civil Rights Act of 1866 and Title VII of the Civil Rights Act of 1964.

Equal Pay Act of 1963

The Equal Pay Act of 1963 requires equal pay for men and women performing substantially equal work. The work must be of comparable skill, effort, and responsibility, performed under similar working conditions. Coverage applies to all aspects of the employment process, including starting salaries, annual increases, and promotions. This law protects women only; men who feel they are being discriminated against in matters of pay may claim violation of Title VII. A criterion for coverage is at least two employees.

Unequal pay for equal work is permitted in certain instances—for example, when wage differences are based on superior educational credentials or extensive prior experience. However, this pay difference should diminish and ultimately disappear after a number of years on the job.

Comparable Worth

An important issue related to equal pay is comparable worth. Several states have implemented programs for comparable worth pay whereby employers are required to compare completely different job categories. Those jobs held predominately by women, such as nursing and secretarial positions, must be compared with those occupied predominately by men (e.g., truck driving and warehouse work). Point systems determine the level of skill involved in the job, as well as the economic value of each position. If the female-dominated jobs are deemed comparable, adjustments are made to reduce the difference in pay.

The important distinction between comparable worth and equal pay is that in order to claim violation of the Equal Pay Act, identical job classifications must be compared. Therefore, if a woman accountant believes that she is not being offered an equal rate of pay to that of her male counterpart—a male accountant performing substantially equal work—she may have sufficient cause to claim violation of the Equal Pay Act. On the other hand, comparable worth compares different job categories. For example, if a clerk-typist believes that her work is of comparable worth to that of a male custodian hired to work for the same employer, she might sue on the basis of sex discrimination. Since there is presently no federal law that deals specifically with comparable worth, she would sue for violation of Title VII.

Businesses are urged to voluntarily assess their employment practices and work toward minimizing designated female or male categories.

Age Discrimination in Employment Act of 1967

The federal Age Discrimination in Employment Act of 1967 (ADEA), as originally written, protected individuals age 40–70. A 1978 amendment permitted jury trials, which gave claimants more power. Effective January 1, 1987, Congress unanimously approved, and President Ronald Reagan signed into law, H.R. 4154, amending ADEA by extending its protection to those beyond age 70. Now, most private sector and federal, state, and local government employees cannot be discriminated against in matters of pay, benefits, or continued employment regardless of how old they may be. The act also pertains to employees of employment agencies and labor organizations, as well as to U.S. citizens working outside the United States.

ADEA contains an exemption for bona fide executives or high-level policy makers who may be retired as early as age 65, provided they have been employed at that level for the preceding two years and meet certain criteria that include exercising discretionary powers on a regular basis; the authority to hire, promote, and terminate employees; and a primary duty to manage an entire organization, department, or subdivision. Contact the EEOC for detailed guidelines.

The general criterion for coverage under ADEA is employment of at least twenty employees. Part-time employees are included when calculating coverage.

Rehabilitation Act of 1973

Section 501 of this federal law prohibits discrimination against persons with disabilities by contractors doing business with the federal government totaling $2,500 or more per year. Those employers who are government contractors, do business totaling $50,000 or more per year, and have fifty or more employees must prepare an affirmative action plan to comply with the Act, although hiring and promotion goals and timetables are not required under this plan. Section 504 requires employers receiving federal financial assistance to take affirmative action in hiring and promoting qualified workers with disabilities.

The act protects "any person who 1) has a physical or mental impairment that substantially limits one or more of the person's major life activities, 2) has a record of such an impairment, or 3) is regarded as having such an impairment." Included in this definition are former drug addicts and recovering alcoholics. Current drug or alcohol users are not protected. Victims of acquired immunodeficiency syndrome (AIDS) and AIDS-related conditions are also covered by this act.

An employer's obligation extends to making a reasonable effort to accommodate the person's disability, as long as such accommodation does not create an undue hardship. Undue hardships are determined by considering such factors as the size of the organization, the type of work involved, and the nature and cost of such accommodation. For example, job restructuring might be required if the person with the disability can perform the essential functions of the job but requires assistance with one remaining aspect of the work, such as heavy lifting. Others aspects of job restructuring may be modification of procedures, providing readers or interpreters, or modification of equipment. Any adjustment, including alterations to facilities that do not create an undue hardship, may be required.

Resources that assist in modifying facilities and equipment to accommodate workers with disabilities can be obtained at:

Job Accommodation Network
Office of Disability Employment Policy
P.O. Box 6080
Morgantown, WV 26506-6080
Phone: 800-526-7234
http://janweb.icdi.wvu.edu/

Americans with Disabilities Act of 1990

In July 1990, President George H. W. Bush signed landmark legislation prohibiting all employers, including privately owned businesses and local governments, from discriminating against employees or job applicants with disabilities. Exempt are the federal government, government-owned corporations, Native American tribes, and bona fide tax-exempt private membership clubs. Religious organizations are permitted to give preference to the employment of their own members. In addition, the law requires every kind of establishment to be accessible to and usable by persons with disabilities. This legislation, entitled the Americans with Disabilities Act of 1990 (ADA), pertains to employers with fifteen or more employees and is monitored by the EEOC.

Under the ADA, the term *disability* is defined the same as in the Rehabilitation Act of 1973; that is, as a physical or mental impairment that substantially limits an individual's major life activities. The definition also encompasses the history of an impairment and the perception of having an impairment. Examples of disabilities that are covered include: impaired sight and hearing; muscular conditions such as cerebral palsy and muscular dystrophy; diseases like cancer, AIDS, diabetes, and epilepsy; cosmetic disfigurements; emotional disturbances; stuttering; smoke sensitivity; tension; and depression. In fact, there are over a thousand different impairments that are covered by this act. Current users of illegal drugs or alcohol are not protected by the ADA. Also, people with contagious diseases or those posing a direct threat to the health or safety of others are not covered. The ADA specifically excludes homosexuals, bisexuals, transvestites, transsexuals, individuals with sexual behavior disorders, compulsive gamblers, kleptomaniacs, and pyromaniacs.

Recently, the EEOC has focused on the issue of discrimination against individuals with intellectual disabilities, such as people with an IQ below 70 and those with significant limitations in adaptive skills. The EEOC has issued a twenty-page guide with examples of situations in which such intellectual disabilities are protected by the ADA.

Under the ADA, employers are required to make a "reasonable accommodation" for those applicants or employees able to perform the "essential" functions of the job with reasonable proficiency. Reasonable accommodation includes job restructuring, allowing part-time or modified work schedules, reassignments, hiring additional workers to aid employees with disabilities in the performance of their jobs, and installing new equipment or modifying existing equipment. An accommodation is considered unreasonable only in those instances where undue physical or financial hardship is placed on the employer. Such hardship is determined according to the overall size of an organization in relation to the size of its workforce, its budget, and the nature and cost of the required accommodation.

Essential functions are loosely defined as tasks that are "fundamental and not marginal," according to the Senate report on the ADA. Employers are encouraged to conduct a detailed review of each job to determine which functions are essential. This review should include an assessment of the amount of time devoted to each task.

The ADA also refers to what an employer may require in the way of preemployment physical examinations. According to the act, employers cannot single out individuals with disabilities for medical exams. If they are shown to be job-related and consistent with the requirements of the business, medical examinations are permitted after an offer of employment has been made, before the start of work. In this instance, an employer may condition an offer of employment on the results of the exam.

Pregnancy Discrimination Act of 1978

The Pregnancy Discrimination Act of 1978 (PDA) recognizes pregnancy as a temporary disability and prohibits sex discrimination based on pregnancy, childbirth, or related conditions. Pregnant applicants may not be denied equal employment opportunities if they are able to perform the essential functions of the available job. Likewise, women must be permitted to work as long as they are capable of performing the essential functions of their current job or any promotional or transfer opportunity.

If an employer insists on establishing special rules for pregnancy, such rules must be dictated by business necessity or related to issues of health or safety.

Fetal Protection

An important concern related to pregnancy discrimination has to do with fetal protection. Whether an employer may bar women of childbearing age from jobs that involve exposure to toxic substances, X rays, lead, or the like is an issue that has been addressed by the EEOC in a series of fetal protection guidelines. The guidelines require employers to determine first if there is substantial risk of harm to an employee's potential offspring from exposure to a workplace hazard. Employers should rely on scientific evidence of the risk of fetal or reproductive harm from exposure and the minimum period of time required for exposure to cause harm. Then, the employer should assess its policy and determine whether there is a reasonable alternative that would be less discriminatory than exclusion, such as a temporary assignment to another, nontoxic job or allowing the employee to wear a personal protection device.

Religious Discrimination Guidelines

The EEOC guidelines define religion and religious practices as "moral or ethical beliefs as to what is right and wrong, which are sincerely held with the strength of traditional religious views. . . ." In 1972, Congress amended that portion of Title VII pertaining to religion in the workplace by expanding the definition to include an individual's right to "all aspects of religious observance and practice, as well as belief, unless an employer demonstrates that he is unable to reasonably accommodate an employee's or prospective employee's religious observance or practice without undue hardship on the conduct of the employer's business." This amendment placed the burden on employers to prove their inability to reasonably accommodate an individual's religious practices.

As with accommodating persons with disabilities, what constitutes an undue hardship depends on a number of factors, including prohibitive cost. Undue hardship must be provable.

Certain work assignments might also require some adjustment if an individual raises religious objections. For example, a foreign work assignment to a country whose prevailing religious practices conflict with the beliefs of an individual might be the basis for that individual's request to work at a different location. Every effort should be made to accommodate such a request.

Balancing an individual's religious beliefs with an organization's dress and grooming practices may also become an issue. Unless safety is a factor, the employer should make a reasonable effort to accommodate religious-based attire and grooming.

Religion and work should be kept separate, meaning that employers have the right to require "quiet and unobtrusive" observance.

National Origin Discrimination Guidelines

The EEOC's "Guidelines on Discrimination Because of National Origin" preclude denial of employment opportunity because of an individual's ancestry; place of origin; or physical, cultural, or linguistic characteristics. There are four main areas pertaining to employment:

1. Citizenship requirements may not be valid if they have the purpose or effect of discrimination on the basis of national origin.
2. Selection criteria that appear to be neutral on first glance may have an adverse impact on certain national groups.
3. English-only rules may be considered discriminatory when applied at all times.
4. Ethnic slurs may be considered national origin discrimination and must not be tolerated.

Immigration Reform and Control Act (IRCA) of 1986

IRCA makes the employment of illegal aliens unlawful and establishes requirements for employers to determine an individual's authorization to work in the United States. The act applies to employers with four or more workers.

The Immigration and Naturalization Service (INS) determines what constitutes an acceptable document proving work eligibility and identity. Some documents establish both identity and employment eligibility; in instances where these are not produced, documents establishing identity in addition to documents establishing employment eligibility are required. A list of these documents may be obtained by visiting IRCA's home page at www.usda.gov/oce/oce/labor-affairs/ircasumm.htm.

Employers must examine documents that establish the individual's identity and eligibility to work in the United States before completing the required I-9 form. This examination should be made subsequent to the final hiring decision to avoid violation of IRCA's antidiscrimination provisions. Employers face penalties for hiring unauthorized employees and for failure to properly complete and maintain I-9 forms.

Drug-Free Workplace Act of 1988

Employers holding contracts with or receiving grants from the federal government of $25,000 or more must meet certain posting and record-keeping requirements and must develop policies prohibiting the unlawful manufacture, distribution, possession, or use of controlled substances in the workplace. The act does not make a definitive statement about requiring drug testing.

Civil Rights Act of 1991

The primary intent of the Civil Rights Act of 1991 is to provide appropriate remedies for intentional discrimination and unlawful harassment in the workplace. It extends beyond the Civil Rights Act of 1964's Title VII "make whole" remedies of providing back pay and reinstatement and paying some attorneys' fees in several ways:

- Coverage is extended to U.S. citizens employed at a U.S. company's foreign site.
- The burden of proof is placed on employers to show lack of discrimination.
- Jury trials are permitted.
- Awards of compensatory and punitive damages are permitted in cases of intentional discrimination.
- Victims of intentional sex discrimination are permitted to seek compensatory and punitive damages of up to $300,000.
- Victims of race discrimination are permitted to seek unlimited damages.
- A "glass ceiling" commission has been established to develop policies for the removal of barriers to women and minorities seeking advancement.
- "Race norming," or the practice of adjusting test scores by race, is banned.

Employment-at-Will and Termination-at-Will

Employment laws and categories of discrimination do not preclude the employment-at-will and termination-at-will doctrines, which grant employers the right to terminate, at any time, for any reason, with or without cause, the employment of an individual who does not have a written contract defining the terms of employment, provided such termination does not violate state or federal laws. In exercising this right, employers are unlikely to incur legal liability.

Employees have additional rights protecting them from arbitrary acts of termination-at-will. The broadest form of protection, the implied covenants of good faith and fair dealing, requires employers to prove "just cause" before terminating an employee. Public policy rights may also protect employees from being fired for exercising rights such as whistle-blowing—public disclosure of illegal actions taken by one's company—or for refusing to perform illegal acts on behalf of an employer. Moreover, the issue of implied contract rights may arise when the protection provided by statements on the employment application form, in employee handbooks, or in other company documents is interpreted as a binding contract. In this regard, employers are advised to develop at-will policies for inclusion in these documents. A sample employment-at-will statement appears in Appendix E: Employment Application Form. It conforms to the following preemployment at-will guidelines:

- *State the at-will principle.* It is important to declare that your offer of employment is neither an employment contract nor a guarantee of employment.
- *Avoid making statements regarding job security.* Steer clear of phrases such as "We treat employees of (company name) like members of our family."
- *Avoid stating a prospective employee's salary in yearly numbers.* A statement of annual salary may imply a one-year employment contract. Instead, use weekly, biweekly, or monthly numbers.
- *Avoid using the term "probationary period."* It implies that, once a given period of time is over, an individual is there to stay. Likewise, avoid the term *permanent employee*; instead, substitute *regular employee*.

In addition to including at-will statements on their job application form, employers can minimize the possibility of wrongful discharge allegations and put the company in a better position to successfully defend against such action by implementing these additional safeguards:

- Make certain that application forms are in full compliance with applicable EEO laws.
- Ensure that everyone having anything whatsoever to do with the employment process is skilled in effective and legal interviewing skills.
- Ensure that applicants clearly understand the content and scope of responsibility of the position they are being considered for, before extending a job offer.
- Make certain job descriptions are accurate and job standards consistent with what is required.

Because the legal issues involving employment-at-will and termination-at-will are still evolving, employers are advised to have all written materials pertaining to the employment process reviewed by counsel annually.

Noncompete Agreements

Also known as *nonsolicitation agreements* or *restrict covenants,* noncompete agreements are designed to protect an employer's trade secrets, customer and marketing lists, and confidential knowledge about the employer, all of which are picked up by employees while on the job. Noncompete agreements are most commonly used in the computer industry, some professional partnerships, high-tech industries, or engineering environments, and they are usually presented for signature when a professional employee is hired or when a worker is promoted to a sensitive position. These agreements are intended to take effect upon termination, at which time employees may be restricted from working for a competitor for a specified period of time (often one to two years); working at the same or a comparable job in the same industry during a certain timeframe; or working in a defined geographical area for a competitor.

The current trend is toward protection of employees by placing limitations on the extent to which an employer can restrict a former employee's right to work. There are no federal laws dealing directly with noncompete agreements, but there are some state laws.

Negligent Hiring and Retention

Negligent hiring and retention may occur when employers fail to exercise reasonable care in hiring or retaining employees. Increasingly, employers are being held liable for harmful acts committed by their employees both in the workplace and away from it. Named in such lawsuits are usually the employer, the employee who caused the injury, and the person directly responsible for hiring. Findings of personal liability are not uncommon. Negligent hiring actions have been brought by employees as well as by innocent third parties, such as customers, visitors, and clients injured by the criminal, violent, or negligent acts of an employee.

Plaintiffs must prove that the employee causing the injury was unfit for hiring or retention, that the employer's hiring or retention of that employee was the cause of the plaintiff's injuries, and that the employer knew or should have known of the employee's unfit condition. Generally, the deciding factor is whether an employer can establish that it exercised reasonable care in ensuring the safety of others. Reasonable care may include conducting preemployment testing, checking references, investigating gaps in an applicant's employment history, verifying academic achievements, conducting a criminal investigation, checking an applicant's credit history, or verifying the individual's driving record. The type of position an employee is hired for often plays a role in how extensive the investigation should be. For example, unsupervised positions in which the employee has a great deal of contact with customers, clients, visitors, or other employees may require more in-depth preemployment investigation than jobs that are highly supervised.

Juries may not be sympathetic to the difficulties an employer might encounter in obtaining relevant background information on which to base a hiring decision. Employers in court because of negligent hiring or retention charges report that juries often find for the plaintiff. The trial of such actions may involve the examination of a number of issues, including what the employer actually knew about the individual, as opposed to what it tried to ascertain; whether the potential risk to others could have been reasonably discovered through the interview or a reference or background check; and whether the risk to others was greater because of the nature of the job. Consideration of these questions may implicate the employer in an act of negligent hiring or retention. Employers should note that such lawsuits might prove more costly than typical employee litigation because of potentially higher awards of punitive damages.

From all that has been said, it's apparent that preventive measures are an employer's best defense against charges of negligent hiring or retention. In this regard, employers are advised to do the following:

- Conduct comprehensive employment interviews.
- Investigate all gaps in employment.
- Conduct job-related preemployment tests.
- Conduct thorough background and reference checks.
- Keep written notes of information received when checking references.
- Decide whether a criminal investigation is warranted, based on information received.
- Immediately investigate any allegations of employee misconduct.
- Consult with legal counsel when in doubt as to what course of action to take.

Federal Record-Keeping Requirements

Employers are obliged to retain documents according to certain federal and state stipulations, and longer if a claim or government investigation is conducted or threatened. This requirement appears in the record retention provisions of most federal and state EEO laws, as well as the Sarbanes-Oxley Act. The latter states that an individual can be imprisoned for up to twenty years and fined if she tampers with records or documents.

As with certain aspects of key employment legislation that may not appear, on the surface, to relate directly to interviewing, closer examination of record-keeping requirements reveals an important correlation with the interviewing process of new hires as well as employees who are promoted or transferred internally. Some of the specific record-keeping requirements for relevant laws are summarized as follows:

Relevant Law	Record-Keeping Requirement
Age Discrimination in Employment Act	Covered employers must keep payroll or any other records containing the name, address, birth date, occupation, rate of pay, and weekly compensation of each employee for three years.
Americans with Disabilities Act	Employers governed by the ADA must retain all HR records involving a person with a disability, whether it has hired him or not. With regard to interviewing, keep requests for reasonable accommodation with job ap-

(continues)

Relevant Law	Record-Keeping Requirement
	plications. All records must be kept for one year from the date the record was made or an employment action is taken, whichever is later.
Executive Order 11246	Covered employers must keep affirmative action programs, utilization analyses, and information on all applicants, including data on race, gender, disability, veteran status, and requested position. While the retention period is unspecified, experts recommend a minimum of three years.
Equal Pay Act	Employers must retain FLSA-required records, as well as wage rates and descriptions of wage differentials for individuals of both genders for an unspecified period of time.
Immigration Reform and Control Act	I-9 forms must be kept for three years or one year after termination, whichever is later.
Rehabilitation Act of 1973	Federal contractors and subcontractors must keep employment records for applicants and employees who have disabilities for one year. Also, keep a record of complaints and actions taken under the act.
Title VII of the Civil Rights Act of 1964	Covered employers must maintain records that would be relevant to any discrimination charge brought by any agency or individual (e.g., all HR documents about the complainant and about individuals in similar positions, application forms, and test papers completed by applicants for the same position). Documents must be retained for one year after the record was made or the action taken or, if a charge is made, until it's resolved. Employers are also required to keep records of selection for apprenticeship programs for two years from the date of application for the program or for the apprenticeship period, whichever is longer.

State Retention Requirements

Nondiscrimination laws in most states have document retention requirements that must be met in addition to federal stipulations. In some states, employers will have to retain files for longer than the federal mandate. Employers with locations in multiple states will need to review the file retention requirements in each state.

Employers may have to retain files for their defense in several types of legal claims actions, including charges of state common law fraud, tort claims, and contract claims. For example, an applicant could accuse an employer of fraud by claiming the employer mislead him about the particulars or availability of a job. Tort claims could result from inferences of defamation and invasion of privacy. Contract laws may be brought into play when employees take issue with their written or oral employment contracts.

This last point—employment contracts—becomes especially complex when you consider that the retention periods for written and oral contracts can vary in the same state. Florida, for example, has a four-year statute for oral contracts but a five-year statute for written contracts. In Illinois, the statute for oral contracts is five years, but for written contracts it is ten. To further complicate matters, some states interpret written contracts broadly, sometimes including e-mail correspondence.

In many states there is something called a catch-all statute of limitations for all claims not covered under a specific statute of limitations. It is usually six years. Hence, rather than trying to follow the myriad rules concerning retention, many employers opt to adopt the six-year rule across-the-board, hoping it will cover most fraud, tort, and contract claims.

With regard to applicants who are not hired, federal nondiscrimination laws require a one-year retention period. However, some states have longer requirements, such as California, where applicant records must be retained for two years.

Employers are advised to consider the risks of failing to retain files for the entire length of a statute of limitations despite the potential administrative costs. If at all possible, retain all records for the longest statute of limitations period and then some.

Affirmative Action

Because Title VII did not immediately have the desired effect against discrimination, a series of executive orders were issued by the federal government, first by President John F. Kennedy in 1961, and later strengthened by President Lyndon Johnson in 1965. The best known, Executive Order 11246, contained an EEO clause that required companies doing business with the federal government to make a series of commitments. Three of the most significant commitments are as follows:

1. *Practice nondiscrimination in employment.* When a company does business with the federal government, it is on the basis of a contract; should the company discriminate in its interviewing and hiring practices, it would effectively be violating its contract. The ramifications could be severe, including contract cancellation and debarment, meaning that the government would no longer do business with that company.

2. *Attain affirmative action goals.* This commits a company to hiring, training, and promoting a certain percentage of qualified women and minorities. The actual percentage is based on the number of women and minorities in a specific geographic location, referred to as a Standard Metropolitan Statistical Area (SMSA). Employers should contact the Office of Federal Contract Compliance Programs (OFCCP) to determine the most recent requirements for separate affirmative action plans pertaining to different establishments.

3. *Obey the rules and regulations of the Department of Labor.* This agreement extends to allowing periodic checking of company premises by labor representatives to ensure compliance with the other two commitments listed here.

Affirmative Action Plans

Increasingly, employers are adopting formal, written affirmative action plans (AAPs) even where they are not required, in an effort to correct racial and gender imbalances in the workplace. (Currently, the OFCCP requires federal contractors and subcontractors to develop written AAPs if fifty or more workers are employed and the employer does $50,000 in business annually with the federal government.) In the absence of a written AAP, it is more difficult to provide credible evidence that the employer is making a bona fide effort to correct real or perceived problems. Minimally, written AAPs should encompass seven key elements:

1. A policy statement
2. Internal dissemination of the policy
3. External dissemination of the policy
4. Positive utilization efforts
5. A review of internal procedures
6. Implementation, development, and execution
7. Establishment of a complaint procedure

Affirmative action guidelines may be obtained by contacting the United States Department of Labor:

Office of Federal Contract Compliance Programs (OFCCP)
200 Constitution Avenue, NW
Washington, D.C. 20210
Phone: 202-219-6666
http://www.dol.gov/esa/ofccp/index.htm

The OFCCP has also published a compliance manual that outlines the specific steps followed by its field staff in reviewing and monitoring AAPs.

Diversity

Any AAP should be temporary only, to be abandoned and replaced by a diversity-driven work environment once workplace equity has been achieved. Diversity-driven work environments go beyond affirmative action by nurturing individuality and making changes to suit the needs of its employees without sacrificing business goals. Diversity reflects all the factors that identify us. The term goes far beyond race, religion, sex, or national origin. It includes the multitude of ways in which we are unique and, at the same time, similar, such as customs, language, lifestyle, mental abilities, personality, physical characteristics, sexual orientation; socioeconomic status, talents, values, and work styles.

The ultimate goal of a diverse workplace is for all involved to work together toward achieving common organizational objectives, while prospering individually. To achieve organizational goals, employees need to be flexible and cooperative; however, the onus for adaptation cannot be placed solely on those employees outside the dominant culture (i.e., the culture to which the people in power belong). For a business to grow and profit, everyone must make a commitment to diversity. This commitment begins with open-mindedness during the interviewing process.

Advantages of Diversity-Driven Work Environments

There are many advantages to seeking a diverse workforce. Employers are able to select from a larger labor pool, enhancing the chances of finding qualified applicants. Such applicants reflect a variety of backgrounds and experiences, increasing the degree of talent and extent of contributions they bring to the organization. Employees will appreciate the multicultural environment provided; consequently, they are likely to be more motivated and have a better attitude, resulting in higher productivity. A diversity-driven work environment can also result in fewer discrimination charges and lawsuits.

Having a diverse workforce is especially critical in companies that reach out to a diverse customer or consumer base. With changing demographics in the United States and many businesses operating on an international level, it makes good business sense to have a workforce that reflects the needs of an organization's diverse customers.

Companies that invest in diversity as a long-term commitment may also enjoy significantly better financial results than those that do not.

Discrimination Charges

Any individual who believes that her employment rights have been violated may file a charge of discrimination with the EEOC. In addition, any individual, organization, or agency may file a charge of discrimination on behalf of another person to protect that person's identity.

The following information is required in order to file a charge of discrimination:

- The name, address, and telephone number of the person or party bringing charges

- The name, address, and telephone number of the organization alleged to have committed the act of discrimination
- A description of the alleged violation
- The date of the alleged violation

It doesn't take much for a lawsuit to get started. All a complainant must prove is that a job existed; that she is a member of a protected group, is qualified for the job, but was rejected in spite of those qualifications; and that the employer continued to look for someone else to fill the job. Charges may be filed by mail or in person at a local EEOC office.

The EEOC has strict requirements with regard to filing dates for charges of discrimination. A charge must be filed with the EEOC within 180 days from the date of the alleged violation. This 180-day filing deadline may be extended to 300 days if a state or local antidiscrimination law covers the charge.

If an organization is deemed guilty of discrimination, whether as a result of intent or by practices that have a discriminatory effect, they may be required to comply with a host of remedies, including:

- Back pay
- Hiring
- Promotion
- Reinstatement
- Reasonable accommodation
- Other actions that will make a person "whole" (i.e., restore them to the status they would have enjoyed had it not been for the discrimination)
- Attorney's fees
- Expert witness fees
- Court costs

Compensatory and punitive damages may also be imposed in matters of intentional discrimination. Damages may compensate for actual monetary losses, future monetary losses, and mental anguish and inconvenience. Punitive damages may be imposed if it is found that an organization acted with malice or reckless indifference (although federal, state, and local governments are exempt from punitive damages).

Employers may also be required to take corrective action to cure the source of the discrimination and minimize the chances of its recurrence. This often translates into government-imposed affirmative action goals and training.

Avoiding Discrimination Charges

With litigation so easy to initiate, your goal should be to prevent lawsuits, not win them. While there is no absolute way of preventing applicants or employees from charging your organization with discrimination, there are guidelines you can follow to help minimize the chances.

* *Make certain your hiring criteria are objective, uniformly applied, and consistent in effect.* By applying job criteria across-the-board that do not have a greater negative impact on any one group, you are demonstrating fair employment practices.
* *Show job-relatedness.* Every standard you set, each question you ask, and every decision you make should be job-related.
* *Focus on making sound hiring decisions that properly match an applicant's skills, knowledge, and interests with a job's duties and responsibilities.* This effort should lead to fewer terminations, which is significant, since firing is the act that triggers many lawsuits.
* *Pay attention to "red flags" on an applicant's application or resume.* As mentioned in Chapter 4, do not proceed with the interviewing process until you're satisfied that these questionable areas have been thoroughly explored.
* *Conduct education and employment reference checks.* While reference checking is not always easy or even possible to do (see Chapter 12), the effort may reveal important information that can influence your decision to extend a job offer, as well as provide protection against charges of negligent hiring and retention should you make the wrong hiring decision.
* *Think like a juror.* To avoid actions that generate lawsuits, think about how a juror would interpret your actions. For example: Did the employee understand, as a result of the interviewing process, what the employer would expect of him once hired? Did the employer follow policies and procedures known to the employee?
* *Treat all employees equally.* Most lawsuits alleging any form of discrimination are based on failure to treat employees consistently, reasonably, and fairly. This includes overt discrimination as well as more subtle forms of discrimination, such as stereotyping, patronizing, and favoritism. Note that "equal treatment" does not mean "identical treatment;" it does mean ensuring that each employee has the same opportunity for consideration as every other employee.
* *Respect an employee's legal rights.* Some employees may have additional rights than listed here as a result of written or implied contracts (e.g., based on the language on employment applications or in employee handbooks), but all employees are entitled to these rights:
  —Civic rights
  —The right to a safe workplace
  —The right to refuse to perform illegal acts without fear of retaliation
  —The right not to be defamed
  —The right to nonharassing treatment
  —The right to participate in certain union activities
  —The right to compensation according to the Fair Labor Standards Act
  —The right to certain benefits under the Employee Retirement Income Security Act (ERISA)

- *Honestly appraise employees.* Negative performance appraisals are difficult to write, but they can save you a lot of trouble later on. It's hard to justify termination on the basis of poor performance with a file filled with glowing reviews. If an employee exhibits performance problems, identify them and together set goals for improvement. If, ultimately, you end up terminating the employee, an unjust termination lawsuit will be more difficult to sustain.

- *Take allegations seriously and act promptly.* Whether allegations are of sexual harassment or other forms of misconduct or illegal acts, a quick and appropriate response will often diffuse a situation and preclude a lawsuit.

Questions to Avoid Asking

Stated in the simplest of terms, if it's not job-related, don't ask. Naturally, this statement begs the question: What's job-related? The answer is equally simple: education and experience, as they relate to the requirements, duties, and responsibilities of the job. That's pretty much it; everything else is off-limits.

Does that sound restrictive? It's really not. The number of subjects you cannot legally inquire about may be great in comparison with the two you can legally question, but those two categories could generate hundreds of legitimate, job-specific questions and answers that will help you determine job suitability. The others will provide limited responses about personal qualities that may be interesting, but have no bearing on ability.

In general the subjects to steer clear of during the employment interview relate to race, religion, sex, national origin, and age. Asking such questions is not, in and of itself, illegal. Rather, once the information is ascertained, you may be charged with applying it illegally. For example, asking a woman applicant if she has children is not illegal. However, if the applicant is not hired because she answers yes and, consequently, you anticipate excessive absenteeism, a charge of discrimination may result.

Bear in mind that just because you do not directly ask an applicant—either via the application form or verbally—for specific information, she may offer it. If this occurs, you are equally liable if a question of illegal use arises. Suppose you inform an applicant that the available position requires travel. You then ask if she foresees any problem in leaving for a business trip with very little advance notice. She responds, "Oh, that will be no problem at all. My mother has been baby-sitting for my three kids ever since my divorce last year." The applicant has just volunteered information regarding two categories that are not job-related: children and marital status. If she is rejected, she might claim discrimination on the basis of this information, even though you did not solicit it.

Should an applicant provide information that you should not have, make certain of three things:

1. Do not, under any circumstances, write it down.
2. Do not pursue the subject with the applicant.
3. Tell the applicant that the information is not job-related and that you want to return to discussing her qualifications in relation to the job opening.

Exhibit 5-1 identifies the most common categories and questions to avoid during the employment interview, both verbally and via the application form. Related recommended questions are also shown. Many of the recommended inquiries appear on the application form in Appendix E.

Bona Fide Occupational Qualifications

Occasionally, the requirements of a position seem to be discriminatory in nature. For instance, jobs that stipulate male or female only appear, on the surface, to be discriminatory. However, upon closer investigation it becomes evident that the EEO concept of bona fide occupational qualification (BFOQ) prevails. By definition, a BFOQ is a criterion that appears to be discriminatory but can be justified by business necessity. For example, an employer may have an opening for a model to show a new line of designer dresses. In this instance, being female would be a BFOQ. An example of an unacceptable BFOQ would be a position requiring heavy lifting where only male applicants are considered. The requirement of lifting may be tested; all applicants—male and female—could be asked to lift the weight normally required on the job. Those unable to perform this task would not be considered, including all men as well as all women not meeting the lifting requirement. Likewise, women able to lift the weight must be given an equal opportunity for the job.

BFOQs may apply to religion, gender, age, and national origin, but never to race. Furthermore, general company preference does not constitute a legitimate BFOQ. The most valid BFOQ or business-necessity defense is safety. When there is doubt, the following business-necessity guidelines should be applied:

- Document the business necessity.
- Explore alternative practices.
- Ensure across-the-board administration of the practice.
- Ensure that the business necessity is not based on stereotypical thinking, arbitrary standards, or tradition.

There are very few instances in which a BFOQ applies. If you believe that your requirements qualify as BFOQs, check with the EEOC before proceeding.

Applicant Tracking

The EEOC requires employers to break down their workforce by job category as well as race, ethnicity, and gender. Private employers of 100 or more employees and some

Exhibit 5-1. Preemployment questions asked verbally and appearing on applications forms.

Subject	Questions Not Recommended	Recommended Questions
Name	What is your maiden name? Have you ever used any other name? Have you ever worked under another name? Have you ever changed your name?	Have you ever worked for this company under a different name? Is additional information relative to a change in name, or use of an assumed name or nickname, necessary for us to check your work record? If yes, please explain.
Address	Do you own or rent your home? How long have you lived at this address?	What is your address? Where do you live?
Age	How old are you? What is your date of birth? Are you between 18 and 24, 25 and 34, etc.?	Are you above the minimum working age of _____?
Physical Appearance	How tall are you? How much do you weigh? What is the color of your eyes and hair?	None
Citizenship and National Origin	Of what country are you a citizen? Where were you born? Where were your parents born? Are you a naturalized or a native-born citizen? What is your nationality? What kind of name is _____?	Are you a citizen of the United States? If you are not a U.S. citizen, do you have the legal right to remain permanently in the United States?
Marital Status	What is your current marital status? Have you ever been married? Divorced? Do you wish to be addressed as Mrs., Miss, or Ms.?	None
Children	Do you have any children? How many children do you have? What child-care arrangements have you made? Do you intend to have children? When do you plan to have children? If you have children, will you return to work?	None

Police Records	Have you ever been arrested?	Have you ever been convicted of a (crime? felony? crime greater than a misdemeanor?) Please explain. (Note: Applicants may not be denied employment because of a conviction record unless there is a direct correlation between the offense and the job, or unless hiring would constitute an unreasonable risk [Correction Law Article 22-A Sec. 754]).
Religion	What is your religious background? What religious holidays do you observe? Is there anything in your religious beliefs that would prevent you from working the required schedule?	None
Disabilities	Do you have any disabilities? Have you ever been treated for any of the following (list of diseases and illnesses)? Do you now have, or have you ever had, a drug or alcohol addiction? Do you have physical, mental, or medical impediments that would interfere with your ability to perform the job for which you are applying? Are there any positions or duties for which you should not be considered because of existing physical, mental, or medical disabilities?	Can you perform the tasks required to carry out the job for which you have applied with or without accommodation?
Photographs	Any question requiring that a photo be supplied before hire.	None
Languages	What is your native language? How did you learn to speak _____?	What is the degree of fluency with which you speak/write any language, including English? (Ask only if job-related.)

(continues)

Exhibit 5-1. Continued.

Subject	Questions Not Recommended	Recommended Questions
Military Experience	Have you ever served in the armed forces of any country? What kind of discharge did you receive?	What is your military experience in the Armed Forces of the United States?
Organizations	What clubs, organizations, or associations do you belong to?	What clubs, organizations, or associations, relative to the position for which you are applying, do you belong to?
References	A requirement that a reference be supplied by a particular kind of person, such as a religious leader.	Please provide the names, titles, addresses, and phone numbers of business references who are not related to you, other than your present or former employers.
Finances	Do you have any overdue bills?	None
Education	Are you a high school or college graduate? When did you attend high school or college?	Questions about the applicant's academic, vocational or professional education, including the names and locations of the schools, the number of years completed, honors, diplomas and degrees received, and the major courses of study.
Experience	Any question regarding experience unrelated to the job.	Any questions regarding relevant work experience.

federal government contractors with fifty or more employees are required to file a report annually.

The EEOC has proposed changes to its major employer reporting form, the EEO-1. One of the proposed changes will increase the number of racial and ethnic classifications from five to seven and allow employees to self-designate as "two or more races, not Hispanic or Latino." The EEOC has stated that self-designation is the preferred method of identifying the race and ethnic information required, although post-employment records or observer identification may be used if self-identification is not feasible. The self-identification procedure may be burdensome for some employers, who will need to use a survey or questionnaire to obtain this information.

Current race/ethnic designations as used by the Equal Employment Opportunity

Commission do not denote scientific definitions of anthropological origins. For the purposes of this report, an employee may be included in the group to which he or she appears to belong, identifies with, or is regarded in the community as belonging. The race/ethnic categories for this survey are:

- *White (Not of Hispanic origin).* All persons having origins in any of the original peoples of Europe, North Africa, or the Middle East.
- *Black (Not of Hispanic origin).* All persons having origins in any of the black racial groups of Africa.
- *Hispanic.* All persons of Mexican, Puerto Rican, Cuban, Central or South American, or other Spanish culture or origin, regardless of race.
- *Asian or Pacific Islander.* All persons having origins in any of the original peoples of the Far East, Southeast Asia, the Indian Subcontinent, or the Pacific Islands. This area includes, for example, China, India, Japan, Korea, the Philippine Islands, and Samoa.
- *American Indian or Alaskan Native.* All persons having origins in any of the original peoples of North America, and who maintain cultural identification through tribal affiliation or community recognition.

The EEOC also proposes increasing the number of job categories by splitting the category of "officials and managers" into three levels: executive/senior level officials and managers; mid-level officials and managers; and lower-level officials and managers. Other categories currently in use are professionals, technicians, sales, office and clerical, skilled craft workers, unskilled operatives, unskilled laborers, and service workers.

Currently, EEO-1 reports must be completed electronically. Single-establishment companies are required to submit only one EEO-1 report form. Multi-establishment companies must file a series of report forms for the principal office or headquarters, separate establishment report forms for each establishment, and a consolidated report that lists all of the cumulated employment data from the headquarters and establishment report forms.

Summary

EEO laws exist to ensure all individuals have the right to compete for all work opportunities without bias because of their race, color, religion, sex, national origin, age, or disability. Employers are urged to familiarize themselves with relevant employment laws and categories of discrimination.

These laws do not preclude the employment-at-will and termination-at-will doctrines, which grant employers the right to terminate the employment of an individual who does not have a written contract defining the terms of employment. However, employees have rights protecting them from arbitrary acts of termination-at-will.

The broadest form of protection, which is the implied convents of good faith and fair dealing, requires employers to prove "just cause" before terminating an employee.

Negligent hiring and retention may occur when employers fail to exercise reasonable care in hiring or retaining employees. Increasingly, employers are being held liable for the acts of their employees both in the workplace and away from it. Plaintiffs must prove that the employee causing the injury was unfit for hiring or retention.

Employers are obliged to retain documents according to certain federal and state stipulations. This requirement appears in the record retention provisions of most federal and state EEO laws. In some states, employers are required to retain employee files for longer than the federal mandate.

Affirmative action is the result of a series of executive orders issued by the federal government to ensure equal employment opportunity. Many federal contractors and subcontractors are required to have written plans.

Diversity-driven work environments go beyond affirmative action by nurturing individuality and making changes to suit the needs of its employees. The ultimate goal of a diverse workplace is for all involved to work together toward achieving common organizational objectives, while prospering individually.

Individuals who believe that their employment rights have been violated may file a charge of discrimination with the EEOC. In addition, any individual, organization, or agency may file a charge of discrimination on behalf of another person to protect that person's identity.

To avoid discrimination charges, ask only job-related questions during employment interviews—that is, questions relating to experience and education as they relate to the requirements, duties, and responsibilities of the job. Make certain, too, that your application forms contain only job-related questions.

The EEOC requires most employers to break down their workforce by job category as well as race, ethnicity, and gender. This is accomplished by filing an annual EEO-1 report.

Note

1. Steven Greenhouse and Constance L. Hays, "Wal-Mart Sex-Bias Suit Given Class-Action Status," *The New York Times* (June 22, 2004), Section C, p. 1; Patrick McGeehan, "Morgan Stanley Settles Bias Suit with $54 Million," *The New York Times* (July 13, 2004), p. 1; and Tina Susman, "Same-sex harass claims rising," *Newsday* (November 8, 2004), p. A18.

CHAPTER 6

Competency-Based Questions

During an interviewing workshop I was conducting, one of the participants, a manager named Dan, firmly stated, "It really doesn't matter what people have done in the past—all that matters is what they're willing to do."

He was taken aback when I told him that I agreed. "You just stated that competency-based questions make the most effective types of questions since they assess an applicant's demonstrated abilities as they relate to the requirements and responsibilities of a particular job," Dan said. "How can you say you agree with me when I say all that matters is what a person is willing to do?"

"That's simple," I replied. "But before I answer, let me ask you a question. How can you determine what a person is willing to do?"

Dan thought briefly and then replied, "This is probably a trick question because the answer is so obvious, but here goes: You ask them!" I smiled. That was exactly what I thought he would say. "Dan," I continued, "suppose you have an opening for a project manager. One of the key qualities is teamwork. What are you going to ask your applicants?" Dan responded, "Well, I could ask them to describe how they work with other members of a team."

"And what do you think they'll say?" I asked. "I guess they'll say they work well with other members of a team," Dan replied. "Right," I said. "What have you learned about how they work with other members of a team?"

"Not much," Dan confessed. But then he thought some more and said, "All right, then, I would ask a specific question. I'd say, suppose you're working as a member of a team and you hit a snag because one of your coworkers isn't doing his share of the work; what are you going to do?" "That's much better," I told him, adding, "But don't you think he's likely to tell you what you want to hear?" Dan was becoming frustrated, so I decided to return to his original question.

I agreed with Dan's assertion that all that matters is what a person is willing to do and, at the same time, I maintain that competency-based questions should form the foundation of any interview. The reason these ideas aren't in conflict is that competency-based questions allow you to project, with a high degree of certainty, just what a person is willing or likely to do. Let me illustrate with teamwork. The last question Dan posed is excellent, but it's incomplete; you still don't know if what the applicant says is what he really will do, or if he's just saying what he anticipates is the "correct" answer. Imagine, however, if you said, "Tell me about a time at your last job when that happened?" The applicant's response is going to entail a specific, job-related experience involving teamwork. Since we're all creatures of habit, it's likely an applicant will approach a similar teamwork challenge the same way in the future as he did in the past.

If you are like Dan, you may be chagrinned but receptive to hearing more about the merits of competency-based questions.

Key Competency Categories

For our purposes, a competency is defined as a skill, trait, quality, or characteristic that contributes to a person's ability to effectively perform the duties and responsibilities of a job. Competencies are the gauges for job success. Identifying job-specific competencies enables you to assess how effective a person has been in the past and, therefore, how effectively she is likely to perform in your organization. While every job requires different competencies, there are four primary categories:

1. Tangible or measurable skills
2. Knowledge
3. Behavior
4. Interpersonal skills

Most jobs emphasize the need for one category over the others, but every employee should be able to demonstrate competencies, to some extent, in all four categories.

Tangible Competencies

For many jobs today, concrete, tangible, or technical skill is critical to success. Tangible competencies demonstrate what applicants have done in past jobs. For example, a sampling of competencies for a technical job includes having overall technical know-how, tailoring technical information to different audiences, applying technical expertise to solve business problems, staying technologically current, understanding the technologies of the organization, optimizing technology, balancing multiple projects, and communicating project status.

Although these concrete competencies are indisputably necessary and should certainly be explored while interviewing a person for a technical job, the other three categories need to be examined as well. The reason is simple: A person brings much more than measurable skills to a job. Complex beings that we all are, we also bring an array of knowledge, behaviors, and interpersonal skills, all of which contribute to our success or failure on the job. This is true regardless of the job or grade level.

Consider this situation: There are two openings for the same type of job and two people are hired, both of them technically competent. One of them, Paul, has slightly more experience than the other, Justine, but both individuals possess outstanding technical know-how. After one year Justine's performance review reveals that she is doing above-average work while Paul's indicates borderline, barely adequate performance. Why? Paul has trouble focusing on the key elements of a project and does not interact well with customers. In addition, while Justine responds well to feedback, Paul views suggestions as criticism. His poor performance evaluation derives from a number of nontechnical issues. What went wrong?

Looking back, the interviewer in this scenario focused all of his questions on the applicants' technical capabilities, erroneously assuming that inquiries relating to the other competencies were irrelevant for a technical job. Had he asked questions about how Paul interacted with customers in past jobs, or asked for examples of how Paul handled past projects, he might not have extended a job offer, in spite of Paul's technical expertise.

Knowledge-Based Competencies

The second competency—knowledge—concerns what applicants know and how they think. Included in this category are project management skills, problem-solving abilities, decision-making skills, the ability to focus on key elements of a project, time management, and the ability to use resources effectively. These are considered intangible qualities, and they are more difficult to measure and quantify than concrete skills, but no less important. Every job, regardless of level, requires a certain degree of knowledge. Even an entry-level position demands some degree of decision making or problem solving. Interviewers should ask knowledge-related questions appropriate to the level and nature of a job to determine not only what applicants know, but also how they think. This is especially important when jobs don't require previous measurable experience, thereby precluding your ability to draw from past job-related experiences.

Behavior-Based Competencies

The third competency concerns an applicant's key behaviors, or how she acts under certain conditions. Suppose the position calls for a high level of client satisfaction. In past client-oriented jobs, was this applicant committed to developing lasting partnerships with clients? Did she keep clients informed of key developments? Did she follow up to ensure client satisfaction? If she worked as part of or led a team, did she help team members focus on client requirements? Did she incorporate client views in decision making? There are numerous questions you can ask applicants with regard to job-specific behaviors that will reveal whether they'll function effectively in your company's environment.

Interpersonal Skills

The fourth and final competency category involves interpersonal skills—that is, how applicants interact with others. Do they actively listen? Can they exercise self-control when upset? Are they self-motivated and able to work effectively with a wide range of people? Do they respect the views and ideas of others? Are they receptive to feedback? Can they manage conflict effectively?

Every job requires some degree of interaction with others. Regardless of how competent they may be at what they can do, what they know, and how they behave, if job applicants are unable to interact effectively with their managers, coworkers, employees, or clients, then their work and the work of others will suffer. Interviewers must ask questions, therefore, that focus on how an applicant interacted in past jobs in situations similar to those that are likely to occur in your organization.

Impact of Competencies

It's not hard to understand how focusing on one set of competencies, at the expense of the other three, can negatively impact your role as a representative for your organization. If the people you hire exhibit problems, it reflects on your judgment and abilities. It also makes your day-to-day job more difficult, creating possible production, morale, and motivational problems. And, of course, hiring the wrong people can be costly.

On the positive side of the ledger, by hiring all-around qualified applicants, you get more out of a person. These people are also more likely to enjoy their work and remain with your company, resulting in a positive impact on turnover rates and recruitment expenses. Productivity is also likely to improve, as will levels of customer and client satisfaction.

Job-Specific Competencies

Each job thus requires competencies from all four categories of tangible skills, knowledge, behavior, and interpersonal skills. It also necessitates a different set of job-specific competencies, based on the particular responsibilities involved.

Several sources will determine which competencies are relevant for each opening. Information about the job is generated primarily by the job description (see Chapter 4). You can also gather additional information from job requisitions and postings. Also, talk with department heads, managers, and supervisors having an in-depth understanding of the opening. They will be especially helpful with the tangible and knowledge competencies. Incumbents can prove helpful, too, since they can probably provide information regarding the behaviors and interpersonal skills needed for the job.

Once you've acquired information about the job, isolate job-specific competencies. This is a two-step procedure: First, make a list of all the required competencies, and second, identify each competency according to its category. By example, consider an account representative. Here is a partial list of competencies needed to successfully perform this job, as determined by examining an HR department-generated job description and posting, and conversations with a director of sales and two incumbents. Note that the list consists of both responsibilities and requirements:

Account Representative: Job-Specific Competencies

- Sells business's products
- Assists in the development and implementation of sales plans
- Documents quote and sales contract review
- Reports sales performance to director of sales
- Interprets technical documents as they relate to sales and contracts for company products
- Is able to effectively interface and communicate with technical and nontechnical staff
- Has experience in managing and executing product sales
- Demonstrates an ability to examine, question, evaluate, and report sales
- Is able to match timelines and meet deadlines

Now you're ready to identify each competency according to its category. Review what each of the competencies represents: "Tangible" reflects what applicants can do; "knowledge" refers to what they know and how they think; "behaviors" reveal how they act; and "interpersonal skills" indicate how they interact. Return to your list and mark each one with a T for tangible, K for knowledge, B for behavior, and I for interpersonal skills. Note that a competency can reflect more than one category:

Account Representative: Competencies by Category

T/K	Sells business's products
T/K	Assists in the development and implementation of sales plans
T/K	Documents quote and sales contract review
T/K	Reports sales performance to director of sales
T/K	Interprets technical documents as they relate to sales and contracts for company products
B/I	Is able to effectively interface and communicate with technical and non-technical staff
T/K/B	Has experience in managing and executing product sales
T/K/B/I	Demonstrates an ability to examine, question, evaluate, and report sales
B	Is able to match timelines and meet deadlines

Now go back over your list to ensure that all four categories are represented. You will no doubt see a greater emphasis of some competencies over others (in the case of the account representative, the emphasis is tangible). Also, where competencies are paired, tangible and knowledge-based skills generally fall together, as do behaviors and interpersonal skills. Sometimes, a competency reflects all four categories. Go back and seek out additional information if all four categories are not represented. Interviewers should perform this critical step before meeting an applicant to ensure that they will probe all relevant areas during the interview.

Having isolated job-specific competencies, you're ready to correlate what the job requires with what the applicant has to offer. Information about the applicant can come from several sources. Two of the most comprehensive sources are the completed employment application form and a resume. Since information appearing on applications and resumes is unlikely to be the same (see Chapter 4), it's a good idea to require an application from everyone submitting a resume. Applicants should be instructed to answer all the questions, precluding the use of "See resume" in response to some questions.

Referrals can also yield valuable applicant-related information. If applicants come to you as a result of staff word-of-mouth recruiting, the referring employee can provide helpful job-related information. Perhaps they worked together as account representatives in the past—that could yield information about an applicant's technical, knowledge, and behavior competencies. Maybe your employee supervised the referral in a past job, in which case important information about interpersonal skills may emerge from that relationship. When considering data from referrals, try not to be influenced by irrelevant factors. For example, if the referral comes from a colleague for whom you have a high regard, don't assume that the applicant will elicit the same response. Likewise, if you hold little regard for the person making a recommendation you could be biased against the applicant before even meeting him. Avoid this trap by adhering to job-related competencies, derived from the four primary competency categories.

References (discussed in Chapter 12) can also provide valuable information about an applicant. Try to contact at least three former employers to establish a pattern. If one former manager indicates that the applicant was a problem from the outset and was glad when she resigned, but two others suggest that she was outstanding, it's probable that there are others issues impacting the first reference. You'll need to probe further to ensure a clear picture.

Characteristics of Competency-Based Questions

Competency-based questions focus on relating past job performance to probable future on-the-job behavior. The questions are based on information relevant to specific job-related skills, abilities, and traits; the answers reveal the likelihood of similar, future performance. The process works because past behavior is an indicator of future behavior. Be careful not to translate this last statement as reading, "Past behavior predicts future behavior," or "Future behavior is the same as past behavior." Proponents of the competency-based approach to employment interviewing plainly point out that past behavior is an indicator only: No one can predict with absolute certainty how someone will behave in a job. There are too many variables that can affect a person's performance, among them:

- A significant change in the work environment
- The approach, attitude, or personality of a manager
- Difficulties in an employee's personal life

- A long-term or degenerative illness or disability
- A department's dramatic departure from established procedures
- Mergers or acquisitions
- The introduction of a new organizational philosophy
- An unfair (real or perceived) performance appraisal or salary increase
- Being bypassed for a promotion

Any of these factors alone can alter how an employee approaches work, and even the most compatible, conscientious, dedicated workers can be affected. Since interviewers cannot anticipate these influences when first meeting an applicant, they need to develop a line of questioning that will project, as accurately as possible, how an employee is likely to behave. This is best accomplished by asking the applicant to draw from the past.

For example, suppose you have an opening that is known for its emergency projects and tight deadlines. You can find out if a person is up to the challenge by asking about similar experiences in the past. Here is how you might phrase the question: "Tell me about a time in your last job when you were given an emergency project with what you believed to be an unrealistic deadline. What did you do?" Suppose the applicant's response indicates a firm grasp of how to handle this type of situation. You still need to know if the applicant was required to interrupt her normal workload frequently to tend to emergencies, or only once in awhile. In addition, you will want to know if the rest of her work suffered while she tended to the emergency project. Some revealing, follow-up competency-based questions would be:

"How many times, in a typical month, did this sort of emergency occur?"

"Describe the system you had for effectively dealing with these emergencies and the impact it had on the rest of your work."

"Who else was involved in meeting these deadlines?"

"What was your role vis-à-vis theirs?"

"Was there ever a time when you felt the deadline could not be met? What did you do?"

Competency-based questions seek specific examples that will allow you to project how an applicant is likely to perform in your organization. If the environment, conditions, and circumstances are essentially the same in the person's current or previous company as in yours, then your task has been made simple. Of course, this is rarely the case. That's why you need to extract information about all four competency categories. You need to know not only if the applicant knew what to do and how to think, but also how to act and interact. Answers to the above-listed follow-up questions will reveal how competent the applicant is in all four categories when confronted with demanding emergency projects.

Competency-based interviews, then, allow you to make hiring decisions based on facts. They are structured, job specific, and focused on relevant concrete and intangible qualities. In addition, they are legally defensible.

Interviewers should note that competency-based interviews do not consist entirely of competency-based questions. Chapter 7 will explore additional employment interview questioning techniques. Nevertheless, competency-based questions should represent about 70 percent of any interview, supplemented by other types of questions. They will improve the interview by:

- Identifying the skills and characteristics needed to succeed in a specific work environment
- Isolating the competencies required for a given job
- Earmarking relevant experiences necessary to have acquired these competencies
- Clarifying what applicants have learned from their experiences
- Determining whether applicants can apply what they have learned to a given job and work environment

Competency-Based Lead-Ins

When preparing competency-based questions remember two things: They require specific examples concerning what the applicant has done in the past, and they should tie in directly with job-specific competencies.

That said, competency-based questions are among the easiest questions to formulate. If the job requires the ability to oversee a project, you could pose the following questions to the applicant:

"Tell me about a time when you had to oversee a project. What was the extent of your responsibilities?"

"Tell me about a specific project you worked on. I'm interested in learning about the roles of everyone involved."

"What did you do in your last job to successfully complete a particularly difficult project?"

Or perhaps the job involves working extensively as a member of a team. The questions in this case might include:

"Describe the circumstances under which you most recently worked as a member of a team."

"Tell me about a specific time when you worked as a member of a disparate team. How did you resolve any differences that arose?"

"Tell me about a specific instance in which you made suggestions that were not acted upon."

"Describe a time when you thought you should have led a team because of your knowledge or expertise, but someone else was selected. How did you feel and what did you do?"

Each of these competency-based questions is introduced by a lead-in phrase that alerts the applicant to an important fact: that you want specific examples. Here's a sampling of competency-based lead-ins:

"Describe a time when you . . ."

"Give an example of a time in which you . . ."

"Tell me about a time when you . . ."

"Tell me about a specific job experience in which you . . ."

"Give me an example of a specific occasion when you . . ."

"Describe a situation in which you were called upon to . . ."

"Describe the most significant . . ."

"What did you do in your last job in order to . . . ?"

"How often in the last year were you called upon to . . . ?"

"Tell me about a time when you didn't want to ———; what happened?"

"Describe a situation in which you felt ———; what was the result?"

By the time you've asked the third or fourth competency-based question, applicants will realize that you expect a specific response whenever you begin with a lead-in phrase.

When to Ask Competency-Based Questions

Effective competency-based employment interviews are structured to ensure that the interviewer stays in control and covers the four key competencies. They are also legally defensible. For maximum effectiveness, competency-based interviews should consist of five stages: rapport building, introductory stage, core stage, confirmation, and closing. Each stage has a specific purpose and should take up a designated approximate percentage of the interview. Competency-based questions are highly effective in some stages, minimally effective in others, and relatively useless in others.

1. *Rapport Building.* This is the stage during which applicants are encouraged to relax and feel at ease with the interviewer. Non-job-related topics are discussed, such as the weather or the applicant's commute. The rapport-building stage should represent approximately 2 percent of the interview. Competency-based questions are ineffective during this stage.

2. *Introductory Stage.* The initial questions an interviewer poses are intended to help still-nervous applicants feel at ease. These questions should encourage the appli-

cant to talk about a familiar topic, such as her current or most recent job. In addition, the first few questions should be broad enough to generate additional questions and to allow the interviewer to begin assessing relevant verbal and organizational skills. This stage should represent about 3 percent of the interview. Competency-based questions during the introductory stage are minimally effective.

3. *Core Stage*. During this stage, interviewers gather information about job-specific skills, knowledge, behavior, and interpersonal skills. It allows for an examination of the applicant's past job performance and projects future performance based on explicit job-related examples. Interviewers can ultimately make hiring decisions based on facts, as opposed to intuitive feelings. The core stage should represent approximately 85 percent of the interview, with as much as 65 percent of it devoted to competency-based questions. The effectiveness of asking competency-based questions in the core stage is high.

4. *Confirmation*. During this stage interviewers can verify what they learned about job-specific competencies during the core stage. Topics of discussion should be limited to those aspects of work experience and education already discussed during the core segment. The confirmation stage should represent approximately 5 percent of the interview. The effectiveness of asking competency-based questions in the confirmation stage is minimal.

5. *Closing*. This final stage is the interviewer's opportunity to ensure that she has covered all relevant competencies needed to make an effective hiring decision. It is also the applicant's last chance to sell himself—to say how and why he would be an asset to the organization. The closing stage should represent approximately 5 percent of the interview, with most to all of it taken up with competency-based questions. The effectiveness of asking competency-based questions in this stage is high.

A summary of the five interview stages, their approximate percentages of time, and the level of effectiveness in asking competency-based questions appears in Exhibit 6-1.

Developing Competency-Based Questions

The information you've gathered through job descriptions and other sources, combined with the applicant's background, will yield a great deal of data about a possible job match—if you know how to phrase your questions properly. Since nearly three-quarters of an interview involves asking for specific examples related to past job performance, employers need to convert topics about which they seek information into competency-based questions. Note that it's not always necessary to ask questions in the interrogative form; statements can often be just as effective.

The best way to develop competency-based questions is to first list the primary duties and responsibilities of the job. Let's assume there's an opening for an assistant to the director of human resources. A partial list of tasks reads as follows:

Exhibit 6-1. The five interview stages.

Stage	Purpose	Percentage of Time	Level of Effectiveness in Asking Competency-Based Questions
Rapport Building	Put applicant at ease	2 percent	None
Introductory	Begin applicant assessment	3 percent	Minimal
Core	Gather information about job-specific skills, knowledge, behavior, and interpersonal skills	85 percent	High
Confirmation	Verify information acquired thus far	5 percent	Minimal
Closing	Last chance for interviewer to cover relevant competencies	5 percent	High

Sample Tasks for Assistant to Director of Human Resources

1. Recruits and interviews applicants for nonexempt positions; refers qualified applicants to appropriate department managers.
2. Performs reference checks on potential employees.
3. Helps director of human resources plan and conduct each month's organizational orientation program.
4. Assists in the implementation of policies and procedures; may be required to explain or interpret certain policies.
5. Assists in the development and maintenance of up-to-date job descriptions for nonexempt positions throughout the company.
6. Assists in the maintenance and administration of the organization's compensation program; monitors salary increase recommendations as they are received to ensure compliance with merit increase guidelines.

Now isolate the first task—"Recruits and interviews applicants for nonexempt positions; refers qualified applicants to appropriate department managers"—and refer to the list of competency-based lead-ins (listed previously in this chapter) and attach them to components of this task. Here is what you will get with very little effort:

"Describe a time when you had a nonexempt position open for an unusually long period of time. How did you eventually fill it?"

"Give an example of a time in which you referred an applicant you believed should have been hired to a department manager, but the referral was rejected. How did you resolve your differences with that manager?"

"Tell me about a time when you had more applicants than you could handle."

"Tell me about a specific job experience in which you hired someone who later didn't work out."

"Give me an example of a specific occasion when you and a department head didn't agree on the requirements for a nonexempt opening. What happened?"

"Describe a situation in which you were called upon to fill several openings in one department simultaneously."

"Describe the most significant recruiting experience you've had to date."

"What did you do in your last job in order to convince a department head to hire someone?"

"How often in the last year were you called upon to recruit for especially hard-to-fill openings? Tell me about the openings."

"Tell me about a time when you didn't want to continue using a long-time recruiting source; *what happened?"*

"Describe a situation in which you felt uneasy with the answers given by a particular applicant; *what was the end result?"*

Of course, you don't have to use all the lead-ins and you can substitute some with your own. This is exemplified with the remaining duties and responsibilities for the assistant to the director of HR position, beginning with the second task: "Performs reference checks on potential employees."

"Describe your process for conducting references. How do you follow-up with former employers who fail to respond to your phone calls or letters?"

"Describe a time when you received negative references on an applicant that the department manager wanted to hire anyway. What happened?"

"Tell me about a time when you went back to a applicant with a negative reference and asked if he could explain why he felt the former employer had given the poor reference."

"Tell me about a reference that sounded too good to be true and later turned out to be just that."

"Tell me how you go about obtaining references with former employers who will only verify dates of employment?"

"Tell me some of the questions you ask former employers to determine job suitability"

"Describe a situation in which you received conflicting references from two of an applicant's former employers. What did you do?"

"Tell me about a time when you called the former manager of an applicant your company was interested in hiring and she referred you to the HR department."

"How do you handle the verification of school records? Please be specific."

"Tell me about a time when an applicant apparently falsified educational credentials. What did you do?"

"Tell me about a time when you received negative references on an applicant after she had already started work. What happened?"

Task 3 on our list is, "Helps director of HR plan and conduct each month's organizational orientation program." Here are some questions related to this task using competency-based lead-ins:

"Describe your role in your organization's orientation program."

"What percentage of your time is taken up with preparing for and conducting your company's orientation program?"

"What is your favorite part of the orientation process? Why? Tell me about your least favorite part."

"Tell me about a time when you were asked questions to which you did not have answers."

"Have you ever been in a situation when speakers you had lined up as part of orientation didn't show up, printed materials weren't ready, or something went wrong with the audio visual equipment? What did you do?"

"Tell me some of the things you did in preparation for your first orientation that you no longer do?"

"Describe the relationship between you and the other orientation developers and participants."

"How do you follow-up with orientation attendees who are required to complete and return forms they received during the session?"

"Tell me about some ideas you might have for making the orientation experience more meaningful and more helpful to new hires."

The next area to probe is task 4: "Assists in the implementation of policies and procedures; may be required to explain or interpret certain policies." Some useful competency-based questions include the following:

"Tell me about your role in implementing and interpreting HR policies and procedures for employees."

"What is the nature of some of the calls you receive from employees with regard to policies and procedures?"

"Describe a situation in which an employee required additional information about an HR policy and became upset with the explanation. What did you do?"

"Has there ever been a time when an employee challenged the accuracy of a policy or procedure? Tell me about it."

"Give me an example of a specific occasion when a long-time policy was revised. What was your role?"

"Describe a company policy or procedure that generates the most questions or concerns. Why do you think that is?"

For the fifth task on our list, "Assists in the development and maintenance of up-to-date job descriptions for nonexempt positions throughout the company," the following competency-based questions will be helpful:

"Describe your responsibilities when it comes to developing job descriptions"

"Tell me about some of the job categories for which you are responsible."

"Describe how you gather information for job descriptions."

"Tell me about a time when you had difficulty developing a job description. Why do you think that was?"

"Have you ever been in a situation where the incumbents and their managers described a job differently? What was the outcome?"

"How do you ensure that job descriptions remain up-to-date?"

"Give me an example of a specific occasion when a job's responsibilities and its corresponding grade and salary range did not seem to coincide. What happened?"

"What do you do to improve your proficiency in developing and maintaining accurate job descriptions?"

The sixth and final task on our list is, "Assists in the maintenance and administration of the organization's compensation program; monitors salary increase recommendations as they are received to ensure compliance with merit increase guidelines." Consider this line of questioning:

"Describe your responsibilities in relation to your organization's compensation program."

"Tell me how performance appraisals relate to salary increases."

"Tell me about a time when you received a salary increase recommendation from a department head for an employee whose documented job performance was below average."

"Describe the most challenging aspect of your compensation responsibilities."

"Give me a specific example of a time when an employee objected to the amount of his recommended increase. What was your role in resolving the dispute?"

"Describe a time when an employee was already at the top of her range, but whose performance warranted a raise. What happened?"

These six tasks alone resulted in more than fifty questions that will yield a great deal of job-related information, reflecting all four competency categories. Additionally, by practicing active listening skills (see Chapter 8), the applicant's answers to these questions are likely to result in even more job-specific questions.

With the half dozen or so preplanned questions described in Chapter 4, and information contained in the job description and the applicant's application and resume, competency-based questions should flow freely during the interview. The process of asking these questions is painless and highly productive, enabling you to ultimately make an effective hiring decision.

Generic Competency-Based Questions

Among the most effective competency-based questions are those that are generated by job descriptions and resumes/applications, because they provide a direct correlation between the position and the applicant. Sometimes, though, interviewers need to explore other aspects of an applicant's eligibility to get a complete picture of how well an applicant will fit within an organizational culture, work on a given team, or function under a certain management style. Job-specific competency-based questions may not be sufficient to determine whether this fit exists.

Isolating some key job-related categories and posing a series of generic competency-based questions can help provide the balance needed to ultimately identify the best person overall for a job.

Exempt Categories and Competency-Based Questions

Here is a list of generic categories that apply to many exempt positions and a series of related competency-based questions.

Decision Making

"Tell me about a time when you had to make an unpopular decision; what was the outcome?"

"Describe a time when you were angry about an unfair decision; how did you react?

"Give me an example of a time when you made a decision that didn't turn out the way you'd planned; what happened? What, if anything, would you do differently?"

"Tell me about a decision that you had to make in order to achieve an unrealistic deadline; what happened?"

"Tell me about the most productive decision you've ever made, and the most unproductive."

Problem Solving

"Tell me about a recent problem at work; how did you resolve it?"

"What did you do in your last job to encourage your staff to resolve their own problems?"

"Describe the most challenging problem you've had to resolve at your current job; what made it challenging and how did you resolve it?"

"Give me an example of what you initially perceived as a problem but later turned out not to be."

"Describe a situation in which you felt overwhelmed by a problem; what was the outcome?"

Communication

"Describe a time when you had to make a presentation to senior management. How did you prepare?"

"Tell me about a time when you were compelled to communicate bad news to an employee. What were the circumstances? What happened?"

"Describe how you keep staff apprised of goings-on in the department and companywide."

"Give me an example of a time when you made a presentation and were asked questions to which you didn't have the answers. What did you do?"

"Describe a situation in which you were called upon to write a memo and the contents were misinterpreted. What happened next?"

Delegation

"Tell me about a time when you delegated tasks to a staff member who failed to follow-through. What happened?"

"Describe an instance in which you opted to perform a task outside the scope of your job description rather than delegate it."

"Give me an example of a time when you delegated a long-term project. How did you determine who would perform certain tasks? Describe your timeline."

"Give me an example of a time when an employee complained about a task you delegated. What happened?"

Time Management

"Describe a time when the amount of time you'd set aside for a task proved insufficient."

"Tell me about an instance when you had to meet several crucial deadlines simultaneously."

"Give me an example of a specific occasion when you were unable to meet a deadline. What, if anything, would you do differently?"

"How do you ensure that you always have enough time in which to accomplish your work?"

"Tell me how you prioritize your assignments and budget your time."

Nonexempt Categories and Competency-Based Questions

Here is a list of generic categories that apply to many nonexempt positions and a series of related competency-based questions.

Ability to Follow Instructions

"Tell me about a time when you were given instructions but had difficulty following them."

"Describe a time when you were given incomplete instructions. What did you do?"

"Tell me about a specific instance when you were given instructions that didn't make sense, but you hesitated to ask for clarification. What happened?"

"Describe a situation in which you disagreed with instructions for completing a task."

"Give me an example of the type of instructions that you find easiest to follow, and the most difficult."

Telephone Skills

"Tell me about a specific job experience in which an irate customer kept calling your boss who told you to 'handle it.' What did you do?"

"Describe a time when your supervisor said the information you recorded on a call slip was incomplete or incorrect."

"Give me an example of a time when you had trouble understanding someone on the phone."

"Tell me about an instance when you had a great deal of work to do but the phones kept ringing. What did you do?"

"Tell me about a time when you were uncomfortable speaking with a particular member of management on the phone, but she frequently called your supervisor. What did you do?"

Juggling Multiple Tasks

"Tell me about a time when you were given assignments by several supervisors, all due at the same time. How did you prioritize the work?"

"Describe an instance when you thought you'd been given too much work to do."

"Tell me about a time when you didn't want to work overtime, but you know it would be the only way you were going to get all your work done. What did you do?"

"Give me an example of a time when you felt you were being asked to juggle more tasks that everyone else in the department."

"Describe an occasion when your supervisor expressed appreciation for your efforts at juggling multiple tasks."

Exempt and Nonexempt Categories and Competency-Based Questions

Here is a list of generic categories that apply to both exempt and nonexempt positions and a series of related competency-based questions.

Ideal Work Environment

"Tell me about the best work environment in which you've ever worked; how did it compare with your concept of the ideal work environment? Now tell me about the worst work environment in which you've ever worked; how did it compare with your concept of the ideal work environment?"

"Tell me about three aspects of your current work environment that you would change if you could."

"Describe a task you've been asked to perform in a less-than-ideal environment. How did you cope?"

"Give me an example of a job which, on the surface, appeared to be ideal, but later turned out to be far less than ideal."

"Tell me about a time when you didn't want to take a job because of the work environment, but you were later glad that you did."

Employer/Employee or Coworker Relations

"Give me an example of a time when you had to deal with a difficult coworker. How did you handle the situation?"

"Tell me about the most productive employer/employee relationship you've ever had. What made it so productive?"

"Tell me about a time in your current job when you made a suggestion about a better way to perform a process. What was your employer's reaction? How did it affect your relationship?"

"Tell me about a specific instance in which you felt a coworker took credit for your work; what did you do?"

"Describe a meeting during which your coworker blamed you, in front of your boss, for an error that you hadn't made."

Strengths and Areas Requiring Improvement

"Tell me about a time when you were able to convert an area requiring improvement into a strength."

"What did you do in your last job to improve one particular area requiring improvement?"

"Identify three of your greatest strengths and tell me about three separate occasions in which you were able to apply them."

"Describe a situation in which an area requiring improvement adversely impacted your coworkers. What would you do differently?"

"Which of your strengths do you apply when faced with a crisis?"

Working Under Pressure

"What do you do at work to relieve stress?"

"Tell me about a time when you made mistakes because you were working under too much pressure. What was the outcome?"

"Describe an instance in which you thrived working under pressure. Please be specific."

"Please provide your personal definition of what working under pressure means; give me an example of when those circumstances prevailed at your last job. How did you handle the pressure?"

"Tell me about a specific job experience in which you were working under pressure because of ineffective leadership. What did you do?"

Motivation

"Tell me about a job that provided a motivating environment; please describe that environment in detail."

"Describe an aspect of your current job that you find especially motivating."

"Tell me how you motivate yourself to perform tasks you dislike."

"Describe a situation in which you felt unmotivated. What happened? What, if anything, did you do to feel motivated?"

"What have you done to improve the motivational levels of other workers?"

Summary

A competency is a skill, trait, quality, or characteristic that contributes to a person's ability to effectively perform the duties and responsibilities of a job. Identifying job-specific competencies allows you to assess how effective a person has been in the past and, therefore, how effectively she is likely to perform in your organization.

There are four primary competency categories: tangible or measurable skills; knowledge; behavior; and interpersonal skills. Most jobs emphasize the need for one category over the others, but every employee should be able to demonstrate competencies to some extent in all four categories. Every job also requires a set of specific competencies, based on its individual requirements and responsibilities.

Competency-based questions focus on relating past job performance to probable future on-the-job behavior. The questions are based on information relevant to specific job-related skills, abilities, and traits; the answers reveal the likelihood of similar, future performance. The process works because past behavior is an indicator of future behavior.

Competency-based questions seek specific examples and are introduced by lead-in phrases that alert applicants to this end. They are also structured, job-specific, and legally defensible. Hence, you are able to make hiring decisions based on facts.

Competency-based questions should constitute about 70 percent of any interview, supplemented by other types of questions.

For maximum effectiveness, competency-based interviews should proceed through five stages: rapport building, introductory stage, core stage, confirmation, and closing. Each has a specific purpose and should take up a designated percentage of the interview.

Although the most effective competency-based questions are those that are generated by job descriptions and resumes/applications, interviewers may need to explore other aspects of an applicant's eligibility to get a complete picture of how well an applicant will fit within an organization's culture. Isolating some key job-related categories and posing a series of generic competency-based questions can create the balance needed to ultimately identify the best person overall for a job.

CHAPTER 7

Additional Types of Questions

A former student of mine recently sent me an e-mail. He had completed one of my courses on interviewing skills about three months before and was pleased to report that he was able to apply much of what he'd learned. He commented that, at the time, he'd thought I was making too big a deal about the importance of asking different types of questions; that, initially, he'd seen nothing wrong with simply asking, "Tell me about yourself." I wrote back that I was delighted he'd found the class useful and asked him, "What's the most important thing you learned about asking questions during an employment interview?" His response came back immediately: "I learned that any thought can be expressed in a number of different ways. The wording you choose will determine how much information you receive and how useful that information is in making a hiring decision."

I knew he was copying that statement from his notes, but I didn't care. His response demonstrated an understanding of the power of words during an interview, and how extensively the wording of a question impacts the end result. I was also thrilled that he no longer used the "Tell me about yourself" question, which I consider to be among the worst ever asked: It lacks direction and structure, and invites applicants to volunteer illegal information.

I wrote back, "Good for you, your organization, and all the applicants you interview! Can you impress me further by telling me the types of questions you ask?" I received his answer within minutes: "In addition to posing competency-based questions during most of the interview, I present open-ended, hypothetical, probing, and some close-ended questions. And even though you didn't ask, I'll tell you what questioning techniques I avoid: trait, multiple choice, and forced choice, because these types of questions usually result in meaningless or misleading information."

Once again, I recognized my own words; and as before, it didn't matter. He'd walked into my class believing that the wording of questions was irrelevant, but he left appreciating the role well-worded questions play in the selection process. I was pleased.

Open-Ended Questions

By definition, open-ended questions require full, multiple-word responses. The answers generally lend themselves to discussion and result in information upon which the interviewer can build additional questions. Open-ended questions encourage applicants to talk, thereby allowing the interviewer an opportunity to actively listen to responses, assess verbal communication skills, and observe the applicant's pattern of nonverbal communication. They also allow the interviewer time to plan subsequent questions. Open-ended questions are especially helpful in encouraging shy or withdrawn applicants to talk without the pressure that can accompany a competency-based question requiring the recollection of specific examples.

The partial interview with a customer representative applicant in Chapter 4 illustrates these points. When asked the open-ended question, "Would you please describe your activities during a typical day at your present job?" the applicant's answer was vague: "Well, let's see," she said. "Each day is really kind of different since I deal with customers and you never know what they're going to call about; but basically, my job is to handle the customer hot line, research any questions, and process complaints." However, her answer yielded four categories for additional questions:

1. Her job requires dealing with a variety of people and situations.
2. She "handles" a customer hot line.
3. She "researches" questions.
4. She "processes" complaints.

Many of the recommended follow-up questions were open-ended:

"What is the nature of some of the situations with which you are asked to deal?"

"Who calls you?"

"What is the process that someone with a complaint is supposed to follow?"

"What is your role in this process?"

"Exactly what is the customer hot line?"

"When you say that you 'handle' the hot line, exactly what do you mean?"

"What do you say to a customer who calls on the hot line?"

"What do you say to a customer who calls with a specific question?"

"What do you do when a customer is not satisfied with the answer you have given him?

"How do you prepare for each day, knowing that you will probably have to listen to several people complaining about a variety of problems?"

Bear in mind that asking open-ended questions such as these allows applicants to control the answers. Such inquiries are most helpful, then, when used to form a foundation for competency-based questions that direct an applicant to provide specific responses supplemented by examples.

Take one of the open-ended questions just listed: "What do you do when a customer is not satisfied with the answer you've given him?" That's a perfectly legitimate question, relative to the responsibilities of a customer service representative.

The applicant may reply, "I tell them I'm sorry they're dissatisfied with my answer and that I wish I could be more helpful." That generic answer tells you very little about how this applicant interacts with customers—which is the essence of her job. Now is the time to follow up with a competency-based question: "Give me a specific example of when this happened." The applicant must now draw from a real situation involving her interaction with a customer. The information her answer yields will help you evaluate a critical job-related skill.

Open-ended questions, then, can result in descriptive monologues that lack substance or verifiable information. Without further probing, such responses are not very useful in painting an accurate picture of an applicant's job suitability.

Any open-ended question can be made more substantive by converting it into or supporting it with a competency-based question. For example, "How would you describe your ability to deal with difficult customers?" is open-ended. The competency-based version reads, "Describe a situation in which an irate customer held you responsible for something that was not your fault. What did you do?"

There are two other possible problems with open-ended questions. The applicant's response may include information that is irrelevant or that violates EEO laws. As soon as this occurs, the interviewer must bring the applicant back to the focus of the question. One way to do this is to say: "Excuse me, but we seem to have strayed from the original question of why you left your last job. I'd like to get back to that." Another effective response might be, "Excuse me, but that information is not job-related. Let's get back to your description of a typical day at the office." This is especially appropriate if information being volunteered has the potential for illegal use.

Another concern is that open-ended questions may be too broad in scope. The classic request to "Tell me about yourself" illustrates this point. Questions that require applicants to summarize many years in a single response are also not effective. When you are addressing an applicant who has worked for over thirty years, don't say, "Describe your work history." Instead, say, "Please describe your work experience over the past five years." This is still open-ended, but it establishes useful boundaries.

Here are further examples of generic, open-ended questions. One set of questions is work-related; another is education-related for applicants who are recent graduates and may have limited or no previous work experience. Note that in those instances where several questions appear as one, they are intended to be asked separately. Also, the effectiveness of many of these queries would be enhanced if followed up with competency-based questions. For example, after the open-ended question, "What is your description of the ideal manager?" the interviewer could, for maximum effectiveness, follow up with, "Tell me about a time when you worked for someone you initially perceived as being the ideal manager, but ultimately was not. What changed?" Or you could say, "Describe someone who was far removed from being your idea of an ideal manager; what were some of the traits that person exhibited?" Or, "Tell me about the effect an ideal manager had on your work, as opposed to a manager who was less than ideal; please be specific." You get the idea.

Generic, Open-Ended Questions Relating to Work Experience

"What is your description of the ideal manager? Employee? Coworker? Work environment? Work schedule?"

"How would you describe yourself as an employee? Coworker? Manager?"

"What kind of people do you find it difficult/easy to work with? Why?"

"What do you feel an employer owes an employee? How about what an employee owes an employer?"

"What were some of the duties of your last job that you found to be difficult? What made them difficult? What about duties that you found to be easy? What made them easy?"

"How do you feel about the progress that you have made in your career to date?"

"Where are you career-wise, in terms of where you thought you'd be five years ago? What happened?"

"How did your last job differ from the one you had before it? Which one did you prefer? Why?"

"Of all the jobs you've had, which did you find the most/least rewarding? Why? What makes a job rewarding?"

"In what ways do you feel your present job has prepared you to assume additional responsibilities?"

"What does the prospect of this job offer you that your last job did not?"

"Why do you want to leave your current job?"

"What are you looking for in a company?"

"How does your experience in the military relate to your chosen field?"

"What immediate and long-term goals have you set for yourself?"

"What would you like to avoid in future jobs? Why?"

"What do you consider to be your greatest strength? What are the areas in which you require improvement? How would you go about making these improvements? What have you done thus far to make improvements?"

"What aspects of your work give you the greatest satisfaction?"

"How do you approach tasks that you dislike? How does this differ from how you approach tasks you like?"

"How do you manage your time?"

"How do you go about making a decision?"

"What have past employers complimented/criticized you for?"

"What types of work-related situations make you feel most comfortable? Uneasy?"

"What is the most difficult/rewarding aspect of being a _____?"

"If you were asked to perform a task that was not in your job description, how would you respond?"

"How do you go about discussing job dissatisfaction with your boss?"

"What, if anything, could your previous employers have done to convince you not to leave?"

Generic, Open-Ended Questions Relating to Education

"What were your favorite and least favorite subjects in high school/college? Why?"

"What subjects did you do best in? Poorest in?"

"Why did you decide to major in _____?"

"Why did you decide to attend _____?"

"What career plans did you have at the beginning of college? How did they change?"

"How did high school/college prepare you for the real world? How did it fail to prepare you?"

"What did you gain by attending high school/college?"

"If you had the opportunity to attend school all over again, what, if anything, would you do differently?"

"How do you feel your studies in _____ have prepared you for this job?"

"Describe your study habits."

"Describe any part-time jobs you had while attending high school/college. Which of your part-time jobs did you find most/least interesting?"

"What advice would you give to someone who wanted to work and attend school at the same time?"

"What did you find to be most difficult about working and attending school at the same time?"

"What could the department head of the course you majored in have done to make the curriculum more interesting?"

"How did you approach required courses that were not of particular interest to you?"

"Describe what you consider to be characteristics of the ideal teacher."

Hypothetical Questions

Hypothetical questions are based on anticipated or known job-related tasks for the available opening. The questions are phrased in the form of problems and presented to the applicant for solutions. The questions are generally introduced with words and phrases such as:

"What would you do if . . .?"

"How would you handle . . .?"

"How would you solve . . .?"

"In the event that . . ."

"If . . ."

"Assuming . . ."

"How would you avoid . . ."

"Consider this scenario . . ."

"What would you say . . .?"

"Suppose . . .?"

"How would you go about . . .?"

Hypothetical questions allow for the evaluation of reasoning abilities, thought processes, values, attitudes, creativity, work style, and one's approach to different tasks.

Although the answers to hypothetical questions can produce important information about the applicant's reasoning and thought processes, interviewers are cautioned against expecting correct answers. Without familiarity with the organization, applicants can offer responses based only on their previous experiences. Such answers, then, are based on how they think rather than what they know.

An important distinction between hypothetical and competency-based questions is that hypotheticals ask applicants to project what they might do in a fictitious, albeit realistic, scenario, whereas competency-based questions draw from the actual experiences of the applicant. The first is based on conjecture; the latter on fact.

Consider the distinction between two differently worded questions on the subject of unreasonable work demands. The first example is worded as a hypothetical question:

> "If you were a manager, and your team complained about having to meet some rather unreasonable demands from one of the company's top clients, how would you go about satisfying both the client and your staff?"

Now let's reword the question to be competency-based:

> "Tell me about a time when, as a manager, your team complained about having to meet some rather unreasonable demands from one of the company's top clients. How did you go about satisfying both the client and your staff?"

The wording of the first question directs the applicant into the realm of possibilities. She is likely to answer using words like "I would" or "I could." There is no way of knowing if she is providing you what she believes is a good answer and the one you want to hear, or if this is actually what she would do. In the second question, however, she must draw from a real situation and describe what happened. Could she make something up? Sure, it's possible, but applicants can't be certain about what you already know or what can be verified. It's more difficult to lie about something that can be referenced than it is to speculate about something that has not yet happened.

Naturally, the competency-based version requires a similar experience to draw from. If, after reviewing the applicant's resume, you're unclear as to whether the applicant has experienced a similar situation in the past, word the question this way:

> **"As a manager, have you ever been in a situation where your team complained about having to meet some rather unreasonable demands from one of the company's top clients? If so, how did you go about satisfying both the client and your staff? If not, draw from your expertise as a manager and imagine such a scenario; what would you do to satisfy both the client and your staff?"**

Here are additional samples of hypothetical questions:

"How would you handle an employee who was consistently tardy?"

"How would you go about discussing job dissatisfaction with your boss?"

"How would you handle a long-term employee whose performance has always been outstanding, but who recently has started to make a number of mistakes in his work?"

"What would you say to an employee who challenged your authority?"

"What would you do if an employee went over your head?"

"Consider this scenario: You've just given a presentation and are asked a series of questions to which you do not know the answers. What would you do?"

"Suppose you are a member of a team and disagree with the way the others want to approach a project; how would you go about trying to change their minds?"

"How would you address an employee whose personal problems are interfering with her work performance?"

"If you were given a task that created an undue amount of pressure, what would you do?"

"How would you avoid conflict with coworkers? Your employees? Your manager? Clients?"

Hypothetical questions are also appropriate for applicants with limited or no work experience (e.g., graduating students). They are also helpful in interviews for jobs with little or no tangible requirements.

Probing Questions

These are questions that let interviewers delve more deeply for additional information. Best thought of as follow-up questions, they are usually short and simply worded. There are three types of probing questions:

1. *Rational probes* request reasons, using short questions such as: "Why?" "How?" "When?" "How often?" and "Who?"
2. *Clarifier probes* are used to qualify or expand upon information provided in a previous response, using questions such as: "What caused that to happen?" "Who else was involved in that decision?" "What happened next?" and "What were the circumstances that resulted in that happening?"
3. *Verifier probes* check out the honesty of a statement. For example: "You state on your resume that you currently work closely with the officers from your customers' firms; please tell me exactly what you have done for them."

Applicants who have trouble providing full answers usually appreciate the extra help that comes from a probing question. These questions also show the applicant you're interested in what she's saying and want to learn more.

Interviewers are cautioned against asking too many probing questions consecutively, since they tend to make applicants feel defensive. In addition, try to show interest with your accompanying body language by maintaining eye contact, nodding, and smiling. Avoid staring, or raising your eyebrows, because these gestures can suggest disapproval. Body language will be discussed more fully in Chapter 8.

Examples of Rational Probing Questions

"What kind of people do you find it difficult/easy to work with? *Why?*"

"Do you take over for your manager when she is away? *How often?*"

"What motivates you? *Why?*"

"What is the greatest accomplishment of your career to date? *Why?*"

Examples of Clarifier Probing Questions

"Who or what has influenced you with regard to your career goals? *In what way?*"

"You said earlier that your team failed to meet the last deadline. *What do you believe caused that to happen?*"

"Before you said that you were part of the decision to revamp your company's compensation structure. *Who else was involved in that decision?*"

"You've described part of what took place when your company downsized. *What happened next?*"

"What are some of the problems you encountered in your last job? *How did you resolve them?*"

"Please give me an example of a project that did not turn out the way you planned. *What happened?*"

"What is your definition of company loyalty? *How far does it extend?*"

Examples of Verifier Probing Questions

"What would your former manager say about how you handled the Grisham deal?"

"How would your former employees describe your management style?"

"What would your coworkers say about your contributions to the last team project you participated in?"

"Earlier you stated that you led a team from your company that had linked up with a team from World Energies, Inc. to work on developing a new communications device. Tell me about the roles and responsibilities of three specific members from World Energies."

Close-Ended Questions

These are questions that may be answered with a single word—generally yes or no. Close-ended questions can be helpful in a number of ways: They give the interviewer greater control; put certain applicants at ease; are useful when seeking clarification; are helpful when you need to verify information; and usually result in concise responses. Also, if there is a single issue that could terminate the interview, such as the absence of an important job requirement, then asking about it up-front in a direct, close-ended way can disclose what you need to know quickly and succinctly.

Interviewers should avoid relying on close-ended questions for the bulk of their information on an applicant's job suitability. Except under certain circumstances, answers to close-ended questions provide limited information, resulting in an incomplete picture of the person's abilities and experiences. Also, you will be unable to assess the applicant's verbal communication skills, if relevant.

Ask close-ended questions to serve the functions described above, but not as a substitute for open-ended or competency-based questions. Any question that can be answered by a single word can be converted into an open-ended question. For example, "Did you like your last job?" can easily be changed to "What did you like about your last job?" In most instances, the open-ended version will yield more valuable information.

Close-ended questions can also be converted into competency-based questions. Asking, "Have you done a good amount of public speaking?" will result in a single-word answer and tell you little about the applicant's experience with public speaking. The open-ended version of this question—"What is your experience with public speaking?"—is better, but still doesn't tell you much. However, a competency-based question on this subject—"Tell me about a time when you had to address a large audience. How did you prepare?''—will provide you with a job-related, detailed response.

Functional Close-Ended Questions Relating to Work

"How often do you travel in your current job?"

"Are you aware that the starting salary for this job is $975 per week?"

"Based on what you have told me so far, can I assume that you prefer working independently rather than as part of a team?"

"How many times did you step in for your manager in the last three months?"

"Earlier you said that the most challenging part of your job is conducting new hire orientations. Just before you indicated you favor conducting interviews—am I to understand that you consider the two areas to be equally rewarding?"

Functional Close-Ended Questions Relating to Education

"What subject did you do best in? Poorest in?"

"What did you major in? Minor in?"

"How many hours a week did you work while carrying a full credit load in college?"

"What was your grade point average in your favorite subject? Least favorite subject?"

How to Relate the Questioning Techniques to Interview Stages

Chapter 6 identified the five stages of a competency-based interview: rapport building; introductory stage; core stage; confirmation; and closing. Competency-based questions comprise as much as 65 percent of the core stage and the entire 5 percent of the closing. The remaining 30 percent of the interview is divided between open-ended, hypothetical, probing, and close-ended questions.

Rapport-Building Stage

This stage, which represents a scant but important 2 percent of the interview, sets the tone for the rest of the meeting. The purpose is to put applicants at ease, thereby encouraging them to communicate openly and allowing you to determine job suitability. Close-ended questions that are casual in nature and focus on non-job-related topics will accomplish this goal.

Here are some examples of neutral, rapport-building, close-ended questions:

"Did you have any trouble getting here?"

"Were you able to find parking nearby?"

"How was the traffic getting here?"

"Were the directions we gave you helpful?"

"Isn't it a beautiful day?"

"When do you think it will stop raining?"

"What do you think about this string of eighty-degree days we're having in late October?"

As you can see, all these questions are about the same two topics: commuting and the weather. Boring? Perhaps. But they are clearly the safest way to start a conversation without running the risk of saying something controversial or job-related. Don't worry about being repetitious in asking the same set of rapport-building, close-ended questions of every applicant; they're not likely to compare notes with one another after their interviews. Chapter 8 will further discuss establishing rapport.

Introductory Stage

The introductory stage represents just 3 percent of the interview and is intended to accomplish two key objectives: to help still-nervous applicants feel at ease and to allow the interviewer to start assessing their job suitability. These objectives are best accomplished by posing two to three open-ended questions. This is the most effective type of question to ask at this stage because the applicant will begin talking and relax more, while you actively listen to her responses and start making some preliminary decisions about the applicant's suitability for the job.

Introductory questions should be about topics familiar to the applicant, so as not to create undue pressure, and broad enough to generate additional questions by you. One question that satisfies both of these criteria is: "Would you please describe your activities during a typical day at your current job?" This question can accomplish a great deal:

- It helps to relax a still-nervous applicant by allowing him to discuss a familiar subject.
- The open-ended nature of the question encourages the applicant to talk, giving you an opportunity to assess verbal and organizational skills.
- It allows you time to begin observing the applicant's pattern of body language.
- It provides information upon which you can build additional questions.

The question is not foolproof, however. An applicant could respond by saying, "Well, that's kind of hard to do. No day is really typical." If this happens, be a little more specific in your wording to help the applicant get started. Try adding, "I can appreciate that. Why don't you just pick a day—say, yesterday—and describe what you did?"

Once the applicant begins to outline specific tasks you can interject, "Do you do that every day?" By breaking the question down and encouraging the applicant to talk, you should be able to get the required information and move on to the next question.

Other effective open-ended questions to start off with include the following:

"Can you give me an overview of your past experiences with benefits administration?"

"Why don't we begin with your current job. Would you describe your involvement in the day-to-day operation of your department?"

"In your job as a public relations manager, how do you go about preparing press releases?"

"Working as a legal assistant sounds very challenging. What are your primary responsibilities?"

"If you were asked to write a summary of your primary duties and responsibilities, what would you include?"

"I'm interested in learning more about what being an internal consultant entails; please tell me what you do in that capacity."

The Core Stage

As the term implies, this is the most substantive segment of the interview. Here, the interviewer gathers all relevant information about the applicant based on the four categories of tangible skills, knowledge, behavior, and interpersonal skills, examining them in relation to the requirements and responsibilities of the job. This stage represents 85 percent of the interview, with as much as 65 percent of it devoted to competency-based questions. That leaves about 20 percent of the time to be divided between four other types of questions: close-ended, open-ended, probing, and hypothetical. The last two should receive shared emphasis, say, about 5 percent each, with open-ended questions receiving about 8 percent of your time and close-ended questions carrying the balance.

Close-ended questions allow you to zero in on specific issues, usually for purposes of verification or clarification. They are useful when you need a tightly worded response in order to proceed with the interview.

Open-ended questions generally focus on how an applicant approaches tasks. They serve as effective set-ups for subsequent competency-based questions, testing out the validity of preceding answers.

Probing questions asked during the core of the interview will allow you to ascertain additional information from answers to competency-based, open-ended, and hypothetical questions. Their main function—whether rational, clarifier, or verifier in nature—is to allow you to delve deeper. Asking too many consecutive probing questions can come across as an interrogation. It also means you're not asking a sufficient number of substantive questions.

Hypotheticals lend balance to competency-based questions. While the competency-based questioning technique focuses on specific examples from past job experiences, hypotheticals present realistic job-related problems for solution. Where one is founded on facts, the other is based on supposition. Interviewers can compare what a person has done with how they might act, looking for similarities and further examining situations that stand out. Hypotheticals are also valuable for applicants with limited or no prior work history. Remember, hypotheticals evaluate how the applicant thinks as opposed to what she knows.

Chapter 6 referred to an opening for the assistant to the director of human resources. Let's revisit this example. The partial list of tasks reads as follows:

1. Recruits and interviews applicants for nonexempt positions; refers qualified applicants to appropriate department managers.
2. Performs reference checks on potential employees.
3. Helps director of human resources plan and conduct each month's organizational orientation program.
4. Assists in the implementation of policies and procedures; may be required to explain or interpret certain policies.
5. Assists in the development and maintenance of up-to-date job descriptions for nonexempt positions throughout the company.
6. Assists in the maintenance and administration of the organization's compensation program; monitors salary increase recommendations as they are received to ensure compliance with merit increase guidelines.

We have already developed more than fifty competency-based questions based on these six tasks. Now let's simulate a segment of the core stage, integrating close-ended, probing, hypothetical, and open-ended questions to support the competency-based questions. Each question is identified as "CB" for competency-based question; "P" for probing; "H" for hypothetical; "OE" for open-ended; and "CE" for close-ended:

Interviewer: How would you describe your ability to handle a disagreement with a department head over the requirements for an opening? (OE)

Applicant: I'd like to think I'm pretty diplomatic.

Interviewer: Why don't you pick a situation that occurred recently; tell me about it. (CB)

Applicant: Well, we had an opening for a security guard at one of our branches two weeks ago. The branch manager wanted me to hire someone who was at least six feet tall and weighed more than 200 pounds.

Interviewer: Why? (P)

Applicant: We'd had a string of attempted robberies at that branch; the manager thought someone who looked big and imposing would threaten would-be thieves.

Interviewer: What happened? (P)

Applicant: I explained that height and weight requirements had a greater negative impact on women and men of certain ethnic groups and therefore could not be justified.

Interviewer: How did the manager respond? (P)

Applicant: Not very well, actually. He insisted that height and weight requirements were job-related.

Interviewer: What did you say to that? (P)

Applicant: I said that if he could show me that, statistically, security guards who were at least six feet tall and weighed 200 pounds were more successful in thwarting robbery attempts, then I would be able to use these as job requirements. Otherwise, I felt we were opening the company up to possible charges of discrimination.

Interviewer: And . . .? (P)

Applicant: He backed off and realized what he was asking for was unrealistic. The job is still open, by the way.

Interviewer: Would you say that your rapport with the manager has been adversely affected by this exchange? (CE)

Applicant: No.

Here's another example:

Interviewer: How would you describe your skills in checking references on applicants under serious hiring consideration? (OE)

Applicant: Good.

Interviewer: Tell me about a time when you checked a reference on an applicant the department wanted to hire, only to find that the person's former employer had several less than favorable things to say about him? (CB)

Applicant: That's never happened.

Interviewer: Imagine that happening, if you will. How would you handle the situation? (H)

Applicant: Well, I'm not sure.

Interviewer: Okay. Let me ask you this: Have you ever received information from an applicant that conflicted with what was on the resume? (CE)

Applicant: Yes.

Interviewer: Think about one of the times that occurred and tell me what you did. (CB)

Applicant: Oh, sure. Okay. I see what you're asking for. I did a lot of probing and comparing of information till I uncovered the truth. In the situation you described, I guess I would ask a series of questions to determine if the former employer was being factual or had a bias.

Interviewer: What are some of the questions you would ask? (P)

Applicant: I'd ask for specific examples to back up his statements. Then I'd compare what he said with what I learned during the interview. I'd also try to contact more than one former employer to see if there was a pattern.

The combination of hypothetical, open-ended, and probing questions in support of competency-based questions in these two examples will allow the interviewer to better evaluate the applicant's job suitability.

Confirmation Stage

The confirming stage offers the interviewer an opportunity to verify what has been learned thus far about an applicant's job-specific competencies; no new topics should be introduced. It represents about 5 percent of the entire interview and should be divided between open- and close-ended questions, with a slightly heavier emphasis on open-ended. A competency-based question may occasionally be appropriate.

Based on the interview for the assistant to the director of HR position, as described in the core stage, here are some appropriate closed-ended questions:

"Based on what you've told me thus far, may I assume that you view yourself as being diplomatic when it comes to handling disagreements with department heads?"

"Am I correct in understanding that you have not experienced checking a reference on an applicant the department wanted to hire, only to find that the person's former employer had several less than favorable things to say about him?"

"When we talked earlier about job descriptions you stated that you assist in their development and maintenance. Is that for exempt and nonexempt job descriptions?"

The single-word answers to these questions will verify whether you have drawn accurate conclusions. The applicant will also have an opportunity to clarify any misunderstood points, if need be.

Sample open-ended questions during the confirmation stage for this same position include the following:

"I'm interested in learning more about your role in your company's monthly organizational orientation program. Would you please clarify for me the extent and nature of your responsibilities?"

"Earlier you stated that you currently assist in the implementation of policies and procedures. What exactly does that mean?"

"I need a clearer picture of when and to whom you explain or interpret these policies and procedures. Would you give me some additional information about this?"

"Tell me more about your responsibilities vis-à-vis your organization's compensation program; specifically, tell me about monitoring salary increase recommendations in relation to compliance with merit increase guidelines."

Not only will these open-ended questions help clarify and confirm preceding information, they let the applicant know that you've been paying attention.

Closing Stage

This the "last chance" stage of the interview. At this point the interviewer needs to make sure she's covered all relevant competencies needed to make a screening or hiring decision, and the applicant has one last opportunity to sell himself. Closing represents 5 percent of the interview, and should be devoted to competency-based questions such as:

"What additional examples of your work with difficult customers would help me make a hiring decision?"

"What else can you tell me about your dealings with the GHK model that will help me understand your level of expertise in this area?"

"What more can you tell me about your work with employee assistance programs to help me understand your experience in this area?"

"What additional examples of your knowledge and/or expertise can you offer in support of your candidacy for this position?"

If applicants leave your office believing they've had every opportunity to present a complete and comprehensive picture of their job suitability, then it probably means you've acquired the information needed to determine a job match.

Questioning Techniques to Avoid

I once received a resume that I later dubbed my "ay yai yai!" resume. Three pages were devoted to a string of no less than fifty "I" statements: "I am analytical . . . ,"

"I have excellent interpersonal skills . . .," "I am good at solving problems . . .," and so on. At the end of the third page, I still didn't know anything about the applicant's skills, abilities, or knowledge. That's because I had just finished reading a classic "trait" resume; that is, one that is big on meaningless rhetoric but short on substance.

Applicants may also provide trait responses during the interview as a substitute for specific examples. This is likely to happen in response to an open-ended question when an applicant lacks sufficient expertise and is hoping to impress you with fancy words and phrases. For example, if you were to ask, "What is your greatest strength?" the applicant could reply, "I excel at problem solving." Good question; good answer, right? Not really. What have your learned about the applicant? Absolutely nothing. If you want to know about a person's strengths, try the two-pronged approach: Ask the open-ended trait question first: "What is your greatest strength?" Then follow up with the competency-based question: "Give me an example of how you've used your greatest strength at your current job." Now if the applicant says, "I excel at problem solving" in response to the first question she must back it up with a specific example. If she cannot, or rambles on with more rhetoric, you know she's giving you just so much verbiage.

Trait responses are also more likely to take you away from exploring a person's "darker side." Applicants naturally stress strengths and attributes, and interviewers have a tendency to focus on the positive, hoping for the perfect match. Consequently, relevant negative characteristics are overlooked, only to surface after the person has been hired. To avoid going down this path, interviewers are urged to explore negative information by asking competency-based questions that will provide evidence about past mistakes and problems. Additional open-ended, hypothetical, probing, and close-ended questions in these areas will also give you a balanced picture of the applicant's strengths and areas requiring improvement.

When applicants are bombarding you with self-praise, it's hard to remember that they probably can't do everything equally well. So as you ask about a person's strengths, examine the flip side and ask: "Tell me, what is something about yourself that you would like to improve on? Be specific about a time when that characteristic surfaced and hindered your ability to achieve desired results."

Another questioning technique to avoid is the use of loaded or multiple-choice questions. Applicants should never feel forced to choose between two or more alternatives. That kind of set-up implies that the correct answer is among the options you've offered, negating any additional possibilities. The applicant is likely to feel inhibited, and you're apt to miss out on valuable information.

Sometimes interviewers resort to loaded questions because they've lost control of the interview. If you want to regain control, ask a series of close-ended questions; then return to more meaningful competency-based questions or one of the other types of questions described earlier in this chapter.

Consider the following examples of loaded questions—ones *not* to ask. Each example is paired with a rewording of the question that is more meaningful.

Don't Ask: "How do you go about delegating tasks? Is it based on what a person has proven he can do, his demonstrated interest, or random selection?"

Ask: "Describe how you go about delegating assignments. Give me an example of when you did this."

Don't Ask: "Would you describe your management style as being proactive, reactive, controlling, or involved?"

Ask: "How would you describe your management style? Give me an example of how and when you recently applied this style."

Don't Ask: "Would you say the greatest motivator for working is money or the pleasure one derives from doing a good job?"

Ask: "What would you say is the greatest motivator for working? Why do you think this is so?"

Don't Ask: "Would you describe your previous manager as easygoing, or was she a stern taskmaster?"

Ask: "How would you describe your previous manager in terms of her work style and interaction with employees?"

Don't Ask: "Would you like to stay in this field for the rest of your career, or do you think you would like to do something else?"

Ask: "What are your short- and long-term goals?"

Another type of question to avoid is the *leading question,* one that implies that there is a single correct answer. The interviewer sets up the question so that the applicant provides the desired response. Here are some examples:

"You do intend to finish college, don't you?"

"Don't you agree that most workers need to be watched very closely?"

"When you were in school, how much time did you waste taking art and music classes?"

It's obvious from the wording of these questions that the interviewer is seeking a particular reply. When leading questions are asked, the interviewer can't hope to learn anything substantive about the applicant.

Summary

Competency-based questions should be supplemented throughout the interview by a combination of open-ended, hypothetical, probing, and close-ended questions.

Open-ended questions, which require full, multiple-word responses, are most meaningful when asked during the introductory, core, and confirmation stages of the interview. Most open-ended questions can be made more substantive when followed by competency-based questions. Hypothetical questions, which are based on anticipated or known job-related tasks, are phrased in the form of problems and presented to the applicant for solutions. They evaluate a person's reasoning abilities and thought processes. Hypotheticals are suitable during the core stage of the interview. Probing questions are short and simply worded, allowing interviewers to delve more deeply for additional information. Like hypotheticals, they are reserved for the core stage. Close-ended questions may be answered with a single word—usually yes or no. They should never be substituted for open-ended or competency-based questions. Close-ended questions should constitute the rapport-building stage and contribute to the core and confirmation stages.

There are three types of questions interviewers should avoid asking: trait, leading, and loaded. Trait questions generate answers that are filled with rhetoric but little substance. They also prohibit you from exploring negative information—that is, examining both an applicant's strengths and areas requiring improvement—which is necessary to provide a balanced picture. Loaded or multiple-choice questions offer limited options from which the applicant is forced to choose. And leading questions imply that there is a single correct answer.

CHAPTER 8

■ Interview Components

Many new as well as experienced interviewers prepare sufficiently for their meetings with applicants, but when they're face-to-face, they don't know how to proceed. What should they do first? Jump right in with the first question? If so, what should that first question be? Should they let the applicant start out by asking a few questions? Or perhaps the interviewer should begin by providing information about the job and the company; but won't that give too much away? Is there a correct order in which information should be provided and received? Maybe no one should say anything at the outset. Allowing silence might let the applicant settle in and feel at ease. But isn't silence awkward? Won't that make the applicant feel even less comfortable? And once the process is under way, how can interviewers encourage applicants to continue talking but still keep them on track? Then there's the matter of ending the interview: Is there a point when interviewers know definitely that it's time to close?

These are all excellent questions concerning the components of an interview. Let's identify and explore these components, thereby making some sense out of how to proceed with the face-to-face meeting.

Establishing an Interview Format

Every interview requires a structured format. The format is beneficial to both interviewers and applicants, providing interviewers with a checklist of sorts, ensuring coverage of all the necessary data, and assuring applicants of a comprehensive exchange of information. The format of an interview should incorporate five critical phases:

1. *Making introductory remarks* about what is to take place during the interview
2. *Asking questions* about an applicant's education and prior work history as they relate to the requirements of the job, as well as about relevant intangible qualities
3. *Providing information* about the job opening, its salary and benefits, and the organization

4. *Answering questions* about the job and the organization

5. *Informing the applicant about what happens next,* before ending the interview on a positive note

The order in which an interviewer covers these five phases is largely a matter of preference, with the exception of the first and last phases. Obviously, telling the applicant what to expect during the interview has to occur at the outset, and informing the applicant about what will happen following the interview needs to take place at the end.

Phase One: Make Introductory Remarks

This phase may seem unnecessary: Both parties know it's a job interview. But the way in which information about the process is conveyed sets the tone for the meeting and alerts the applicant as to what to expect over the next hour or so. Here's one example of how you might start out:

> "Good morning, Mr. Turner, my name is Dan King. I'm going to be interviewing you for the position of marketing representative with Walsh Enterprises. I'll begin by giving you an overview of the company and then ask you some questions about your background and qualifications. Then I'll describe the responsibilities of the job. At that point, I'll answer any questions you may have about the opening and the company. Before we end, I'll let you know what happens next and when you can expect to hear from me."

This is a highly structured approach that can come across as overly formal unless accompanied by the appropriate body language and tone of voice. Certainly, with this format there will be no doubt as to what the interview will cover. New interviewers tend to favor this approach because it clearly conveys that the interviewer is in control.

Here's another example of how you might start things off:

> "Hi, Bob. I'm Dan King. I see you're applying for a marketing rep opening here at Walsh. Excellent! Why don't I talk a little bit about our company while you tell me some things about yourself. If you think of any questions as we're talking, just jump right in and ask me—no need to wait until the end."

This opening reflects a casual, unstructured approach, putting a greater onus on the applicant to be a partner in the interview process. Seasoned interviewers unconcerned about losing control of the meeting often opt for this approach.

Here's a third sampling of how to begin the interview:

> "Hello, Mr. Turner; nice to meet you—I'm Dan King, vice president of human resources. As you know, we're here today to dis-

cuss your application for the marketing representative opening
with Walsh Enterprises. We'll do that by talking about your experience and qualifications, the job itself, and our organization. I encourage you to ask any questions you might have; it's important
that we're both on the same page in terms of what the job entails
and what we're looking for in our next marketing representative.
Before you leave I'll let you know the next step.''

This is a softer approach, but no less comprehensive. The specific components
are blended together so that the order in which areas are going to be covered is
unclear. The applicant understands that the interview will be comprehensive, the
interviewer is in the driver's seat, and that he needs to pay attention to ensure getting the most out of the session. As with the second example, this approach is best
used by interviewers with a fairly high level of confidence in their ability to maintain
control of the meeting.

Some interviewers have a preferred opening that they use consistently. Others
are flexible, quickly assessing an applicant's general composure and comfort level
before beginning and adjusting their approach accordingly. Practice and develop a
style that works best for you. It's as important that you're comfortable with the
format as it is for the applicant to feel at ease.

Phase Five: Informing the Applicant About What Happens Next

Before looking at phases two, three, and four, let's turn to the final stage—telling an
applicant what happens after the interview is over. This is the other aspect of the
format that has a fixed place at the end of the interview, when you're sure you have
all the information needed to make an informed decision. Just as some interviewers
have trouble knowing how to begin interviews, others are uncertain as to how to end
them. To help you decide if it's time to close an interview, ask yourself the following
questions:

- Have I asked the applicant enough questions about her education and previous experience to determine job suitability?
- Have I adequately described the available position and provided sufficient
  information about this organization?
- Have I discussed salary, benefits, growth opportunities, and other related
  topics to the extent the policy of this company permits?
- Have I allowed the applicant to ask questions?

As with the first stage, what one says at the conclusion of an interview may seem
obvious. "We still have several applicants to consider; we'll be in touch when we've
completed the interviews," or some variation thereof, seems sufficient. But there's
more that can be said or implied, depending on your level of interest in the applicant.
Consider these possibilities:

High Level of Interest

"Thank you for coming in today, Mr. Turner. I've enjoyed talking with you and learning about your qualifications. I'd like to confirm your continued interest in this job before continuing [pause while, presumably, the applicant replies affirmatively]. As the next step in the interview process, I'd like to arrange for you to meet with our vice president of marketing. I'll call you by the end of the week with a date and time. Meanwhile, please feel free to call me with any questions you may have. Once again, thank you for your time."

Moderate Level of Interest

"Thank you for coming in today, Mr. Turner. I found our meeting to be quite informative. We're in the process of interviewing a number of qualified applicants and hope to reach a decision within the next several weeks. Please feel free to call me with any questions in the interim. You'll be hearing from me, regardless of our decision."

Low Level of Interest

"Thank you for coming in today, Mr. Turner, and for allowing me to review your qualifications for the position of marketing representative. It's been most informative. We're nearing the end of our interviewing process and expect to be reaching a decision by the beginning of next week. I'll contact you at that time. Please feel free to call me if you have any questions."

Each of these closings, even the one reflecting a low level of interest, has a positive tone. That's important from a public relations standpoint; you never know if you'll be considering a rejected applicant for another position or if he might refer a friend. However, notice the distinction in the wording between the three closings. The closing for the applicant for whom there is a high level of interest is the only one that commits to a subsequent interview, thereby revealing continued interest. The closing for the applicant for whom there is a moderate level of interest leaves the door open by allowing an indeterminate period of time before reaching a decision. The closing for the applicant for whom there is a low level of interest identifies a short period of time by which he will be notified.

Phases Two, Three, and Four: Asking Questions, Answering Questions, and Providing Information

Interviewers have flexibility with regard to the order of phases two, three, and four. Here are some popular options:

Option One

- Make introductory remarks.
- Ask questions.
- Answer questions.

- Provide information.
- Inform the applicant as to what happens next.

Asking questions immediately following your opening remarks gives you an advantage in that the applicant can't parrot anything he's heard you say about the job as part of his answers. This approach also reveals the applicant's knowledge of the company. It can, however, be unnerving for applicants feeling uneasy and needing more time to settle in.

Option Two

- Make introductory remarks.
- Provide information.
- Answer questions.
- Ask questions.
- Inform the applicant as to what happens next.

With the interviewer doing most of the talking at the beginning of the interview, applicants are likely to feel more at ease. However, providing too much information before applicants can describe their capabilities may give away the job and feed applicants key information. For example, interviewers may inadvertently describe the kind of person they're looking for to such an extent that applicants simply repeat this information later on in the interview when describing their skills. If the interviewer is unaware of what he's done, he may erroneously assume that he's just found the ideal applicant.

Option Three

- Make introductory remarks.
- Answer questions.
- Ask questions.
- Provide information.
- Inform the applicant as to what happens next.

Some interviewers like to invite applicants to ask questions before proceeding. The interviewer is usually looking for some insight as to the person's current level of knowledge about the job and the company. In all fairness, however, your statements may generate many of the applicant's questions. Asking questions before providing information gives some interviewers a greater sense of control.

Any order you select for phases two, three, and four will work, as long as it reflects your own personality and style. If you feel comfortable, the applicant is likely to respond well to whatever format you select.

Putting Applicants at Ease

Regardless of the format you select, devote a few moments at the beginning of the interview to putting the applicant at ease. During the rapport-building stage (as discussed in Chapter 7), you want to use icebreakers: comments and questions that have no direct bearing on the job. Their sole purpose is to put the applicant at ease before the actual interview begins. The most popular icebreakers are comments about uncontroversial subjects, such as the weather or traffic conditions. Here are some neutral questions and remarks:

"Did you have a smooth commute?"

"When we spoke last week you indicated that you were going to take the train in; how did that work for you?"

"That was some blizzard we had last week! How much snow did you get where you live?"

"It's nice to see the sun shining for a change. Five consecutive rainy days is enough for me!"

Some questions and comments may seem neutral on the surface, but nonetheless should be avoided. Topics such as sports, politics, and religion are sensitive by their very nature. An applicant's response can therefore trigger strong reactions on the part of the interviewer; these reactions can inadvertently skew the interviewer's view of the applicant's job suitability. Here, therefore, are some icebreakers to avoid:

"So, the Red Sox finally won the World Series! Thank goodness!"

"Which team are you putting your money on for the Super Bowl?"

"Say, did you happen to catch the Yankees game last night? Are you as tired as I am this morning? I stayed up for all fourteen innings!"

"Did you have any trouble at the train station on your way over here? I understand there's a group of antiwar protesters tying up traffic. What are those people thinking?"

"Did you read the headlines in this morning's paper?

"Tonight's debate looks like it's shaping up to be a real doozy!"

"I see you stopped off at church on your way over here—I forgot it's Ash Wednesday."

"I take it today isn't one of those less popular religious holidays that you celebrate; me neither. I guess that's why we're both here!"

Just how much time should be spent on icebreakers depends on how comfortable the applicant appears to be. In most instances, fifteen to thirty seconds is sufficient, although sometimes more time will be needed. Under no circumstances should this stage of the interview continue for more than a couple of minutes. Applicants who are still uneasy after this amount of time will probably not respond to additional small talk. The best thing to do in this instance is to get started.

Getting Started

Regardless of whether you opt to begin the core of the interview by asking questions, providing information, or answering questions, getting started can be challenging. Some interviewers get caught up in small talk and seem unable to move on, or they don't know how to transition from the icebreaker comments to the next stage. Others who want to begin by asking questions simply don't know what to ask first. Regardless of which format you favor, consider integrating the topic of your icebreaker into a transitional statement. For example:

"I'm glad you didn't have any trouble getting here. I'm anxious to begin talking with you about your interest in our opening for a marketing representative."

"I'm sorry you had trouble finding parking. I know that those meters where you finally found a space allow only ninety minutes. Why don't we get started, so that you can be sure to get back to your car before the meter expires?"

"With the weather so beautiful, I'm sure that you're anxious to get back outside, so why don't we get started?"

"Why don't we get started with the interview; perhaps it will help take your mind off the fact that you got soaked coming over here!"

Each of these statements creates a bridge between one stage of the interview and another, thereby eliminating the awkward silence or stammering that can easily occur.

Listening Versus Talking

Interviewers need to balance the amount of talking they do with listening. Many interviewers talk too much, erroneously believing that they're more in control of the interview as long as they're talking. In reality, no more than 25 percent of your time should be devoted to talking. This time should be spent asking questions about the applicant's qualifications, clarifying points, providing information about the job and the organization, and answering job- and organization-related questions. The remaining 75 percent of the interview should be devoted to listening.

Listening to what the applicant says in response to the icebreaker questions at the beginning of the interview is very different from actively listening during the rest of the interview. Icebreaker listening is very causal; active listening requires greater concentration. Following are some guidelines for active listening:

- *Listen for connecting themes and ideas.* By not focusing on every word, interviewers are better able to concentrate on key job-related information.

- *Summarize periodically.* Applicants don't always provide complete answers to questions at one time. Frequently, you need to fit the pieces together. To make certain that you have a clear picture of what the applicant is telling you, periodically stop and summarize. To illustrate: "Let me make certain that I understand exactly what you've accomplished in this area. You weren't directly responsible for running the department, but your boss was away about 25 percent of the time, and during that time you ran the department. Is this correct?" The applicant may then say, "Well, I didn't exactly run the department; if there were any problems, it was up to me to get in touch with the boss to find out what we should do." This clarifies the scope and extent of the applicant's responsibility.

- *Filter out distractions.* Distractions can include people coming into your office, the phone ringing, and focusing your thoughts elsewhere, which can easily occur when applicants aren't interesting to listen to. Maybe the work they do strikes you as being dull, or perhaps they speak in a monotone. At these times, you may find yourself thinking about that last vacation in Mexico and how you'd prefer being there right now. If that happens to you, consider that not all positions require effective verbal communication skills. The fact that an applicant is not a skilled speaker may be irrelevant to the job. It's unfair to judge people on the basis of how well they're able to hold your interest, unless verbal communication skills are job-related. By not listening actively, you're likely to miss important information that could influence the final hiring decision.

- *Use free information.* Every time an applicant opens his mouth, you get free information. If you don't listen actively, you're going to miss valuable insights. Free information should be the foundation for many of your interview questions.

- *Screen out personal biases.* Don't allow personal views or opinions to interfere with active listening.

- *Acknowledge any emotional states.* Maybe you had a fender bender en route to work this morning and now you're in a foul mood; or perhaps you're depressed because you just learned that you didn't get the promotion you'd hoped for. Emotional states can overshadow your ability to be attentive during an interview. Acknowledge any unusual emotional states and exercise self-discipline until after the interview is over.

Thought Speed

This is a wonderful tool that enables interviewers to hone their active listening skills. Here's how it works: Researchers have determined that most people think at a rate of approximately 400 words per minute; we speak at a rate of approximately 125 words per minute. In short, we think faster than we speak. While the applicant is talking, you can use thought speed to accomplish a great deal, including the following:

- Prepare your next question.
- Analyze what the applicant is saying.
- Piece together what the applicant is saying now in relation to something said earlier in the interview.

- Glance down at the application and/or resume to verify information.
- Observe the applicant's body language.
- Mentally check your own body language to ensure that you're conveying interest and understanding.
- Consider how this applicant's background relates to the job requirements.
- Take notes.

Thought speed can also work to your detriment, if you anticipate how applicants are likely to complete their responses before they finish, jump to conclusions too soon, compare an applicant's responses with those of a previous applicant, or get too involved in note taking. When applicants ramble or speak in a monotone, your mind can also wander, causing you to tune out. Guard against such responses by periodically recapping what the applicant has said.

Interpreting Nonverbal Communication

Nonverbal communication is vital to the interview process. Often interviewers can learn as much about applicants through their nonverbal messages as from verbal ones. Nonverbal messages that are misinterpreted by the interviewer can result in poor selection or rejection decisions. This usually occurs when body language is interpreted according to the interviewer's own gestures or expressions. For example, just because you have a tendency to avoid eye contact when you're hiding something doesn't mean that the applicant is avoiding your eyes for the same reason. It may very well be a sign that she's deep in thought.

Each of us has our own pattern of nonverbal expression, attributable to a combination of cultural and environmental factors. These factors influence our gestures and posture, whether we engage in or avoid touching, and the distance we maintain from one another. With regard to distance, or proxemics, our culture recognizes a distance of from two to five feet as being an appropriate distance between interviewer and applicant. Someone with a different cultural experience might regard this as too great a distance and immediately pull his chair up much closer to the interviewer. That action might be interpreted as a violation of space or as an act of aggression or intimacy, leaving the interviewer with feelings of discomfort, hostility, or intimidation. Some interviewers may go so far as to move their chairs back or actually get up during instances of excessive proximity.

Another aspect of nonverbal communication, chronemics, has to do with the amount of time that passes between verbal exchanges. In our culture, we expect people to respond to our questions immediately. In other cultures, people deliberately wait before answering. An applicant who appears to pause might be perceived by her interviewer as being bored, inattentive, confused, or nervous.

Be careful not to draw conclusions too early in the interview process, based on an applicant's nonverbal messages. Allow time for the individual's patterns to emerge, and then relate these patterns to the other factors involved in making a selection.

Here are some additional points to keep in mind about nonverbal communication and body language. To begin with, body language encompasses more than facial expressions, body movements, and gestures. The term also refers to pauses in speech, speech rate, vocal tone, pitch, and enunciation. Together, all of these factors "speak" to an interviewer from the very first moment of contact. Often the message can be confusing. For example, body movements such as finger or foot tapping can contradict facial expressions such as smiling. Similarly, an applicant may maintain direct eye contact while answering a question, an indication that she has a high degree of self-confidence, but the vocal tone conveys just the opposite.

The situation may be further complicated when the interviewer tries to assess the content of what's being said. The conflict between the verbal and nonverbal message can be confusing, leaving the interviewer wondering which message is the more accurate. Since verbal messages are clearly easier to control than nonverbal ones, when there is a conflict between the verbal and the nonverbal, the nonverbal is often more persuasive. This may be accurate, however, only to the extent that the person's nonverbal messages are being accurately interpreted.

Very few gestures can be interpreted the same cross-culturally. One such gesture is the smile, which is universally accepted as a welcoming gesture. Even so, with eighty facial muscles that influence the smile, there are more than fifty different types of smiles. And people in different cultures smile on different occasions. Some people smile to mask embarrassment (Thailand), others smile when confused (Japan), and for still others excessive smiling signals shallowness or thoughtlessness (Korea).

Body language, then, cannot be universally translated. That is, a gesture or movement that you use to express a certain feeling may mean something entirely different when someone from another country or culture uses it. For example:

- *Nodding.* In the United States, it is commonly assumed that nodding the head up and down indicates "yes" and shaking it back and forth means "no." In Bulgaria, nodding the head up and down means "no" and shaking the head back and forth means "yes."
- *Eye Contact.* Americans tend to look others directly in the eye when greeting and conversing with others. In Japan and Korea, direct eye contact is considered intimidating.
- *Shaking Hands.* Americans are taught to shake hands with a firm, solid grip. To Middle Easterners and many Asians, a firm grip suggests aggressiveness.
- *Closed Eyes.* In the United States, closed eyes signify boredom or sleep. In Japan, closed eyes may mean that the listener is concentrating deeply.
- *Waving.* In the United States, raising the arm and moving the open hand back and forth signals "hello" or "good-bye." Throughout much of Europe, this same action signifies "no."

This difference in interpretation doesn't just occur across diverse cultures. As a result of our individual socialization processes, each of us develops our own pattern of nonverbal messages: We tend to react to a situation in the same nonverbal way each time that it occurs. For example, the applicant who nervously clasps his hands while waiting to be interviewed is likely to do the same thing each time he's nervous. Therefore, although there are no universal interpretations to body language cues, each of us has our own nonverbal pattern that may be consistently translated if observed over a period of time.

The following is a list of common nonverbal messages exhibited during interviews and how Americans tend to interpret certain movements:

Nonverbal Message	Typical Interpretation
Making direct eye contact	Friendly, sincere, self-confident, assertive
Avoiding eye contact	Cold, evasive, indifferent, insecure, passive, frightened, nervous
Shaking head	Disagreeing, shocked, disbelieving
Yawning	Bored
Patting on the back	Encouraging, congratulatory, consoling
Scratching the head	Bewildered, disbelieving
Biting the lip	Nervous, fearful, uneasy
Tapping feet	Nervous, anxious
Folding arms	Angry, disapproving, disagreeing, defensive, aggressive
Raising eyebrows	Disbelieving, surprised
Narrowing eyes	Disagreeing, resentful, angry, disapproving
Flaring nostrils	Angry, frustrated
Wringing hands	Nervous, anxious, fearful
Leaning forward	Attentive, interested
Slouching in seat	Bored, relaxed
Sitting on edge of seat	Anxious, nervous, apprehensive
Shifting in seat	Restless, bored, nervous, apprehensive
Hunching over	Insecure, passive
Having erect posture	Self-confident, assertive

Paul Ekman, a psychologist and researcher in nonverbal communication, focuses on facial expressions as a means for interpreting certain emotions. For instance, he maintains that disgust is shown in the nose, cheeks, and mouth; fear appears in the eyes; sadness, in the brows, mouth, and eyes; anger is shown in the forehead and brows; and surprise may appear in any facial area.

Interviewers are cautioned against assigning a specific meaning to a given move-ment or facial expression until they have identified an individual's nonverbal pat-terns and can therefore be fairly certain that such interpretation is correct.

Interviewers should be aware of any sudden changes in nonverbal communica-tion. For example, if an applicant has been sitting quite comfortably for twenty min-utes or so, and then suddenly shifts in her seat when you ask why she left her last job, this is a clue that something is amiss. Even if the applicant offers an acceptable response without hesitation, the sudden change in body language should tell you that something is wrong. Additional probing is necessary. The conflict between the verbal and the nonverbal should not be ignored.

Also be careful not to erroneously interpret a person's body language according to his reaction to yours. If you are not aware of your own body language, you may incorrectly assume that an applicant is initiating a nonverbal message, instead of reacting to yours. It's critical, therefore, to be aware of your own body language in terms of how you react to certain emotions or situations. Your nonverbal responses can be controlled once you're aware of them.

During an interview, your goal is to evaluate the applicant as objectively as possi-ble. It's hard enough to make a value judgment; adding elements that may not be valid can only serve to make it more difficult. For example, suppose you just learned that the deadline for a major report had been moved up, putting you in a bad mood. If you're not conscious of the body language that you're projecting as a result of this news, the applicant may assume that you're reacting negatively to something on his resume or to something that he's said in response to one of your questions. This is perfectly understandable. After all, how many of us are so secure or self-confident that we would think, "Oh, I know it couldn't possibly have anything to do with me"?

Also remember that when it comes to perception versus how you really may be feeling, it's perception that counts. Try asking a friend or colleague to observe you during a meeting or throughout a typical workday. Periodically ask for feedback. Ask the person what she perceives your mood to be at a given moment based on your nonverbal messages. Remember, the interpretation may differ from what you're ac-tually feeling. This simple exercise can help you understand your patterns and thus help you control your body language during an interview.

By being aware of your own nonverbal communication, you can consciously choose to project certain nonverbal messages to applicants. For instance, by knowing that nodding one's head is generally interpreted as a sign of understanding, you can use this gesture to encourage an applicant to continue talking. Likewise, if you are aware that leaning forward in one's chair implies interest or attentiveness, you can assume this position when interviewing in order to convey interest in whatever the applicant is saying.

Encouraging the Applicant to Talk

One of the greatest challenges for an interviewer is encouraging applicants to talk. Of course, some applicants are well prepared, self-confident, and more than willing to answer your questions. Indeed, it's difficult to prevent some of them from talking too much and for too long. With others, however, talking to an interviewer can be intimidating and unnerving; regardless of how much they may want the job, selling themselves may be very difficult. Therefore, they're going to need your help. Here are six ways in which you can encourage applicants to speak freely:

1. *Use repetition.* This encourages applicants to continue talking and also helps to clarify certain points. Repeating the last few words of an applicant's statement and letting your voice trail off as a question mark will encourage the person to elaborate. For example, suppose that an applicant has just finished making a point: "The most difficult part of being a manager was that I was in charge of twenty-five people." You could follow up by saying, "You supervised twenty-five people . . . ?" The applicant might then reply, "Well, not directly. I was in charge of three supervisors, each of whom monitored the work of about seven workers." To further clarify, you might then say: "So, you were directly responsible for supervising three people. Is this correct?" The applicant would then state, "Yes, that's correct, although my supervisors always came to me when they were having trouble with their workers."

   This dialogue presents a far more accurate picture of the applicant's supervisory responsibilities than did the original statement. Using repetition encouraged the applicant to provide valuable additional information.

2. *Summarize.* Like repetition, summarization allows the applicant to clarify points made thus far in the interview and to elaborate as necessary. It further ensures an accurate understanding on your part. Summarization may be used at specific time intervals in the interview—say, every ten minutes or after a certain topic has been fully discussed. For instance, you and the applicant may have just devoted ten minutes to reviewing his prior work experience as it relates to the available position. At that point, you might say: "Let me make certain that I understand what you've said thus far. All of your employment since high school has been as a mechanic. This includes the time that you spent in the Marine Corps. You enjoy this line of work and want to continue doing it. However, you feel that you were underpaid at your last job and that's why you left. Is all of this correct?"

   The applicant can now confirm all or part of what you've just summarized. Be careful not to include more than four or five statements in your summary. This way, if part of it is inaccurate or requires clarification, it won't be difficult to isolate. Also, to ensure accuracy, make certain to employ the active listening guidelines outlined earlier.

3. *Ask close-ended questions.* Asking competency-based questions will yield the most information, but some applicants have difficulty talking and may initially respond better to a series of direct, close-ended questions. Such questions are effective when used for the limited purpose of allowing the applicant to achieve a certain comfort level before moving on to more information-producing forms of inquiry.

4. *Employ certain phrases to encourage applicants to continue talking.* These phrases include "I see," "How interesting," "Is that right?" "Really?" and "I didn't know that." It's important to note that none of these phrases express an opinion or show agreement or disagreement; they merely show interest and understanding.

5. *Use encouraging body language.* In order for these phrases of understanding to be effective, they must be accompanied by body language that expresses encouragement—for example, nodding, smiling, making direct eye contact, and leaning forward. Conveying these nonverbal messages consistently throughout the interview will establish your interest in what the applicant is saying, thereby encouraging the person to provide additional information.

6. *Try silence.* Most people find silence to be awkward and uncomfortable. Consequently, interviewers often feel compelled to talk whenever the applicant stops. However, unless prepared to ask another question, talking when you need additional information from the applicant will not help you reach a hiring decision. When the applicant stops talking and you want him to continue, try silently and slowly counting to five before speaking. This pause often compels an applicant to go on. Of course, you must be careful not to carry silence too far. The interview can easily become a stressful situation if you simply continue to stare at an applicant who has nothing more to say or needs your encouragement to continue. However, if you combine silence with positive body language, the applicant should continue talking within a few seconds. Silence clearly conveys the message that more information is wanted.

Keeping Applicants On Track

During most interviews, applicants are responsive to the questions asked and the format laid out by their interviewers. Sometimes, however, applicants try to take over or distract the interviewer by going off on a tangent. This may be deliberate (e.g., to cover up a lack of job-specific knowledge or experience) or inadvertent (e.g., resulting from an inability to provide detailed responses to challenging competency-based questions). Whatever the reason, interviewers need to be able to keep applicants on track.

In addition to the preparation steps identified in Chapter 4, there are other measures interviewers can take to keep the face-to-face meeting moving steadily forward. Following are ten situations during which applicants may try to divert your attention from a discussion of their qualifications, and suggestions for keeping them on track:

1. When an applicant asks you to elaborate on your history with the company, say: "Perhaps we could talk about my history with the company at another time. This is your opportunity to convince me that you're the best person for this job. Let's return to our discussion of your qualifications."

2. When an applicant tries to change the subject from a discussion of her qualifications to the pictures on your desk, ask: "Since we only have a limited amount of

time for this interview, don't you think it would be a better use of our time if we focused on your qualifications rather than my pictures?"

3. When an applicant goes off on a tangent while answering a question, interject by saying, "I'm not sure I see how what you're saying relates to the question I asked. Allow me to restate it."

4. When an applicant answers your questions with questions of her own, say: "It would be beneficial to us both if you could just answer my question before asking one of your own."

5. When an applicant insists on discussing positions other than the one she's applying for, pull out the job description and ask that she review it. Then say, "I need to know before proceeding any further if you are, in fact, interested in being considered for this position. If you are, we need to focus our attention on how you qualify for this job—not others."

6. When an applicant presses for an answer as to whether you're going to hire her, say: "I'm sure you can appreciate the fact that I need to weigh each applicant's responses to key questions before I can make a decision. That said, I'd like to return to those key questions so I can give you equal consideration."

7. When an applicant avoids answering questions directly, say: "I'm having difficulty relating your answers to my questions. That's going to cause problems for me later when I'm evaluating all the applicants' responses. Is there any way you can help me out here, perhaps by answering my questions more directly?"

8. When an applicant starts touching or playing with items on your desk and commenting about them, say: "Let me know when you're done so we can return to the interview."

9. When an applicant starts talking about personal matters in lieu of her job experience, interrupt and say, "We need to discuss job-related matters."

10. When an applicant says or does anything that compels you to stray from the interview format, say: "Tell me again why you're here and why I should hire you."

Keep your body language neutral throughout instances such as these and remain calm. Remember that you're in charge of the interview and it won't take more than a statement or two by you to get an applicant back on track. Try, also, to get through the interview without forming overly negative impressions. As an interviewer, you are obliged to remain objective and evaluate a host of tangible and intangible factors. Wait until after the interview is over before making a final determination.

Providing Information

Ascertaining information about the applicant is only part of the interview; providing information to the applicant is also important. Just as interviewers must decide if applicants are appropriate for a job, applicants too must decide whether the job and company are right for them. This is particularly true when unemployment is low and applicants can afford to be selective about job opportunities.

Many interviewers assume that applicants come to the interview armed with information about both the company and the job opening. Perhaps there was a detailed description in the newspaper advertisement to which the applicant responded; maybe the applicant has been referred by a long-term employee who has extensive knowledge of the company and the available job; or perhaps, while waiting in the reception area, the applicant was seen perusing the company's annual report or newsletter. It's also possible that the applicant is a former employee or has been away on a leave of absence. Regardless of how much the applicant may know beforehand, interviewers are responsible for informing all job applicants about certain aspects of the company and the available position. In this way, applicants will be certain to understand key elements of their prospective employment.

As previously stated, information about the job and company may be provided at the beginning of the interview or offered between asking and answering questions. However, care must be given not to give away too much regarding the characteristics of an ideal applicant in the early stages of the interview.

Generally, interviewers should inform applicants about what the organization does and how long it's been in business, as well as provide brief statements about its origins, current standing among competitors, and projected growth. They should also provide a brief summary of company benefits. Then offer more specific information concerning the department that has the opening, including its function, the different tasks performed, how it interrelates with other departments, a description of who's in charge, the chain of command, and the work environment.

This naturally leads to a description of the specific job opening, details of which may be offered by providing the applicant with a copy of the job description. Allow him a few moments to read it and then encourage questions based on its contents. If the job description is comprehensive and well written, it will ensure a clear understanding of what the job entails and requires. Be certain to cover growth opportunities available through job posting, career planning, training programs, tuition reimbursement, or other in-house or outside means for career development. Also review any negative features as they pertain to, say, working conditions or the work schedule. Let the applicant react now, during the interview, rather than later as a disgruntled employee.

Whether salary is discussed depends on your company's policy. It's advisable for interviewers to provide at least general information about the range for an given job. Tell the applicant, too, if the salary is fixed and nonnegotiable.

Also offer a brief description of the neighborhood surrounding the workplace. Most people like to know about transportation options, restaurants, stores, and any health/exercise facilities in the area.

Finally, be certain to inform the applicant what will happen after the interview is over. State approximately when the applicant may expect to hear from you, whether it's likely that there will be additional interviews, and what to do if she has additional questions. Be certain you have a current telephone number and address so that there will be no problem with future communication. If you're concerned that all of this will take too long, prepare a fact sheet that you can hand to an applicant before concluding the interview.

Perception

Before meeting an applicant, interviewers should briefly review the four primary ways in which we formulate our perceptions and ideas about people. These four aspects of perception—first impressions, information from others, single statements, and ethnocentrism—together form a valuable interview component. Briefly reviewing them when meeting with an applicant can help you avoid hasty hiring or rejection decisions based on nonfactual, subjective factors.

First Impressions

This is the most prevalent and often most damaging way of formulating ideas about people, since we often form first impressions without even realizing it. Interviewers unaware of the importance of perception frequently boast, "The minute he walked in the door, I could tell he was right for the job."

This is a mistake. You cannot determine job suitability by sizing up people in a split second based on their appearance. Of course, appearance (e.g., clothing, colors, and grooming) does play a role in the selection process. After all, employees represent an organization, therefore the image that they project is a direct reflection on that company. The problem is that interviewers have a tendency to form preconceived notions of how employees in certain job classifications should look. An accountant, for example, conjures up a different image than does a mechanic. If a person applying for a mechanic's opening came to an interview dressed in a suit, you would be surprised but probably not turned off. However, if an accountant appeared in your office wearing overalls, it's far more likely that you would form a negative first impression.

First impressions should play a role in your decision-making process, but not at the exclusion of all the other factors to be examined. Don't allow them to act as a substitute for judgment, and try not to form a complete impression until after you've conducted the interview. You may find that the applicant's attire or grooming is the only problem. The person's job skills may be superior to those of all other applicants. At this point you can talk to the applicant about the image your organization wants its employees to project. Then schedule a brief follow-up interview to see if she got the message.

Information from Others

An applicant who comes highly recommended by someone for whom you have high regard can elicit a positive response from you even before the actual face-to-face meeting. On the other hand, someone you dislike may make a referral to you, automatically creating a negative bias toward the person being recommended. In both instances you're allowing yourself to be influenced by information from others. Instead of assessing the applicant on her own merits, you're assessing the person making the recommendation, thereby transferring your opinion from the referral source to the applicant. As with first impressions, information from others does play a role in the decision-making process. Anything that might supplement the data on an application or resume can be helpful, but it's premature to make an evaluation based on this highly subjective aspect of perception at this stage of the employment process.

Single Statements

Suppose an applicant's response to one of your questions rubs you the wrong way. If you're unaware of the impact that a single statement can have, it could bother you to the extent that you eliminate the person from further consideration, even though the comment doesn't constitute a valid reason for rejection. Be particularly careful if this should happen during the initial stage of the interview, when you're trying to put the applicant at ease and establish rapport. If you err and mention something relating to, say, politics, the applicant might express a view contrary to yours. If you're not careful, this difference could influence your objectivity in assessing the applicant's job suitability. You will then have taken a single statement—one that is totally irrelevant to the decision-making process—and allowed it to affect your judgment.

Even single statements that are job-related must be weighed in relation to other qualifying factors. Keep in mind that it's usually a combination of factors that results in the rejection of an applicant.

Ethnocentrism

Ethnocentrism refers to applying our values, standards, and beliefs to judge or evaluate others. Overall, this is a perfectly natural result of the cultural conditioning process to which we are all exposed. In our early years, well-intentioned parents, teachers, and religious leaders teach us to think and act according to certain guidelines. At the age of five or six, few of us question the validity of these guidelines. Unfortunately, many people grow up believing that this is the only way to think. The result is stereotypical misperceptions whereby we assign specific attributes and roles to others based on surface characteristics, such as sex, age, or ethnic origin.

Other factors also come into play. For example, the interviewer sees from a resume that the applicant graduated from Harvard. The interviewer's general assumptions about Harvard graduates could lead her to hastily conclude that the person would be an asset to the organization. Negative reactions may also occur. For instance, an applicant may presently be working for an organization from which your brother was recently fired. This negative association could bias your assessment of the applicant's job suitability.

When perceptions are based on ethnocentric thinking, objectivity falls by the wayside. The chances for open, effective communication are blocked whenever an applicant's responses or nonverbal messages deviate from the interviewer's preconceived notions. Keep in mind that ethnocentrism does not pertain to work-related standards established by the company; rather, it comes into play through the intangible qualities of an individual's style and approach to doing work. It conflicts with objectivity, which is an interviewer's number-one obligation.

Summary

The contents of this chapter can best be summarized with the following guidelines:

1. Establish a format that encompasses all of the important ingredients of an interview, and be sure that it reflects your own style and personality.

2. Establish rapport by taking a few moments at the beginning of an interview to put the applicant at ease.

3. Carefully select your first question so that the answer will yield additional categories to explore.

4. Practice active listening skills, concentrating closely on what the applicant says and talking no more than 25 percent of the time.

5. Practice positive nonverbal communication skills, by employing those gestures and movements that are likely to be interpreted as encouraging. Also, strive for consistency between verbal statements and nonverbal expressions.

6. Encourage applicants to talk by using the techniques of repetition, summarization, direct close-ended questions, encouraging phrases, positive body language, and silence.

7. Provide information, making certain that the applicant has a clear and complete understanding of both the available job and the organization.

8. Consider the role of perception, and try not be unduly influenced by first impressions, information from others, single statements, and ethnocentric thoughts.

CHAPTER 9

Types of Employment Interviews

Nick Dawkins is the HR manager for Clarisse Inc., a communications company with about 900 employees, located outside of Boston, Massachusetts. He currently has several openings to fill, including one for a business office supervisor. Nick has cast a wide recruitment net, using a variety of sources. As a result, he has identified several possibilities, all of whom look impressive on paper. Nick is ready to begin the interview process. He knows that he has to first carefully screen the applicants before bringing them in for interviews. To do this, he plans on conducting either face-to-face exploratory, telephone screening, or video interviews. Assuming there is continued interest, Nick plans on scheduling each applicant for a series of comprehensive interviews. First, there will be the HR interview with himself; next there will be either a departmental interview with the business office manager or a panel interview with the business office manager and other selected managers; finally, there might be a peer interview with business office colleagues and other supervisors.

By selecting a combination of different types of interviews, Nick is confident that he will find the most suitable business office supervisor for Clarisse.

Exploratory Interviews

Exploratory interviews may be conducted under many circumstances, such as during job fairs, at open houses, with applicants responding to an ad, with professional applicants traveling a significant distance at considerable expense (usually yours), during campus recruiting, and with walk-ins. In each instance the objective is the same: to establish continued interest on both sides and to determine preliminary job suitability. Assuming these two conditions are satisfied, the next step is to set up a job-specific interview. Under no circumstances should interviewers substitute exploratory interviews for the in-depth job-specific interview, or make a decision to hire based on the exploratory meeting. On the other hand, exploratory interviews can screen out applicants in whom you definitely have no further interest.

While some exploratory interviews are conducted over the phone (discussed in a subsequent section of this chapter), most are conducted face-to-face. What distinguishes an exploratory interview is the amount of time allotted to asking questions. Interviewers must focus on key job-related issues—usually in a period of fifteen to twenty minutes for nonexempt applicants and about thirty minutes for professional applicants—and decide if a full follow-up interview is warranted.

Under these conditions, interviewers often feel pressured into making a decision based on what they perceive to be limited information. Consequently, it can be tempting to dismiss a person for giving an inappropriate answer, or even because of the way he dresses or shakes your hand. Using such non-job-related reasons as the basis for rejection, even at this early stage in the interview process, can be counterproductive for a number of reasons: You may be passing up a viable applicant; the applicant leaves with negative feelings about your organization (which he may well share with others); and it could lead to claims of discrimination based on "intent" (e.g., the minute you saw the applicant was a woman, she contends she was excluded from further consideration).

Time is limited in an exploratory interview, yet you can still make decisions based on solid, job-related information. The process of deciding who "passes" an exploratory interview begins with the all-important job description. First, segregate those tasks that are essential; then, from that list, try to identify tasks that require 20 percent or more of the incumbent's time. Many companies write their job descriptions so that each duty is coded as being essential or nonessential. Additionally, they note an approximate percentage of time devoted to each task. If there are none or just a few tasks that require 20 percent or more of the incumbent's time, adjust the percentage downward so that you have somewhere between four and eight essential tasks isolated. If necessary, isolate all essential tasks, even those requiring 5 percent or less time, in order to come up with half dozen or so duties.

To illustrate, here is a sample job description for a business office supervisor. Preceding each task is an "E" signifying an essential task or "NE" for nonessential task. Following each task is the approximate percentage of time devoted to each task:

(E)   1. Plans, organizes, and controls the billing, receiving, and paying functions for the office. (25 percent)

(E)   2. Reviews financial resources and collects delinquent accounts by direct contact or referral to collection agency. (20 percent)

(E)   3. Prepares and distributes the payroll; establishes and maintains payroll records. (15 percent)

(E)   4. Maintains flow of financial information with other departments. (10 percent)

(NE)   5. Keeps current on new systems, methods, and equipment. (5 percent)

(NE)   6. Performs HR functions in absence of manager; specifically, hiring, training, evaluating performance, and recommending salary increases. (5 percent)

(E)   7. Ensures compliance with government regulations and participates in audits, as required. (5 percent)

(E)   8. Informs management of current financial position and effect of operations by preparing and analyzing various reports. (10 percent)

(NE)   9. Revises policies and procedures relevant to the business office function. (5 percent)

By segregating the essential functions, we end up with this list:

1. Plans, organizes, and controls the billing, receiving, and paying functions for the office. (25 percent)
2. Reviews financial resources and collects delinquent accounts by direct contact or referral to collection agency. (20 percent)
3. Prepares and distributes the payroll; establishes and maintains payroll records. (15 percent)
4. Maintains flow of financial information with other departments. (10 percent)
5. Ensures compliance with government regulations and participates in audits, as required. (5 percent)
6. Informs management of current financial position and effect of operations by preparing and analyzing various reports. (10 percent)

Now we can isolate those essential tasks that encompass 20 percent or more of the incumbent's time:

1. Plans, organizes, and controls the billing, receiving, and paying functions for the office. (25 percent)
2. Reviews financial resources and collects delinquent accounts by direct contact or referral to collection agency. (20 percent)

Since only two duties take up 20 percent or more time, other tasks need to be isolated:

3. Prepares and distributes the payroll; establishes and maintains payroll records. (15 percent)
4. Maintains flow of financial information with other departments. (10 percent)
5. Informs management of current financial position and effect of operations by preparing and analyzing various reports. (10 percent)

Now we have five out of the nine primary responsibilities that represent 80 percent of the job. This condensed job description will allow you to focus on the salient aspects of an applicant's experience and qualifications to determine preliminary job suitability.

Look, too, at the category of "education, prior work experience, and specialized skills and knowledge." Eliminate excess verbiage and separate key requirements. For the business officer supervisor's job, you might extract the following:

1. Extensive experience in billing, receiving, payroll, and collection
2. Ability to prepare/analyze/present financial reports
3. Accounting degree desirable

Now, when interviewing applicants in a limited amount of time, you can focus on just five key tasks and three requirements.

The final step in preparing for an exploratory interview is to plan your format and the types of questions you'll ask. Begin by explaining the purpose of the meeting, then verify the available position and, if your company policy permits, the starting salary or salary range. Ask what the applicant currently does (open-ended question) and what her current salary is (close-ended question). Then, based on the isolated tasks and educational requirements, ask a series of about six competency-based questions to determine the level and nature of her expertise. Wind down with one or two open-ended and/or close-ended questions to confirm what she's told you. Your final question should be, "What else should I know about you in relation to your application for this job?" Probing questions are rarely introduced in exploratory interviews, unless the applicants' responses to competency-based questions are incomplete. Hypotheticals are omitted as well, except where the applicant has no prior work experience to draw from.

Here's a sampling of questions from an exploratory interview with an applicant for the business office supervisor's position:

> "Good morning, Jesse. Thank you for stopping by today. I understand you're interested in our opening for a business office supervisor. Is that correct?" (answer) "Very good—let's get started."
>
> "Jesse, this is an exploratory interview. That means we spend a few minutes discussing your interest and qualifications. Then, if it appears that there is a sufficient match between your skills and the position requirements, and you're still interested in continuing, we can arrange a more in-depth interview for another time. How does that sound to you?" (answer)
>
> "Let me also confirm that you understand the salary range for this job is $48,500 to $56,000. Do you want to proceed?" (answer)
>
> "Okay, fine; I'm going to ask you a few questions now. First, why don't you begin by telling me about your activities in a typical day at your current job as an office supervisor." (answer)
>
> "What are you currently earning?" (answer)
>
> "I'm interested in learning more about your billing, receiving, and paying responsibilities. Give me one example to illustrate each of these areas." (answer)
>
> "Tell me about a particularly difficult collection you had to make by direct contact." (answer)
>
> "Describe a time when the payroll was delayed; what did you do?" (answer)
>
> "Tell me about another department with which you maintain a

steady flow of financial information and the nature of that information.'' (answer)

"Describe the contents of the most recent financial report you
prepared.'' (answer)

"May I safely assume from what you have told me that the bulk
of your work is in billing and receiving?'' (answer)

"Am I also to understand that you have not had any experience
in direct contact collections?'' (answer)

"What else should I know about you in relation to your application for this job?'' (answer)

"All right. Thank you for your time and interest. I need to review your answers and will get back to you no later than Friday.
Enjoy the rest of the day.''

This sample exploratory interview would probably last about twenty minutes. Regardless of the outcome, the applicant should leave feeling that she had an opportunity to present her qualifications and will be judged on her abilities in relation to the job requirements. The interviewer, too, can leave the interview knowing he's asked enough relevant questions to make a preliminary decision to reject the applicant or continue with a more comprehensive job-specific interview.

Telephone Screening Interviews

Telephone screening is intended to accomplish one of two objectives: to establish continued interest in a job applicant that results in the scheduling of an appointment to meet in person for an in-depth interview, or to determine that an applicant's qualifications do not sufficiently meet the job's specifications. Under no circumstances should telephone screening be viewed as a substitute for the face-to-face interview.

Successful telephone screening depends on establishing and following a certain format. To begin with, it's usually wise to contact applicants at their home during nonworking hours. Identify yourself and explain the purpose of your call. Also, confirm the individual's interest in the specific job. Suggest that the applicant allot anywhere from fifteen to forty-five minutes for the screening call (again, fifteen to twenty minutes is considered sufficient for a nonexempt-level applicant and thirty to forty-five minutes for a professional).

When the specified time arrives to call the applicant back, describe the available position, being careful not to identify the qualities being sought in the desired applicant. Encourage the applicant to ask questions related to the specific opening or the company. Have a series of questions ready to assist you in determining whether continued interest is warranted. Some questions to ask *nonexempt-level applicants* are:

- Why are you leaving your present (or last) employer?
- What do (or did) you do in a typical day?
- What do you like (or did you like) most and least about your present (or last) job?

- Why are you applying for this particular position?

In addition, ask questions relative to any significant aspects of the job. For example, if the job requires standing for long periods of time, ask applicants to describe jobs where they've had to meet a similar requirement. In addition, describe a typical situation that is likely to occur with this job and ask the applicants to describe how they've handled similar situations in the past.

Appropriate questions to ask *exempt-level applicants* include:

- Why are you leaving your present (or last) employer?
- Why are you applying for this particular position?
- What do you know about this organization?
- What have you contributed in past positions?
- What contributions do you anticipate being able to make in this position?
- What do you expect to receive from this company?
- How does this position fit in with your long-term goals?

Next, based on the particulars of the job, ask a series of questions regarding how the job applicant has handled certain situations in past positions. As the applicant responds, remind yourself of the purpose of the call: You're deciding whether a face-to-face interview is in order, not whether the individual should be hired. Take notes as the applicants talk; if the conversation itself is not determinative, reviewing their responses after the call can help you decide whether to schedule an interview. If you do decide to bring them in, these notes can be used as a point of reference and comparison as you repeat some of the questions asked on the phone, seeking more in-depth information.

Be careful not to judge the quality of an applicant's telephone presentation if effective verbal communication skills are not a job-related criterion. On the other hand, some people, especially those in sales or marketing, do very well communicating on the phone; consequently, you must be able to separate style from substance.

Before concluding the conversation, go over a brief checklist:

- Does the applicant understand the job?
- Did you ask questions that will allow you to determine whether further interest is warranted?
- Did the applicant ask pertinent questions?
- Has the applicant expressed interest in the job?
- Does the applicant meet the basic qualifications for the job?
- Is there consistency between the information on the resume or application and what the applicant has told you?

If there's no doubt in your mind that the person should be invited in for an interview, do so before the conversation is completed. If you are not certain and want to review your notes before making a decision, thank the applicant for his time, describe the next step, and estimate when he may expect to hear from you. If you are absolutely certain that the applicant is not suitable for the job, you have one or two choices: Be honest and say that his qualifications are not suitable or that there is a lack of specific expertise or knowledge necessary for the job, or say that you will be reviewing the results of your conversations with all the applicants before taking any further action. If you do reject the applicant outright, be certain to explain your policy on keeping applications and resumes on file and encourage the individual to apply again in the future for other openings. If you have handled the situation tactfully, the person can hang up feeling good, even though no job interview is forthcoming.

Telephone screening offers numerous benefits. The process lets you to weed out applicants who are not qualified, thereby allowing you more time to devote to viable potential employees. It's also an impartial process; that is, neither party can be influenced or distracted by such visual factors as appearance, clothing, or grooming. While these assessments can be important job-related intangibles, they are irrelevant at this screening stage.

Video Screening Interviews

Video screening is growing in popularity as businesses expand their applicant searches nationally and even internationally. That's because video screening allows interviewers to observe long-distance applicants while simultaneously talking with them. It also results in cost savings achieved by eliminating travel and administrative costs. Video screening is used primarily as a tool for screening mid- and executive-level applicants.

Currently, video interviewing is typically used by the following organizations:

- Colleges and universities, to assist visiting employers with campus recruitment
- Executive recruiters, to sort through applicants throughout the United States
- Corporations, typically high-tech companies and those in the communications industry, for screening applicants in remote locations

Businesses that are interested in video screening often hire the services of an outside source. These sources generally either facilitate a live videoconference between applicants and an employer, or they provide the company with an unedited videotape of a screening session conducted by a professional interviewer. The tape is unedited to simulate, as closely as possible, a face-to-face meeting.

One drawback to video screening is that the audio portion of the interviews are generally superior to the visual. Pictures are often unclear, lacking broadcast quality. Sometimes, too, the video is out of sync with the audio portion of the presentation.

Applicants who find themselves in front of a video camera are usually coached, so they learn to maximize how they come across. Here are some of the tips they're typically offered:

- Watch how newscasters dress and dress similarly.
- Speak clearly and succinctly.
- Don't fidget.
- Pretend that the camera is a real person and maintain "eye contact."
- Avoid sudden movements.

The Human Resources (HR) Interview

Employment interviews conducted by HR specialists are both broad-based and job-specific: They are broad-based in that the HR interviewer covers a great deal of general territory, including goals and interests; and job-specific because the interviewer delves into the applicant's education and experiences as they relate specifically to the available job opening (e.g., whether an applicant qualifies sufficiently skill- and knowledge-wise to pass on to the department for further consideration). HR practitioners also need to consider whether a person is a good fit for the organization. Typically, then, the HR interview is the longest and most comprehensive of all interview types.

Let's look at some of the questions Nick, the HR manager at Clarisse, Inc., would ask of Kira, an applicant for the position of business office supervisor. Kira is currently a business office supervisor but doesn't feel she's receiving adequate compensation. She's also frustrated because she wants to learn new skills, but there are no training opportunities at her current job.

For purposes of this example, we'll skip over the steps of establishing the format, putting the applicant at ease, providing information, and answering questions. Our focus is solely on asking a series of competency-based, hypothetical, open-ended, probing, and close-ended questions. Once again, let's start with the job description.

Primary Duties and Responsibilities of Business Office Supervisor

(E)   1. Plans, organizes, and controls the billing, receiving, and paying functions for the office. (25 percent)

(E)   2. Reviews financial resources and collects delinquent accounts by direct contact or referral to collection agency. (20 percent)

(E)   3. Prepares and distributes the payroll; establishes and maintains payroll records. (15 percent)

(E)   4. Maintains flow of financial information with other departments. (10 percent)

(NE) 5. Keeps current on new systems, methods, and equipment. (5 percent)

(NE) 6. Performs HR functions in absence of manager; specifically, hiring, training, evaluating performance, and recommending salary increases. (5 percent)

(E)   7. Ensures compliance with government regulations and participates in audits, as required. (5 percent)

(E)   8. Informs management of current financial position and effect of operations by preparing and analyzing various reports. (10 percent)

(NE) 9. Revises policies and procedures relevant to the business office function. (5 percent)

Requirements: Education, Prior Work Experience, and Specialized Skills and Knowledge

1. Extensive experience in billing, receiving, payroll, and collection
2. Ability to prepare/analyze/present financial reports
3. Accounting degree desirable

Job-Specific Experience and Education Questions

"Kira, please describe your activities at your current job in a typical day."

"Are there any other activities you might be asked to perform? What are they?"

"Of these activities, which would you identify as your primary responsibility?"

"Approximately what percentage of your time would you say you devote to this responsibility?"

"You've indicated that organizing the billing for your office is your primary responsibility; do you also plan and control the billing?"

"What are your responsibilities with regard to the receiving and paying functions?"

"Tell me about a time when you ran into a problem with regard to organizing the billing for your office; what happened?"

"What would you identify as your second most important responsibility?"

"With regard to this responsibility of preparing payroll, can you tell me about an instance when you couldn't get the payroll out in time?"

"What were the repercussions of not getting the payroll out in time?"

"What procedures are in place as a result of that incident?"

"What was your roll in putting those procedures in place?"

"Do you review financial resources and collect delinquent accounts? If not, who does?"

"Describe how you keep current with regard to new systems, methods, and equipment."

"How do you ensure compliance with government regulations?"

"Have you ever participated in an audit? Tell me about it."

"Tell me about your responsibilities as they pertain to the flow of financial information between departments."

"Describe an instance when one of the other departments didn't receive important financial information in a timely manner and held you responsible—what happened?"

"What HR responsibilities, if any, do you perform in the absence of your manager?"

"Let me make certain I understand what you just said: You don't perform any HR responsibilities, but that's one of the tasks you're interested in taking on. Is that correct?"

"Tell me more about your interest in HR—and please be specific."

"Am I to understand that you'd like to eventually move from what you're currently doing into HR? If so, do you have a timeline in mind?"

"I have a few more questions about your current responsibilities. Are you at all involved with management in terms of preparing or analyzing financial reports? If not, who is?"

"Tell me about a time when you disagreed with something your manager wanted you to do. What was the end result?"

"Can you describe an instance in which you were asked to perform a task that wasn't in your job description?"

"Of all the tasks you've identified, which do you enjoy the most? The least?"

"Which of these tasks do you find especially easy? Difficult?"

"Before working at your current company, did you perform any billing, receiving, payroll, or collection tasks?"

"Am I correct in understanding that all of your experience with accounting is in your current capacity as a business office supervisor?"

"Kira, I have a few questions I'd like to ask you about your education as it pertains to this job. You've indicated that you graduated with a degree in accounting. Tell me about some of the accounting courses that you took."

"Which of these courses did you do well in?"

"Were there any courses that were especially challenging? Why?"

"Why did you decide to major in accounting?"

Generic Questions to Establish the Right Fit

"Kira, can you give me your definition of the ideal manager? How about the ideal work environment?"

"What would you like to avoid in future jobs?"

"From what I've said, combined with what you've read in the job description for this position, what does this job offer that your current job does not provide?"

"Is there anything your current boss could say that would make you want to stay there?"

"What do you consider to be your greatest strength? Give me an example of a time in your current job when you applied this strength."

"Tell me about an area in which you'd like to improve. How do you plan on making these improvements?"

"How would you describe yourself as an employee?"

"How do you approach tasks that you dislike?"

"If you had two tasks due by the end of the day—one that you excel in and enjoy, the other more challenging and less interesting—which would you do first?"

"How would you go about discussing job dissatisfaction with your boss?"

"In what way do you feel your work experiences to date have prepared you to assume additional responsibilities?"

"Tell me about your short- and long-term goals. I'm especially interested in learning more about your interest in HR."

"How can you link your current set of skills with your interest in HR?"

"What educational or training opportunities are of interest to you?"

"What kind of people do you find it difficult to work with? Easy to work with?"

"What do you feel an employer owes an employee? What about what an employee owes an employer?"

"If you could design the dream job, what would it be? What would you be doing?"

"What else would you like me to know about you before we conclude?"

The Departmental Interview

Unlike the HR interview, department heads or managers are less likely to probe general areas of interest or education. Their main focus is, "Can this person do the job?" The departmental interview, then, emphasizes job specifics. For this reason, the departmental interview should entail open-ended, competency-based, and hypothetical questions based on specific job-related duties and responsibilities.

Following his interview with Kira, Nick sits down with the job description for the business office supervisor, Kira's resume, and his interview notes. Based on her experience and responses in relation to the requirements of the job, Nick is hesitant to refer her on. She lacks expertise in a number of essential areas and seems more interested in pursuing a career in HR than continuing with business. Still, Millicent, the department head, wants to meet with her, so Nick sets up an interview.

Here are some of the job-specific questions Millicent could ask Kira:

"Tell me how you go about organizing the billing for your office—please be specific."

"How do you handle receipt errors?"

"What about payment overages?"

"Describe your logging system."

"What's your approach to collecting delinquent accounts?"

"I have some questions about your responsibilities with regard to your company's payroll system: How do you prepare the payroll? When do you distribute it? How do you maintain payroll records?"

"What's your take on the Schematic 5500?"

"Describe your system of financial record keeping."

"What do you think of the new Jackal record-keeping system?"

"Tell me about a time when you were blamed for a financial error that wasn't your fault."

"What would you do if I wasn't around and one of the company's VPs started screaming about not having received important financial documents?"

"I need someone to revise policies and procedures relevant to the business office function—have you ever done that?"

"How would you go about revising policies and procedures? Who would you talk to? How would you gather the information you'd need?"

"What's the most important ingredient in preparing a financial report?"

"What would you do during a government audit if you were held responsible for an error?"

After Kira leaves Millicent's office, she reflects on the interview. Nick was right; Kira is lacking experience with some critical job-specific areas. She will not consider her further.

Panel Interviews

Most interviews involve two people: the interviewer and the applicant. Occasionally, however, the team or panel approach is used. Ideally, this method involves up to three interviewers—usually an HR representative, the department manager, and the department head. Panel interviews are commonly conducted for one of two reasons: 1) to save the time it would take to schedule three separate interviews and 2) to compare impressions of applicants as they answer questions.

The role of each participant should be agreed upon ahead of time. Perhaps the HR representative will begin by introducing everyone, making small talk to establish rapport, and asking some open-ended and competency-based questions to determine overall job suitability. Then the manager will ask more detailed, job-specific questions; the department head may also ask job-specific questions as well as assessing the applicant's fit within the department and company. The HR representative might continue by exploring the applicant's fit as well as looking at relevant intangible factors. While the panel members need not have a list of specific questions they plan on asking, everyone should agree in advance on their general areas of coverage. It's awkward and unprofessional to have members of a panel bickering over who's going to ask which question, or having more than one person asking the same question.

Applicants should always be advised in advance that the panel approach will be used. Otherwise, it can be unnerving to find more than one interviewer in the room.

Seating should be carefully arranged. Unlike a one-on-one interview, where the proximity of the interviewer's chair to the applicant's is inconsequential, improper seating in a panel interview situation can create an uncomfortable environment. Do not, for example, surround the applicant's chair by placing one seat on either side and one directly in front. As Exhibit 9-1 illustrates, this arrangement results in a "tennis match" sort of interview, with the applicant continually turning his head from one side to the other, trying to address all members of the team. Instead, offer the applicant a seat and form an arc in front of him. As Exhibit 9-2 illustrates, this setting is less structured and more conducive to a productive exchange.

If carefully planned, panel interviews can be highly effective. They tend to be more objective because there's less singular interaction with the applicant. In addition, while one of the panelists is talking, the other two can more carefully observe the applicant's body language and take additional time to assess responses to specific questions. Also, if there are three different personality types on the panel, you'll be able to see how the applicant responds to and interacts with these different types.

Exhibit 9-1. Surrounding the job applicant.

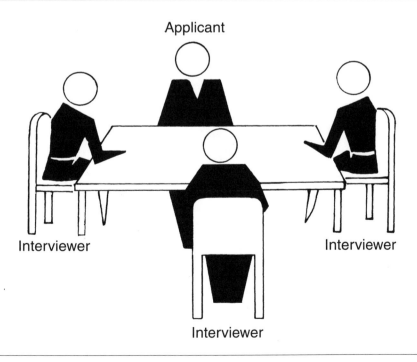

Applicant

Interviewer

Interviewer

Interviewer

Exhibit 9-2. Suggested seating arrangement for team or panel interview.

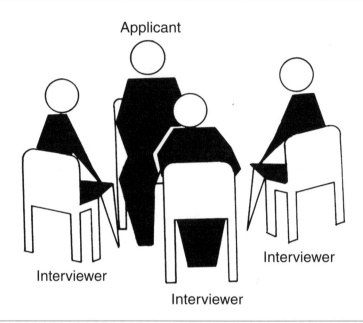

Most important, assessments tend to be more accurate and consistent, since everyone is basing their decisions on the same information.

Peer Interviews

Peer interviews involve the colleagues of a potential employee. The approach has grown in popularity, especially in those work environments in which teamwork is vital. Most peer interviews are in the form of panels, although some are one-on-one. They should take place at the end of the interviewing process; that is, following any screening interviews, the applicant's interview with HR, and the individual or panel departmental interview.

Participants in a peer interview should be:

- Experienced in the details of the available job
- Aware of job-related intangible factors
- Clear about the relationship of the available job with other jobs in the department and within other departments
- Aware of specific problems associated with the job
- Well-versed in how the department functions
- Familiar with the culture of the department in particular, and the organization in general

- Aware of departmental and company goals
- Familiar with the history of the organization
- Sensitive to the issue of diversity
- Free of bias

Structure is critical for peer interviews to succeed. Since most participants of peer interviews are not skilled interviewers, an HR representative usually prepares them in advance. At its most basic level, preparation includes a review of critical factors, a discussion of questions to avoid from a legal standpoint, and a list of recommended general questions to ask. Beyond that, some peer interviews are broken down into specific components, with each participant responsible for probing a particular area. For example, one person could explore a skill assessment; another could examine how well the applicant is likely to fit in with the rest of the team; and a third could examine the relevance of past experiences to the tasks at hand.

Some companies hold mock peer interviews to ensure preparedness. Others invest in extensive training, complete with a detailed checklist of dos and don'ts. Free-form questioning is generally discouraged.

As with panel interviews, three participants are considered ideal for peer interviewing. Four is acceptable; five is the absolute maximum. An HR representative should be present during the process. She would function as the "moderator" of the interview, introducing the applicant to the participants and explaining the process. Beyond that, the HR representative is usually silent, unless one of the interviewers poses an illegal or inappropriate question.

Following a peer interview, participants should compare their observations, using a prepared checklist of relevant topics and corresponding ratings. These ratings should be kept simple—for example, highly qualified, qualified, or not qualified. At the end, participants can summarize their individual evaluations, again using simple terms: highly recommend for hire; recommend for hire; do not recommend for hire.

The HR representative should be present during these discussions to ensure adherence to relevant topics and objective evaluations. Observations by the peer interview participants should then be compared with those of all preceding interviews. The HR representative, departmental representatives, and members of the peer interview sometimes meet to discuss a particular applicant. This type of meeting generally occurs when there is a lack of uniformity between everyone's evaluations. If there is disagreement over who would make the best employee, the hiring manager, hopefully backed by HR, should have the final say.

Interviewing Less-Than-Ideal Applicants

Most applicants are eager to make a good impression on their interviewer. They try to answer all questions as fully as possible, project positive body language, and ask appropriate questions. Occasionally, however, you'll find yourself face-to-face with a less-than-ideal applicant who falls into one of the following categories: excessively shy or nervous, overly talkative, overly aggressive or dominant, or highly emotional or distraught.

At the first indication that you're dealing with a less-than-ideal applicant, make certain adjustments in how you proceed with the interview.

Excessively Shy or Nervous Applicants

Within the first few seconds of the rapport-building portion of the interview, it will become apparent if an applicant is especially shy or nervous. Avoid drawing attention to the person's state by saying something like, "I can see that you're really nervous; just try to relax!" Or, "Don't be shy—I'll try to go easy on you!" Statements such as these are only going to make matters worse. Believe it or not, shy or nervous people don't think others notice; calling attention to their behavior could drive them to a point of near implosion.

Because this type of person needs to be drawn out slowly, a broad, open-ended question might be too intimidating if asked right off the bat. Instead, try a few close-ended queries to put the applicant at ease. Make them simple questions, relating to areas likely to make the applicant feel comfortable. Also, make certain that your first competency-based or open-ended question pertains to a topic within the individual's realm of experience, thereby ensuring a certain degree of ease. In addition, try using a softer tone of voice, exaggerated positive body language, and words of encouragement. Let the applicant know that you're interested in what she has to say.

Overly Talkative Applicants

Some applicants seem capable of talking nonstop. They not only answer your questions, but volunteer a great deal more information, much of which is irrelevant, unnecessary, and sometimes illegal. Applicants who are overly talkative may just be extreme verbalizers; on the other hand, they could be engaging in excessive verbiage to distract you from their lack of job-related skills.

Such people are often very personable and really quite delightful to speak with. However, you must remind yourself that you're not there to engage in a social conversation. Your goal is to acquire sufficient information upon which to base a hiring decision.

The key to effectively dealing with applicants who talk too much is to control the situation. You must remember that you're in charge of the interview and control the amount of time devoted to questions and answers. When you've gathered enough data, say to the applicant: "Everything you've told me is very interesting. I now have enough information upon which to base my decision. Thank you very much for your time. You'll be hearing from us by the end of this week."

Sometimes applicants don't respond to this cue to that the interview is over. They remain seated and resume talking. If this occurs, escalate your efforts somewhat. Tell the applicant, "I'm afraid that's all the time we have. I have other applicants waiting. I'm sure you understand." At this point, stand up and extend your hand. As you shake hands, gently guide the applicant to the door.

Overly Aggressive Applicants

Some applicants present themselves in an overly aggressive or hostile manner. Perhaps they've been out of work for a long time, or maybe they've applied for a job with your company before and were rejected. Whatever their motivation, the resulting behavior makes interviewing difficult.

When confronted with an angry applicant, stay calm and maintain your objectivity. Try to find out why the applicant is so upset. Explain that you cannot continue the interview as long as he remains agitated. Your goal should be to complete the interview and judge the applicant as fairly as possible, taking into account any extenuating circumstances. If the applicant's behavior escalates or he remains hostile, ask the applicant if he's still interested in the position; if so, tell him you need to reschedule the interview.

Dominant Applicants

Sometimes an applicant will try to gain control of the interview, usually to cover up for a lack of sufficient job experience. The attempted takeover may manifest itself in a variety of ways, for instance, by steering the conversation to a discussion of the interviewer's career or hobbies, or discussing books or plants in the office. All is not lost if this happens. Remind yourself that you're in charge and assertively say to the applicant: "Excuse me, but we seem to have strayed. Let's get back to . . ." If she continues trying to dominate the interview, wait for an opening and state, "We only have a limited amount of time remaining and I still have a number of questions to ask you. Shall we get back on track?"

Highly Emotional or Distraught Applicants

Have you ever had an applicant begin to cry during an interview? Needless to say, it can be quite unnerving. If this ever happens, extend empathy rather than sympathy; this approach will allow you to remain objective, in charge, and better able to help the individual regain composure. Resist patting the person on the back or asking her to elaborate on whatever it was that set her off. In all likelihood, you'll get an earful of personal information to which you have no right. Offering the person a few moments of privacy usually helps most applicants to continue with the interview. In some instances, however, it may be preferable to reschedule the interview.

Occasionally, applicants become emotional or distraught when you challenge an answer to a particular question. If this happens, change directions and return to the question later in the interview, perhaps after a better rapport has been established. Emphasize to the applicant that the information is important for continued consideration. This message is usually sufficient encouragement for even the most reluctant applicant. Sometimes it's helpful to pose a series of very specific, close-ended questions. Another way to encourage applicants to answer is to indicate that you'll be verifying the information she provides during a reference check.

Stress Interviews (How and Why to Avoid Them)

In a stress interview the applicant is deliberately put on guard, made to feel ill at ease, or "tested" for some purpose known only to the interviewer. *This technique is not recommended under any circumstance.* Proponents of stress interviewing claim that they're able to ferret out significant job-related traits, such as how applicants will handle uncomfortable situations that cannot be discovered through questioning, assessing nonverbal communication skills, or weighing intangible factors. In truth, stress interviews are often nothing more than a subterfuge for ineffective interviewing skills.

The examples of stress interviews that follow are provided so readers can learn to identify and recognize these bad tendencies. *Readers are urged to view these as illustrations of what to avoid.*

Stress Interviews in the Office

Stress interviews in the office usually involve various "props," such as chairs, exaggerated body language on the part of the interviewer, or unnecessary, sometimes inappropriate comments. Here are some examples:

- The interviewer slowly eyes the applicant from head to toe, staring for some time at the applicant's feet. Finally he says, "I never would have worn those socks with those shoes."
- The interviewer makes certain that his chair is elevated considerably higher than that of the applicant.
- The interviewer invites the applicant to sit in an oversize chair, making it difficult for the applicant to rise up out of it.
- The interviewer invites the applicant to sit in a chair with one leg slightly shorter than the others, causing it to wobble anytime the applicants shifts in her seat.
- The applicant is offered a chair better suited for a five-year-old.
- The applicant is offered a chair that faces the window. On a sunny day, with the drapes open, the interviewer repositions the chair according to the time of day so that the sun will shine directly in the applicant's eyes.
- The interviewer positions himself in front of a window on a sunny day with the drapes open, thereby causing a "halo" effect around her head.
- The interviewer begins firing questions at the applicant as soon as he enters the room.

- The interviewer doesn't ask the applicant any questions; rather, he simply stares at the applicant, waiting to see what the person will say or do.
- The interviewer asks questions while looking down at her desk or doing other work.
- The interviewer answers the phone during the interview, puts the person on hold, turns to the applicant and says, "Go ahead; he can wait for a minute."
- The interviewer makes a series of phone calls during the interview.
- The interviewer leaves the room for several minutes.
- The interviewer begins by saying, "Go ahead—impress me."
- The interviewer begins by saying, "Is there anything you'd like to tell me?"
- The interviewer asks the applicant, "Do you always wear your hair that way?"
- The interviewer takes her watch off, places it on the desk, and says, "We have exactly forty-five minutes."
- The interviewer stares at the applicant's watch and says, "You must be rich. Why would you want to work here?"
- After the applicant responds to a question, the interviewer asks, "Are you sure that's the answer you want to give me?"
- The interviewer stares at the applicant for some time and finally says, "You're rather young, aren't you?"

Mealtime Stress Interviews

Mealtime interviews are generally reserved for professional-level applicants. They can be appropriate and quite comfortable for both the interviewer and the applicant if the same guidelines that govern office interviews are adhered to. Unfortunately, meals also provide an ideal arena for proponents of stress interviews, based on their perceived justification that eating and drinking habits may be a valid reflection of the applicant's decision-making skills on the job. Consider these examples:

- The interviewer waits until the applicant has a mouthful of soup before asking a question.
- The applicant is rejected because he orders a cheeseburger or some other food that requires direct handling with one's hands. The premise here is that an applicant should assume that he'll be asked to review papers during the course of a mealtime interview, which cannot be done with greasy fingers.
- The applicant is rejected because she orders shrimp scampi when the interviewer orders a chef's salad. The point here is that the scampi takes less than a dozen bites to complete while the salad requires many more bites to consume; therefore, the applicant will be finished eating long before the interviewer, leaving the interviewer feeling rushed.

- The applicant accepts an offer of an alcoholic beverage and is rejected on the basis that he might have a tendency to drink too much.

- The applicant refuses an offer of an alcoholic beverage and is rejected on the basis that she might be a recovering alcoholic.

- The applicant is rejected for refusing to check his coat upon entering the restaurant, the assumption being that he's insecure about parting with possessions.

- The applicant is evaluated on her knowledge of the correct utensils to use during various courses of the meal.

- The applicant is found acceptable because he orders something from the menu that costs the same or less than what the interviewer orders.

- The interviewer fires a steady stream of open-ended questions at the applicant as soon as her food arrives, to see whether she can eat and talk at the same time.

- The interviewer tries to slip in some non-job-related, illegal questions during the meal.

- The interviewer assesses the applicant's level of assertiveness based on how she deals with a disagreeable waiter.

- The interviewer identifies several other diners who work at the same organization; later in the meal, she asks the applicant about them to determine how closely he was paying attention.

Interviewing Pitfalls

Regardless of the type of interview you're conducting, there are some pitfalls that all interviewers should be mindful of:

- Avoid interrupting the applicant, as long as he is saying something relevant.
- Avoid agreement or disagreement; instead, express interest and understanding.
- Avoid using terminology with which the applicant is unlikely to be familiar.
- Avoid reading the application or resume back to the applicant.
- Avoid comparisons with the incumbent, previous employees, yourself, or other applicants.
- Avoid asking unrelated questions.
- Avoid talking down to an applicant.
- Avoid talking about yourself.
- Avoid hiring an unqualified applicant simply because you are desperate to fill an opening.

- Avoid trying to duplicate someone else's interviewing style.
- Avoid allowing applicants to interview you or to control the interview.
- Avoid hasty decisions based solely upon first impressions, information from others, a single response, body language, or your biases.
- Avoid asking questions even in a roundabout way that might be considered violations of EEO laws.
- Avoid judging applicants on the basis of cultural or educational differences.
- Avoid conducting stress interviews of any sort.

Summary

There are many different types of interviews, each serving a specific function in the hiring process. Three of these are screening interviews:

1. *Exploratory interviews* establish continued interest—on the part of both the interviewer and the applicant—and determine preliminary job suitability. Assuming these two conditions are satisfied, the next step is to set up a job-specific interview.
2. *Telephone interviews* are intended to accomplish one of two objectives: to establish continued interest in a job applicant that results in the scheduling of an appointment to meet in person for an in-depth interview, or to determine that an applicant's qualifications do not sufficiently meet the job's specifications.
3. *Video interviews* allow employers to observe long-distance applicants in addition to simultaneously talking with them.

Under no circumstances should exploratory, telephone, or video screening interviews substitute for the face-to-face interview.

Other types of interviews constitute comprehensive meetings between the applicant and one or more representatives of the hiring organization:

- *HR interviews* conducted by HR specialists are both broad-based and job-specific. They are broad-based in that the HR interviewer covers a great deal of general territory, including goals and interests, and job-specific because the interviewer delves into the applicant's education and experiences as they relate specifically to the available job opening.
- *Departmental interviews,* which are conducted by department heads or managers, focus on whether the person can do the job; that is, they emphasize job-specifics.
- *Panel interviews* generally involve three interviewers—usually an HR representative, the department manager, and a department head. Panel interviews save time and allow interviewers to compare impressions of applicants as they answer questions.

- *Peer interviews* involve the colleagues of a potential employee. Most peer interviews are in the form of panels, although some are one-on-one. An HR representative should be present.

Most applicants are eager to make a good impression on their interviewer. They try to answer all questions as fully as possible, project positive body language, and ask appropriate questions. Occasionally, however, you'll find yourself face-to-face with a less-than-ideal applicant who falls into one of several categories: excessively shy or nervous, overly talkative, overly aggressive or dominant, or highly emotional or distraught. At the first indication that you're dealing with a less-than-ideal applicant, make certain adjustments in how you proceed with the interview.

Proponents of stress interviews claim that the process allows them to ferret out significant job-related traits by deliberately putting the applicant on guard or at a disadvantage. Stress interviews are not recommended under any circumstance.

Regardless of the type of interview you're conducting, there are certain pitfalls (as outlined in this chapter) that all interviewers should learn and try to avoid.

Selection

CHAPTER 10

Documenting the Interview

One benefit of active listening is that interviewers can take notes while the applicant is talking without losing track of what's being said. Thanks to thought speed, you can write down keywords and ideas during the interview, then immediately after, develop your notes more fully. Revisiting your notes right away will ensure that you retain important facts.

The Role of Documentation in the Selection Process

Some interviewers believe that note taking will offend applicants or make them uneasy. If you feel this way, tell the applicant at the beginning of the interview that you'll be taking some notes to make certain that you have sufficient information upon which to base an effective evaluation. Most applicants will not mind, even preferring that you do take notes. After all, jobs have many applicants competing for them; with so many people being considered for each position, how can the interviewer differentiate among applicants without referring to notes? In fact, not taking any notes could convey a lack of interest; consequently, the applicant may lose interest in the job.

Notes taken are a permanent record of your interview and should be written with care. Whether you use a separate preprinted form (Appendix F) or a blank piece of paper, the same guidelines relating to documentation apply. Interviewers are cautioned against writing directly on the employment application. This is considered a legal document and should bear the handwriting of the applicant only. Likewise, have the applicant fill in any blanks or make any corrections on the application form.

In addition to serving as a permanent record of an interview, documentation enables interviewers to measure each applicant's job suitability against the requirements of the job. Following the interview, place your notes next to the job description. Then simply compare your notes about the applicant's relevant experience, skills, and accomplishments with the requirements, duties, and responsibilities of the available opening. This should make it easy to identify areas in which the applicant shines as well as any skills or experience he's lacking, especially if your job description identifies tasks as being essential or nonessential.

Documentation may also be used to compare applicants in the final running with one another. Place your post-interview notes on each finalist next to one another, with the job description at the end. Compare the background and qualifications of one person with the other applicants and with the job requirements.

Post-interview notes will additionally prove useful to the original and any future interviewers when considering rejected applicants for jobs down the road. Finally, post-interview documentation is frequently scrutinized as potential evidence in employment discrimination suits.

Avoiding Subjective Language

Effective post-interview documentation should avoid the use of subjective language, even if complimentary. Stated another way, all language that is written down should be objective. For example, saying that an applicant is attractive is a subjective statement. On the other hand, writing that "the applicant's appearance is consistent with the employee image desired by the organization for this position" would be objective.

As you can see from this example, objective language generally takes longer to write and requires greater effort. It's easier to say that someone is attractive than it is to write the objective version of the very same thought. However, the term *attractive* may not mean the same thing to everyone as it does to you; hence, it would not be useful to future interviewers reviewing your notes or even to you, since your opinion as to what constitutes attractiveness may change over time. In addition, it could create an issue in an EEO investigation.

Following are some additional examples of subjective language that should be avoided:

Abrasive	Acted high	Acted like a real know-it-all
Appears to be rich	A real sales job	A real workaholic
Arrogant	Bad dresser	Boring
Calculating	Careless	Chip on his shoulder
Cocky	Cultured	Curt
Diligent	Easily distracted	Eccentric
Energetic	Erratic	Fake smile
Fidgety	Full of hot air	Good sense of humor
Greedy	Has a bad attitude	Ideal applicant
Ingenious	Interesting	Jovial
Lackluster	Looks like a model	Looks too old
Makes lots of mistakes	Manipulative	Money-hungry
Narrow-minded	Needs polish	No roots
No sense of humor	Not serious about working	Perfect
Personable	Polished	Pompous
Pontificates	Pretentious	Refined
Reserved	Restless	Rude
Sarcastic	Sharp	Shrewd
Sloppy	Sluggish	Smart
Snappy dresser	Somber	Tactful

Too hyper	Too much makeup	Too nervous
Too pushy	Tried too hard	Uptight
Vain		

In contrast, here are some examples of objective language:

- This job requires prior customer service experience; applicant has two years' experience as a customer service representative.
- This job calls for excellent verbal skills; applicant exhibited clear and concise verbal skills during our sixty-minute interview.
- This job includes working with highly confidential matters; applicant has never worked with confidential matters before.
- This job requires employees to be on-call; applicant said one of the reasons he was leaving his current job was because he was on-call and found it "disruptive" to his personal life.

As you can see, these objective versions actually reference relevant portions of the job description, leaving no room for doubt with regard to the applicant's qualifications.

Avoiding Recording Unsubstantiated Opinions

Interviewers are cautioned against recording their opinions without sufficient job-related backup. Opinions that stand alone without concrete support imply that the interviewer has drawn some conclusions, but fail to identify what information these conclusions were based on. These statements generally begin with phrases such as:

"I feel . . ."

"In my opinion . . ."

"I believe . . ."

"It is apparent to me that . . ."

"In my judgment . . ."

"I am of the opinion that . . ."

"I think . . ."

"It is my view that . . ."

"To my way of thinking . . ."

"It is obvious to me that . . ."

"To me it is clear that . . ."

"Without a doubt, this applicant . . ."

Such broad, summarizing statements do not refer to specific requirements and matching qualifications. Interview notes containing statements such as these would not be useful in determining the applicant's job suitability.

Following are some expressions that illustrate the ineffectiveness of recording opinions. None of the original statements tells us anything about the applicant's qualifications for a given job; all such statements should therefore be avoided. However, these statements become effective when they are followed by job-related information:

Don't Say: "I feel Ms. Jenkins would make an excellent manager of product planning."

Say: "I feel Ms. Jenkins would make an excellent manager of product planning based on her experience in her present capacity as manager of product planning at Avedon Industries."

Don't Say: "In my opinion, Mr. Martin doesn't have what it takes to be a sales representative."

Say: "In my opinion, based on his lack of sales experience and failure to answer key questions, Mr. Martin does not have what it takes to be a sales representative."

Don't Say: "I believe Ms. Salamander is just what we're looking for!"

Say: "Based on her test scores and accounting expertise, I believe Ms. Salamander is just what we're looking for!"

Don't Say: "It is apparent to me that Mr. Brock can't do this job."

Say: "It's apparent to me that Mr. Brock can't do this job due to his lack of experience in a high-volume working environment."

Don't Say: "In my judgment, Ms. Princeton will make an excellent project manager."

Say: "In my judgment, after assessing her two years' experience as a project coordinator, Ms. Princeton will make an excellent project manager."

Don't Say: "I am of the opinion that Mr. Valentine will make a good addition to our staff."

Say: "I am of the opinion that Mr. Valentine will make a good addition to our staff based on his experience in dealing with crises and working under pressure."

Don't Say: "I think Mr. Turner will make a good mechanic."

Say: "I think Mr. Turner will make a good mechanic based on his three years' previous experience as a mechanic."

Don't Say: "It is my view that we would be making a mistake if we hired this applicant."

Say:	"It is my view that we would be making a mistake if we hired this applicant due to her lack of public relations experience."
Don't Say:	"To my way of thinking, Ms. Davis appears to be just right for the office assistant position."
Say:	"To my way of thinking, because of her demonstrated interpersonal skills, Ms. Davis appears to be just right for the office assistant position."
Don't Say:	"I consider Ms. Hastings to be excellent secretarial material."
Say:	"I consider Ms. Hastings to be excellent secretarial material based on three outstanding references and high test scores."
Don't Say:	"It is my view that Ms. Heller will do quite well as a data processing operator."
Say:	"It is my view that Ms. Heller will do quite well as a data processing operator after having worked in this capacity for the past two years."
Don't Say:	"As I see it, Mr. Green is just right for this job."
Say:	"As I see it, Mr. Green is just right for this job due to his accounts receivable background."
Don't Say:	"To my way of thinking, Ms. Mendosa will make a great programmer/analyst."
Say:	"To my way of thinking, Ms. Mendosa will make a great programmer/analyst because of her experience with multiprocessing systems."
Don't Say:	"If you ask me, we've found our next assistant vice president of marketing."
Say:	"If you ask me, after assessing his background in marketing for the past five years, we've found our next assistant vice president of marketing."
Don't Say:	"I believe that with a little training, this applicant will work out fine."
Say:	"I believe that with a little training to supplement her limited sales experience, this applicant will work out fine."

You can abbreviate the preferred versions of each of these statements by eliminating their opinion lead-in portions altogether. So, for example, instead of writing, "It is my view that Ms. Heller will do quite well as a data processing operator after having worked in this capacity for the past two years," drop the lead-in and state,

"Ms. Heller will do quite well as a data processing operator after having worked in this capacity for the past two years." Likewise, instead of stating, "As I see it, Mr. Green is just right for this job due to his accounts receivable background," drop the lead-in and simply state, "Mr. Green is just right for this job due to his accounts receivable background." And in the case of Ms. Mendosa, instead of recording, "To my way of thinking, Ms. Mendosa will make a great programmer/analyst because of her experience with multi-processing systems," write instead, "Ms. Mendosa will make a great programmer/analyst because of her experience with multi-processing systems." Not only are these versions less wordy and therefore easier to write, they convey a stronger message and appear less tentative.

Referring to Job-Related Facts

There are two documentation techniques that best enable interviewers to assess job suitability, compare the qualifications of several applicants, measure the applicant for future job matches, and preclude the possibility of referencing any information that might violate EEO laws.

The more effective of these two techniques requires referring only to job-related facts. This is a rather simple process, especially if the job descriptions are well written and if you practiced active listening techniques throughout the interview. As soon after the interview as possible, refer directly to each duty and requirement of the position and then indicate whether the applicant has the necessary skills and experience. In addition, you may want to record direct quotes made by the applicant.

The latter technique—directly quoting the applicant—is of particular significance when an applicant possesses all of the concrete requirements of the job but is lacking in some intangible, nonrecordable quality. For example, you're about three-quarters of the way through an interview; even though the applicant can clearly handle the duties of the job, you have an uneasy feeling about her attitude concerning a number of tasks. Since recording that the applicant has a "bad attitude" would be subjective, you continue to probe until you either resolve or confirm your sense of uneasiness by discovering some job-related reason for rejecting her. For example, among other things, you explore with her the fact that this job requires extensive overtime with little advance notice. Your question to her in this regard might be, "Describe a time in your last job when you were asked to work overtime at the last minute. How did you react?" She replies, "I told my boss I didn't like the idea of being asked at the last minute! I mean, obviously I stayed, but I didn't like it." You might then say, "Are you saying that you have a problem with working overtime, especially on short notice?" She might then reply, "Don't get me wrong; I'll do it—but I would appreciate receiving sufficient advance notice. After all, there is life after work!"

When it's time to write up this interview, you might state: "This job requires extensive overtime with little advance notice. When asked how she felt about this, applicant replied, 'I'll do it—but I would appreciate receiving sufficient advance notice.'"

By writing up your notes in this manner, you've clearly indicated that the applicant has effectively eliminated herself because she finds objectionable one of the requirements of the job—working overtime with little advance notice.

Recording direct quotes can also be helpful when comparing several applicants with similar backgrounds and qualifications.

Let's consider another, more comprehensive illustration of the usefulness of referring directly to the position's duties and requirements and recording direct quotes made by the applicant: Jody is trying to fill the position of administrative assistant to the president of your company. Here is a partial list of essential duties and responsibilities that encompass approximately 85 percent of the job:

- Schedules all appointments and meetings for the president
- Arranges the president's travel itinerary, including commuting, reservations, and accommodations
- Screens all calls and visitors to the president's office
- Opens, reroutes, and disposes of all electronic and paper correspondence directed to the president
- Replies to routine inquiries
- Supervises maintenance of all correspondence and reports sent in and out of the president's office, including confidential information
- Supervises the work of the president's clerical staff
- Prepares formal minutes of all board of directors meetings, as well as shareholders and executive committee meetings
- Prepares various reports required for meetings of the board of directors, shareholders, and executive committee

As Judy interviews each applicant applying for this position, she refers to the specific job requirements. A partial interview with an applicant named Josh, who is currently working as a senior secretary for the vice president of public relations, might go something like this:

Jody: What are your responsibilities with regard to scheduling appointments and meetings?

Josh: Oh, I do all of that.

Jody: Please be more specific.

Josh: It's my job to see to it that the vice president's calendar is in order; that is, I schedule her appointments and meetings and then every morning, first thing, I go over her calendar with her. If she needs me to make any changes, I get on it right away.

Jody: What about with regard to arranging the vice president's travel itinerary?

Josh: That's my job, too. I even arrange international trips, because my boss travels to Europe about a half dozen times a year. It's up to me to book her hotel reservations, travel plans, and everything like that.

Jody: Tell me about a time when you thought her travel plans were all set, but then something went wrong.

Josh: Well, one time she flew to Rome, but when she arrived at her hotel they didn't have her reservation. It took them over an hour to straighten out the mess and find her a room in another hotel; by then, it was too late for her to change before making a big presentation. She was pretty mad at me, but it wasn't my fault."

Jody: "Why do you think she was mad at you?"

Josh: "Because I was supposed to make the reservation—which I did. But I can't be held responsible for what some hotel clerk in Rome does!"

Jody: What do you do when someone calls or stops by your office and wants to speak with or see your boss?

Josh: By now, I pretty much know who she wants to see and who I should turn away. I use my judgment and may tell someone she's in a meeting and can't be disturbed. I also offer my help. Sometimes the person has a question that I can answer.

Jody: Tell me about a time when someone insisted, saying it was urgent that he see her?

Josh: That actually happened last Friday morning. I remember because she really was in a meeting—her weekly staff meeting. The VP of human resources said it was an important matter concerning one of her employees. I buzzed her and she came right out.

Jody: What are your responsibilities with regard to the vice president's mail, including e-mail?

Josh: I open all the mail, including anything marked "confidential." Then I sort and prioritize everything so she can review it. Even though I know what can be discarded and what's important, she likes to go through everything herself. She's kind of a control freak.

Jody: What do you mean when you say she's a control freak?

Josh: Well, she likes to add her personal touch to most things.

Jody: Like what?

Josh: In addition to sorting through her own mail, she likes to place her own phone calls. She also likes to greet people rather than having me take them in to her. I guess that's about it.

Jody: How do you feel about that?

Josh: I don't mind. It's that much less for me to do!

Jody: Let's turn our attention to another aspect of this job. What is the extent of any supervisory responsibility you may have?

Josh: I don't have any.

Jody: Am I correct in understanding, then, that you do not delegate work to anyone else?

Josh: Right. I do it all myself.

Jody: Describe your responsibilities with regard to meetings.

Josh: I prepare memos and reports for distribution at staff meetings and for the executive committee—by that, I mean I coordinate the materials and collate everything. Sometimes she asks me to prepare PowerPoint presentations. I enjoy that. But of course she checks each slide and usually ends up changing something.

Jody: What do you enjoy about preparing PowerPoint presentations?

Josh: I like being creative.

Jody: But you mind when your boss changes some of the slides?

Josh: I guess I do—I mean why ask me to do something if you're going to change it?

This partial interview illustrates the importance of writing down facts as they relate to the duties and requirements of a job. Jody correlated each question to a particular responsibility listed in the job description. As the applicant responded, Jody might have jotted down the following keywords and phrases:

Sr. sec'y—VP PR

Schedules appointments, meetings and trips—prob. w/hotel in Rome: ". . . can't be hld respon. 4 clerk/ Rome does."

Screens visitors; offers help; puts through if urgent

Opens, sorts and prioritizes all mail, including confidential

Boss = "control freak" re: mail, calls, greeting peo. O.K. with app.—". . . less 4 me 2 do!"

No super/delegation

Coord./collates memos/reports for meetings (staff & executive)

Occas. preps. PP slides—likes creative; doesn't like when boss changes slides: "why ask me . . . if ur going to change it?"

After the applicant has left, Jody can review these thoughts and elaborate on her notes. By once again referring to the position's requirements, she can determine overall job suitability. The final set of notes, based on this portion of the interview, might read like this:

Applicant has worked as secretary to VP, public relations, for 3 years.

Job requires scheduling appointments and meetings: Applicant schedules appointments and meetings.

Job requires making travel arrangements: Applicant makes travel arrangements. Concerning problem with hotel in Rome, he said, ". . . can't be held responsible for what some hotel clerk in Rome does."

Job requires screening calls and visitors: Applicant screens visitors; offers help; puts through if urgent.

Job requires opening, rerouting, and disposing of correspondence: Applicant opens and prioritizes all mail, including "confidential."

Refers to boss as "control freak" re: mail, calls, greeting people; O.K. with applicant—". . . less for me to do."

Job requires supervising and delegating work to clerical staff: Applicant has no supervisory/delegation experience

Job requires preparing reports for meetings of board of directors, shareholders, and executive committee: Applicant coordinates and collates memos and reports for staff and executive meetings.

Occasionally prepares PowerPoint slides—likes creative aspect; doesn't like when boss changes slides: "Why ask me to do something if you're going to change it?"

Everything written is a job-related fact, including the three quotes. Since Josh lacks experience with some of the essential tangible and intangible requirements of this job, Jody feels confident about rejecting Josh from further consideration. Should her decision be challenged, she can confidently turn to her documentation of the interview for validation.

Being Descriptive

A second documentation technique enables interviewers to better recall specific applicants. It entails recording a description of the applicant's behavior, speech, attire, or appearance. Interviewers conducting interviews for entry-level jobs as well as volume interviews in excess of twenty a week may find this technique helpful. After meeting with so many people, interviewers may have difficulty differentiating one applicant from another when referring to each person's application or resume alone. Even notes that are objective, factual, and job-related may not succeed in jogging their recollection of a specific applicant.

To help you better recall specifics, consider the occasional use of descriptive phrases. Their purpose is limited to identifying the person and aiding you in remembering the particular interview. Take care when using such phrases for two primary reasons: First, descriptive phrases can easily become subjective; and second, even though factual, they're not job-related. For example, noting that the "applicant was dressed entirely in yellow" is an objective descriptive phrase. The addition of just one word, however, makes it subjective: "Applicant was garishly dressed entirely in yellow." Even the objective version, however, is not job-related.

Here are additional examples of objective descriptive phrases:

- Smiled during the entire thirty minutes of the interview
- Hair extended below waist
- Wore black nail polish
- Wore pearl cuff links
- Twirled hair through entire ninety minutes of the interview
- Played with paper clips
- Tapped fingers
- Taller than six-foot-six (the same height as the office doorway)
- Laughed frequently
- Chewed gum
- Rocked in chair

Interviewers are cautioned against using any of these descriptive terms as part of the selection process. They are intended only to help you remember the applicant, not to determine job suitability.

Notes Versus Forms

Interviewers should have three documents in front of them at the beginning of every interview: the applicant's resume and/or application; the corresponding job description; and either a blank piece of paper for note taking or an interview evaluation form. Interviewers who are comfortable with a piece of paper need to restrict their comments to objective, factual, and job-related information, with occasional distinguishing notes as needed. Many interviewers, however, feel anxious about the sight of a blank piece of paper and are uncomfortable about being left on their own to write notes. They prefer instead to have some guidance by way of a form, especially one that incorporates a point system. In this method, the interviewer typically assigns a numerical value to each factor evaluated. Factors appear on a preprinted form with a key that briefly explains the point value of each rating.

Each individual factor might be evaluated according to a five-point scale:

1   Outstanding
2   Very good
3   Good
4   Fair
5   Poor

The overall rating for a five-point value system might look like this:

1   Superior overall skills and qualifications
2   Above-average skills and qualifications
3   Meets the requirements of the job
4   Fails to meet all of the requirements of the job
5   Not qualified

There are four primary problems with this kind of system:

1. The accompanying point value form may contain factors that are subjective and not job-related—for instance, appearance, personality, awareness, maturity, tact, and self-confidence. Even if these intangible factors are job-related, it's hard enough to justify the relationship of intangibles to job performance; quantifying them by assigning numerical values is even more difficult to substantiate.

2. Using subjective terms such as *outstanding* or *poor* to judge someone is meaningless. At the very least, a key with a description of each term should appear on the form. This description should include language that is clear and likely to be interpreted uniformly by anyone reading it.

3. Busy interviewers who are relying on forms with several preprinted categories tend to check off boxes quickly, without giving ample thought to each person's actual skill level.

4. Without written details concerning each applicant, it will be extremely difficult to distinguish one person from another at a later date.

If forms are used, they should include only job-related categories, such as various aspects of education and experience. In addition, sufficient space should be allotted for the interviewer's notes. Overall evaluation categories of "meets job requirements" and "fails to meet job requirements" may be included as well. A sample interview evaluation form appears in Appendix F, minus numerical values.

Documenting Applicants with Limited Experience

You may find yourself recruiting for jobs that carry limited experiential or educational requirements, such as entry-level positions, which usually require simple, repetitive tasks. Naturally, when this occurs you can't evaluate someone's demonstrated skill level. In these instances, consider posing hypothetical questions relative to the specific tasks of the job and recording the applicant's reply.

For instance, suppose you have an opening for a messenger. The position calls for picking up presorted mail from the mailroom and distributing it to each employee. During the course of the interview, you might ask an applicant, "What would you do if an employee told you that she was expecting a very important letter, but it wasn't included in the mail you had just brought to her?" The applicant might reply, "I would give her the name and extension of my supervisor to check on it." Your notes for this interview might then include the following reference to the job-related activity: "When asked how he would handle missing mail, said, 'Tell employee to check with supervisor.'"

This way, even interviewers with applicants who lack prior work experience can yield post-interview documentation that is objective, factual, and job-related.

Effective Versus Ineffective Notes

At this point it's helpful to illustrate both effective and ineffective note taking. Let's revisit the abridged job description for the position of assistant to the director of human resources, as discussed in Chapter 6 and Chapter 7, and expand upon it, adding portions from an interview for the position. Note that the interview excerpts include only questions asked by the interviewer and responses by the applicant. They do not include detailed information provided about the job and the company, nor do they include questions asked by the applicant. Following the interview excerpts are examples of effective and ineffective note taking.

Job Description for the Assistant to the Director of Human Resources

1. Recruits applicants for nonexempt-level positions using various recruitment sources.
2. Interviews and screens all applicants for nonexempt positions; refers qualified applicants to appropriate department manager/supervisor.
3. Assists department manager/supervisor with hiring decisions.
4. Performs reference checks on potential employees, by telephone and in writing.
5. Processes new employees in terms of payroll and benefits; informs new employees of all pertinent information.

6. Is responsible for conveying all necessary insurance information to employees and assisting them with questions and processing of claims.

7. Assists in the implementation of policies and procedures; may explain or interpret certain policies as required.

8. Assists in the maintenance and administration of the organization's compensation program; monitors salary increase recommendations as they are received to ensure compliance with merit increase guidelines.

9. Advises managers/supervisors of employee performance review schedule; follows up on delinquent or inconsistent reviews.

10. Is responsible for the orderly and systematic maintenance of all employee records and files.

11. Assists EEO officer with advising managers/supervisors on matters of equal employment opportunity and affirmative action as they pertain to the interviewing and hiring process and employer/employee relations.

12. Assists in the maintenance of up-to-date job descriptions of positions throughout the company.

13. Maintains all necessary HR records and reports, including unemployment insurance reports, flow-log recording, EEO reports, change notices, and identification card records.

14. Conducts exit interviews for terminating nonexempt employees.

15. Assists HR manager and HR director with the planning and conducting of each month's organizational orientation program.

16. Performs other related duties and assignments as required.

Prior Experience and/or Education

1. Thorough general knowledge and understanding of the HR function

2. Prior experience as a nonexempt interviewer, preferably in a manufacturing environment

3. Ability to work effectively with all levels of management and large numbers of employees

4. Ability to deal effectively with applicants and referral sources

Partial Interview for Human Resources Assistant

Interviewer: Good morning, Ms. Oliver. Thank you for coming in. Please be seated.

Applicant: Thank you. I'm glad to be here and, by the way, it's Mrs. Oliver, but you can call me Sandra.

Interviewer: Did you have any difficulty getting here, Sandra?

Applicant: No, my daughter attends school about two miles from here, so I'm very familiar with the area.

Interviewer: Well, I'm glad that you didn't have any trouble. I'm anxious to begin talking with you about your interest in our opening for the assistant to the director of human resources.

Applicant: Oh, I'm ready! I've been looking forward to this all week. I really want this job!

Interviewer: Fine. Then why don't we begin discussing your qualifications as they relate to the responsibilities of this job.

Applicant: Sure; no problem.

Interviewer: To begin with, this job requires recruiting, interviewing, and screening applicants for all of our nonexempt positions. Please describe your experience in this regard.

Applicant: Well, that's exactly what I've been doing for the past year at Circuits, Inc.

Interviewer: Please explain what you mean.

Applicant: Well, whenever I receive an approved job requisition, it's up to me to start recruiting. The first thing I do is talk with department heads to make sure that I understand the requirements and duties of the job. I also try to visit the department in order to get a feel for the work environment and to see firsthand what the person will be doing. It also helps beef up my rapport with the department head. Let's see, where was I? Oh, yes—then I start to explore different recruitment sources.

Interviewer: Such as?

Applicant: The usual: agencies, want ads, employee referrals, you know.

Interviewer: Any others?

Applicant: That's usually all it takes. We don't have any trouble attracting applicants. We have a fine reputation in the manufacturing industry, as I'm sure you know.

Interviewer: Please, continue.

Applicant: Well, I interview and screen all the applicants and then refer those qualified to the department head.

Interviewer: Where did you learn to interview?

Applicant: I have a degree in HR administration, as you can see from my resume, and then I received on-the-job training when I first joined Circuits, Inc.

Interviewer: How much time was devoted to on-the-job training?

Applicant: About three months; then I was left on my own.

Interviewer: I see. Please go on.

Applicant: Okay. As I said, I refer qualified applicants to the department head. Then, we get together and decide on who to hire.

Interviewer: Who finally makes the actual hiring decision?

Applicant: The department heads and I usually agree, but if we disagree, then they decide. After all, they're the ones who have to work with the person.

Interviewer: What are your responsibilities with regard to reference checks?

Applicant: I conduct both written and telephone references on only those applicants we're interested in.

Interviewer: Tell me about a reference check that didn't confirm the information you had on an applicant; what happened?

Applicant: That's happened several times, actually. Each time I tried to get at least two additional references to confirm either the employer's information or the applicant's. Then I turned all the information over to the department manager for a final decision.

Interviewer: Tell me about a time when you felt it appropriate to discuss the conflicting information with the applicant; what happened?

Applicant: There was this applicant who warned me in advance that I might get some negative information from his old boss. He was right. I called the applicant and told him what his former employer had said. He called the guy who ended up calling me to explain why he said what he did. It was pretty amazing. We ended up hiring the guy; he worked out fine.

Interviewer: Once an applicant is selected, what do you do?

Applicant: I arrange the starting date and schedule them for orientation. It's also my job to put them on payroll and take care of their benefits.

Interviewer: So then, is it your responsibility to explain all of the company benefits?

Applicant: No, not exactly. I just process the paperwork. Someone from the benefits department explains all of that during orientation.

Interviewer: I understand. Tell me. Sandra, does Circuits, Inc. have a policies and procedures manual?

Applicant: Yes, it does.

Interviewer: What are your responsibilities with regard to this manual?

Applicant: Sometimes if my boss, the human resources manager, isn't around, I try to answer questions from department heads.

Interviewer: Give me a specific example.

Applicant: Well, last week one of the managers from accounting called for clarification on our vacation policy for part-timers.

Interviewer: Were you able to help?

Applicant: Yes.

Interviewer: Good. Tell me, in addition to recruiting, interviewing, screening, and processing payroll and benefits paperwork, what other areas of human resources are you involved with?

Applicant: Well, let's see. Let me think for a minute. Oh yes, I'm in charge of performance reviews.

Interviewer: In what way are you in charge of performance reviews?

Applicant: I keep a log of when each nonexempt employee's review is due and notify the department head if they don't get them in on time.

Interviewer: Tell me about a time when a department head didn't submit a past due review, despite repeated requests.

Applicant: We have this one department head—I won't name names—who never gets anything in on time. So what I did was start bugging him about two months before the review was really due. By the time he finally got around to sending it in, it was only a little late!

Interviewer: I see. That's certainly an interesting approach. Tell me about your responsibilities with regard to salary administration.

Applicant: I don't have any. We have a compensation manager who takes care of that.

Interviewer: What about equal employment opportunity and affirmative action?

Applicant: Nope. Our EEO officer handles that. I know a lot about those areas, though.

Interviewer: You know a lot about EEO and affirmative action?

Applicant: Yes. I studied it in school and attended a three-day seminar on it about six months ago. I'd like to specialize in EEO some day.

Interviewer: That's very interesting. What other human resources responsibilities do you have at Circuits, Inc.?

Applicant: Well, I help with job descriptions.

Interviewer: In what way?

Applicant: Whenever there's a nonexempt job opening, I check with the department head to make sure that the job hasn't changed significantly and that the existing job description is still valid. If it needs revamping, I tell my boss and she takes over from there.

Interviewer: What are your responsibilities with regard to HR record keeping?

Applicant: I keep an applicant flow-log and make sure employees update their records online.

Interviewer: Do you personally process any other forms?

Applicant: None that I can think of.

Interviewer: What about your involvement with exit interviews?

Applicant: Oh, yes, I forgot about that! I do all exit interviews for nonexempt employees. I enjoy that!

Interviewer: What is it that you enjoy about it?

Applicant: I like finding out why a person is leaving and what the company might do in the future to prevent good people from leaving.

Interviewer: I see. That's very interesting. Describe for me a specific exit interview and what you learned as a result.

Applicant: We recently lost a great programmer/analyst because we ignored his request for a transfer to a less technical department. He didn't care about making less money; he just wanted to change fields. Even though he was really good at being a techie, he just didn't enjoy it. I felt badly about that; we should pay attention to what people want to do as much as what they can do.

Interviewer: What other aspects of your work do you enjoy?

Applicant: I like the interviewing: You know, talking to so many different people.

Interviewer: Tell me about one of the most interesting people you ever interviewed.

Applicant: There was an applicant who came in with a snake draped around her neck—honest! She said it was her pet and that she took it wherever she went!

Interviewer: That's certainly unusual. What don't you like about your job, Sandra?

Applicant: If I had to pick one thing, I guess it would be making sure employees update their records via the intranet; you know, like when they've completed a course at school or learned a new skill. All that has to go into their files and they're responsible for doing it, but I'm kind of a watchdog over the entire process.

Interviewer: What aspect of your job do you find to be the most difficult?

Applicant: I guess that would be my part in the monthly orientation program.

Interviewer: You participate in the orientation program?

Applicant: Yes, didn't I mention that? I have to give an opening talk of about twenty minutes about the history of Circuits, Inc., why it's such a great place to work, that sort of thing.

Interviewer: What is it about doing this that you find difficult?

Applicant: I get nervous talking in front of people.

Interviewer: I see. Sandra, I'd like to get back for a moment to your educational training in HR administration. What made you interested in this field?

Applicant: It seemed challenging and varied. It also seemed to offer a lot in the way of growth opportunities.

Interviewer: What level do you ultimately want to achieve?

Applicant: I think I'd like to be an EEO officer.

Interviewer: If we contacted your college, what would they tell us about your grades, both in HR courses and other courses?

Applicant: I graduated with a 3.0 average. I did pretty well in everything except math. I got a "D" in statistics.

Interviewer: What did your HR curriculum consist of?

Applicant: Everything—the degree prepared me to be a generalist.

Interviewer: I know you said that you particularly like EEO. What aspects of human resources do you enjoy the least?

Applicant: That would have to be benefits. I really find it kind of dry and boring.

Interviewer: I understand. Sandra, I have just a few more questions to ask you. Can you tell me about a time when an applicant acted up? By that I mean, became aggressive or otherwise emotional.

Applicant: I did have a guy start screaming at me when I told him the job he was applying for was already filled. I tried to calm him down by telling him we could still talk; then if something suitable opened up in the future, I could call him. It worked. I knew I had to remain objective if I was going to evaluate him fairly.

Interviewer: It sounds like you got a good handle on the situation. Sandra, what does the prospect of this job offer you that your present job does not?

Applicant: It's time for a change.

Interviewer: A change?

Applicant: Yes. One year in Circuits, Inc. is long enough. It's not the most exciting place in the world to work.

Interviewer: What's your idea of an ideal work environment?

Applicant: One where employees who prove themselves can grow; also, where managers don't look over your shoulder all the time. Of course, I'd like to be paid more, too!

Interviewer: What type of employee are you?

Applicant: I like to work independently. I don't need close supervision.

Interviewer: What do you feel you could offer our company, Sandra? Please be specific about three of your attributes, with examples of when you've applied them in your current job.

Applicant: Let's see. Well, I'm objective; I gave you an example of that before with the applicant who was screaming at me. I'm also a hard worker. In the last month alone I've worked overtime at least a dozen times without getting paid for it. And I care about keeping good people once we hire them—that's why I get so much out of exit interviews. I also want to say that I love the field of human resources.

Interviewer: Is there anything else I should know about your qualifications that would help me to make a hiring decision in your favor?

Applicant: I can't think of anything else.

Interviewer: Fine, Sandra. I'd like to thank you again for coming in. We'll be interviewing for the next five days or so, and will make our decision at the end of that time. If you have any questions in the interim, please feel free to call or e-mail me. I've enjoyed talking with you.

Applicant: Thank you. I've enjoyed talking with you, too. I really want this job!

Interviewer: I understand. Good-bye, Sandra.

Applicant: Bye.

Example of Ineffective Note Taking

Here are the *ineffective* notes taken during the course of the interview with Sandra, followed by the interviewer's summarizing statement:

Interviewer's Notes

Married; young daughter

Too anxious

Tends to ramble

Only nine months' real experience; degree okay

Likes P&P involvement

Had trouble remembering what else she does

Interested in EEO; I smell trouble

No real J.D. experience

Light record keeping

Sounds like a troublemaker; loves to find out why people leave

Dislikes doing orientation

Dislikes benefits

Light experience with problem applicants

Bored with present job; didn't give it much of a chance

Wants more money and to move up in a hurry

Doesn't like supervision

Summarizing Statement

I don't feel Sandra would make a very good HR assistant. She just doesn't seem reliable. Also, she hasn't demonstrated a thorough knowledge of HR.

As you can see, these statements are highly subjective. In addition, many of the comments are not job-related and some violate EEO regulations.

Example of Effective Note Taking

Now, let's review *effective* notes based on the same interview (to be subsequently elaborated upon in relation to job-specific requirements and responsibilities as identified in the job description):

Interviewer's Notes

Circuits, Inc., manufacturing

Nonexempt interviewing experience: 9 mos; 3 mos. OJT

Degree in HR admin.

Recruiting, interviews (enjoys), screens, and recommends for hire

Telephone and written references

Processes payroll and benefits form

P&P manual; most questions handled by HR mgr. (boss)

No salary admin. respon.

Expressed interest in pursuing field of EEO

Checks on accuracy of existing JD's

Flow-log and employee updates (enjoys least)

Exit interviews for all nonexempt employees (enjoys)

Participates in monthly orientation prog.: "nervous talking in front of people"

Least favorite: benefits

Reason for leaving: "time for a change"

Has dealt with applicants who have acted up; knew it was important to remain objective

"Likes to work independently"

"I'm a hard worker; I love the field of human resources"

Summarizing Statement

This job calls for a thorough general knowledge and understanding of human resources, as well as prior experience as a nonexempt interviewer. Ms. Oliver has had three months' on-the-job training and nine months' actual experience in the following areas of HR at Circuits, Inc.: nonexempt recruitment, interviewing, screening, references, processing payroll and benefits forms, checking accuracy of job descriptions, flow-logs and employee updates, exit interviews, monthly orientation. Also has a degree in HR administration. Recommends hiring; interested in EEO; enjoys exit interviews; least favorite—benefits. "Wants a change," "Likes to work independently," "Hard worker," "Loves HR."

These statements are all objective, factual, and job-related. Anyone reading them would have an immediate understanding of the applicant's skill level as it relates to the requirements of the job.

Documentation Guidelines

Effective documentation requires adhering to a set of ten simple yet critically important guidelines:

1. Take notes on a blank piece of paper or an interview evaluation form, not on the application form. The application is a legal document and should bear the handwriting of the applicant only.

2. Write only keywords or phrases during the interview; elaborate immediately afterward.

3. Refer to the job description to relate accomplishments with specific requirements.

4. Take notes reflecting positive as well as negative attributes and comments.

5. Use objective language, avoiding subjective terminology.

6. Provide concrete support for all opinions.

7. Record job-related facts.

8. Write down portions of specific questions and directly quote applicants' responses.

9. Record descriptive terms, if needed, to distinguish applicants from one another.

10. Use terminology likely to be understood by anyone, never codes that may be misconstrued.

Summary

Notes serve as a permanent record of an interview. They also help interviewers assess an applicant's job suitability in relation to the job description and as compared with other applicants; they are useful to the original interviewer and others considering rejected applicants for future openings; and they can be used as evidence in employment discrimination suits.

Effective documentation relies on objective language. Additionally, any personal opinions should be supported by job-related information.

There are two effective documentation techniques that enable interviewers to assess job suitability. The first requires that only job-related facts be referred to. The second technique relies on a description of the applicant's behavior, speech, attire, or appearance to help interviewers differentiate between applicants.

Interviewers are urged to avoid using point value systems tied to forms that cite subjective categories.

Directly quoting applicants' responses can prove useful for those jobs that do not carry any experiential or educational requirements. Quotes are also helpful when an applicant meets the concrete aspects of a job but falls short with regard to one or more intangible requirements.

Preemployment Testing

Following World War II, testing was used extensively as a means for selecting new hires. The popularity of testing as a selection tool continued for several decades, only to decline toward the end of the 1990s. However, due in part to a globally competitive economy, heightened security concerns, and a shortage of skilled labor, preemployment tests are once again becoming a favored means for selection. For HR practitioners, this may mean reexamining existing or previously used tests to support an increasing array of online test options, while remaining sensitive to certain applicant populations, such as older workers, who may be more comfortable with traditional paper and pencil tests. It may also mean revisiting areas to be tested: Quantifiable skills, such as computer knowledge, and personal qualities, like honesty, are among the most common testing categories; but also popular are interest tests, and tests that purport to measure learning and thinking ability. HR test givers must also be ever vigilant about possible adverse impact, job-relatedness, and over-reliance on test scores as the basis for selection.

Can tests accurately predict how individuals are likely to perform in any given job? Even the strongest supporters of tests will agree that not all tests are created equal and care must be exercised in their selection, implementation, and interpretation.

How Preemployment Tests Are Used

Employers typically use preemployment tests to accomplish two primary objectives: eliciting an applicant's undesirable traits and identifying characteristics that most closely match the qualities required in the available job. Specifically, tests given to prospective employees may help to:

- Predict acceptable or unacceptable on-the-job behavior
- Minimize or eliminate bias in the interview and selection process

Portions of this chapter are excerpted from Diane Arthur, *Fundamentals of Human Resources Management, Fourth Edition* (New York: AMACOM, 2004).

- Allow employers to identify potentially unfit workers
- Identify responsible individuals, capable of working under certain working conditions
- Reduce the cost of recruiting, hiring, and training
- Identify future "superstars"
- Identify additional job factors that should be taken into account
- Safeguard against so-called professional applicants who pride themselves on being able to mislead interviewers
- Identify workers who will need extra assistance or training
- Flush out factors that could prove to be detrimental on the job

Advocates of preemployment testing believe that employers can acquire this information through the use of a wide range of tests, including skills and aptitude testing, integrity tests, personality tests, psychological tests, drug tests, and physical tests. The exams may be conducted at any point in the selection process, depending on the extent of an employer's commitment to test scores. Firm believers in testing generally require applicants to complete one or more tests as the first step. If the applicants achieve a predetermined minimum score, they will be interviewed and given further consideration. Otherwise, they are rejected. Employers who place a greater value on the face-to-face meeting usually require tests only after the interview process is completed. These employers give little weight to test performance unless it conflicts with information ascertained during the interview or through reference checks. Those employers who place an equal emphasis on each of three main tangible aspects of the selection process—interviewing, testing, and references—usually first discuss various aspects of the job with the applicant, then conduct tests, talk further with the applicant, and, finally, conduct reference checks. At this point, the results of each phase are studied and a hiring decision is made.

HR practitioners are urged to work closely with their hiring managers and come to an agreement as to the role preemployment testing plays in the selection process.

Testing Advantages and Disadvantages

In simplest terms, preemployment and employment tests are defined as procedures for determining job suitability. This is accomplished by examining the skills, knowledge, or physical capabilities of employees or employment applicants according to a predetermined set of objective guidelines. The results are assessed in relation to the requirements and responsibilities of a given position and conclusions are drawn as to the appropriateness of the applicant's qualifications.

Testing Advantages

Proponents of workplace testing maintain the process allows employers to match an individual's abilities and potential with the requirements of a given job. It also identifies certain desirable and undesirable traits. Among the positive traits are honesty, reliability, competence, emotional stability, integrity, and motivation. Negative characteristics to be screened out include substance dependency and a propensity to steal. In security-sensitive jobs, ferreting out such traits becomes particularly important. Another popular reason for workplace testing is to protect against charges of negligent hiring—the charge sometimes faced by employers who fail to exercise reasonable care in hiring or retaining employees. Increasingly, employers are being held responsible for the criminal, violent, or negligent acts of their employees, both in and away from the workplace. Generally, the deciding factor is whether an employer can establish the exercise of reasonable care in ensuring the safety of others. One way of achieving that objective is through preemployment and employment testing.

Some test proponents also support workplace testing as a substitute for reference checks. Fear of being charged with invasion of privacy and defamation of character has led many employers to refuse to divulge all but the most basic of information about former employees, such as dates of employment and job titles. This is unfortunate; more information than is commonly given could, in fact, be shared, not only because truth is a complete defense, but because the common-law doctrine of qualified privilege states that an exchange of job-related information is in the best interest of both employers and the general public. Still, the fact remains that the sharing of reference-related information is limited, and consequently, employers are turning to other ways—like testing—to determine job eligibility.

Another advantage of workplace testing is its overall objective nature. Assuming it's been validated, a test can help employers make unbiased job-related decisions. When tests are fair representations of the skills and knowledge needed to perform a given job, employers are likely to be portrayed as impartial; this, in turn, may serve to enhance the overall image of an organization.

Finally, tests may help distinguish between otherwise similarly qualified applicants. Although no two applicants may ever be perceived as identical in terms of skills, abilities, and potential, it is sometimes difficult to choose the one person likely to be the best overall. Tests may help with the final decision.

Testing Disadvantages

One of the greatest concerns expressed by testing opponents is a tendency to rely too heavily on tests. Certainly this is true when employers conduct tests prior to interviewing applicants, immediately dismissing those who do not score at a minimum level. This practice occurs frequently when the interviewers are not confident in their ability to ask questions and interpret answers, because of a lack of training or experience. Also, it's often seen in organizations that have been "burned"—that is, involved in some sort of legal action that may have been avoided by a more thorough selection process.

Another common complaint about preemployment testing stems from the tendency to believe that tests can point to people who *will* do well, as opposed to those who are *likely* to do well in a given job or work environment. The predictive abilities of any exam are limited; results can only indicate which individuals are most likely to succeed. This is true even if a test is well designed and properly used.

Opponents to testing additionally point out that many people react negatively to the mere idea of a test. There are individuals who may in fact be qualified but do not do well on tests, resulting in a distorted or incomplete picture of their abilities if test scores are overemphasized. Rejecting such an applicant is a disservice to the person and possibly to the organization.

Concern that tests may be misused is also on the negative side of the testing ledger. Test misuse may occur when employers are interested in seeing what abilities an applicant possesses beyond those called for in a given job. This is usually done to help evaluate potential and future growth; after all, what employer doesn't want its employees to stay for a long time? This motivation cannot be faulted, but the method is inappropriate. Tests should be given only to evaluate specific skills, abilities, and traits as called for in the available job.

Testing may also be inappropriate when the qualities being sought can be acquired through a minimal amount of on-the-job training or education. In such instances, testing is an unnecessary expenditure of time, money, and energy. Finally, testing is too commonly viewed as the solution to virtually every employment problem. Sometimes, improved employer/employee relations is the best way to address workplace conflicts.

A summary of testing advantages and disadvantages appears in Exhibit 11-1.

Test Validation

In 1978, the Uniform Guidelines on Employee Selection Procedures were adopted by the U.S. Equal Employment Opportunity Commission (EEOC), the U.S. Civil Service Commission (renamed the Office of Personnel Management), the Office of Federal Contract Compliance of the U.S. Department of Labor, the U.S. Department

Exhibit 11-1. Testing advantages and disadvantages.

Advantages

- Enables employers to match an individual's abilities and potential with the requirements of a given job
- Identifies certain desirable and undesirable traits
- Protects against charges of negligent hiring
- Substitutes for reference checks
- Is inherently objective, if validated
- Distinguishes between otherwise similarly qualified applicants

Disadvantages

- Substitutes for effective interviewing skills
- Attempts to predict who will do well
- Screens out qualified individuals who do not test well
- Attempts to evaluate future job suitability
- Substitutes for on-the-job training in jobs requiring minimal learning
- Is viewed as solving multiple employment problems

of the Treasury, and the U.S. Department of Justice. The primary purpose of the Uniform Guidelines is to provide a framework for determining the proper use of tests and other selection procedures when they are to be the basis for any employment decision. The term "test" covers all formal, scored, quantified, or standardized techniques of assessing job suitability. "Other selection procedures" refers to application forms, interviews covering education and work experience, reference checks, performance evaluations, and training programs, as well as any other means for determining job suitability.

The guidelines are also intended to preclude the use of any selection procedure that has an adverse impact on the hiring, promotion, or other employment opportunities of members of either sex of any race or ethnic group. When two or more substantially equal selection procedures are available, employers are expected to use the procedure that has been shown to have the lesser adverse impact on members of any protected group. These guidelines apply to private employers with fifteen or more employees, to state and local governments, and to most employment agencies, labor organizations, and contractors and subcontractors of the federal government.

Validation studies are required as a means of "proving" that a certain test or other selection procedure really works and does not unfairly discriminate against groups of protected individuals. The keys to proving validity are job-relatedness and evidence that the test is a proven indicator of job success.

In broad terms, validation begins with a thorough job analysis to identify the requirements of a job. The next step entails identifying selection devices and standards that will isolate applicants or employees who meet the job requirements. Employers should then prepare a detailed validation report that outlines and documents the steps taken. The last part of the study is a summary explaining the study's conclusions and stating that the study found the selection procedure used to be valid and nondiscriminatory. Validity studies should be carried out under conditions ensuring the adequacy and accuracy of the research and the report.

Types of Validity Studies

The Uniform Guidelines recognize three specific methods of determining validity:

1. *Criterion-related validity* refers to a statistical relationship between scores on a test or some other selection procedure and the actual job performance of a sample of workers. There must be evidence that the selection procedure is predictive of job performance. For example, a study proving that college graduates perform a particular job better than high school graduates would be criterion-related.

2. *Content validity* pertains to selection procedures that test a sample of significant parts of a particular job—that is, a demonstration that the content of a selection procedure is representative of important aspects of job performance. For example, the analysis of computer skills for an administrative assistant's position would constitute a content validity study.

3. *Construct validity* describes a relationship between something believed to be an underlying human trait or characteristic and successful job performance. Honesty, for example, might be such a characteristic, the presence and measure of which might be assessed by a given selection procedure.

For all three methods, the Uniform Guidelines specify that cutoff scores must be "set so as to be reasonable and consistent with normal expectations of acceptable proficiency within the workforce."

Although the Uniform Guidelines do not state a preference of one validity method over the others, it is generally agreed that the criterion-related process, though effective, can be a long and expensive procedure. Construct validity has been the source of much debate and is considered to be the most difficult of the three to establish. Consequently, most employers rely on content validation, believing that it most accurately predicts job success.

The guidelines do not specify how frequently or under what conditions validity studies should be reviewed for currency. They do, however, urge employers to keep abreast of changes in the labor market, relating such changes to the validation strategy originally used, and to revise their validation studies accordingly.

Employers may use tests and other selection procedures that have not been validated, provided a legitimate validation study is under way. Until it is completed, however, employers are discouraged from making hiring decisions based on invalidated test results.

Test Administration

Test administration encompasses a number of components, including who should take tests, who should administer tests, test standardization, test security, and language consistency. Exhibit 11-2 highlights each of these components.

Test Takers

Many people believe that it's most equitable to require testing across the board; that is, a test should be administered to every applicant applying for every job. Each external job applicant should be tested, as should each employee under consideration for transfer or promotion. Across-the-board testing precludes claims that certain individuals have been singled out for testing. This method may seem fair on the surface; however, it is actually laden with bias, since not all positions require tests. It's far better to identify the specific skills required to perform a particular job as written out in a job description. Next, ask yourself a simple but crucial question: "What do I hope to accomplish by conducting a test?" The answer—"I hope to identify those individuals who possess specific skills and knowledge deemed essential for the successful performance of a given job"—should help determine who should take tests.

Exhibit 11-2. Components of test administration.

Test Takers	Applicants and employees who need to demonstrate specific skills and knowledge essential for the successful performance of a particular job
Test Administrators	Rely on professionals on staff Send someone on staff for professional training Hire outside professionals
Test Standardization	Same environment

Same conditions:
- Duration
- Instructions
- Materials
- Physical factors

No distorting influences:
- Tools in poor repair
- Excessive noise
- Interruptions
- Uncomfortable seating
- Poor lighting
- Poor ventilation

Test Security	Separate those who have taken tests from those who have not yet been tested Limit access to tests and answer sheets Keep tests locked away Assign random seating
Language Consistency	Avoid unfamiliar words or word usage

Test Administrators

According to the American Psychological Association (APA) Standard 6.6, "Responsibility for test use should be assumed by or delegated only to those individuals who have the training and expertise necessary to handle this responsibility in a professional and technically adequate manner."

The level and type of expertise of the tester should be commensurate with the complexity and level of the job in question and with the type of test involved. For example, individuals with a minimal degree of training and test administration knowledge can generally conduct multiple-choice tests. On the other hand, administering tests that assess personality or mental ability usually requires extensive training. Test publishers generally indicate the degree of psychological training required to administer and interpret their tests. A third type of testing, work sample tests, may be conducted and rated by individuals who are knowledgeable about the details of the job. Line supervisors may therefore conduct work sample tests, as long as they are also familiar with basic testing procedures, including how to set up for the test, give instructions, and determine scoring.

Depending on the type of test in question, employers may either select a professional already on staff to manage their testing programs, send someone on staff for professional training, or hire outside professionals. Employers need to carefully evaluate the credentials of outside vendors and should check their reputation in the field. In addition, it is prudent to review the test's underlying research and its relevance for meeting an organization's goals.

Test Standardization

Each time a test is administered it should be given in exactly the same way, in the same environment and under the same conditions, including duration, instructions, materials, physical factors, and any other aspect that might affect testing outcome. It is only when precise standards are adopted and all applicants are allowed to react to the same set of stimuli that legitimate conclusions may be drawn about test scores and job suitability. A possible exception may be made for certain online tests that are computer-adaptive, meaning answers to the current question determine what the next question will be. But this method of testing is more difficult to design in an equitable way and may be challenged for being invalid or having an adverse impact.

Every effort should also be made to eliminate or minimize distorting influences, including test administrators who mumble or speak with a pronounced accent, the use of tools that are in poor repair, excessive noise, interruptions during the test, uncomfortable seating, or poor lighting or ventilation. Of course, if a particular job is routinely performed in a noisy atmosphere, then simulating that environment as part of the test would be appropriate.

Test Security

APA Standard 15.3 calls for "reasonable efforts to be made to assure the validity of test scores by eliminating opportunities for test takers to attain scores by fraudulent means." To meet this standard, some employers opt to keep all exams locked away in a safe location and to limit the number of people who have access to copies of the tests and answer sheets. During exams, they may separate individuals who know one another to minimize cheating. Although such measures could result in negative feelings on the part of some test takers, they are often necessary for fair and meaningful test results.

Language Consistency

Linguistic factors may adversely affect the test performance of people who speak dialects or are unfamiliar with certain terms or situations. Unfamiliar words or word usage may prove to be a distraction or may create negative attitudes toward the test and testers, thereby having a negative impact on test results. Employers must make every effort to ensure that there is no bias in the language of their tests. Maintaining consistency of language helps ensure equitable testing conditions.

Preemployment Testing Policies

Organizations that conduct tests should have written testing policies. The policy should specify the primary objective of testing, the organization's commitment to compliance with relevant employment laws, which applicants will be tested, who will conduct and interpret test results, a description of testing conditions, and a description of all tests currently used. Everyone concerned with conducting or interpreting tests, as well as all those involved in any stage of the employment process, should become familiar with the policy through training workshops in which all the components of the organization's testing program are fully discussed and explained.

- *The primary objective of testing.* A general statement will usually suffice. For example: "As part of _____ company's commitment to hire qualified individuals to fill positions as they become available, selected preemployment testing may be conducted. Resulting test scores will contribute to making the final selection."
- *The organization's commitment to compliance with employment laws.* A clear and concise statement will express the company's position: "It is _____ company's policy to employ qualified individuals regardless of race, creed, religion, national origin, sex, age, or disability status. When an equally valid means of assessing applicants is known to be available, it will be used if it has less of an adverse impact on groups that are subject to discrimination."
- *Information pertaining to which applicants and employees will be tested.* First, a statement regarding the testing of similarly situated applicants should appear: "All applicants applying for a position identified as suitable for testing will be given the same test. Such tests will be job-related and relevant to the selection process. Reasonable accommodations will be made for individuals with disabilities." This statement should then be followed by a list of those positions that currently require tests.
- *Who will conduct and interpret test results.* A general remark concerning the competency of test administrators should begin this section: "All testing will be carried out by those individuals having the training and expertise necessary to assume this responsibility in a professional and technically competent fashion. The actual degree and type of expertise will be commensurate with the complexity and level of a given job."
- *Description of testing conditions.* Begin by addressing the issue of standardization: "Each time a test is administered it must be given in exactly the same way, in the same environment and under the same conditions, including identical duration, instructions, materials, and physical factors." Next, provide a detailed description of where tests are administered. If tests are not always conducted in the same place, describe the ideal testing environment. Include information about the type of seating, lighting, ventilation, tools, and materials that test takers can expect. In addition, this section should address the issue of security to ensure fair test results, as well as the importance of eliminating any linguistic factors that may adversely affect test performance.

- *Description of all tests currently used.* Begin with an introductory comment concerning the validation status of tests in the organization. For instance: "All tests used by this organization have been found to be valid and nondiscriminatory, both in content and in practice." Then identify all of the tests presently being used, noting that these tests are reviewed on a regular basis for currency.

Testing Categories

Several tests are classified in more than one way. For example, some achievement tests measure physical abilities and could therefore be categorized with physical testing; other achievement tests measure knowledge, placing them under the heading of psychological testing. Similarly, motor work samples may be considered a form of physical testing; however, they are also a type of achievement test and could therefore be classified as psychological. Drug tests are clearly physical tests; however, because of their popularity, they are frequently given as their own category. The same holds true for integrity testing: Although technically a form of personality testing, integrity tests usually stand on their own. Exhibit 11-3 organizes these tests into categories.

Drug Testing

The controversy over whether to test applicants and employees for drug use remains unresolved. Sound arguments may be made both for testing and not testing. Proponents point to the risks linked to substance abuse and maintain that testing will ferret out offenders, thereby ridding the workplace of numerous ills. But those who oppose drug testing are quick to point out that some courts have criticized a "zero tolerance" policy, designed to deter drug use off the job as well as on the job, as an unwarranted invasion of privacy. Popular methods used for detection, such as urine analysis, may also be considered invasive, thereby violating an individual's privacy.

Opponents also object to drug testing because they fear it will subject companies to potential legal liability. Applicants or employees who have been accused of drug use may allege that positive test results do not prove any act of wrongdoing. For example, urine can retain traces of drugs for anywhere from a few days, in the case of cocaine and amphetamines, to a month, as with the drugs classified as cannabinoids. Consequently, although a urine test may indicate use of an illegal drug, it cannot establish with certainty that the drug was used during working hours, impaired the employee's ability to perform his work, interfered with the work of colleagues, or endangered the safety of others. Lawsuits may also stem from false-positive test results caused by the use of legitimate and common over-the-counter drugs. When urine-screening tests are used, they frequently report "drug detected" without distinguishing which drug is present. To reduce this possibility, it is advisable to ask test takers to identify all drug products used in the weeks prior to the test.

In addition, no matter how sophisticated a test may be, it does not always cor-

Exhibit 11-3. Testing categories.

Drug

- Urine (screening; confirmatory)
- Blood
- Hair analysis
- Critical tracking (assesses on-the-spot employee fitness by measuring fine hand-eye coordination and reaction time)
- Papillary reaction (tests pupil's reaction to light)

Psychological

- General intelligence
- Aptitude (what a person can accomplish on the basis of what she knows)
- Achievement (measures current skills, knowledge, and accomplishments)

Personality

- Projective tests (evaluate how a person describes, interprets, or attaches meaning to certain unstructured stimuli)
- Personality inventories (seek to uncover personal characteristics, thoughts, feelings, attitudes, and behavior)
- Graphology (handwriting analysis)

Integrity Testing

- Polygraphs and other mechanical lie-detector tests (legal under certain circumstances, such as in some security-sensitive jobs)
- Written honesty tests, including:
    Overt tests (target an applicant's attitudes about specific aspects of dishonesty)
    Veiled-purpose tests (pose seemingly irrelevant questions)

Physical Testing

- Preemployment physical exams
- Tests of physical ability (psychomotor tests)

rectly identify all individuals who use drugs. Temporary abstinence, faked samples, and false negatives are all obstacles to accurately identifying drug abusers. Additionally, few tests are able to differentiate users from abusers—an important distinction. Hence, the relationship between testing positive for substance abuse and job performance is debatable.

To help you determine whether testing is appropriate for your company, consider these questions:

- Are there safety- or security-sensitive jobs where substance abuse might endanger lives or property?
- Are other companies in my field conducting drug testing?

- How successful have other companies with drug testing programs been?
- How receptive are members of management and the workforce to drug testing?
- If my organization decides to implement a drug testing program, will it be part of an overall workplace antidrug program?
- If we make job offers conditional on passing a drug test, will word spread, thereby affording applicants ample opportunity to "test clean"?

Applicant Drug Test Consent

If your company adopts a drug testing policy for applicants, it's advisable to test all job applicants as a condition of employment. Acquire the permission of applicants before conducting drug tests. Applicant consent forms can be simple and straightforward. A statement such as the following may suffice:

> **I agree to submit to drug testing as part of Avedon Industries' employment selection process. I understand that positive test results, refusal to be tested, or any attempt to tamper with test samples or results will result in the withdrawal of my employment application, withdrawal of an offer of employment, or termination of employment, depending on when the results are made known.**

Consent forms might also call for applicants to list current medications, including over-the-counter drugs. Additionally, the consent form could include a statement whereby the applicant agrees not to file any action against the company or its laboratory testing service. Legal counsel should review consent forms before they are issued and before any drug testing program begins.

Psychological Testing

Psychological tests, defined here as measures of general intelligence or mental ability, are seen by proponents as tools for identifying and predicting behaviors that are relevant to a given position. For example, many industrial psychologists believe that an individual's propensity to leave an organization prematurely may be anticipated through testing. Similarly, in evaluating applicants for sales positions, a psychological test instrument might be used first to identify the characteristics judged most valuable in a sales representative and then to assess the likelihood that each applicant will exhibit those traits. Psychological tests are also increasingly being used to evaluate specific traits, such as managerial effectiveness, business ethics, company loyalty, stability, cooperation, and independence.

To determine whether such testing is appropriate, employers need to explore answers to these questions:

- Can psychological tests really identify traits and predict behavior?
- Are they effective measures of intelligence or ability?
- Can employers rely on their projections?

Objectors and Supporters of Psychological Testing

Here are the most commonly voiced objections to psychological testing in the workplace:

- The tests are intimidating.
- They invade the privacy of individuals.
- They set a negative tone for the workplace.
- They cannot accurately measure intelligence because intelligence defies definition.
- They promote labeling—for example, referring to someone as "bright" or "slow."
- They may contain questions on topics with which test takers are uncomfortable.
- The results may be misleading or misused.
- They promote reliance on testing, to the exclusion of other selection factors.

On the other hand, employers who are fearful of charges of negligent hiring, unsuccessful at obtaining comprehensive references, or uncomfortable with the subjective nature of interviews are turning to psychological tests as a means of "knowing" a person before making a hiring decision. They argue that responsibly administered psychological tests designed to select employees whose abilities match the requirements of a job can be more objective than other selection procedures. In addition, they reason that psychological tests:

- Can be more cost-efficient than other screening devices
- Have a deterrent effect on deviant conduct among those hired
- Produce a more productive workforce
- Provide employers with peace of mind
- Provide employers with a competitive edge

Types of Psychological Tests

Employers may choose from numerous types of psychological tests, including general intelligence tests that measure a wide range of traits; aptitude tests that predict what a person can accomplish on the basis of what she knows; achievement tests that measure current skills, knowledge, and accomplishments; job knowledge or trade tests that require applicants to demonstrate their degree of existing knowledge on how a given job is performed by answering written or oral questions; and work sample tests that require test takers to demonstrate their existing level of skills using actual or simulated job-related equipment.

Employers must make certain that the tests selected comply not only with federal and state laws, but meet with appropriate ethical principles as well. The ethical use of tests can be controlled to some extent by a code of ethics to which professional testers and publishers subscribe. Both the American Psychological Association (APA) and the American Personnel and Guidance Association (APGA) are bound by ethical codes pertaining to test administration and other psychological services. These codes cover such issues as test validity, reliability, standardization, and administration. Test publishers must also control the release of tests to qualified persons only—those trained to use tests for their intended purposes alone. Publishers and distributors of psychological tests must make certain that the tests they market are designed properly and are of potential value to a particular organization and society as a whole.

Employers obtaining psychological test results must understand exactly what is being measured by the tests given to prospective employees, as well as what is not being measured. It is especially important for employers to realize that test scores are not fixed measures of an individual's mental status; rather, tests of general intelligence and special aptitudes reveal only the probability that a test-taker will succeed in a particular job or field. In addition, test scores are susceptible to errors of measurement and to changes in abilities and achievements.

Personality Testing

Should personality, defined as that combination of qualities and characteristics distinguishing one individual from another, be a consideration when making a hiring decision? The answer to this question will vary with each job. Clearly, some tasks will be carried out more effectively if the incumbent possesses certain intangible traits. For example, a friendly receptionist is certainly more desirable than someone who is abrasive or abrupt, because a receptionist is generally the first contact a client or visitor has with a company. Similarly, an interviewer who appears disinterested or judgmental could make an applicant feel uneasy and hesitant about revealing important background information. In these instances, certain aspects of an applicant's personality are job-related. On the other hand, personality has little relevance for programmers or those hired to conduct research, since they will have minimal interaction with others.

Job-relatedness, then, is the key to whether personality should be a consideration when making a hiring decision. But how can the job-relatedness of an intangible be determined? Start by asking yourself if one applicant without certain traits can perform a given job as effectively as another possessing those traits. If the answer is no, and you can go on to document why, then the personality requirements are probably valid. If the answer is yes, but an applicant with certain characteristics could probably do a better job, then the answer is less clear. If the answer is yes, but you would prefer to hire a particular personality type, then the requirement is probably invalid.

Even when personality traits are job-related, employers are cautioned that judgments about personality are subjective and, as such, susceptible to challenge. Care must be taken to avoid weighing personality too heavily or using it as the sole basis for selection or rejection. As stated earlier, intangible qualities are most useful when there are two applicants with similar tangible skills or when there are no concrete requirements at all.

Advocates and Opponents of Personality Testing

Advocates of personality testing view it as a valid indicator of job success, maintaining that a workforce comprised of individuals who have been selected, in part, because of their responses to personality test questions will work harder and more efficiently, thereby improving productivity. Additionally, having been properly "matched" with their jobs, members of such a workforce are more inclined to stay with one employer for a longer period of time. Proponents also argue that personality tests provide employers with a more complete picture of an applicant than do other selection criteria, such as application forms, resumes, face-to-face interviews, or reference checks. In addition, supporters of personality testing maintain that information may be gathered in such a way that applicants are unaware of exactly what is being revealed. Hence, there is little potential for allegations of discrimination and resulting lawsuits. Finally, supporters claim that personality tests reduce recruitment costs, since tests can accurately identify those workers best suited for specific jobs, virtually eliminating wasted time, effort, or money.

Opponents of personality tests strongly disagree with all these claims. They argue that personality is extremely difficult to measure and that labeling personalities is an imprecise process. Even if it is shown that a particular quality prevails over others, there may be unusual circumstances to take into account, perhaps a significant event in the applicant's life that, after a certain period of time, ceases to be influential. Opponents express concern over the assumption that personalities do not change over time, so they reject the idea that matches deemed appropriate or inappropriate at one time will necessarily remain so. Opponents also voice concern that employers who conduct personality tests might erroneously assume that a given job can be successfully performed by only one specific personality type. This kind of thinking not only discriminates against qualified applicants, but also may hurt the company.

Employers who decide to use personality tests to help make better hiring decisions should make certain the tests are developed in full compliance with the Uniform Guidelines on Employee Selection Procedures, are validated, and are administered by individuals skilled and knowledgeable in matters of personality testing. Test questions should also be constructed in such as way as to minimize the potential for violating an individual's privacy and an individual's protection against self-incrimination.

Integrity Testing

Polygraphs, other mechanical lie-detector tests, and written honesty tests may reveal significant information concerning an applicant's attitudes about specific aspects of dishonesty.

Polygraph Tests

In 1988, the Employee Polygraph Protection Act all but banned private-sector employers from using mechanical lie-detector tests as screening devices for job applicants. There are certain exceptions where polygraph testing is still permitted. Employers hiring workers for security-sensitive jobs are exempt, as are employers involved in manufacturing, distributing, or dispensing controlled substances, such as pharmaceutical work. In addition, the Employee Polygraph Protection Act does not apply to the federal government, state or local governments, or industries with national defense or national security contracts. Moreover, businesses with access to highly classified information may continue to use polygraph tests. However, although these employers are exempt, they may not use the results of the polygraphs as the sole basis for making an employment-related decision.

Use of polygraph tests to investigate employees reasonably suspected of stealing or committing other infractions may also be permitted. Access to stolen property alone, however, is not considered a reasonable basis for suspicion. An employee believed to have committed an infraction must first receive a written notice that identifies the loss being investigated, states the employer's basis for suspicion, and explains the employee's statutory rights under the act. Employees must also be advised of their right to consult with counsel before and during the examination.

Employees and applicants may refuse to take the polygraph test or may terminate it at any time. No test is allowed to last longer than ninety minutes. In addition, upon learning of the test results, employees and applicants may request a second test or hire an independent examiner for a second opinion. Test takers must not be asked degrading or intrusive questions, including questions about sexual behavior, union activities, or religious, racial, or political beliefs. They must be given advance notice relative to testing conditions and, before the test begins, must be permitted to review all questions. Afterward, they must receive a written copy of the test questions, their responses, and any opinions based on the test results.

Employers may test according to these exceptions and guidelines, only if they use the services of licensed and bonded examiners.

Violators of the Employee Polygraph Protection Act may be fined; required to hire, reinstate, or promote the employee or applicant; and required to pay lost wages and benefits, as well as attorney fees. Employers must post a notice of this law conspicuously where all applicants and employees can see it.

Some states have polygraph laws that are even more restrictive than the federal statute. Federal law will not preempt such state laws unless the state provisions conflict with the federal act. Therefore, employers who use polygraph tests unlawfully risk not only violation of federal and state statutes, but also legal liability on the basis of defamation and invasion of privacy.

Written Honesty Tests

Not surprisingly, since the Employee Polygraph Protection Act virtually banned the use of the most popular form of lie-detector test, there has been an increase in the use of written honesty or integrity tests. Most of these tests pose a series of direct and indirect questions related to thievery and deceit; other forms of these tests also seek out the potential for unsafe work habits, drug abuse, and counterproductivity. These tests generally take about twenty minutes to complete and are scored by computer in approximately six seconds.

While most people would agree that written honesty tests are less intimidating than polygraphs, there is a great deal of concern expressed over their validity. Indeed, there are reports of companies simply transferring polygraph questions onto paper.

Test publishers argue that their written honesty exams are highly accurate and based on extensive research. However, many experts express concern about the over-reliance on such test results to determine job suitability.

Physical Testing

Physical tests are intended to ensure that a company's workforce is physically capable of performing the essential functions of each job and does not threaten the health or safety of others. Physical exams and physical ability and psychomotor tests are the two primary forms of physical testing used by employers as preemployment hiring tools.

Preemployment Physical Examinations

Preemployment physical exams can identify individuals who are not physically able to perform the essential functions of a job in a safe and effective manner. More specifically, such exams may disclose a person's past and present state of health, or prior exposure to harmful substances or an injurious environment. Predictive screening, while controversial, can also assess an applicant's susceptibility to future injury.

Employers are subject to the preemployment physical restrictions and guidelines of their respective states. Generally, the employer is required to pay for the entire cost of the exam, to provide the employee with a copy of the results, and to maintain the confidentiality of the results. State regulations may also control the timing of tests and who may not be tested. Some states restrict preemployment physicals to those applicants receiving an offer of employment. In these instances, employment is generally conditioned on the successful completion of the medical exam. Other jurisdictions stipulate that preemployment medical exams must be given to all applicants, including applicants with prevailing disabilities. Depending on the test results, accommodation for those with physical or other impairments may be required, barring undue hardship to the employer. People with disabilities cannot be singled out for physical exams, as stipulated in a provision in the Americans with Disabilities Act.

Employers are advised to ascertain relevant state requirements before implementing or continuing with preemployment physicals by reviewing state fair employment or civil rights acts, or by consulting with an attorney.

In these litigious times, more employers are requiring applicants and employees to sign a waiver acknowledging that the company does not guarantee the accuracy of its physician's conclusions. This sort of waiver is an attempt to limit the employer's liability for negligence, if the employee later suffers an on-the-job injury as a result of a condition that was not detected during the preemployment physical.

Preemployment physical exams can be significant detective and evaluative tools, assuming the administering physician is familiar with those tasks that are essential to the performance of each applicable job and the evaluation is limited to the applicant's ability to perform those tasks. Test results are not always accurate, however, and offer limited predictive qualities. Consequently, physicals are effective, but only as one of several selection devices.

Physical Ability and Psychomotor Tests

Many on-the-job injuries occur because the tasks require more strength and endurance than the employee can exert without excessive stress. These injuries can lead to increased absenteeism and turnover, not to mention claims for workers compensation and health insurance. Since it is extremely difficult, if not impossible, to judge a person's strength and level of endurance on the basis of body size and appearance, physical ability tests, also known as strength and endurance tests, can be helpful preemployment selection devices when hiring people for positions requiring physical performance.

The preferred validation method for physical ability tests is content validity. A thorough job analysis must determine that a given test accurately reflects the primary duties and responsibilities of a job. Many employers contact private agencies or clinics for assistance with physical ability testing.

Psychomotor tests measure abilities such as manual dexterity, motor ability, and hand-eye coordination. They are used primarily for semiskilled, repetitive work, such as packing and certain forms of inspection. Most psychomotor tests are simulation tests, although relevant written exams may be useful. The most valid psychomotor test should call for the use of the same muscle groups as required on the job. Custom-made tests that reproduce the combination of motor abilities needed have been shown to have fair validity.

Computer-Based Testing

With more than 880 million active Internet users worldwide, it's not surprising to learn that computer-based testing (CBT) is growing in popularity. By definition, a CBT is a test or assessment that is administered by computer. CBTs are not to be confused with Web-based testing; the latter lacks a regulated testing environment, since tests delivered via the Web can be taken anytime, anytime, and without observation by a proctor.

CBTs allow test takers to read the instructions and questions from a computer monitor and then respond by using either a light pen, which allows "writing" directly on the screen; a "mouse," to click on items on the screen; or a keyboard, for typing out answers. Regardless of the method used, the answers to test questions are then keyed directly into the computer.

CBTs come in many forms, the most popular of which is the computerized adaptive test (CAT). With CATs, the computer "adapts" itself according to the test taker's ability by selecting the next question based on the performance of the previous question. If the test taker answers a question correctly, the level of difficulty increases for the next question. On the other hand, if the test taker answers a question incorrectly, the next question is less difficult. The process continues until either the accuracy of the test score reaches a certain level or the test ends after a predetermined number of questions are administered.

Questions for CATs are chosen from a pool of possible questions categorized by content and difficulty. Individual test takers are exposed to specific questions that are appropriate to their ability level. Hence, CATs are highly personalized.

Computerized classification tests (CCTs) are a variation of CATs in that they are also adaptive. The goal with CCTs is to classify the test takers into two or more broad categories, such as pass or fail, rather than to determine a specific score. Some CCTs provide an immediate pass or fail score, and then provide detailed scoring two to three weeks later.

Advantages of CBTs

Proponents of computer-based tests maintain that these procedures eliminate any possibility of administration bias, thereby ensuring standardized testing procedures. Other advantages include:

- *Convenience.* CBTs offer test takers a wider choice of testing locations and testing dates.
- *Consistency.* Well-controlled test environments and consistent test administration are by-products of CBTs.
- *Efficiency.* CBTs offer shorter test-taking time and faster score reporting. In fact, results are usually available immediately.
- *Ease.* The tests are reportedly easier to take than pencil-and-paper tests because tutorials demonstrate how to take the test and one can simply click on an answer.
- *Security.* CBTs offer increased multiple levels of security through encryption and password protection.
- *Diversity of Questions.* CBTs offer a wide range of question types pulled from numerous types of exams. They can randomize the order of questions or

devise exams instantaneously by selecting questions from a variety of subjects.

- *Varied Presentation.* Information is presented in a wide range of formats, using graphics, voice-activated responses, and split screens to simultaneously display text and questions.
- *Accuracy.* There is a reduced chance for the type of transcription errors that accompany "bubble" answer sheets required of pencil-and-paper tests.

Disadvantages of CBTs

There are three primary concerns about using CBTs:

1. *Computer Literacy.* People who are not computer-savvy worry that CBTs favor test takers who are more computer-literate, despite the availability of tutorials that allow users to become familiar with the computer and learn how to read the questions and indicate their responses prior to taking the actual test.
2. *Lack of Flexibility.* Some test takers complain that CBTs prevent them from returning to a previously answered question. In addition, they can't jump around within a section.
3. *Cost.* Costs related to the start-up and maintenance of CBTs, including software and help desk/support costs, are perceived by some as being prohibitive.

All variations of CBTs are subject to the standards and requirements for selection procedures as outlined in the Uniform Guidelines on Employee Selection Procedures.

Summary

Employers typically use a wide range of preemployment tests to accomplish two primary objectives: eliciting an applicant's undesirable traits and identifying characteristics that most closely match the qualities required in the available job.

There are numerous testing advantages and disadvantages that should be weighed before using any test. Proponents argue that testing is inherently objective, and that in addition to matching an individual with a job and identifying specific traits, tests can protect against charges of negligent hiring. Opponents maintain that there is no substitute for effective interviewing; in addition, tests cannot predict who will perform well in a job or evaluate future job suitability. Furthermore, tests may screen out qualified individuals who simply do not test well.

Tests and other selection procedures must be validated. The keys to proving validity are job-relatedness and evidence that the test is a proven indicator of job success.

Proper test administration includes identifying who should take tests, who should administer and evaluate them, standardization of testing conditions, security, and language consistency. All of these factors should be covered in an organization's testing policy.

There are a vast array of testing tools from which to choose, including aptitude tests designed to measure a person's potential ability, achievement tests intended to measure current skills, and physical tests that may ensure performance of tasks without threatening the health or safety of others. There are several significant types of exams within each of these broad testing categories, including drug, psychological, personality, integrity, and physical tests. These, in turn, are broken down further into hundreds of specific tests.

Computer-based tests are growing in popularity. Because CBTs eliminate any possible administration bias, they are thought to ensure standardized testing procedures. Opponents worry that CBTs favor test takers that are more computer-literate.

All tests are subject to the standards and requirements for selection procedures as outlined in the Uniform Guidelines on Employee Selection Procedures.

CHAPTER 12

Background and Reference Checks

Most interviewers know it's unwise to make a hiring decision without first checking an applicant's references and, in many instances, conducting a thorough background check. Despite well-honed recruiting, screening, and interviewing skills, interviewers feel uncomfortable in extending a job offer, at any level of employment, without more closely examining the background of the person selected. Reliance on background checks has dramatically increased over time. In 1993, slightly over 50 percent of all employers said that they conducted background checks on prospective employees; in 2005, that number rose to 96 percent.[1] This percentage encompasses small, midsize, and large organizations.

In part, this increase is due to concerns over charges of negligent hiring and retention. In addition, following the 9/11 terrorist attacks, there is greater concern over identity theft. News of executive embezzlement and unscrupulous behavior has also left employers wary of hiring without first conducting background checks on all individuals, regardless of position or level.

Employers conducting background and reference checks need to consider legal guidelines, establish a background check policy, and select a reputable vendor. When conducting reference checks, employers need to know how and what to ask, and develop guidelines for releasing and obtaining information.

Legal Guidelines

Despite acknowledging the importance of conducting background checks, some employers fail to probe as thoroughly as they're entitled to. In addition, few employers readily provide detailed information to other employers, with some going so far as to refuse to give references for former workers for fear of being sued for invasion of privacy or defamation of character.

Invasion of Privacy and Defamation of Character

Because of the fear of being sued by former employees for giving less than flattering references, many employers verify only dates of employment in an effort to mitigate any legal exposure on the basis of invasion of privacy or defamation of character. Indeed, even if an applicant was off by a month when recording his dates of employment, a former employer may simply state that these dates are incorrect, without offering the correct dates or an explanation. This leaves you to wonder how far off the applicant was and if he was trying to conceal something.

Although it's difficult to blame employers for being careful in this regard (no company wants to be sued), they may be overly cautious, failing to realize that a great deal of information can be legitimately and legally imparted without fear of retaliation from the former employee. Understanding the meaning of the term *defamation* should alleviate this concern somewhat. Defamation occurs when one person makes a statement about another that is false or harms the person's reputation. The statement may be either oral or written. In employment situations, allegations of defamation frequently arise when a former employer tells a prospective employer why an individual was terminated. The key to whether defamation has actually occurred is truth or falsity of the information. To be actionable, a statement must be a personal attack, lacking in veracity. Thus, if a former employer gives a prospective employer a false and damaging reason for an employee's termination, or gives the discharged person a false basis for the discharge, and the applicant repeats this information to a prospective employer, then the applicant may have been defamed. For example, a former employer who tells a prospective employer that a certain worker was terminated because of poor performance when, in truth, the worker quit over a dispute with his supervisor, could be guilty of defamation.

Employers fearing charges of defamation should also be aware that, based on case law, truth is an absolute defense, even if the statements made about a former employee are negative. However, the truth, too, may be actionable if it is volunteered with malicious intent to do harm. Disputable opinions or statements are also protected by a limited privilege; that is, such communications must be malicious to be actionable.

Common-Law Doctrine of Qualified Privilege

Employers are further protected by the common-law principle of qualified privilege. This doctrine is premised on the public policy that an exchange of information relative to the job suitability of employees is in the best interest of both employers and the general public. Consequently, if such information is defamatory but without malice, it is deemed privileged.

This privilege is not without certain limitations, however. The information must be provided in good faith and in accordance with the questions asked. For example, if a prospective employer asks about a former employee's ability to work unsupervised, the voluntary statement that she had a problem getting in on time is not protected. Also, information about an individual's private life should not be offered unless relevant to work performance. Moreover, former employers should ensure that the information is being provided to the appropriate party and is relevant to the requirements of the job. Failure to comply with any of these conditions could eliminate the protection provided by the qualified privilege.

Good-Faith References

The number of states with background-checking laws is increasing. These laws protect employers that provide good-faith job references of former and current employees. This added protection allows employers to give and receive references, going beyond the typical "play it safe" policy of verifying only dates of employment for former employees. Even with such legal protection, however, the trend is to proceed cautiously by providing only documented information that can be easily defended in court. In addition to dates of employment, salary ranges, promotions, transfers and demotions, performance evaluations, and attendance records are documented information and thus can also be shared.

References and Negligent Hiring

Despite the degree of protection afforded former employers by case law, the common-law doctrine of qualified privilege, and individual state laws, many employers still fear liability and hesitate to provide references. The result has been a proliferation of lawsuits based on negligent hiring and retention (see Chapter 5). The only effective defense against charges of negligent hiring is based on a complete investigation of all job-related facets of an applicant's background prior to employment. This investigation may include background checks of previous convictions and driving record violations, where deemed appropriate. Workers compensation records for positions requiring physical labor may also be checked to alert future employers to potential problems. Educational records should additionally be reviewed, if relevant.

This situation presents quite a dilemma for employers: Former employers can be sued for defamation or invasion of privacy for providing improper references; prospective employers can also be sued for negligent hiring and retention if references are not properly checked. By way of a solution, some employment experts suggest that job applicants be required to sign waivers, relieving former employers of liability if they are not hired because of unflattering references. However, such waivers would be of questionable legal enforceability.

The Fair Credit Reporting Act (FCRA)

This federal law, enforced by the Federal Trade Commission (FTC), governs the acquisition and use of background information on applicants and employees. Employers need to check to see if they have additional state regulations governing background information and/or investigative reports. As of this writing, the states that regulate background checks are Arizona, California, Colorado, Georgia, Kansas, Louisiana, Maine, Maryland, Massachusetts, Minnesota, Montana, New Hampshire, New Jersey, New Mexico, New York, Oklahoma, Rhode Island, Tennessee, Texas,

Virginia, and Washington. Of these, California has the most stringent requirements, including a set of unique procedural steps for compliance. Organizations with multi-state locations are advised to comply with the laws of the states where the individual investigated resides and the employer requesting the information has its principle place of business. Full text of the FCRA can be obtained by visiting www.ftc.gov/os/statutes/fcra.htm.

Consumer Reports

The FCRA applies to two types of reports. The first is the consumer report, which impacts an applicant's or employee's credit worthiness, credit standing, credit capacity, character, general reputation, personal characteristics, or mode of living, when such information is used for employment purposes. Examples of consumer reports include checks on criminal background, Department of Motor Vehicle inquiries, and credit history. The report must be prepared by a consumer reporting agency, such as Equifax, to qualify as a genuine consumer report under the FCRA. In some instances, drug test results may also qualify as a consumer report.

Investigative Consumer Reports

The second type of report is the investigative consumer report. These are defined by the FCRA as a subset of consumer reports in which information about an applicant's or employee's character, reputation, personal characteristics, or mode of living is acquired through interviews with the person's friends, neighbors, or business associates. Examples of investigative consumer reports include employment reference checks and interviews with former employers and coworkers, as conducted by a consumer reporting agency.

Employers can learn more about consumer reports and investigative consumer reports by accessing a document entitled "Notice to Users of Consumer Reports: Obligations of Users Under the FCRA," available at the FTC website (www.ftc.gov/os/statutes/2user.htm).

Three Steps of Basic FCRA Compliance

Employers are obliged to comply with three steps whenever they or a third party conduct a background check or investigation under the FCRA:

1. Employers must provide applicants or employees with a special notice in writing that they will request an investigative report, and obtain signatures of consent. In addition, employers are required to present a summary of rights under federal law. Individuals wanting a copy of the report must so indicate.
2. Employers must certify to the company conducting the background check or investigation that they will comply with applicable federal and state laws by signing a form typically provided by the investigation company.

3. Employers must provide a copy of the report to the individual investigated if an adverse action is to be taken as a result of the report. Employers should include a description of the adverse action, which could be, for example, withdrawing an offer of employment. Employers are further obliged to wait a reasonable period of time (generally three to five days) before taking adverse action to allow the individual investigated time to dispute the accuracy or completeness of any information in the report.

When hiring the services of investigation companies to conduct background checks, employers are cautioned to ensure that the agencies are aware of prevailing laws. In addition, employers need to ensure that these agencies do not reveal information they are not entitled to disclose. For example, agencies are not permitted to divulge information about bankruptcies that are more than ten years old or tax liens that exceed seven years.

Background Checks Policy

Organizations that intend to conduct their own background checks should have a written policy, along with accompanying procedures, for HR or others to follow.

Purpose

The policy should begin by stating its overall purpose. For example:

> **Avedon Industries is committed to hiring individuals whose skills and backgrounds are compatible with the position for which they are applying. In addition, we are obliged to provide a safe environment in which our employees work. Accordingly, background checks will enable Avedon Industries to obtain and confirm job-related information that will, in turn, help us determine an applicant's overall employability, ensure the protection of Avedon's employees and its property and information.**

Contents

The policy should next identify what background checks could cover. List those areas likely to be investigated, such as prior employment history, educational experiences, and, if desired, personal references. Be sure to stipulate that you are only collecting information that pertains to the quality and quantity of work performed. If you are planning on going beyond the "basics" and will be using a third-party agency to gather information about an individual's criminal record, credit, character, finances, and the like, be certain to reference the required steps for compliance with the FCRA, as described earlier.

Be certain, also, to identify any prevailing laws. For instance, if you plan to collect credit information, your policy might state:

Avedon Industries is permitted to collect credit-related information consistent with the guidelines of the FCRA, provided Avedon (1) certifies to the consumer reporting agency that they are in compliance with the FCRA, (2) obtains written authorization from the applicant, (3) informs the applicant of his right to request additional information as to the nature of the report, (4) informs the applicant as to what the report will encompass, (5) provides the individual with a summary of his rights under the FCRA, and (6) informs the applicant as to any negative results, intended adverse action, and sufficient time in which to contest the negative results.

Perhaps you plan on conducting a criminal investigation as part of your background check. In that event, your policy might state:

It is the policy of Avedon Industries to conduct a criminal investigation as part of its background check on potential employees. As part of this investigation, Avedon Industries is permitted to make inquiries concerning criminal records as long is it does not violate Title VII of the Civil Rights Act of 1964, with regard to using information acquired as a basis for denying employment, unless it is determined to be job-related or dictated by business necessity.

Dissemination of the Policy

Organizational policies concerning background checks should be clearly communicated to all applicants. The most obvious location for this information is the employment application form. Here's a sample statement:

I understand that background checks are an integral part of the selection process; as such, I hereby authorize Avedon Industries to conduct a background check of all previous places of employment. In the event that Avedon Industries is unable to verify any reference stated on this application, it is my responsibility to furnish the necessary documentation.

Generally, there are separate statements for permission to contact an applicant's current employer and to acquire educational records. For example:

☐ You may ☐ You may not contact my present employer.

☐ You may ☐ You may not contact the schools I have attended for the release of my educational records.

Finally, it is worth noting that some businesses also place this kind of notice in their employee handbook, reasoning that some promotions of employees could warrant a background check.

Record Keeping

Your policy should clearly stipulate that the information acquired as a result of any background check will only be used as part of the selection process and will be kept strictly confidential. Here's a sample:

> Avedon Industries recognizes the potentially sensitive nature of information that may result from background checks. As such, Avedon assures its applicants that all information acquired as a result of any background check will only be used as part of the selection process and that said information will be kept strictly confidential. Only selected human resources individuals will be permitted access to this information.

Selecting a Vendor

Here are some helpful guidelines when selecting a vendor to conduct background checks:

- *Be patient.* Most credible vendors will require as many as five days to conduct a thorough background check, although some can be accomplished effectively in as few as three. Rushing through the process could result in overlooking important information; hence, if a third-party agency tells you that it requires a week to do a thorough job, be patient and think about how you'll feel knowing you didn't cut any corners.

- *You get what you pay for.* Conducting background checks can be pricey. The average cost for a basic search is under $100; however, a background check on an executive can be more than double that amount. That's because most vendors charge by the state. If an applicant has moved around from one company, or company location, to another, the price is going to be higher. If a vendor offers to conduct a search for considerably less money, be wary.

- *Be vigilant about how the vendor acquires its criminal history information.* There are three main methods that vendors use to acquire this data: using in-house researchers, contracting local court retrieval service companies to go to the courts for them, and doing database searches. Most credible firms rely on a combination of the three methods. If you are considering a vendor that relies on third-party databases to conduct criminal history record checks, ask if the court sanctions the database and how often the material is updated.

- *Make certain that the vendor is well insured.* Insurance is an important component, especially in the event of a negligent hiring lawsuit, because employers typically want to assign liability onto the vendor.

- *Ensure the legal knowledge base of the vendor.* For example, any credible firm that conducts background checks should be knowledgeable about the FCRA, which governs how credit information can be used. It should also be willing to consult with HR to ensure the company knows how to legally use the information it supplies.

- *Conduct a test run.* Some experts recommend testing the abilities of a vendor before signing on with them by providing a name of someone known to have a criminal record. An employer can then assess how thorough and accurate the vendor's findings are.

Reference Checks

While some employers conduct background checks, more are likely to conduct reference checks that explore previous employment, education, and possibly personal recommendations. Reference checks can yield valuable job-related information, provided you can get former employers to talk to you. Despite the laws protecting employers that truthfully provide factual, job-related information about former employees, many employers still hesitate to verify much more than dates of employment, for fear of being sued for invasion of privacy or defamation of character (as discussed previously in this chapter). As such, many employers sigh and say, "Why bother trying?"

There are a number of very good reasons to bother. You could head off many problems if you succeed in acquiring reference information, among them falsified credentials, possible charges of negligent hiring and retention, workplace violence incidents, poor productivity, and employee theft.

Let's consider what happened at a small advertising agency in Chicago, as it illustrates how it can be well worth the effort to conduct reference checks. The ad agency retained the services of an executive search firm to hire a temporary bookkeeper. The woman they hired did such an excellent job that the advertising agency offered her a permanent bookkeeper position. They assumed that the search firm had checked her references and, hence, did not run any checks themselves. Besides, they reasoned, she was doing such an excellent job, what could they possibly learn that would be relevant? That turned out to be a huge mistake. Within months of hire, the woman began taking blank checks from her employer and forging signatures, ultimately making off with more than $70,000 before being caught. It turns out that just two months before taking the initial temporary assignment with the agency, she had pleaded guilty to embezzling nearly $200,000 from another employer and was sentenced to four years' probation and 100 hours of community service. That was a lesson learned the hard way.

Internet-Based Reference Checking

There is some indication that Internet-based reference-checking processes are becoming integrated into HR management technologies with the goal of making the process nearly effortless for employers. As more record holders create Internet-friendly databases that employers can easily access, the turnaround time for acquiring information is likely to be reduced significantly, as will the attendant costs connected to the process. For example, the Social Security Administration is looking into an Internet program that will enable verification of a person's name and Social Security number within two days. Since Social Security numbers are entrées to virtually everything about us, this initiative could, potentially, revamp background checking. It is particularly significant in the wake of 9/11, since the issue of identity theft has become a major concern. Whether employers will be permitted to access this information, however, remains to be seen. Until then, most employers continue to conduct reference checks by telephone and in writing.

There is one Internet-related approach to reference checking that can yield relevant information, although it's a bit of a shot-in-the-dark technique. Suitable only for executive-level applicants, some experts recommend using online search engines such as Google or Yahoo! to seek out press releases or news reports that show an applicant was once affiliated with a company that was not included on her resume. This, in turn, can result in learning about connections or traits that make the person a bad risk or otherwise undesirable for hire.

For instance, a firm used this technique to check the background of a high-level executive under consideration for hire by an insurance company. They checked through FCC filings and press releases and found that he had been affiliated with a number of companies that he had failed to include on his resume. Upon further investigation, it turns out that all of these companies had gone bankrupt. Since he was applying for a position where he would be authorized to pay out insurance claims, the firm felt uneasy about granting him access to money, given his history of being affiliated with failed businesses.

Telephone References

Telephone references are considered to be the most effective means for gathering information about an applicant under consideration for hire. Telephone reference checks will permit you to evaluate the former employer's tone of voice and voice inflections. They also allow for clarification of comments that may have a double meaning, such as "You'll be lucky to get him to work for you." Not only is a telephone reference likely to produce valuable information, it takes less time to conduct than written references.

Conducting telephone reference checks is similar to conducting an interview. Many of the same skills, such as active listening and encouraging the other person to talk, are employed. In fact, just about the only facet of an employment interview that cannot be incorporated into a telephone reference check is nonverbal communication. Because of this similarity to an interview, preparation for a telephone reference check is key.

Begin by deciding whom to call. Ask the applicant for the names of her former manager and anyone else qualified to comment on the quality of her work. Also get the name of someone to contact in the HR department. It may be necessary to speak with more than one person: The manager and others with whom the applicant directly worked will be able to discuss work performance; HR will provide information regarding such matters as job title, dates of employment, absenteeism, tardiness, and salary history.

Bear in mind that even if it turns out that you're unable to speak with an applicant's former employer, the applicant can't be certain of this. Sometimes, just asking an applicant for a reference can inspire her to volunteer valuable information. I recall an instance when I was nearing the end of an interview that had gone fairly smoothly, although I had some concerns about the applicant's ability to work under pressure. When I asked her for the names of three managers with whom she'd had regular dealings, she immediately became agitated. That was a huge red flag. I waited for a moment; then she began to explain: "I guess I might as well tell you, since you're going to find out anyway." She proceeded to describe a recent incident involving a team of managers and an assignment that she said she had "botched." Her account revealed a great deal about her ability to meet deadlines while working under pressure and confirmed some of my concerns about her. As it turned out, I was unable to speak to any of the managers she'd named. Had she not described the incident, I never would have learned about it.

It's important to prepare a phone-reference form in advance. As with written reference forms, you may want to have one for exempt positions and another for nonexempt positions. The same form can be used for both written and phone references. However, in designing the forms, keep in mind that phone references will yield more information and therefore will require more space for your notes. It is also likely that you'll ask questions other than those on the form. Therefore, allow ample room between questions to take notes. A sample reference form for exempt positions is provided in Appendix G and a sample for nonexempt positions is found in Appendix H.

When conducting a telephone reference check, begin by identifying yourself, your organization, and the reason for your call. To illustrate:

> "Good morning, Mr. Salerno. My name is Peter Fisher. I'm the HR manager at Valdart, Ltd., and I am conducting a reference check on your former employee, Ms. Susan Downey."

If there is any reluctance on the part of the previous employer, offer your phone number and suggest that he call back to verify your identity. If it's a long-distance call, offer to receive the call collect.

Always begin by verifying the information provided by the applicant. This will help the former employer recall specific information about the person. For example:

> "Ms. Downey has informed me that she worked for your organization as an industrial engineer from June 2003 through December 2005. She indicated that she regularly fulfilled four key responsibilities during that time: analyzing current operating procedures; developing flowcharts and linear responsibility charts to improve operating procedures; implementing systems by programming

> personal computers and by training staff; and advising manage-
> ment of project feasibility after conducting studies. Would you
> agree with this summary of her primary responsibilities?''

While listening to your opening statement, the respondent's thought speed will allow him to think about other aspects of the former employee's work. At this point, you'll be able to proceed with the other categories on the reference form. As soon as you anticipate that the former employer is willing to volunteer information, shift from close-ended questions to competency-based and open-ended questions. Be prepared to ask probing questions when more in-depth information is needed.

If the person is close-mouthed, refusing to provide any information beyond verification of dates of employment and, possibly, eligibility for rehire, try this approach:

> ''I understand you're hesitant to say anything, for fear of being
> sued, but did you know that truth is an absolute defense, even if
> the statements made about a former employee are negative, as
> long as the truth is communicated without malice? Not only that,
> but employers are protected by the common-law principle of quali-
> fied privilege. That means an exchange of information relative to
> the job suitability of employees is in the best interest of both em-
> ployers and the general public. So even if such information is de-
> famatory but without malice, it's deemed privileged. You just have
> to make sure the information is provided in good faith and in re-
> sponse to job-related questions.''

Referencing specific legislation can be daunting, but it may be just what's needed to get the person talking.

Another tactic you can try is to say something like, "Put yourself in my shoes. Wouldn't you want to verify a person's work experience before extending a job offer?" That, too, might just do the trick.

If the person still hesitates to answer your questions, try asking her if there's someone else with whom you can talk—another manager, perhaps—or any other parties familiar with the former employee's work, even if they're no longer with the company. Sometimes that will work. Even if the former employer still won't communicate, you may get the name of someone who will.

Written References

Written references usually consist of form letters designed to verify facts provided by the applicant. Unless directed to the attention of a specific manager or department head, these forms are usually routed to, and completed by, HR staff relying on the former employee's file for information. Even when addressed to the applicant's former manager, these inquiries may routinely be turned over to the company's HR department for response.

Another drawback to a written reference is the amount of time it takes to obtain a response. Even if the request is marked "Rush," it generally takes a minimum of one to two weeks for a reply. This is valuable time lost if you're waiting for the reference to be returned before making a hiring decision. In fact, the person you finally select may have accepted another job offer in the interim.

Make certain that your written request is comprehensive, but not time-consuming. Each question should be straightforward, easy to understand, and work-related. It's also advisable to have two separate form letters: one for exempt employees and another for nonexempt employees. In addition, try to direct your request to the applicant's former manager. You may also want to call this person before sending the letter. This way, you can make certain that she's still employed with the company and you can stress the importance of a speedy reply. Follow-up with a phone call three to four days after mailing your request to help expedite a reply.

While faxing is certainly faster than the mail, and e-mail is even faster, these methods are not recommended when conducting written reference checks. References contain confidential information and their contents should not be casually disclosed.

Educational References

Applicants must provide written consent before a school can release educational records to a prospective employer. The Family Education Rights and Privacy Act (Buckley Amendment) allows students to inspect their scholastic records and to deny schools permission to release certain information. A space for this permission should appear on the application form or a separate release form. Once the proper release has been obtained, the prospective employer, usually for a small fee, may ascertain academic information.

Be certain to collect the following information when you check educational credentials: dates attended, major and minor courses of study, specific courses relevant to the position applied for, degree and honors received, attendance record, work-study program participation, and grade averages.

When considering grade averages, remember that the value of scholastic achievement varies from school to school. An overall index of 3.5 at one college might be equivalent to an index of 2.8 in another. Therefore, it's important to know something about the standing and reputation of a particular school before weighing the grade point index. Also factor in the degree of difficulty of the courses they studied.

Be careful, too, about drawing conclusions based on grades. Not everyone does well on tests or in a classroom setting. That doesn't mean, however, that the applicant hasn't gained the knowledge needed to perform a particular job. Likewise, outstanding grades do not, in and of themselves, mean that someone will excel in a position.

Educational references are generally most useful in confirming the validity of information provided by an applicant. This can be important, since applicants have been known to claim degrees that they don't possess. Educational references may also prove to be valuable when an applicant has had little or no previous work experience. Remember, however, that these references should only be conducted when a job description clearly calls for specific educational achievements.

Personal References

Some application forms ask job seekers to provide names of personal references. Usually, three names are called for, along with their relationship to the applicant, titles, phone numbers, and addresses. Although asking someone to provide the names of references certain to offer only praise seems like a waste of time, many interviewers check personal references and maintain that the information gleaned is valid and useful. Specifically, personal references may reveal significant data relevant to the issue of negligent hiring and retention. Some employers go so far as to ask the references to refer still others who can discuss certain qualities and behavior characteristics. By talking with people not directly referred by the applicant, employers are more likely to get a complete and accurate picture. Still others believe that the type of person used as a reference is significant, whether the person is a doctor, lawyer, teacher, or whatever.

As with employment references, personal reference checks may result in charges of discrimination, if potential employers do not abide by the legal guidelines described earlier. Incorrectly, some employers believe that these guidelines do not apply when talking with a reference not connected with the applicant's former employment, prompting non-job-related and even illegal questions, in the belief that an acquaintance is more likely to reveal information relevant to the intangible qualities being sought.

Generally speaking, personal references should be avoided unless interviewers have absolutely no other source of employment or educational information. When personal references are checked, the information acquired should be sifted carefully, and any data that appears biased or not factual should be filtered out.

Evaluating References

While obtaining reference information is important, it has no real value if it's not properly evaluated. By and large, reference checks should be viewed as an interview; that is, the person conducting the check must listen to or read the information carefully in relation to the requirements and responsibilities of the job. In some ways, references are more difficult to assess than are interviews, because they tend to be more subjective. Regardless of how well your questions are worded, former employers may provide biased, albeit truthful, positive and negative responses, which may cloud the picture of an applicant and justify additional checking. Also, loss of one job does not necessarily mean failure in another, nor does it indicate employee deficiencies. It's conceivable that termination could have been avoided if there had been a more appropriate job match or if the employee's personality had been more compatible with that of her manager.

The safest way to approach and evaluate reference checks is to view them as just one of the factors to consider in making a final selection. This doesn't diminish their value; it merely puts them in proper perspective.

Guidelines for Releasing and Obtaining Information

When it comes to references, most employers have been on both the giving and receiving ends. When contacted about a former employee's work performance, they're probably stingy with information; but when trying to get information, they want to know everything possible about a potential hire and are undoubtedly frustrated when their efforts are inhibited.

It would be ideal if every employer worked from the same set of guidelines governing both the release and ascertainment of reference information. That way, everyone would be abiding by the same rules. Of course that's not likely to happen; however, you can set up a set of workable guidelines to eliminate any internal confusion as to what to do when asking for or providing reference-related information.

Guidelines for Releasing Information

When it comes to releasing work-related information about a former employee, consider the following guidelines:

- One person, or a limited number of persons, should have the responsibility of releasing information about former employees. These individuals should be trained in matters relating to laws, such as those pertaining to invasion of privacy, defamation of character, and qualified privilege. Typically, this task falls to HR practitioners.
- During exit interviews, tell terminating employees what information will be provided during a reference check. If the employee is being asked to leave, make sure she knows the reason.
- Try to obtain a signed consent form from a terminating employee, authorizing you to provide relevant reference information to prospective employers.
- Always tell the truth, and make certain you have documentation to back it up.
- Provide factual, job-related examples to support your statements.
- Make certain that the person to whom you are providing reference information has a legitimate and legal right to it.
- Be certain all information provided is job-related.
- Do not provide unsolicited information.

Guidelines for Obtaining Information

To increase your chances of obtaining meaningful information about potential employees, consider these guidelines:

- Conduct all reference checks in a uniform manner. Never single out only women or minorities for reference checks or follow up on only those applicants who strike you as "suspect." Inconsistency may be viewed as discriminatory.
- If an applicant is ultimately rejected because of a negative recommendation, be prepared to document the job-related reason.
- If, while conducting a reference check, you discover that an applicant has filed an EEO charge against her former employer, keep in mind that it is illegal to refuse to employ someone for this reason.
- Obtain permission from applicants, on the application form, to contact former employers.
- Carefully question the validity of comments made by former employers. Despite possible legal ramifications, it's not uncommon for employers to express negative feelings toward a good employee who resigned for a better position. Likewise, employees terminated for poor performance sometimes work out a deal with their former employers that ensures them of positive reference checks. Therefore, probe for objective statements regarding job performance.
- Exercise caution when interpreting a respondent's tone of voice, use of silence, or implication. Be aware, too, of phrases that may be interpreted in more than one way. For example, if a former employer were to say, "She gave every impression of being a conscientious worker," it would behoove you to probe and ask for clarification.
- Since reference checks are generally reserved for applicants making it to the final stage of consideration, give these individuals the opportunity to refute any information resulting from the reference check that contradicts impressions or information obtained during the interview.
- If possible, check with a minimum of two previous employers to rule out the possibility of either positive or negative bias. This may also disclose patterns in an individual's work habits.
- Ideally, allow the person who interviewed the applicant to do the reference checks as well. If representatives from both HR and the department in which the opening exists conducted the interview, the HR specialist usually does the checking.
- Do not automatically assume that a reported personality clash is the applicant's fault.
- Do not assume that an applicant who has been fired is necessarily a bad risk. Employees are terminated for many reasons; get an explanation before jumping to conclusions.
- Tell applicants that any job offer will be contingent upon a satisfactory reference from their current employers. This is a wise step to take since most applicants do not grant permission to contact their present employers.

Reference and Background Checklists

Whether you use an outside vendor for background checks or conduct your own reference checks in-house, there can be a lot of tracking to do, especially if you have periods of high volume interviewing. It's not unusual for references to "get lost" or for interviewers to think the process is complete when it hasn't even started.

A colleague of mine winces when he's asked to retell a horror story that happened because he didn't stay on top of the background-checking process. As the HR manager for his company, he felt his job ended when the hiring manager made her final selection. At that point, he turned the paperwork over to his assistant, whose job it was to contact the company's regular vendor for a routine background check while she conducted educational and experiential reference checks. Meanwhile, a letter offering employment was sent to the new hire, contingent upon a satisfactory background and reference check. In this particular instance, the vendor apparently needed additional time for its investigation, but didn't say why. My colleague's assistant didn't think anything of it and proceeded with her part of the process, calling the applicant's former employer. She was unable to acquire any information and was told instead that his employment records were sealed. When she asked why, she was told it was "a confidential matter." She later said she'd intended to bring the matter to the attention of her manager, but became busy and simply forgot. Time passed, and the applicant's starting date rolled around. There were still no references on him or feedback from the vendor. Again, no one followed up. The individual started work; six months later he was caught stealing computers and other office equipment during the night. Another employee, working late, confronted him and was assaulted for his efforts. Later, it was revealed that the employee had been fired from his previous job for his part in a physical altercation with another worker. In addition, the criminal background check that the vendor had failed to conduct unveiled two previous larceny-related convictions. The last time I spoke with my colleague, he was knee-deep battling charges of negligent hiring and retention brought by the assaulted employee.

In this regard, two simple checklists could have helped prevent a most unfortunate situation. Once an applicant is selected for hire, use these checklists in conjunction with the exempt and nonexempt reference forms (Appendices G and H). Whether you use one or both checklists depends on whether you contract with outside vendors for background checks. The reference checklist appears as Exhibit 12-1; the background checklist is Exhibit 12-2.

Summary

Most interviewers know it is unwise to make a hiring decision without first checking an applicant's references and, in many instances, conducting a thorough background check. However, these steps are not always easy to accomplish.

Employers often hesitate to disclose reference information about former employ-

Exhibit 12-1. Reference checklist.

Name: *Date:*

Conducted by:

Reference Checklist Instructions:

- Beginning with the most recent work or education experience, list all experiential and educational reference checks to be attempted.
- Identify each attempt by date, and assign each a number according to the following:

  (1) Reference information received and consistent with information the applicant provided.
  (2) Reference information received and inconsistent with information the applicant provided; further action required.
  (3) Reference information received that causes concern; further action required.
  (4) Reference information requested and pending; follow up required.
  (5) Reference request denied. Reason given is _____.

- Document the results of each attempt and place in the individual's file.
- Determine applicant's job suitability based on the results of the reference checks, and choose one of the following:

  (1) Results of applicant's reference checks confirm job suitability.
  (2) Results of applicant's reference checks raise some concerns—additional action is required.
  (3) Results of applicant's reference checks refute job suitability.

Exhibit 12-2. Background checklist.

Name: *Date:*

Vendor:

Monitored by:

Background Checklist Guidelines:

- Have I clearly communicated to the vendor conducting the background check exactly what it is expected to determine? _____ Yes _____ No
- Have I submitted information required for the vendor to conduct its background check? _____ Yes _____ No
- Date information submitted to the vendor: _____
- Date information received from the vendor: _____
- Results of background check (choose those results that are appropriate and follow up, accordingly):

  (1) Background check is complete; results are satisfactory.
  (2) Background check is complete; results are questionable.
  (3) Background check is complete; results are unsatisfactory.

ees, fearing lawsuits stemming from charges of invasion of privacy or defamation of character. Others are afraid to explore background information because of prevailing legislation, such as the Fair Credit Reporting Act. Concerns prevail, despite what employers are entitled to know, according to the Common-Law Doctrine of Qualified Privilege, and regardless of state laws protecting employers that provide good-faith job references.

Organizations that intend to conduct background checks should have a written policy, along with accompanying procedures, for HR and others to follow. The policy should state its purpose, identify what background checks could cover, be clearly communicated to all applicants, and stipulate how any acquired information will be used.

Carefully select a vendor to conduct your company's background checks. Considerations should include how the vendor acquires its information, whether the company is insured, and assurance that the vendor is knowledgeable about relevant legislation.

While some employers conduct background checks, more are likely to conduct reference checks that explore previous employment, education, and possibly personal recommendations. Reference checks can yield valuable job-related information.

While obtaining reference information is important, it has no real value if it's not properly evaluated. The safest way to approach and evaluate reference checks is to view them as just one of the factors to consider in making a final selection. This does not diminish their value; it merely puts them in proper perspective.

Workable reference guidelines can eliminate any internal confusion about what to do when asking for or providing information. Likewise, reference and background checklists can help with information tracking, especially during periods of high volume interviewing.

Note

1. Jennifer Schramm, "Background Checking," *HR Magazine* Vol. 50, No. 1 (January 2005), p. 128.

CHAPTER 13

The Selection Process

You've conducted legal, competency-based interviews, effectively documented each interview, conducted relevant tests, and run comprehensive background and reference checks. In addition, you've factored in all job-specific tangible and intangible qualities, considered your company's affirmative action goals, and assessed its organizationwide and departmental diversity levels. Hopefully, the hiring manager and HR representative agree on whom to hire; if they don't, the manager should make the final decision, with the HR person documenting his reasons for disagreeing. At last, it's time to extend an offer of employment to the one applicant who stands out among the rest.

This final step of extending an offer of employment should be fairly effortless, although there are still some critical components remaining to ensure a smooth transition from the status of applicant to employee. Some organizations handle this step electronically. Applicants are sent the job offer letter online that they're expected to accept or decline immediately. If the answer is yes, they're directed to a welcome page, complete with a greeting from the chief executive officer. With the exception of entry-level positions, specific salaries have probably not yet been discussed and agreed upon, so the person may not be interested in your final offer. If he is interested, the applicant undoubtedly has numerous questions requiring dialogue between the employer and prospective employee. Hence, this procedure is ill advised.

While you may have determined that a particular individual is the right person for the job, it's unwise to assume that she feels the same way. Depending on how much time has passed since you and she last spoke, a lot could have happened: The applicant may have spoken with employees who said something about the company culture that struck her as undesirable. She may have gone on other interviews and received a more tempting offer, or she may have decided to stay where she's currently working. It could be, too, that she wasn't as impressed with your company as you were with her. It's presumptuous to assume, therefore, that she's sitting by her computer, phone, or mailbox waiting for your offer of employment.

Any delay in action could cause you to lose your first choice. As such, the HR representative (ideally, the person involved in the interviewing process) should call the prospective employee as soon as the decision about whom to hire has been reached. Tell her you'd like to offer her the job and ask that she come in so you can discuss some of the particulars. Your conversation might go something like this:

> "Hello, June? This is Marty Stonewell, from Avedon Industries. We've completed our interview process for the marketing representative opening and reviewed everyone's skills and qualifications. I'm pleased to say that we'd like to offer you the job [pause while, hopefully, she accepts]. I'd like to set up a mutually convenient time for you to come in so we can review some of the particulars of the job, such as your duties and reporting relationship, as well as discuss your salary, some of your benefits, and, of course, a starting date. We can also go over any questions you might have."

As soon as you get off the phone, begin preparing for the meeting.

Preparation for the Final Meeting

This is a crucial step. So often, employers assume new employees know certain, basic information about the job, only to learn, after they've started, that they do not. Here's one of my favorite stories to illustrate this point:

A young woman named Delia was selected to work as a public relations assistant for a small publishing company. She was thrilled and looked forward to starting her new job. Because she was concerned about the commute, Delia allowed plenty of time to make sure she wouldn't be late on her first day. As it turned out, she'd planned her travel schedule exceedingly well and arrived at her new job by 8:15 A.M.—forty-five minutes early. The next day she left home at the same time; once again, she arrived early, this time at 8:18. She did this for the remainder of the week with the same results, give or take a few minutes on either side of 8:15. She then began to relax somewhat. Delia was the only one arriving that early, and she was no longer concerned about being late. She decided to take a later train from that point on. The following Monday, she arrived at 8:45—still fifteen minutes early, allowing her ample time to get settled and ready to begin work. She noticed that others were already at their desks, but she didn't give the matter much thought. She'd arrived in plenty of time to begin her day and that's all that mattered.

For the next three mornings she was at her desk no later than 8:50 A.M. On Friday, Rupert, her manager, summoned her into his office, clearly agitated. She didn't have much time to try to figure out what was wrong because he started right in by bellowing, "What exactly is it that you think you're doing? You've been here for two weeks and have shown up late five days in a row! I hope you've got a good explanation, because this is not the way to make a good impression on me!" Delia was stunned. "What are you talking about? I've been early every morning since I've started. True, I'm not as early this week as I was last week, but I'm still here ten to fifteen minutes before I'm supposed to be!" Rupert quieted down and looked at her. Then he had a disquieting thought: "Delia, what time did they tell you in HR that we start in this department?" Delia replied, "They didn't tell me anything, so I just assumed the job was nine to five. Aren't those the hours I'm supposed to work?" Rupert signed. "No, Delia; our hours are eight-thirty to five."

Reading this scenario you might think that Delia should have asked HR what her hours were supposed to be. But Delia had only worked at one other job before this one in an office where the schedule was nine to five. Since no one had said otherwise, she assumed the hours were the same at this job. Yes, she should have confirmed the actual hours of work; however, the onus was on HR to communicate all the particulars about the job before she began, including something as basic as her schedule.

To avoid creating employer/employee rifts such as the one between Rupert and Delia, develop a checklist that reflects all the particulars of the available position. The checklist should represent a review of topics previously discussed with the applicant; indeed, nothing said at this final stage should come as a surprise, with the exception of the actual starting salary figure. Exhibit 13-1 is a comprehensive generic checklist that can be used as a model. Some of the topics may not apply to all jobs, but it's better to start out with more than less.

Once you and the prospective employee sit down and go over the list together, check off each topic discussed. It's a good idea to give the individual a copy of the list, so she can also keep track of everything discussed. It's most important to indicate whether you and the individual are in agreement concerning each topic. If there are any discrepancies, clearly indicate the nature of the disagreement, as well as the next step to be taken.

For example, the employee may have assumed that she was entitled to the same number of vacation days as she enjoys at her current job. If this becomes an area of contention, make a note before moving on to the next topic. Toward the end of the meeting, return to the matter of vacation days and see if you can come to an agreement. If not, you may need to get back to her. The reason it's a good idea to move on and then return to the subject is that you don't want to get bogged down at any point. Get through all the topics on your checklist and then revisit any that require additional discussion. This approach will also give you an overview of how many areas of contention there are, as well their levels of severity. In this way, you'll have a better sense of where you can afford to yield, thereby gaining leverage to hold out regarding more significant points.

Exhibit 13-2 on page 275 shows how the discussion relating to vacation might be indicated on the final meeting checklist.

The Final Meeting

The procedure to follow during the final meeting between the HR representative and soon-to-be-employee is simple: Use the checklist as a guide, review each topic as it relates to the job he's about to fill, and answer any remaining questions he may have. Then, as indicated earlier, return to any areas of disagreement at the end of the meeting and try to reach resolution.

Exhibit 13-1. Final meeting checklist.

Topic	☑ Discussed	☑ Agreed	☑ Disagreed
Job title:			
Department:			
Report to:			
Name:			
Title:			
Primary duties and responsibilities:			
(List or attach a job description)			
Start date:			
Schedule:			
Hours:			
Shifts arrangements:			
Days:			
Location:			
Fixed:			
Rotate:			
Salary:			
Base salary (in weekly, biweekly, or monthly terms):			
Bonus:			
Commissions:			
Signing bonus:			
Overtime:			
Comp time:			
Travel allowance:			
Schedule of salary reviews:			
Employment-at-will relationship:			
Conditions of employment:			
Satisfactory background check:			
Satisfactory references:			
Satisfactory results of company-issued physical:			
Satisfactory results of company-issued drug test:			
Union/Nonunion status and requirements:			
Benefits (to be covered in detail during orientation):			
Holidays			
Personal days			
Sick days			
Vacation (eligibility; number of days)			
General health benefits including:			
Medical			
Dental			
Vision			

Insurance: life, accidental death,
   disability
Profit sharing, stock options,
   ESOPs
Pension plan, 401(k)
Tuition reimbursement
Additional perks:
  Health club membership
  PDA
  Cell phone
  Laptop computer
  Company car
Noncompete agreement
Other topics relating to the terms and
   conditions of employment

Exhibit 13-2. Final meeting checklist, with notation about "vacation" disagreement.

Topic	☑ Discussed	☑ Agreed	☑ Disagreed
Vacation (eligibility; number of days)	☑		☑ # of days. Applicant currently gets 20 days; level of job warrants 15. App. is adamant. Suggest allowing 5 unpaid days, if dept. mgr. agrees, but cannot take 20 consecutive days. App. will consider & call w/in 24 hrs.

This process, while simple, sometimes unveils significant discrepancies to the extent that some of the most seemingly benign areas of dispute can become deal breakers. For instance, a man I know was interviewing for the position of director of human resources—the topmost position in the department, reporting directly to the president of the company. Eli was satisfied with the job description, had no argument with the salary or benefits, but wanted a title change: Instead of director of HR, he requested "vice president of HR." This title would be in line with the heads of other departments companywide, all of whom were vice presidents. Anything less, he argued, would diminish the credibility of the HR function. The company's president would not budge. Despite acknowledging that one of her goals was to position HR to take on a more strategic role in achieving the organization's missions, she remained steadfast: The HR department had never been headed up by an officer and she felt it would represent too dramatic a departure to do so now. Eli grew concerned that the president's thinking was reflective of how the organization functioned; if she refused to get on board with a title change, how was he going to be able to convince her to implement the many improvements he knew were needed to increase productivity? He ultimately decided to decline the company's offer.

With this illustration in mind, let's look at the final meeting from the perspective of the job applicant, in terms of some of the problem areas that could develop, along with potential solutions. Note that the discussion that follows presumes that the HR representative avoids presenting anything new or different about the job during the meeting.

Topic: Job Title

Possible Problems: The title fails to accurately reflect the full scope of responsibilities, it is not comparable to other titles with similar levels of responsibility, or certain words in the title (e.g. *clerk* or *assistant*) are objectionable.

Possible Solutions: Explain how job titles are part of specific job families—to change a specific title would impact the entire job family, as well as incumbents performing similar functions. Suggest that the applicant begin work at the existing job title, with the commitment that HR will review its continued appropriateness after three months. Confirm that the applicant will accept the existing job title, as well as any suggestions, before proceeding.

Topic: Primary Duties and Responsibilities

Possible Problem: The primary duties and responsibilities encompass tasks the applicant didn't realize were part of the job.

Possible Solutions: First, explain that it is the same job description that she reviewed during the interview. Then, together, focus on identifying the real problem: Are these tasks that the applicant doesn't feel qualified to perform? Perhaps on-the-job training or an outside workshop is the solution. If, on the other hand, these are responsibilities that the applicant doesn't feel should be part of the job, then make clear that the job description reflects the tasks expected of all incumbents hired for this position. If she is uncomfortable with any of the duties identified, ask her what she realistically expects to happen. This is a critical point in the meeting. If she expresses a high level of discomfort, then you may have to ask if she's no longer interested in the job. If, however, she says she initially misunderstood certain aspects of the job but is now clear about and fine with them, confirm that she is willing to accept the responsibilities as identified in the job description before proceeding.

Topic: Start Date

Possible Problem: Applicant requires more time before beginning work than you consider reasonable.

Possible Solution: Find out why he needs more time. If it's because he feels obliged to his current employer, offer to talk with his manager once he's given notice. If, however, it's because he wants a lengthy break between jobs, suggest a compromise, such as an abbreviated break coupled with an initial modified work schedule, such as two to three days per week for the first two weeks.

Topic: **Schedule**

Possible Problem: Agreed-upon hours, shift arrangement, and/or workdays are no longer acceptable to the applicant.

Possible Solution: Be careful that the problem doesn't have to do with a religious conflict; if it does, you're obliged to try and make a reasonable accommodation. If the problem does not concern religion, explain that the schedule is the same as the one described during the interview. Ask what has happened since that time to make it problematic. If the applicant's explanation strikes you as plausible, see if there are alternative work schedules you can explore. For example, does your company offer flextime, a compressed workweek, or telecommuting? If so, and if the applicant were to opt for one of these alternatives, consider the impact it would have on the rest of the workforce and the workload in the department.

Topic: **Salary**

Possible Problem: Applicant's expectations have increased since the time of the interview.

Possible Solution: Salary is a thorny topic. The final salary agreed upon has to be acceptable to both parties: If either side feels disgruntled, the employer/employee relationship is doomed to fail before it even begins. Depending on the level of the position, most employers have some latitude in terms of what they can offer. In fact, many applicants believe they're expected to reject your first offer and negotiate. Therefore, before the final meeting you need a clear idea of just how much base salary you're prepared to offer and what additional aspects of salary—such as bonuses, commissions, or travel allowance—invite discussion. Consider this multistepped approach:

1. Listen closely to everything the applicant's saying while asking yourself if there is a sound basis for his demands.
2. Ask meaningful questions, including: Why do you feel you're worth the additional money? What's changed since our last interview? Why do you think your current employer doesn't pay you this amount? Did you consider how I would react to your request for more than I'm prepared to offer? What will you do if I tell you right now that we cannot pay you more than the sum I've offered? If you were me, what would you do?
3. Look for areas of compromise. For example, if the applicant's dissatisfied with the base salary, a one-time signing bonus could alleviate the problem. Or perhaps adjusting the method of calculating commissions might prove satisfactory.
4. Keep in mind how much "wiggle room" you have. How much beyond what you were prepared to offer are you willing to pay in order to have this person work for you?

5. Consider the likely impact this person's salary will have on incumbents functioning in a similar capacity at a lesser rate of pay.

6. Consider how badly the organization wants or needs this person. Was the position open a long time before you finally found the right match? Is this a hard-to-fill position such that only a handful of individuals possess the skills and knowledge required? What can this person offer that someone requiring less compensation cannot?

Topic: **Conditions of Employment**

Possible Problem: Applicant does not want her current employer contacted for references until she receives a letter extending an offer of employment, at which time she will give notice.

Possible Solution: This shouldn't be a problem. Explain that conditions of employment could extend to beyond her start date; in other words, under certain circumstances, a person could start work without all of the conditions being met, with the understanding that appropriate action would be taken post hire, if need be. For example, all reference checks may not come back prior to the agreed-upon start date, but you're confident enough with the information you have to proceed.

Topic: **Benefits**

Possible Problems: There could be any one of a number of issues regarding benefits, including number of and eligibility for vacation days, general health benefits, profit sharing, and tuition reimbursement.

Possible Solutions: Most benefits are set by the company, leaving HR little room to negotiate, although some benefits, such as number of vacation days, can sometimes be amended. State this clearly, suggesting that the applicant raise specific benefits-related questions during the employee orientation. If, however, the applicant has concerns that preclude his ability to proceed beyond this point, pause and, if plausible, set up a meeting or phone call between the applicant and someone in benefits. Hopefully, you'll be able to proceed shortly thereafter.

Topic: **Additional Perks**

Possible Problem: The applicant wants the company to furnish more "stuff," such as a PDA, cell phone, or laptop computer.

Possible Solution: If you decide to grant additional perks, bear in mind the likely impact such acts of generosity are likely to have on the new hire's colleagues. These extras may make her happy (for now), but there could be repercussions, including a negative effect on the morale and productivity of other employees.

Topic: **Noncompete Agreement**

Possible Problem: The applicant refuses to sign this kind of contract.

Possible Solution: Noncompete agreements (discussed in Chapter 5) are for a specified period of time, often one to two years, and are intended to take effect upon termination. Employees may be restricted from working for a competitor; working at the same or a comparable job in the same industry; or working in a defined geographical area for a competitor. Because these are often intricately worded agreements, you may need to get your lawyers involved if applicants refuse to sign or require modifications to your organization's standard noncompete agreement.

As you wade through the details of the final meeting checklist, try not to get bogged down by issues to the extent that you lose sight of your main objective: that is, to make this applicant an employee. As such, if you hit a snag, take a step back and remind yourself, as well as the applicant, about some of the benefits of working for your company. Mention any awards or recognition bestowed upon your organization (e.g., "Malstrom Electronics has been voted one of the top ten places to work in Vermont for three years in a row"). Also, bear in mind that prospective employees want to hear about staff recognition, advancement possibilities, and any unique aspects of the corporate culture.

To exemplify this last point, the HR manager from a small business in upstate New York recently contacted me regarding an interesting choice her company offers new hires. Since they know they can't afford to offer the same salaries as their competitors, they look for other ways of attracting and retaining employees. They came up with an idea whereby applicants are offered the following unusual choice: If hired, they can either have fully paid pet insurance and enjoy other pet-related services, such as dog walking, or they can receive fully paid, comparably priced, on-site child care and at-home baby-sitting services. If they opt for the pet package, employees can bring their pets to work one day a month; likewise, if they prefer the child-care perk, they can have their children at their workstations once a month. According to the HR manager, applicants seem to love having a choice, and so far, no one's been bitten.

Notifying Selected Applicants

Assuming all goes smoothly during the final meeting and you've exchanged a verbal agreement concerning the terms of employment, it's time to extend an official offer in writing.

The HR representative should send two copies of the letter to the prospective employee: one for him to sign and return to the employer, the other for him to keep. Also, send a copy to the hiring manager.

The contents of the letter should be concise and clear, leaving no room for misunderstanding. Much of what was discussed during the final meeting should be included:

- Job title
- Department
- Primary duties and responsibilities (list or attach a job description)

- Start date
- Schedule
- Location
- Salary in weekly, biweekly, or monthly terms
- Statement concerning the employment-at-will relationship
- Conditions of employment, including arrangements regarding:
  Preemployment physical (may warrant a separate letter)
  Preemployment drug test (may warrant a separate letter)
- Union status, if relevant
- Benefits highlights
- Identification and instructions for the completion of any materials enclosed, such as benefits forms
- Additional perks
- Noncompete agreement (may warrant a separate letter)
- Whom to contact with questions

Exhibit 13-3 is a sample letter reflecting this plethora of topics. As you can see, it is a highly formalized, comprehensive letter of considerable length. Depending on the nature of the job, certain aspects may not be necessary, such as referencing the signing bonus. Also, your company may not require preemployment physicals or conduct drug tests for all potential employees. It may also not have a noncompete agreement requirement. Even without these references, however, this is a long letter. You may choose, therefore, to remove certain segments and communicate them under separate cover. In addition to the noncompete agreement, sections suitable for isolation and individual reference include any requirements concerning physical exams and drug tests.

Some companies opt not to reference the employment-at-will statement in their offer of employment, reasoning that it renders the letter too formal. After all, the individual signed the application form containing the at-will clause; also, the statement probably appears in the employee handbook that the person will receive soon after starting work. Others, myself included, recommend including the employment-at-will statement in the letter offering employment. This is a critical document and the at-will statement is a vital part of the employer/employee relationship; as such, they belong together. Duplication of effort is preferable over omission.

Notifying Rejected Applicants

Once you've received a signed letter from the applicant accepting your offer of employment it's time to notify the other applicants. Except for those individuals whom you knew absolutely would not be considered as soon as their interviews ended, it's best to wait to send out letters of rejection until you have a firm commitment from the person you want to hire.

Exhibit 13-3. Sample job offer letter.

January 23, 2XXX

Mr. Richard Reason
20 Foxrun Circle
Secona, Nevada 55555

Dear Mr. Reason:

We are pleased to confirm our offer for the nonunion position of industrial engineer in the operations department of Hardcore Industries. The attached job description reflects the primary duties and responsibilities for this job, as discussed during our meeting on January 21, 2XXX.

As agreed, you will begin work on February 28, 2XXX. At 9:00 A.M. on that date, kindly report to your manager, Claire Hinton, in the operations department, at Hardcore's headquarters located at 477 Jackson Boulevard, in Secona. For your convenience, you may park in space number 47 in the south employee parking lot. This will be your regular parking space as long as you're employed by Hardcore. When you are required to visit any of Hardcore's other locations, you will be able to park in their rotating employees' parking lots.

Your regularly scheduled core hours will be 10:00 A.M. to 4:00 P.M., Monday through Friday, with an additional two hours of work preceding and/or following these hours each day. These additional hours will be determined between yourself and your manager. This will total eight hours of work daily, including a one-hour lunch period.

As agreed, your base starting salary will be $2,250 per week, which, if annualized, is equivalent to $117,000 a year. In addition, you will receive a signing bonus of $5,000, payable in a lump sum, effective immediately upon hire. The entire amount will be returned should your relationship with Hardcore be severed either by you or us, according to the terms and conditions of Hardcore's at-will agreement (see below), within six months of the date of hire. The signing bonus has no bearing whatsoever on any salary increases for which you might be deemed eligible, during your unspecified term of employment.

Hardcore's at-will agreement reads as follows:

"Employees hired by Hardcore Industries may terminate their employment at any time, with or without notice or cause. Likewise, Hardcore may terminate the employment of any of its employees at any time, with or without notice or cause.

"I understand that my employment is for no definite period of time, and if terminated, Hardcore Industries is liable only for wages earned as of the date of termination.

"I further understand that no representative of Hardcore Industries, other than the president or a designated official, has any authority to enter into any agreement, oral or written, for employment for any specified period of time or to make any agreement or assurances contrary to this policy.

"Nothing in this letter, in the employee handbook, or any other Hardcore document shall be interpreted to be in conflict with or to eliminate or modify in any way the employment-at-will status of Hardcore's employees."

(continues)

Exhibit 13-3. Continued.

This offer of employment is contingent upon certain conditions: (1) satisfactory results of a Hardcore-initiated background check; (2) satisfactory results of a Hardcore-initiated reference check; (3) satisfactory results of a Hardcore-issued preemployment physical; (4) satisfactory results of a Hardcore-issued drug test.

With regard to items (3) and (4), the nursing office has been advised of your start date and will be expecting you for your preemployment physical exam and drug test anytime within one week of that date; that is, no later than February 21, 2XXX. The nursing office is open Monday through Friday, between 8:00 A.M. and 12:00 noon. Please call extension 6488 for an appointment and instructions as to how to prepare for these two exams.

The extension of an offer of employment is also contingent upon your agreement to abide by Hardcore's noncompete clause. You will receive a letter under separate cover from Hardcore's legal department essentially asking that you commit to (1) being free of any agreement limiting your ability to work for Hardcore, and (2) upon termination from Hardcore, agreeing not to work at the same or a comparable job for a competitor for a period of one year. Upon receipt, please call Jocelyn Wright in the legal department at extension 6420 with any questions concerning the noncompete agreement.

The attached schedule of benefits identifies such matters as holidays, personal days, sick days, vacation, general health benefits, insurance, Hardcore's pension plan, and tuition reimbursement. As discussed during our meeting on January 21, 2XXX, all of these and other benefits will be fully explained and your questions answered during employee orientation, beginning on February 28, 2XXX. At that time you will also be asked to complete certain benefits and payroll forms. Should you have any questions that you would like addressed prior to that date, please feel free to contact Hardcore's benefits manager, Lou Briscoe, at extension 6499.

As part of your employment package, you are entitled to free membership in the LiveLong health club, a PDA, cell phone, and laptop computer. You will also receive reimbursable expenses in conjunction with approved Hardcore-related business, according to the enclosed schedule. These entitlements will continue until either party evokes their employment-at-will status.

As agreed, you will resign from your current position upon receipt of and agreement with the conditions of this job offer. Upon doing so, please notify this office in writing so that we may conduct a reference check with your current employer.

Kindly indicate your understanding and acceptance of the terms of Hardcore's offer by signing below and returning a signed copy of this letter in the enclosed envelope, no later than February 1, 2XXX.

It is my sincere pleasure to extend this offer of employment with Hardcore Industries. If you have any non-benefits, -health, or -legal questions, please do not hesitate to contact me at extension 6815.

Sincerely,

Wes Lohan
Manager of Human Resources

Rejection letters should refer to the specific position for which an individual applied. In other words, don't reject the person overall; you may want to consider him for another position in the future.

The tone of a rejection letter should be professional and sincere. Avoid including detailed information about the successful applicant—doing so without permission of the new hire could be considered an invasion of privacy. In addition, a rejected applicant could use your disclosures as the basis for a discrimination claim.

Rejection letters should be brief, beginning and ending on a positive note. As with letters offering employment, the HR representative who interviewed the applicant usually sends them. Following is a sample letter encompassing these points:

July 29, 2XXX

Mr. Alfred Morris
128 Field Avenue
Union City, Nevada 55535

Dear Mr. Morris:

Thank you for taking the time to meet with us to discuss Hardcore Industries' opening for an industrial engineer. We learned a great deal about your accomplishments and aspirations, and appreciate the interest you expressed in our company.

When filling an opening, Hardcore looks at a number of factors, such as experience, demonstrated skills, knowledge, and the ability to handle key job-related situations. This can make the selection process difficult when we are fortunate enough to attract many qualified applicants. With only one opening, however, we are forced to turn away many fine interviewees. Accordingly, we regret that we are unable to extend an offer of employment to you at this time.

Thank you again for your time and interest, Mr. Morris. We hope you again consider us for employment in the future.

Sincerely,

Wes Lohan
Manager of Human Resources

What Could Go Wrong?

Congratulations! You're all done! The letter offering employment has been sent out; all that's left is for the applicant to sign and return it to you. Then you'll proceed with any remaining steps, such as the physical and drug test, schedule the new employee for orientation, and that will be that. Right?

Well, technically, there is nothing left to do. But that doesn't mean things can't still go wrong. Let's look at three possible last-minute scenarios and what you can do to avert a disaster. In each instance, bear in mind that even if the worst possible scenario seems imminent—that is, that you're going to lose the applicant—it may be preferable to being held hostage by unreasonable, last-minute demands that could be a sign of trouble later on.

Scenario 1: The applicant calls you upon receipt of the offer letter, claiming you changed the mutually agreed-upon salary.

Response: Ask her what figure she believes should have been recorded and offer to call her back. Immediately check your notes. It's possible, although unlikely, that you made a mistake. Upon confirming that the figure in her letter is the salary you both agreed to, call her. You should state: "Ms. Chisholm, I've reviewed my notes; the salary I referenced in the letter is correct. In addition, I recall our discussion concerning salary and that you agreed to a starting salary of $85,000 per annum, or $1,634.62 a week." At this point, do not say anything further. Here's a possible response from the applicant: "I remember that $85,000 is what you offered, but I said I was worth more—at least $5,000 more." In that case, you must respond by saying, "Yes, Ms. Chisholm, you did say you believed you were worth more money; but if you'll recall, I clearly stated that I can offer you the equivalent of $85,000 at this time." Again, don't say anything more—the ball is in her court. She could come back with any number of responses, including rejecting your offer outright. In the time between your last, and her next, statement, you need to decide what you're prepared to do: You can either stand your ground, compromise, or acquiesce. My recommendation is to stand pat. If she continues to argue, say, "Ms. Chisholm, this is not a matter for further discussion. I must know at this time if you are comfortable accepting the agreed-upon salary of $85,000. Our offer is firm."

Scenario 2: The applicant calls to say that he's received a better offer. He prefers working for you, however, and wants to know if you can sweeten the pot.

Response: This is a take-off of the first scenario because this applicant, too, wants more than was agreed to. In this case, it could be more money, greater benefits, or additional perks. Whatever the case, unless this person is a one-in-a-million find for a hard-to-fill position, my advice is the same: Do not alter your offer. The time for negotiations is past; the applicant agreed to your original offer and last-minute grandstanding is only going to make a bad impression. Accordingly, you could respond by saying, "I'm sorry to hear that you're not interested in keeping your oral commitment to us. I'll send you a letter confirming this conversation and withdrawing our offer." The applicant might come back with, "That's not what I said; I want to work for you. It's just that I have this other offer and they're making it very tempting." Again, remain firm: "I understand, Mr. Stars, but the time for discussing the particulars of your employment is past; we both agreed to the same terms of employment." If the applicant really does have another offer, he may withdraw his verbal commitment. Chances are, though, that he doesn't have another offer and was just trying to get more from you. If that's the case, he may then say something like, "I was hoping to get you to match their offer, but I'd rather work for you even though I'll be earning less."

Scenario 3: The applicant calls upon receiving the offer letter and says she needs more time before making a final decision.

Response: Ask her if there are any specific questions you can answer that will help. She might say, "I don't know what it is; I'm just not sure if I really should leave my current job. They really need me here." It's tempting to get annoyed with this response, but you need to remain objective. As such, consider asking, "Ms. Polymer, are you saying that you're rejecting our offer of employment?" At this point she might ask for more of an incentive to switch jobs, or she might actually say, "Yes, I guess that's what I'm saying. I'm sorry, but I realize I'm better off staying here."

Having the applicant reject your offer at the last minute is probably the worst thing you can imagine happening at this point. You'd closed the book on this job and now you're faced with the prospect of starting all over again. But the picture may not be as grim as you might think. First, have the applicant formally reject your offer of employment, in writing. Then, go to your pile of rejected applicants and look at anyone who came in a close second. If you're lucky, you'll find someone who will work out as well, or nearly as well, as your first choice. It may add some time to the start date, but at least you were smart enough not to send out rejection letters before you received a firm commitment.

Sometimes unforeseen things happen and there's nothing to be done. I once had an applicant that accepted our job offer, reported for work, and then during lunch simply got into her car and didn't return. We called her home, to no avail. We sent a telegram—again there was no response. Finally, a week later, she sent a curt note: "Sorry—it didn't work out."

Summary

The final step of extending an offer of employment should be fairly effortless, although there are still some critical components remaining to ensure a smooth transition from status of applicant to employee.

Call to extend a verbal offer. Then, assuming the applicant accepts, set up a meeting so you can discuss some of the particulars, such as duties and reporting relationship, salary, benefits, and a starting date.

In preparation for this meeting, and to ensure coverage of all the salient points, develop a checklist representing a review of topics previously discussed with the applicant. Nothing said at this final stage should come as a surprise. Once you and the prospective employee go over the list together, check off each topic discussed and indicate whether you and the individual are in agreement. If there are any discrepancies, clearly indicate the nature of the disagreement. Before ending the meeting, return to any areas of dispute and try to come to an agreement.

Sometimes significant discrepancies are unveiled during the final meeting. Typical problem areas that can result in disputes include job titles, primary duties and responsibilities, start dates, schedules, salary, conditions of employment, benefits, additional perks, and noncompete agreements. Some of these disputes can mushroom into deal breakers.

As you wade through the details of your checklist, try not to get bogged down by issues to the extent that you lose sight of your main objective: that is, to make this applicant an employee. As such, if you hit a snag, take a step back and remind yourself *and* the applicant about some of the benefits of working for your company.

Assuming all goes smoothly during the final meeting and you've exchanged a verbal agreement concerning the terms of employment, it's time to extend an official offer in writing. The contents of the letter should be concise and clear, leaving no room for misunderstanding. Much of what was discussed during the final meeting should be included.

Once you've received a signed letter from the applicant accepting your offer of employment, it's time to notify the other applicants. Except for those individuals whom you knew absolutely would not be considered as soon as their interviews ended, it's best to wait to send out letters of rejection until you have a firm commitment from the person you want to hire.

After you've sent out the letter formally offering employment there's really nothing left to do, but that doesn't mean things can't still go wrong. If this should happen and it looks like you're going to lose the applicant, it may still be preferable to being held hostage by unreasonable, last-minute demands. If someone is grandstanding, it could be a sign of trouble later on.

PART IV

Orientation

The Fundamentals of Employee Orientation

About five years ago, I came across a great cartoon about orientation. It depicted a man standing rather tentatively in the partially open doorway of his manager's office. His boss was seated at a desk that brandished a large banner reading, WELCOME TO THE TEAM! He was turned in the direction of the employee, apparently replying to a query posed by the worker. The caption read, "I don't have the time to show you how to do the job. I don't even have the time to show you where to find the file that shows you how to do the job."[1]

Sound familiar? Did you ever start a new job without having anyone to provide guidance or information? If so, you're not alone. One survey reports that nearly half of all new employees say they failed to get much-needed support when they joined a new company.[2]

Everyone knows that starting a new job can be unnerving. Until an employee becomes familiar with his surroundings, feels comfortable with the details and routine of a typical day, and develops an understanding of company and departmental expectations, it's likely to be difficult for him to focus on job performance. Most businesses recognize this and provide some form of employee orientation covering a range of topics and varying considerably in duration. Do orientation programs manage to put new hires at ease and familiarize them with their work environments? Some do; others fail. Programs that succeed are well planned and thoughtfully organized in terms of format and content. But for those employers to whom the term *orientation* means sending new hires to a brief meeting during which someone from HR describes the company's history, rules, and benefits, leaving little if any time for questions or interaction among attendees, there's little hope for success. After all the time, effort, and expense you invested in finding the best possible person for a job, why risk losing her at the outset?

Objectives

Let's eavesdrop on a conversation between Richard Reason, Hardcore Industries' newest industrial engineer, and his wife, Lydia. It's the evening of Richard's first day of work and Lorna is anxious to hear how things went. "So how was your first day at Hardcore?" she asks. Richard answers without hesitation: "I couldn't have asked for a better day. I had the first part of my orientation in the morning and learned a great deal about the company, without feeling overwhelmed. Then I met everyone in my department and had lunch with my manager, Claire Hinton. She took me on a tour of operations and I started to get a feel for how my department interacts with other functions in the company." "Wow," says Lydia. "It sounds like an ideal introduction to a new job." "It was," replies Richard. "Best of all, I felt welcomed—like I belonged there. There's no doubt in my mind that this was a smart move for me; I feel as if I have a real future at Hardcore."

If you could listen to employees talk about their first day of work at your company, that's the kind of conversation you'd want to hear. First and foremost, orientation programs should focus on affirming a person's decision to join your company. There's nothing worse than making a career move, only to have regrets shortly thereafter. As such, the orientation process should embellish what the employee learned during his interviews. Topics to be expanded upon may include the organization's mission, values, and corporate culture, and how individual goals can coexist with those of the organization while supporting this culture. The affirmation process also includes encouraging the person to feel like a contributing member of your company team from the outset. Overall, then, your goal is to have new employees leave at the end of their first day feeling like a valued employee—not a new hire.

With this objective in mind, some employers work proactively at converting a person's new hire status to that of employee well before orientation begins. Some send a Welcome packet to the individual's home, including a checklist of topics to be covered during orientation. Others send out the individual's new business cards in advance, as a means of beginning the psychological conversion process. One company sends a box called a "Logo Lottery." Inside, new hires find T-shirts, hats, mugs, and other paraphernalia inscribed with the company logo. The reasoning for these offerings is simple: The company wants people to feel like they already work for the company before walking through the door on their first official day on the job.

Orientation programs also help with employee retention. With employee turnover costing as much as two and a half times an employee's annual salary, it behooves any organization to do what it can to keep high performers motivated and interested in staying put. In a survey conducted by Manchester Inc., an HR consulting firm in Jacksonville, Florida, nearly 60 percent of the responding companies reported that improved orientation programs increased retention rates among frontline employees; 33 percent said orientation improved retention among executives; and 43 percent reported help with middle manager retention.[3] In another study about the correlation between orientation and employee retention, a consulting group from San Anselmo, California, named Deliver the Promise, determined that organizations conducting comprehensive orientation can look forward to a decline in turnover by as much as 50 percent within two years.[4]

In addition to affirming a person's decision to join your company and helping with employee retention, orientations serve to reduce the possibility of costly litigation and unnecessary disciplinary action in the future by clearly communicating organizational policies and relevant employment legislation. Also, orientations often ensure that new employees receive the benefits to which they're entitled by allocating sufficient time for reviewing their options, answering questions, and helping them sign up. While critically important, discussing benefits can be tedious. A popular alternative, then, is to provide new hires with benefits information for independent review in advance. Then, during orientation, benefits experts address any remaining questions and help employees complete their forms. Consider, too, having this information available online, with access to a benefits expert for additional help as needed.

Benefits of Orientation Programs

As stated, employee orientations accomplish a great deal more than explaining the dos and don'ts of the workplace. Whether organizational or departmental (both to be described later in this chapter), orientations benefit employers and employees alike.

Benefits of Orientation Programs to Employers

Many employers don't realize the multitude of ways in which they can benefit from well prepared and implemented employee orientation programs. To begin with, orientation sets the tone for overall effective employer/employee relations. Savvy employers view this forum as an opportunity to convey their strong commitment to the well-being and development of the company's workforce. In return, new hires are motivated to reciprocate by contributing maximally. Demonstrate your dedication to the development of the workforce by describing some of the employee-friendly programs in place. Select examples that go beyond what employees are likely to expect, like basic medical coverage, to demonstrate how great it is to work for your organization. Instead of beginning an organizational orientation session by describing the rules of the company (boring), begin with something like this:

> "We care about what our employees want! How do we know what you want? We ask you! Just last year as a result of surveys, our employee suggestion program, and one-on-one conversations with members of our management team, we revamped our cafeteria menu and set up an employee lounge. The year before that we implemented our 'walk in our shoes' program whereby managers volunteer to perform an employee's least desirable task for a day. That's been a huge hit! So welcome to Hardcore Industries everyone—we know we can count on you to work hard for us; in return, we want you to start thinking about ways we can make your experience at Hardcore the best possible!"

While it's not advisable to start off by describing company rules (information retention can be as low as 15 percent on the first day[5]), new employees certainly need to know what's expected of them, as well as what happens if they fail to comply with these expectations. But there are ways of discussing these matters that are more palatable than others. For instance, define the topic as "policies and procedures," not "rules and regulations." The first sounds informative; the latter, punitive. Consider introducing this subject by saying something like the following:

> **"You've all been given a copy of Hardcore's employee handbook. In it you'll find many company policies concerning such matters as vacation schedules and holidays. You'll become familiar with all that Hardcore offers its workforce, as well as what we expect in return, regarding such matters as attendance and punctuality.**
>
> **"In just a few moments, we'll begin to review its contents. But first, I want to stress that all of Hardcore's policies reflect our strong belief in a reciprocal relationship between employer and employee."**

Introducing company expectations in this manner benefits employers by establishing an atmosphere of mutual respect—a cornerstone for productivity.

Orientation programs can also help shorten a new employee's learning curve. Learning entails a great deal more than how to do one's job. Departmental orientations help employees become indoctrinated in the workings of their unit, learning how it interrelates with other functions in the company. They can also help employees become familiar with where things are (such as copy and fax machines), how equipment works (such as computers and the phone system), and who to go to for help (such as with ordering supplies). This information significantly reduces the amount of time it might otherwise take if new employees have to constantly look for someone to ask or try to manage on their own.

Departmental orientation also begins the process of promoting open communication between a manager and her staff. Being prepared for your new hire's arrival, having an agenda prepared for her first day, and being available for questions sets a positive tone suggestive of open communication. Contrast that description with what happened to one employee, who we'll call Eric. Told to report to his manager's office on Monday morning at 9:00 A.M., he arrives promptly and is asked by the receptionist to please have a seat. He sits and waits. After fifteen minutes pass, he again approaches the receptionist who says, "She knows you're here; it'll just be another minute." Fifteen minutes stretch into forty-five. Eric feels uneasy and is left to wonder if he's made a mistake accepting this job. Finally, his manager emerges from her office, carrying a folder and a key. Eric stands up, ready to follow her, when she says, "Sorry—I'm already running behind this morning. Here's a folder with some departmental procedures. You can go through them and if you have any questions, ask Cora." "Who's Cora?" asks Eric. "She's the other analyst in our department. I'll try to catch up with you later. Oh, I almost forgot. Here's the key to the men's room. Welcome aboard!"

Benefits of Orientation Programs to Employees

Employees tend to look at the benefits of orientation programs somewhat differently than employers. Whereas employers take a long-term, holistic view of the process, employees want, first and foremost, to feel welcome. Contrast these two scenarios: Our first employee is greeted cheerfully and escorted to her office, where she finds a nameplate on the door, a vase of lovely flowers on the desk, her drawers filled with supplies, and an agenda of that day's activities, including organizational orientation in the morning, lunch with her manager, and a department orientation in the afternoon. Our second employee arrives only to discover that HR has forgotten to notify the department that he was starting that morning. His office is still being used for storage, so there's no place for him to sit. His manager is out of town and no one knows quite what to do with him. He's sent to HR for orientation, which, it turns out, consists of filling out benefits forms.

Making employees feel welcome can be accomplished with little effort, as evidenced by the first scenario. Prepare to welcome new hires by providing information about those factors that will affect employees personally. Think about the details of a typical day and consider all that you know innately. The list of items that most employees want to know about include:

- *Clothing.* What attire is appropriate? Do we have casual-dress Friday? What's considered appropriate to wear on that day? What if there's an important meeting on a Friday—is attire still casual?

- *Parking.* Where am I supposed to park? Do I have an assigned space? Are there certain spaces where I shouldn't park? Which lots fill up first? How long does it generally take to get out of the parking lot at quitting time?

- *Office Location.* What's the best way to get to my office? Am I better off taking the stairs?

- *Supplies and Equipment.* Where do I go for supplies? Are there forms to fill out for special supplies? Where's the copy machine? Do I do my own copying? What about the fax machine? What's the number for the fax machine? Am I supposed to keep a log of all faxes sent and received?

- *Phones.* How does the phone system work? What should I say when answering the phone? Where can I find phone numbers for key staff members? What's my phone number?

- *Computers.* How do specific programs work? How do I access the intranet? Who should I contact if I have questions about using my computer? Is e-mail the preferred method of communication? What's my e-mail address? Where can I find a list of e-mail addresses for my department? What about the rest of the company?

- *Food.* Where can I go to eat? If I eat in the company cafeteria, is there a proper "etiquette," such as who typically eats with whom and at which tables? What about restaurants in the area?

- *Personal Hygiene.* Where are the rest rooms? What about an employee lounge? What are the "rules" concerning use of the lounge?
- *Salutations.* How am I to address coworkers? Managers? Members of senior management?

Some of this information can be provided during the general organizational orientation, while the rest can be conveyed during the departmental orientation by the new employee's manager or assigned "partner" (see Chapter 15). Regardless of when you do it, proactively providing the answers to seemingly insignificant questions is likely to make new hires feel comfortable and welcome.

In addition to learning about those things that enable them to function at a most basic level on a daily basis, employees look to glean additional benefits from orientation. Departmentally speaking, they want to know about the people with whom they will be working; how their work will be judged; how what they do fits in with departmental goals; who to go to with questions, suggestions, or concerns; and the proper communication channels. Organizationally, they're interested in policies and procedures that affect them; repercussions for violating policies; what the company expects of them; and what warrants reward and recognition.

If all of this sounds self-serving, it is. Only after employees feel secure about their place in the organization are they likely to turn their attention to more global concerns, such as the company's goals. Then they will want to know: What is my role in helping to achieve these goals? Who are our competitors? How are we positioned in relation to our competitors? And what are the major external issues that affect us?

As an employer, recognize that your employees may have different items in mind that they want to take away from orientation, or they may put the issues on your agenda in a different order of importance. If you do that, you are ahead of the employer/employee relations game and more likely to nurture a healthy, long-term relationship.

Preparation: Before the Employee Starts

Preparations for the arrival of a new employee can vary considerably. As described in the previous example, some new employees receive a warm greeting and flowers or, in the worst-case scenario, absolutely nothing because HR forgot that the person was scheduled to begin work. Some companies go to extreme measures. For example, one employer stated that he could never understand why people throw parties when employees leave. He thought it made more sense to have a "welcome aboard" party. Now that he's a manager, that's just what he does. Every time someone new joins his department of about twenty employees there's a celebration, complete with balloons, noisemakers, and cake. The entire event lasts only about fifteen minutes, but it makes a huge impact on the new hire. She gets to meet everyone on an informal basis and feels truly welcome. The staff likes it as well: It's a brief break from work, and they also get to meet the newest member of their team. Employees working in other departments at this company, reportedly jealous, are trying to convince HR to draft a "new hire party" policy.

It's up to you to plan how elaborate an arrival you want, as long as you accomplish some basic preparatory steps. Begin with a welcome letter to the new hire. The contents should be brief, with no reference to job responsibilities, instructions regarding tests, or enclosed forms to be completed. It is, plain and simple, a letter welcoming the person to the organization. Here's a sample:

February 22, 2XXX

Mr. Richard Reason
20 Foxrun Circle
Secona, Nevada 55555

Dear Mr. Reason:

I just wanted to drop you a line to say that we're all looking forward to having you join us on February 28. I'm sure your first few days will be filled with many new and exciting challenges and, as such, you'll be quite busy. Still, if you have a moment, please stop by the human resources department and say "hello."

I'm available should you ever have any questions or concerns concerning your job or the organization. Stop by or call me at extension 6815.

Best of luck as you embark on what we look forward to being a rewarding and productive experience at Hardcore Industries.

Sincerely,
Wes Lohan

Manager of Human Resources

At about the same time as HR sends this welcome letter, the new hire's manager should distribute an internal memo or e-mail to members of the department. The purpose of this correspondence is to inform existing staff of the new employee's starting date, his responsibilities, and a brief statement about his background. The tone should be friendly, the content informative. Here's one approach:

From: Claire Hinton
To: Operations staff

Subject: Richard Reason

We are pleased to announce the hiring of Richard Reason to the position of industrial engineer in our operations department. Richard has six years' prior experience as an industrial engineer, working first at Zanza Corp., and most recently at Boma Products. Richard will come aboard, beginning on February 28.

Please try to be available on that date to give Richard a warm welcome to our staff!

Thus far, preparation has consisted of sending a letter to the new hire and communicating news of the new hire to existing staff about one week before his start date. Around this same time, HR should complete all prehire forms and set up any necessary files, including payroll and benefits. HR should also determine when the new employee will be scheduled to participate in the organizational orientation, communicating this information to his manager.

Meanwhile, the manager has an important preparatory task to perform: She needs to make ready the employee's workstation or office for his arrival. At minimum, you want to supply the new employee with:

- *An Agenda of the Person's First Day.* Here's an example of a simple agenda:

9:00 A.M.	Welcome!
9:15 A.M.	Meet with Claire Hinton
10:00: A.M.	Organizational orientation
12:00 NOON	Lunch with Claire Hinton and other members of the operations department
2:00 P.M.	Departmental orientation
4:00 P.M.	Meeting with Claire Hinton

  This sparsely written agenda gives the new hire an overview of how his time is going to be spent on his first day. The agenda could be more detailed and extend beyond the first day, depending on what the manager has planned; what matters is that the employee has some sense of what to expect.

- *Essential Supplies.* If the manager is uncertain about what supplies to provide, then let her look around the work area of someone performing a similar job. Have someone stock the new hire's work area with supplies and information relating to his computer, including a list of e-mail addresses (don't omit the employee's own e-mail address) and instructions for accessing the company intranet. Provide writing materials and instruments, as well as basic office supplies such as paper clips. In addition, provide a telephone directory, a list identifying the employee's phone number and key personnel with their extensions, and instructions on how to use the phone system, including how to access voice mail. If relevant, provide a calculator and any other equipment that may be needed. Also, provide the name and extension of the party the employee needs to call if any supplies are missing.

- *Map/Floor Plan.* Provide a map and/or floor plan to help the employee navigate during the first few days. Be sure to highlight certain locations, including emergency exits, rest rooms, the employee lounge, medical office, child- and elder-care facilities, vending machines, and the cafeteria.

- *Organizational and Departmental Charts.* While these will probably be reviewed during orientation, it's a good idea to provide the new hire with an overview of reporting relationships throughout the organization and the department in which he'll be working. Along these lines, it would be helpful if he could see faces to go along with names. You never know when he might be in the elevator, standing alongside the company's president.

- *Reading Materials.* Supply the new hire with company literature and any required departmental documents, such as a procedures manual, as well as recommended readings that may enhance his ability to do his job. In addition, prepare a glossary of industry- or company-specific terminology and acronyms. Be sure to remove any files that belonged to the new hire's predecessor if not relevant to his work.

   Some companies provide a stack of "dumb question" cards designed to be used any time the new hire has a question but feels uncomfortable about asking it. Be generous in the number of cards you provide and omit an expiration date.

- *Access Materials.* Provide any keys or access passes, along with security codes needed to enter the building.

- *Food/Beverage Locations.* If you have a company cafeteria, provide its hours of operation and a menu or list of typical offerings, along with their prices. Indicate, too, where he can grab a cup of coffee in the morning, along with a list of favorite restaurants in the area.

In making these preparations, the manager also needs to ensure that she'll be able to spend ample time with the new hire on his first day. In addition, she should identify a "partner" to accompany and assist the new hire as needed (see Chapter 15).

Organizational Orientation

Organizational orientation is a process—not an event to be accomplished in a day or even a week. Indeed, consultant Charles Cadwell says it can take up to a year for an employee to feel fully integrated into a new company.[6] That said, careful thought should go into what's covered during an employee's formal introduction into her new work environment, how the information is presented, and how much time to devote to its coverage.

Purpose

Noting what was said earlier about orientation objectives from the dual perspectives of the employer and the employee, it's safe to say that a well-planned organizational orientation should make new employees feel welcome and knowledgeable about their new organization. Typically, the purpose of organizational orientations is to:

- Give new employees an overview of the organization's history, products, and services

- Describe how the organization sets itself apart from its chief competitors
- Explain the organizational structure
- Describe the organization's philosophy, mission, and goals
- Explain how vital each employee is in helping to achieve company goals
- Discuss the organization's culture (e.g., its commitment to work/life balance)
- Explain career development opportunities, including available training, mentoring programs, tuition assistance, and promotional opportunities
- Describe the benefits and employee services offered
- Identify the organization's commitment to equal employment opportunity, diversity, nonharassment, health, and safety
- Review the interrelationship between various departments
- Outline the company's standards of performance and policies and procedures
- Outline safety and security practices

Participants

There are mixed views as to the best composition of an orientation program. There are those who favor the "one size fits all" approach; after all, everyone is working for the same company and should therefore be exposed to the same information about its history, goals, and the like. Others prefer to have one program for exempt employees and another for nonexempt employees. This is typically done when there is a substantial difference in the specific information offered, such as managerial benefits and policies pertaining to executives. Still other companies separate employees new to the workforce from those with prior work experience. The former group usually consists of new graduates needing help in making the transition from the academic to the business world. Then there are companies that have special orientation sessions for sales and marketing staff, while some segregate technical employees. Conducting separate sessions for employees with disabilities is ill advised. Make every effort, instead, to provide suitable accommodations for their disabilities.

While orientation programs are designed with new employees in mind, consider inviting existing staff to attend as well. A refresher on such matters as corporate goals and standards of performance can prove to be useful to all employees. It can also motivate existing employees to feel that they are of continuing importance to the company. Having existing staff attend the same session as new employees also allows for an exchange between the two groups.

Because discussion is an important element of an effective orientation program, the number of participants should be limited to a maximum of twenty. The ideal group size is from twelve to fifteen. Limiting the group size encourages an exchange between the new employees, while allowing for questions to be asked and responded to. However, having too small a group can make the participants feel conspicuous and self-conscious.

Location and Setting

The site selected for your organizational orientation program should be centrally located and convenient for most employees. It should easily accommodate the number of people scheduled to attend, but not be too large. Tables should be provided, since literature is likely to be distributed and employees will probably want to jot down notes during the course of the presentation. Tables and chairs should be arranged in a casual manner; round tables are preferable over a classroom-style arrangement. For these reasons, auditoriums should be avoided.

Content

Basically, all topics covered during an organizational orientation fall into one of two categories: what employees can expect from the organization and what the organization expects to receive from employees. Beyond these two broad areas, organizations can choose from a wide selection of additional topics, suitable to their work environment and relevant to a particular group of participants.

When identifying the specific content of an orientation program, keep in mind that employees want, first and foremost, to feel welcome. They're also interested in knowing the policies and procedures that affect them, the repercussions for violating policies, what the company expects of them, and what warrants reward and recognition. Remember, too, that information retention can be as low as 15 percent on the first day of work.

That said, it's not advisable to start off by describing the organization's history, products/services, or organizational structure; also, don't begin with an explanation of how the organization sets itself apart from its chief competitors, or its philosophy, mission, or goals. The employer who starts off by describing its employee-friendly programs has the right idea. It's an attention-grabber and establishes the organization's commitment to its workforce. When it's time to discuss programs, policies and procedures, and the like, focus first on those that benefit employees—such as e-mail and Internet usage—while also describing the ramifications for violations. Ease into a discussion of company objectives by talking about how individual goals can coexist with those of the organization while also supporting the prevailing corporate culture.

Employee Handbooks

One of the most important documents to be discussed during organizational orientation is the employee handbook, for the following reasons:

- It provides a written declaration of a company's commitment to fair employment practices and equal employment opportunity with regard to all employees in all work-related instances.

- It expresses the basic philosophies of senior management, through both content and tone.
- It serves as a basic communication tool pertaining to various areas of work.
- It clarifies an organization's expectations of its employees.
- It outlines the benefits and privileges of working for an organization.

An employee handbook contains many of the topics typically discussed during orientation. While all subjects covered should be written so that they're self-explanatory, it's advisable to encourage employees to ask questions and seek clarification. In addition, because of possible legal ramifications, companies must ensure that recipients understand the handbook's contents. Employees should be asked to sign a statement that they have received a copy of the company handbook and have read and understood its contents. Consider the sample shown in Exhibit 14-1.

Departmental Representation

The next area to consider in orientation planning is departmental representation; that is, who should conduct or be actively involved with the program. Ideally, the

Exhibit 14-1. Handbook acknowledgment.

This is to acknowledge that I have received and read Hardcore's employee handbook in its entirety. Any statements, rules, policies, or procedures I did not understand were explained to me.

I understand that the contents of this handbook do not constitute a binding contract, but comprise a set of guidelines concerning my employment with Hardcore Industries.

I understand that these guidelines are not intended to confer any special rights or privileges upon specific individuals or to entitle any person to any fixed term or condition of employment.

I understand that no Hardcore employee has the authority to enter into a contract with me, binding upon Hardcore, unless such contract is in writing and signed by the president or the president's delegate.

I understand that Hardcore may modify any of the provisions in this handbook at any time. I further understand that I am to observe and abide by all policies and regulations contained herein, as well as any and all amended policies and regulations that may be given to me in writing and made a part of this handbook.

I acknowledge receipt and retention of a copy of this signed statement and Hardcore's employee handbook. A copy of this signed statement will be placed in my HR file.

Name _____

Signature _____

Department _____

Date _____

following people should be included: 1) members of HR, 2) experts in specific topics, and 3) members of management representing different departments.

Someone from HR is usually in charge of the overall program, which entails:

- Planning the content
- Scheduling speakers
- Preparing the presentation media and supplemental material
- Reserving space
- Scheduling attendees
- Making opening and closing remarks
- Introducing each speaker
- Conducting tours

Because of this wide range of responsibilities, the HR representative selected should be have in-depth knowledge of the organization and possess effective presentation skills. Set up a rotational schedule if you have more than one HR person who meets these dual qualifications; this way, they can keep their respective presentations fresh.

Experts in various topics should also be involved in the orientation. Bring in benefits experts, salary administrators, and a member of the training and development department to discuss growth opportunities. These topical experts, too, should be well versed in the workings of the company and possess interpersonal skills. This is especially important with experts who are discussing topics that many other people may consider somewhat "dry," such as insurance. Regardless of the subject, if it's important enough to be included in the orientation, you should have someone on hand to present the material and generate interest.

Finally, presentations by senior members from various departments demonstrate involvement and interest on the part of management. In addition to welcoming new people into the organization, officers might briefly describe the primary functions of their respective departments and discuss how each unit relates to the organization as a whole. This information will add to the employee's holistic view of the company. Having minority and women representatives from senior management may serve to promote an organization's EEO and diversity-driven work environment.

Format

Orientation information can be imparted in a variety of ways. In fact, variety is considered essential to the success of a program when a great deal of information is presented.

It's especially important to appeal to different learning styles: visual, auditory, and kinesthetic (i.e., where someone learns through physical involvement). Presentation techniques that appeal to people whose primary method of absorbing information is visual include the use of flip charts, PowerPoint presentations, written materials, videos, samples or models, and visual representations of what they're learning. For those who are primarily auditory in how they learn, provide brief lectures, soft instrumental music during any group discussions, and sound effects to highlight certain points. Also, be certain to speak clearly and vary vocal speed and volume. Orientation participants who learn best through a kinesthetic style will prefer small group or paired discussions, demonstrations, and tours.

Timing and Duration

Employees should be encouraged to begin orientation as soon as possible, usually on the first day of work. Employees are not yet caught up in the details of their jobs and there's little chance of their receiving inaccurate information from other sources.

A thorough coverage of all key topics will take several days. Ideally, consider breaking discussions up over a series of half days; better yet, conduct several two- to three-hour modularized sessions. The employee's retention rate is bound to be higher and fatigue is less likely to set in. Also, managers are probably more receptive to releasing their employees for a few hours at a time. Take a progressive approach, going from general to detailed information to ensure greater retention.

In direct contrast with this modularized approach is the total immersion or "boot camp" format. Proponents of this approach admit that there are parallels to armed services basic training in terms of how new hires are indoctrinated in the ways of the organization. The program can run anywhere from three days to a month or longer, depending on the composition of the group. The emphasis is on breaking employees of what are considered to be bad work habits and showing them how the company does business. There are also team-building exercises, such as running obstacle courses and relay races. At the end, there is usually a test reflecting material presented over the course of the program. Questions typically center around the company's products and corporate structure.

Departmental Orientation

Departmental orientations need not be as structured as organizational orientations. Sometimes, there's only one new hire in a department at any given time, so the session is informal, albeit no less important.

Introductions

Introducing a new hire to others with whom she'll be working should be one of the first objectives of any departmental orientation. These introductions should include individuals from the same department as well as employees in other units. If there are more than a half dozen introductions, prepare a sheet in advance with everyone's name, title, office location, telephone number, e-mail address, and fax extensions. This way the new hire won't feel pressure to memorize everyone's name upon introduction.

As you take the new employee around, be careful not to express your opinions about others. For example, "Janet, the next person you're going to meet is Bob Johnson. Watch out for him during staff meetings; he's notorious for stealing ideas and submitting them as his own." Or, "When I introduce you to Fred Waters, don't take it personally if he acts as if he doesn't like you. He applied for your position but was rejected. He thinks you cheated him out of a promotion."

Seemingly positive statements should be avoided as well. For example, "Janet, I'd like you to meet Rod Perret. Rod can always be counted on to help you meet impossible deadlines."

New employees should be permitted to form their own opinions about coworkers. Therefore, avoid statements that are subjective or judgmental. Instead, focus on being descriptive. As you approach the office or workstation of each employee, briefly describe his overall function. Think in terms of action words, as described in Chapter 4. For instance, you might want to say, "The next person you'll be meeting is Terry Carson. Terry is our office manager. She receives all the work prepared by the department's assistant vice presidents, distributes it among the secretaries, reviews the final product, and then returns it to the appropriate AVP." If the new hire is taking notes, she could quickly write, "Terry Carson: office manager: receives, distributes, and returns work to AVPs." You could also have this information written out for the new hire in advance.

Familiarization with the Office

Take the new hire on a walking tour of the office. Along the way, point out rest rooms, water coolers, the employee lounge, child- and elder-care facilities, the medical office, and any other site likely to be of importance or interest. Identify any patterns to how the office is laid out: for example, all the managers' offices lined up along the wall of windows with their respective assistants' desks directly outside. Include a tour of all company floors and offices, whether or not the employee is likely to have dealings with them. Providing a printed floor plan is helpful.

Try to time your walking tour so that it ends in the employee cafeteria at the beginning of the lunch hour. This will enable the new hire to develop familiarity with its layout and offerings. It also allows for informal introductions to other employees who may be eating at the same time.

Content

So far we've seen that proactive managers prepare to welcome new hires by announcing their arrival to the rest of the staff and providing a well-outfitted workspace. They also address some of the questions posed earlier in the chapter concerning clothing, parking, supplies and equipment, phones, computers, and salutations. In addition, they provide employees with appropriate printed materials. Now that the person is onboard and the introductions and tour are completed, the emphasis shifts to departmental- and job-specific matters. Here are some topics considered relevant for inclusion in this stage of a departmental orientation:

- *Departmental Responsibilities.* Discuss the department's origins, overall function, and long- and short-term goals.

- *Interrelationship Between the Employee's Department and Other Departments.* Talk about the flow of work between departments and key individuals to contact in other departments.

- *Department Structure.* Identify specific functions by task and incumbent.

- *Departmental Culture.* Describe any unique features of the department, including "rituals" such as birthday celebrations.

- *Job Duties and Responsibilities.* Together, review the new employee's job description, discussing her specific areas of responsibility and how these tasks interrelate departmentally and intradepartmentally.

- *Confidentiality.* Identify areas of work considered confidential and the ramifications of violating confidentiality.

- *Performance Expectations.* Discuss the concepts of ongoing coaching and counseling when warranted. Also define regularly scheduled performance evaluations and salary reviews.

- *Hours of Work.* Remind the employee of starting and quitting times and any alternative schedule options.

- *Meal and Break Periods.* Describe how meal times are scheduled, as well as the frequency and duration of breaks.

- *Payroll.* Explain how often the employee can expect to get paid (e.g., monthly, weekly) and any information relevant to direct payroll deposit. Also, if the employee will spend a significant amount of time in the field, explain the company's travel and entertainment policy, as well as its expense reporting procedures.

- *Personal Telephone Calls and Personal Use of the Computer.* Identify circumstances under which personal telephone calls are permitted and stipulations concerning the use of company computers for personal use (e.g., sending and receiving personal e-mails, surfing the Internet, playing computer games, or entering chat rooms).

- *Reporting Relationships.* Define direct and indirect reporting relationships through the department and organizationwide, as well as who's typically in charge when key personnel are out of the office.

- *Vacation Scheduling.* Explain how vacations are scheduled, who approves vacation requests, and how far in advance requests should be made.

To prevent information overload, break up the discussion of these topics, talking for no more than an hour at a time. Encourage the employee to take notes or follow along with a preprinted sheet with each of these topics and corresponding key points.

Proactive managers will also have arranged for someone to partner with the new employee, as described in Chapter 15.

How Are We Doing?

You may think your company's organizational orientation program is great, but if employees don't find it worthwhile or fail to come away with an understanding of the salient features, then your efforts will have been wasted.

Your program should be continuously evaluated in terms of its content, presentation, and overall impact. Obtain feedback by surveying participants at the end of each session. Then review and compare the survey results over a period of time. Sample questions and statements might include:

1. Which segment of the orientation did you find most informative? Least informative?

2. Which segment of the orientation did you find most interesting? Least interesting?

3. Was the order in which topics were presented effective?   Yes   No

4. List three things you learned about this organization as a result of the orientation.

5. On a scale of one to five, with one representing excellent and five signifying poor, rate each session according to the following:
   * Duration   1   2   3   4   5
   * Format   1   2   3   4   5
   * Location   1   2   3   4   5
   * Number of participants   1   2   3   4   5
   * Quality of printed materials   1   2   3   4   5
   * Quality of visuals   1   2   3   4   5
   * Range of topics   1   2   3   4   5
   * Relevance of topics   1   2   3   4   5
   * Room set-up   1   2   3   4   5
   * Selection of speakers   1   2   3   4   5

6. As a result of the orientation, do you fully understand your benefits? Yes   No

7. As a result of the orientation, do you fully understand the contents of the employee handbook?   Yes   No

8. For each of the following categories, indicate whether you feel there was 1) too little time spent, 2) just enough time spent, or 3) too much time spent:
   * An overview of the organization's history and present status   1   2   3
   * The company's overall functions   1   2   3
   * The organizational structure and culture   1   2   3
   * The organization's philosophy, goals, and objectives   1   2   3
   * Each employee's role in helping to achieve company goals   1   2   3
   * Benefits and employee services offered   1   2   3

- Standards of performance, policies, procedures, and
  regulations   1   2   3
- Safety and security practices   1   2   3

9. On a scale of one to five, with one representing the most effective and five signifying the least effective, rate each presenter in terms of the presenter's ability to
   convey the subject matter, sustain your interest, and respond to questions. (List
   presenters by title, and the topics each presenter addressed.)

10. On a scale of one to five, with one representing the most helpful and five signify-
    ing the least helpful, rate the usefulness of the tour.   1   2   3   4   5

11. On a scale of one to five, with one representing the highest and five signifying
    the lowest, describe your level of interest in the orientation overall.
                                                          1   2   3   4   5

12. What suggestions do you have for improving the organizational orientation pro-
    gram? Please be specific.

13. Please provide a summarizing statement reflecting your overall evaluation of the
    orientation program.

Ask presenters for their feedback as well. In addition to responding to the same
questions asked of participants, query presenters about:

- The overall structure of the program
- The balance of information
- The completeness of information
- The clarity of information
- The relevance of information
- The tone of the program

Some organizations also approach employees several months after they've attended orientation to conduct follow-up surveys. Follow-up surveys might read as
follows:

Dear Valued Hardcore Employee,

Our records show that you attended our New Hire Organizational Orientation
on (date). Now that you've been on-the-job for (number of months), we'd like
your input concerning the degree of usefulness of some of the topics that were
covered.

Please react to the following categories by circling a number from one to three.
One signifies "extremely helpful," two signifies "helpful," and three signifies
"not at all helpful."

- Made me feel welcome   1   2   3
- Allowed me to get to know other employees   1   2   3
- Benefits   1   2   3

• Compensation	1	2	3
• Policies and procedures	1	2	3
• Career development opportunities	1	2	3
• Organizational commitment to equal employment opportunity, diversity, nonharassment, health, and safety	1	2	3
• Company history, products, and services	1	2	3
• Organizational structure	1	2	3
• Company philosophy, mission, and goals	1	2	3
• My role in helping to achieve company goals	1	2	3
• Organizational culture	1	2	3

- Do you have any suggestions as to how orientation can be improved?

Thank you for your feedback. Your signature on this questionnaire is optional.

_____

(optional signature)

Summary

Everyone knows that starting a new job can be unnerving. Until an employee becomes familiar with his surroundings, feels comfortable with the details and routine of a typical day, and develops an understanding of company and departmental expectations, it's likely to be difficult for him to focus on job performance. Most businesses recognize this fact and provide some form of employee orientation covering a range of topics and varying in duration.

Well-developed organizational and departmental orientation programs should affirm a person's decision to join your company. They can also help with employee retention and reduce the possibility of costly litigation and unnecessary disciplinary action. In addition, they set the tone for effective employer/employee relations, shorten a new employee's learning curve, and promote open communication between a manager and her staff.

During organizational orientations, employees look forward to learning about policies and procedures, the repercussions for violating policies, what the company expects of them, and what warrants reward and recognition. In this regard, one of the most important documents to be discussed during orientation is the employee handbook.

Departmental orientations allow new employees to meet those with whom they will work, become familiar with the office, and learn about job-specific matters.

Businesses that evaluate the content, presentation, and overall impact of their orientation programs will ensure more productive employer/employee relations.

Notes

1. Jennifer Hutchins, "Getting to Know You," *Workforce Management* Vol. 79, No. 11 (November 2000), pp. 36–40.

2. Barbara Morris, "The Cost of a Bad Start," *Salary Benchmarks* (October 27, 2003).

3. Charlotte Garvey, "The Whirlwind of a New Job," *HR Magazine* Vol. 46, No. 6 (June 2001), pp. 110–118.

4. Alicia Abell, "Practical Tips for New-Employee Orientation," *The Chronicle of Philanthropy's Philanthropy Careers* (January 14, 2004).

5. Ibid.

6. Jennifer Hutchins, "Steps to Effective Orientation," *Workforce Management* Vol. 79, No. 11 (November 2000), p. 40.

CHAPTER 15

Beyond the Fundamentals of Employee Orientation

Recently, a client asked me to help redesign his company's organizational orientation program. I agreed. As part of the process, I spoke with many employees about various facets of orientation. Among other questions, I asked, "For comparative purposes, can you briefly describe the orientation program at your last place of employment?" Here's a sampling of some of the answers I received:

- "What orientation? At my last company all we did was sit around for three hours and fill out a bunch of forms in human resources."

- "Orientation lasted a week—I wanted to cry, it was so boring. The only good part was the tour."

- "I shadowed an employee from my department for a couple of days. He took me on a tour, introduced me to everyone, and took me to lunch. Then there was a general orientation for all new hires the following week. That lasted three days and I really learned a lot. My only complaint was that my manager was virtually invisible throughout the entire process. In fact, I didn't even meet with her until the end of my first week on the job."

- "Orientation at my last company was online; it was cool. I learned at my own pace and no one made me participate in dumb, getting-to-know-you types of activities. Sorry—I guess that's the techie in me talking. I just prefer learning on my own."

- "I worked at a large corporation where the orientation program you participated in depended on your job: Technical employees had their own session, executives met separately, and so on. The process made me feel kind of isolated. I couldn't help but wonder what the others were learning in their sessions."

- "My last job was keen on keeping up with the latest trends. With regard to orientation, that meant going a step further and implementing an 'onboarding' program. It was intense but very effective. It really enhanced employer/employee relations."

This sampling of responses confirmed what I know to be true: Orientation can embrace and be enhanced by a wide range of techniques and approaches. Let's look at some of them, beginning with the partner program.

The Partner Program

The partner program, also referred to as the buddy system, sponsor system, or shadowing, is a one-on-one relationship between a new hire and another employee from the same department, whereby the latter is assigned to answer questions, offer encouragement, and provide whatever personal assistance may be needed as the new employee becomes acclimated to his work environment. The buddy helps ease the new employee's transition into the new work environment, lessening the stress of "fitting in" by providing access to someone who is both familiar and comfortable with the culture, attitude, and expectations.

While some employees are lucky enough to immediately link up with someone who's willing to help them out during their first few days on the job, most are not. Outside of organizational and departmental orientation programs that may or may not be beneficial, new workers are usually left to fend for themselves. A formalized partner program guarantees that every individual has one person to guide them through the confusion of functioning in a new work environment. Here are just a few of the benefits of a partner program:

- The initial confusion and uncertainty experienced by all new employees is greatly reduced.
- New hires can be assured of receiving comprehensive, straightforward answers to important questions about day-to-day matters.
- Managers have more time to deal with employees on work-related issues.
- New employees are likely to develop increased confidence and self-esteem, leading to greater productivity.

Whereas managers provide valuable information about the organizational structure and departmental guidelines, partners take new hires "behind the scenes," offering a peek at some of the company's unwritten rules. In no way is the partner's role to substitute for that of the manager.

Partner programs are similar to mentoring in that the process is a developmental, helping relationship: One person invests time, ability, and effort in enhancing another person's knowledge and skills in preparation for greater productivity or future achievement. As with mentoring, everyone wins in the end: The new hire gains expedited insights about the inner workings of the company; the partner gains additional recognition by the organization and adds another dimension to her leadership skills; and the organization benefits by building a stronger team.

Partner programs can range from a casual transfer of information or ideas from one person to another, to a structured system with a specific agenda. Regardless of how informal or ordered the program is, the new hire's partner should take a proactive stance; that is, the partner must regularly approach the new employee with information, rather than waiting for the employee to come to him, asking for help.

Ideally, partner programs should begin before new hires begin work. Just as the manager should send out a letter of welcome, so too should a person's assigned partner. It could read something like this:

February 22, 2XXX

Mr. Richard Reason
20 Foxrun Circle
Secona, Nevada 55555

Dear Richard,

My name is Allie Rowens. I'm an industrial engineer in Hardcore's operations department, and I've been with the company for three years. As part of Hardcore's Partner Program, I'm going to be available to you during your initial weeks on the job to answer any questions you may have. View me as a friendly source of advice, information, and introductions. If you want to call me before starting next week, my extension is 6339.

Hardcore is a great place to work, and I'm looking forward to making your introduction to the company as smooth and pleasant as possible. I look forward to meeting and working with you.

Sincerely,

Allie Rowens

This same message can be conveyed in a phone call or e-mail; what matters is that contact is made before the person's first day on the job.

Depending on the complexity of the job and nature of the work environment, the partner relationship typically lasts from a minimum of a week to as long as three months. By then, the employee should have developed solid relationships with his colleagues and learned all the basics of the work environment.

Selecting a Partner

Some employees make better partners than others. Their length of service and knowledge of the company and organizational and departmental goals are important, but those factors should not be the sole basis for selection. Select a peer who will make a lasting impression—someone who is personable, patient, and can explain things clearly and concisely. Also, select an employee with high personal standards of performance and a positive attitude. Ideally, a partner should be someone whose style of communication and approach to work is flexible enough to suit that of the new hire. In this regard, partners are encouraged to familiarize themselves with the approach to learning preferred by the new hire. Some people need examples, some need to talk, and others need to experiment with different methods for learning and accomplishing tasks. Regardless of the preferred methodology, partners need to practice active listening, offer information and ideas, and provide frequent feedback.

Make certain, too, that the employee selected is able to budget her time and not fall behind in her work as she takes time away from her job to assist the new hire with his. Managers are responsible for ensuring that this doesn't happen. They are also responsible for overseeing the partner relationship to ensure that the two are properly matched. If, for any reason, it appears that the partner's style or personality is ill suited to the new employee, managers shouldn't hesitate to assign a new partner midstream.

Ideally, HR should conduct a brief training session for employees interested in joining the partner program. The purpose of the training is to teach coaching skills and reinforce the most salient points about partnering. The agenda for this session should include explaining or defining:

- The purpose and anticipated results of the program
- The role of the partner and the nature of the relationship
- Mandatory aspects and topics of the program
- A partner's availability requirements
- Partners' reporting responsibilities to management
- Confidentiality
- Duration of the program

Employees who volunteer their time to be partners should be appropriately recognized and rewarded.

While personalized one-on-one partnering has the greatest potential for trust and learning, sometimes it's not as practical as group or team partnering. During times of mass hiring, for example, having one partner available to a group of up to six new employees is by far more cost- and time-effective. In these instances, participants can learn from one another as well as from their assigned partner.

Online Orientation

Another approach to orientation for newly hired employees is offering it to them online. This process allows employees to log on to a guide that takes them through any one of several areas typically covered during conventional orientation programs. Of course, missing from this approach is the opportunity for two-way communication. For example, often an employee's question will trigger an additional, relevant thought that the presenter may offer to enhance a topic currently under discussion. Still, online orientation may be helpful when standard orientation is not practical because of time or other restraints.

Some companies use online orientation to enhance the face-to-face process. They may conduct a series of comprehensive person-to-person sessions and then post online all the materials presented to reinforce the messages and the content. Typically, companies include a gallery of names and photos to help employees remember important contacts.

Just as on-site orientation programs can vary considerably in terms of content, format, and duration, so too can online orientation. There are, however, key components that typically appear in most company's online systems:

- Introduction
- Instructions
- Employee checklist
- Overview of contents
- Equal employment opportunity and diversity workplace statements
- Organizational information
- Benefits information
- Policies and procedures
- Workplace health and safety
- Technology resources
- Employee assistance program
- Employee amenities
- Training and development
- Confirmation of completion
- Online orientation evaluation

That said, let's take a slightly more detailed look at an online orientation program at a retailer headquartered in the southeast, employing approximately 3,500 employees:

Introduction

- Welcome to the company
- Purpose of the online orientation
- Orientation requirements

Instructions

- Order of topics
- Importance of not skipping any subjects
- What employees will be asked to do at the end of each section
- What to do if employees encounter problems or have questions

Employee Checklist

- Purpose
- Recommended/required timeline
- What to do upon completion

Overview of Contents

- Topics to be covered
- Relevance of each topic
- Reference to name, telephone extension, and e-mail address for person to contact with questions regarding each topic

Equal Employment Opportunity and Diversity Workplace Statements

- Statement of commitment to EEO by the senior-most member of management
- Statement concerning zero tolerance for sexual and other forms of harassment
- Description of diversity and its benefits to the organization

Organizational Information

- History of the company
- Organizational structure
- Description of services and products
- General industry information and special terminology
- Comparison with chief competitors
- Information concerning number of locations and employee composition at each location
- Mission statement
- Company philosophy, goals, and objectives
- Unique organizational features
- Importance of each employee in helping to achieve company goals
- Company culture

Benefits Information

- Statement concerning importance of submitting completed benefits forms to the benefits office within thirty-one days from their start date to receive health insurance coverage
- Identification of benefits-related topics to be covered, including: child and elder care, dental insurance, disability insurance, employee discounts, holidays, life insurance, medical insurance, paid and unpaid leave, retirement and investment plans, savings plans, tuition reimbursement, and vacations

Policies and Procedures and Employee Handbook

- Purpose
- Identification of topics to be covered, including: EEO and affirmative action policies, employment and termination-at-will, general expectations of all employees, growth opportunities, standards of performance, performance re-

view process, salary increase guidelines, employee recognition, conflict of interest, drug-free workplace, and workplace violence

- Employee accountability
- Management accountability

Workplace Health and Safety

- Who is responsible
- Procedure to follow in an emergency
- What to do if there's a work-related injury or illness
- Protecting personal property

Technology Resources

- Definition of technology resources
- Proper use
- Guidelines to e-mail usage, including laws governing right to privacy in e-mail correspondence
- Internet and intranet usage
- NetID
- Computer security standards
- Computer-related employee self-services
- Technology labs
- Repairs

Employee Assistance Program

- Purpose
- Services
- Procedure
- Confidentiality

Employee Amenities

- Eligibility
- Services, including: cultural arts discounts, health club membership, and store discounts
- Eligibility of family members
- Procedure

Training and Development

- Eligibility
- Options, including: in-house workshops, outside seminars, and tuition reimbursement
- Release time

Confirmation of Completion

- Final steps, including opportunity to revisit certain topics and responding to questions about each topic to ensure understanding
- Procedure to follow in order to receive certificate of completion

Online Orientation Evaluation

- Purpose
- Instructions for completion

In addition to the online orientation portions of these programs, companies often require or suggest informal welcome events where employees are greeted in person and have an opportunity to meet other new hires. Depending on the size of the organization and how many employees on average they hire in any given month, these functions can be held anywhere from weekly to once a month.

Blended Learning

Blended learning refers to the formal combination of two or more delivery modes to meet a specific set of learning objectives. Typically, the delivery modes are technology-based lessons and traditional classroom instruction. The goal of blended learning is to simultaneously support organizational objectives and meet the unique developmental needs of each individual while optimizing the cost of program delivery.

Applying blended learning to employee orientation is growing in popularity. The process allows companies to impart critical information about an organization in an efficient yet still personalized way. It integrates different learning styles (e.g., visual, auditory, and kinesthetic), recognizes the limited computer comfort level of some individuals, acknowledges that time and money restraints prohibit many organizations from devoting the requisite number of hours to classroom orientation, while still respecting the indisputable benefits of face-to-face communication and interaction.

Here's a step-by-step example of how the concept of blended learning might apply to organizational orientation:

Step 1. New employees meet for an introductory session. After introductions are completed, an HR representative presents an overview of the orientation process, including its format, content, and duration. She describes the blended learning approach, explaining how the process will impact each stage.

Step 2. Employees complete a series of self-paced, online tutorials covering organizational information, benefits, policies and procedures, health and safety, employee programs, and training and development. While step 2 is self-paced, there's still an outside date for the completion of all tutorials.

Step 3. As employees complete step 2, they fill out a questionnaire reflecting their understanding of the contents of each tutorial.

Step 4. As the outside date for the completion of all the tutorials approaches, the HR representative contacts the original group of attendees and arranges a meeting. The purpose of this meeting is to discuss any questions employees may have as a result of the online tutorials. Employees will bring the online questionnaires they completed as the basis for this discussion.

Step 5. Employees return to the intranet and complete an additional questionnaire that solidifies their understanding of all that they learned in the classroom and online.

Step 6. Employees complete an online orientation evaluation, providing feedback about the blended learning process and making suggestions for future improvements.

The particulars of each step will vary depending on a number of factors, including the preferred learning style of attendees. For instance, if your organization separates its orientation programs according to special interest groups, you might skew your blended learning approach to favor classroom over online learning. This might be the case if the group consisted of sales professionals who tend to respond best to collaborative, visual, and verbal methods of learning. On the other hand, a group of IT professionals would probably be more responsive to a linear, factual, and individually directed means of orientation.

Since most organizations do not have sufficient numbers of new hires in one particular job classification to warrant a specialized organizational orientation session, blended learning becomes more challenging. Determining how much emphasis to place on traditional classroom versus online learning can be made easier if you isolate and evaluate certain variables about your organization. Exhibit 15-1 provides a preliminary blended learning guide to help you with this process.

Experts project that organizations will become increasingly comfortable with blended learning as it pertains to employee orientation. As the process becomes more refined, companies will learn to better combine the best features of classroom instruction with the most desirable aspects of online learning.

Onboarding

Some employers use the term *onboarding* interchangeably with orientation, along with alignment, assimilation, integration, and transition. But onboarding differs from these processes—especially traditional orientation—in several ways:

- Onboarding continues far beyond the point at which orientation programs typically end, lasting as long as a year. (Successful executive transitions can take more than two years, depending on the number of variables.)

Exhibit 15-1. Preliminary blended learning guide for organizational orientation.

Instructions: Read each statement following these instructions and identify its degree of applicability to your organization. Circle the most appropriate number from 1 through 5, in keeping with this scale:

1 = Completely applicable
2 = Applicable in most instances
3 = Applicable in many instances
4 = Applicable in some instances
5 = Rarely applicable

After responding to each statement, add up your scores and divide that total by 20. Locate where your answer fits according to the following key:

• A score of 1.0–2.0 suggests that your organization would probably benefit from a greater emphasis of online learning blended with a small amount of classroom instruction.
• A score of 2.1–3.5 suggests your organization would probably benefit from a balanced blend of online learning and classroom instruction.
• A score of 3.6–5.0 suggests your organization would probably benefit from a greater emphasis on classroom learning blended with a small amount of online learning.

1) Our employees have demonstrated a keen interest in and high comfort level with electronic learning.	1 2 3 4 5
2) Collectively, our employees have demonstrated a high level of resiliency and receptiveness to change.	1 2 3 4 5
3) Members of the management team have demonstrated a keen interest in and high comfort level with electronic learning.	1 2 3 4 5
4) Collectively, members of the management team have demonstrated a high level of resiliency and receptiveness to change.	1 2 3 4 5
5) Members of the HR department have demonstrated a keen interest and high comfort level with electronic learning.	1 2 3 4 5
6) Collectively, members of the HR department have demonstrated a high level of resiliency and receptiveness to change.	1 2 3 4 5
7) Observations of employee learning styles suggest that blended learning would be well received.	1 2 3 4 5
8) Overall evaluations of our current organizational orientation program suggest that blended learning would be well received.	1 2 3 4 5
9) Evaluations of our current organizational orientation programs suggest a low level of responsiveness to its interactive aspects.	1 2 3 4 5
10) Evaluations of our current organizational orientation programs suggest a low level of responsiveness to presentations by management.	1 2 3 4 5
11) Evaluations of our current organizational orientation programs suggest a low level of responsiveness to completing forms.	1 2 3 4 5
12) Current orientation content is conducive to blended learning.	1 2 3 4 5
13) Our current orientation content is due for a major overhaul.	1 2 3 4 5

14) The online aspect of blended learning would not be problematic because of employee access to or ability to use computers.	1	2	3	4	5
15) The classroom aspect of blended learning poses logistical problems since not all employees are in a central location.	1	2	3	4	5
16) Current orientation sessions must adapt to employee schedules.	1	2	3	4	5
17) Managerial preference is of utmost importance.	1	2	3	4	5
18) Employee preference is of utmost importance.	1	2	3	4	5
19) Keeping up with our competitors by integrating technology into our orientation program is of utmost importance.	1	2	3	4	5
20) Keeping orientation costs low is of utmost importance.	1	2	3	4	5

- Onboarding links new employees with more colleagues and introduces them to other aspects of the company.
- Onboarding provides specialized resources and intensive support. The onboarding process supports a closer connection between an employee and her manager.
- Onboarding programs are customized to focus on the areas of greatest need for an individual's role in the company.

You might say, then, that orientation leads to, and lays the foundation for, onboarding.

Onboarding Programs for Executives

Successful executives are often thought of as quick thinkers and effective decision makers, backed by a knowledgeable support team. But it's unreasonable to expect even the best among them to start with a new company functioning at maximum capacity. Even if an executive brings in some of his own staff, it takes time to establish new working relationships and learn the intricate details of how a company functions. Experts report that newly promoted or hired executives face many major challenges during their first four months. Some executives often get off to a slow start or fail in the execution of their new responsibilities due to a lack of clear direction. Others take on too many tasks and try to meet unreasonable deadlines. Some executives, anxious to please, fail to think through decisions before implementing them, or they err by placing their priorities before those of their boss's. Executives can avoid making these mistakes if they receive the proper guidance.

In some organizations, onboarding targets employees hired for or promoted into leadership roles. In this regard, onboarding is intended to:

- Ensure that new leaders are thoroughly indoctrinated in the workings, priorities, objectives, brand identity, strategic direction, decision-making processes, initiatives, results achieved, and culture of the company
- Offer in-depth information relevant to how the company measures success
- Provide a systematic approach to ensure that new hires succeed in their jobs and remain with the company

- Ensure alignment between organizational and individual goals
- Foster increased exchange of information between members of the leadership team
- Focus on creating and nurturing solid employer/employee relationships
- Increase job satisfaction
- Decrease job turnover

An example of a formalized approach to onboarding incoming leaders may be seen at Johnson & Johnson in New Brunswick, New Jersey.[1] Their objective is to help executives learn about and adapt to the ways of the company as quickly as possible. To accomplish this, the company has developed three separate programs for different levels of executives:

1. *Transitions Coaching Program.* This agenda is for new executives.
2. *Transitions Leadership Program.* This course is for vice presidents and executive vice presidents taking on new functional roles.
3. *New Business Leader Program.* This plan is designed for senior-level executives moving from functional responsibilities to more complex positions.

A survey of more than 125 executives who went through these onboarding programs reported that they felt "better prepared" for their jobs as a result of the training they received. Specifically, 95 percent said they were better able to prioritize their work; 83 percent built successful new partnerships; and 82 percent said the program helped clarify expectations of their new boss. Overall, the executives reported that they felt they'd performed 30 percent to 40 percent better during their transition as a result of having participated in the programs.

Some onboarding programs for new leaders combine personal coaching with the use of a Web-based application, allowing the executive to access onboarding resources and advice online. Others bring in professional onboarding consultants to work one-on-one with new executives over a period of months, providing feedback along the way.

Onboarding and Managerial Relations with Employees

With regard to the relationship between onboarding and a closer connection between managers and their employees, managers should foster six critical categories.[2]

1. *Relationships.* Managers need to talk to their new hires about what each of them can do to develop their employer/employee relationship. Each should be frank about observations they've made concerning the other person's strengths and areas requiring improvement. A map or timeline can be used to identify points at which they will sit down and discuss progress and/or problems encountered to date.

2. *Interests.* A manager attending one of my interviewing seminars once said that he asked all applicants interested in working for him the same question: "Do you like to read mysteries?" He explained his reasoning as follows: "I like to read mysteries. I know that one of my responsibilities as a manager is to interact socially with my employees. I figure if they also like reading mysteries we'll have something in common."

Making a hiring decision based on a person's reading preferences is, of course, inappropriate. However, the manager was on the right track with regard to understanding that his responsibilities extend beyond issuing work assignments. The most effective managers learn about their employees' interests. What aspects of work do they most enjoy? What is it about these tasks that they enjoy? What are their passions outside of work? Is there a way to integrate what they enjoy off the job with work?

Experts agree that employees are most productive when they're able to combine what they excel in with what they like doing. Managers need to understand that both are equally important for maximally effective employer/employee relations.

3. *Challenge.* How often have you been excited about the talents of a new hire only to be chagrined to learn that she was leaving to work elsewhere? What went wrong? Chances are, she became bored. Top performers need to remain challenged if they're going to remain productive. A manager is responsible for learning what motivates or challenges his employees so they'll want to continue working at an optimum level of output.

4. *Focus.* Employees who function within the confines of their department and lack a thorough understanding of their role toward achieving organizational goals are not going to be maximally motivated or productive. Managers are responsible for keeping employees informed of goings-on companywide and how each individual's contributions make the organization that much stronger and more successful.

5. *Work/Life Balance.* Even the most dedicated workers need to balance their jobs with family and outside interests and obligations. The most effective managers understand this and—without prying—show an interest in and support for each individual's life outside of work.

6. *Follow-Through.* As managers and employees learn more about one another and develop a greater sense of mutual trust and understanding, it should become easier for everyone to complete work assignments, follow through on commitments, and meet deadlines.

Because of the significant commitment of time and energy required of program participants, onboarding requires the unconditional and ongoing support of senior management, as well as direct involvement by HR.

Best Practices: Sample Orientation Programs

By now it should be evident that a one-size-fits-all approach to employee orientation doesn't work. Whether you opt for a purely classroom instruction or online approach, or decide instead to apply a blended learning methodology, every organization has specific variables that drive its orientation program's contents, format, participants, and duration. For comparative purposes, here's a sampling of four orientation programs.

Bausch & Lomb

Bausch & Lomb Incorporated is an eye health company with headquarters in Rochester, New York. The company has three primary product lines: vision care, surgical, and pharmaceuticals. Founded in 1853, it has a workforce of approximately 12,400 people located throughout thirty-five countries.

Bausch & Lomb's orientation program consists of an interactive online video that stresses organizational issues; HR management guidelines that focus on the employee's workgroup; and a mentoring program that addresses job issues. Together, these three components are designed to promote company values and culture. The emphasis is on communicating principles and how new employees can participate and contribute. This, in turn, increases employees' sense of belonging and strengthens their commitment to the company.

The three-tiered approach allows employees to transport the acquired principles with them when they move within the company to different jobs. Since Bausch & Lomb operates on a global level, the skills and knowledge are transportable to multiple international locations.

The Container Store

The Container Store, an originator and leading retailer of storage and organization products, has occupied a prestigious spot at the top of *Fortune* magazine's list of the "100 Best Companies to Work for in America" for the past six years. Founded in 1978, the retailer employs approximately 2,500 employees. The privately held company currently has thirty-three locations throughout the United States.

Orientation at The Container Store consists of "Foundation Week." A layered approach to conveying information reinforces whatever employees learned the day before. By the end of the week, new hires have been exposed to the same information in several different ways from a host of different people.

Part of the first day is devoted to discussing the company's philosophy; the balance of the time is spent with the store manager. Day two is "hands on" and visual: Employees learn how the products get into the store and onto the shelves by actually working as store employees. On the third day, employees hook up with salespeople learning about the different sections of the store and various selling techniques. Day four takes new hires through different roles, such as store greeter and cashier. And on the final day, employees learn about inventory and backroom operations. They also meet, once again, with their managers.

Whole Foods Market

Founded in 1980 as a small store in Austin, Texas, Whole Foods Market, Inc. is now the world's leading retailer of natural and organic foods, with 167 stores and 32,000 employees throughout North America and the United Kingdom. The company has appeared on *Fortune*'s "100 Best" list for eight consecutive years.

New hires at Whole Foods Market work for thirty days before they're voted by existing employees onto a specific team. During that time, they're assigned a buddy and required to complete orientation and a skills-based checklist. Each location has its own orientation agenda, tailored to fit its member base. For example, some locations support a large population of team members who don't speak English as their first language; as such, orientation videos are translated into their native language.

Despite regional differences, every orientation begins with "Start with the Cart." Employees get a shopping cart and a list of questions they have to answer, such as, "What is quinoa and how do you cook it?" The process is highly interactive. Another aspect of their orientation is called "Hit the Floor Running." New hires are taken on a tour of the store, watch a video, play team-building games, and eat in the store. Other topics covered during their orientation include customer service, company history, core values, and safety.

Whole Foods Market believes in a constantly evolving orientation process, changing the content as new issues arise.

Intel Corporation

California-based Intel Corporation is the world's largest chip maker and also a leading manufacturer of computer, networking, and communications products. It can boast of many distinguished awards, among them being named to *Fortune*'s 2004 list of Blue Ribbon companies, one of the world's most sustainable corporations, and one of the Best Workplaces for Commuters, as recognized by the U.S. Environmental Protection Agency. It has also been voted one of the 100 Best Corporate Citizens five years in a row, and one of the 100 Best Companies for Working Mothers for three consecutive years.

Intel provides a great deal of information during a new hire orientation session. At its conclusion, employees are provided with relevant online links so they can access additional information. While the company supports a blended learning approach, it is a strong advocate of the human interaction that comes from classroom instruction.

The first part of Intel's orientation consists of a full day devoted to providing administrative data as well as information about the corporate culture. This session is followed by matching new hires with buddies who show them around and help reduce their anxiety. One to three months later, employees are required to attend a one-day "Working at Intel" class where they're taught *how* to work at Intel. The process may best be described as a fast-paced, application-learning experience using interactive techniques where employees learn about core practice tools, such as team development and how to conduct effective meetings. After an additional three to six months have passed, employees meet in an "Executive Staff Member New Hire

Forum" where they can ask strategy and product questions of senior staff. These senior staff members query the now not-so-new employees as well.

Intel believes this approach stresses the importance of treating orientation as an ongoing process rather than an event. The company also believes it's important to stress two issues that are most important to employees: "Did I make the right decision?" and "How will I succeed in this work environment?"

Summary

Orientation can be enhanced by a wide range of techniques and approaches. Among the most popular is the partner program—a one-on-one relationship between a new hire and another employee from the same department. The established employee is assigned to answer questions, offer encouragement, and provide whatever personal assistance may be needed as the new employee becomes acclimated to his work environment. Whereas managers provide valuable information about the organizational structure and departmental guidelines, partners take new hires "behind the scenes," offering a peek at some of the company's unwritten rules.

Another approach to orientation for newly hired employees is offering it to them online. This process allows employees to log on to a guide that takes them through any one of several areas typically covered during conventional orientation programs. Just as on-site orientation programs can vary considerably in terms of content, format, and duration, so too can online orientation.

Blended learning refers to the formal combination of two or more delivery modes to meet a specific set of learning objectives. Typically, the delivery modes are technology-based lessons and traditional classroom instruction. The goal of blended learning is to simultaneously support organizational objectives and meet the unique developmental needs of each individual while optimizing the cost of program delivery.

Orientation can lead to and lay the foundation for onboarding. Onboarding continues far beyond the point at which orientation programs typically end, lasting as long as a year or more. Onboarding also provides specialized resources and supports a closer connection between an employee and her manager.

A one-size-fits-all approach to employee orientation rarely succeeds. Whether you opt for a purely classroom or online approach, or decide instead to apply a blended learning methodology, every organization has specific variables that drive its organization program's contents, format, participants, and duration. A sampling of four orientation programs used by a cross-section of companies from various industries has been provided for comparative purposes.

Notes

1. Susan J. Wells, "Diving In," *HR Magazine* Vol. 50, No. 3 (March 2005), pp. 54–59.
2. Stephenie Overman, "Onboarding: Making a Connection Beyond Orientation," SHRM Forum, Employment Management Association, February 2005; available through http://www.shrm.org/ema/library with SHRM member log-on.

Appendixes

Appendix A:
Job Posting Form

Job Title:
Department/Manager: Location:
Primary Duties and Responsibilities:

Exemption Status: Grade/Salary Range:
Work Schedule:
Working Conditions:
Minimum Qualifications and Requirements:

Closing Date:

Job Posting Eligibility Requirements

1. You must be an employee of JavaCorp for at least twelve consecutive months.
2. You must be in your current position for at least six consecutive months.
3. You must meet the minimum qualifications and requirements listed above.
4. Your most recent evaluation must reflect a minimum overall rating of satisfactory.
5. You must notify your manager of your intent to submit a job posting application.

Job Posting Application Procedure

1. Complete a job posting application form, available online and in the HR department.
2. E-mail or take the completed form to HR with a copy to your manager, by the closing date.
3. Someone in HR will contact you within three working days of receipt.

Appendix B:
Job Posting Application Form

Position Applied For:
Date of Application: Closing Date for Available Position:
Name: Tel. Ext./E-Mail Address:
Job Title: Manager's Name:
Dept.: Location:
Summary of Duties and Responsibilities:

Grade/Salary: Work Schedule:

Job Posting Eligibility Requirements

1. You must be an employee of JavaCorp for at least twelve consecutive months.
2. You must be in your current position for at least six consecutive months.
3. You must meet the minimum qualifications and requirements listed on the job posting form for this position.
4. Your most recent evaluation must reflect a minimum overall rating of satisfactory.
5. You must submit a copy of this job posting application to your manager.

Job Posting Application Procedure

1. E-mail or take this completed form to HR with a copy to your manager, by the closing date on the job posting for this position.
2. Someone in HR will contact you within three working days of receipt.

Appendix C:
Work Environment Checklist

Physical Working Conditions
    Extensive standing or sitting
    Ventilation
    Exposure to chemicals or fumes
    Workspace
    Noise level
    Extensive video display terminal use
    Types of machinery or equipment

Geographic Location and Status of the Job
    Central office
    Satellite branch
    Permanent
    Temporary
    Rotational

Travel
    Purpose
    Degree of advance notice
    Locations
    Frequency
    Duration
    Means of transportation
    Reimbursement of expenses

Work Schedule
    Full-time
    Part-time
    Contingency
    Job sharing
    Flextime
    Compressed workweek
    Telecommuting
    Days of the week
    Shifts
    Meal breaks and other scheduled breaks

Appendix D: Job Description Form

Job Title: Location:
Work Schedule: Department:
Reporting Relationship:
Salary Range: Grade: Exemption Status:

Summary of Duties and Responsibilities:

Primary Duties and Responsibilities:
(E) = Essential Functions; (N) = Nonessential Functions

Percentage
of time
devoted to
each task

_____%	1.
_____%	2.
_____%	3.
_____%	4.
_____%	5.
_____%	6.
_____%	7.
_____%	8.
_____%	9.
_____%	10.

Performs other related duties and assignments as required.

Education, prior work experience, and specialized skills and knowledge:

Physical environment and working conditions:

Business machines and computer software used:

Other factors, such as access to confidential information or contact with the public:

Job Analyst:

Date:

Appendix E: Employment Application Form

Note to readers: The following information is suitable for paper or electronic employment application forms. To adapt to a paper format, use color, borders, columns, boxes, varying type sizes, boldface, heads and subheads, and upper and lowercase lettering. To adapt to electronic use, modify the design to reflect selected fields and offer job seekers the option of submitting a text-based application that they can copy and paste into an e-mail.

JavaCorp
Application for Employment

JavaCorp is an equal opportunity/affirmative action employer and abides by all federal, state, and local laws prohibiting discrimination in employment based on race, color, religion, sex, national origin, age, disability, veteran status, citizenship status, and all other protected groups.

Please answer all of the following questions, even if you have attached your resume.

Name _____ Social Security No. _____
Position applying for _____ Date _____
Current Address Street _____
   City, State, Zip Code _____
Phone Number _____ E-Mail Address _____
Availability   ( ) Full-Time   ( ) Part-Time   ( ) Days
                    ( ) Evenings   ( ) Overtime   ( ) Seasonal
Referral Source _____
Have you ever worked for JavaCorp before?   ( ) No ( ) Yes Dates _____
Have you ever applied at JavaCorp before?   ( ) No ( ) Yes Dates _____
Have you ever been convicted of a crime?   ( ) No ( ) Yes
If yes, please explain _____
(A positive response will not necessarily affect your eligibility for employment. Applicants are not obliged to disclose sealed or expunged records of conviction.)

Are you able to perform the tasks required to carry out the job for which you have applied, with or without accommodation?   ( ) No ( ) Yes

As related to the position applied for, what language(s) do you speak, read, and/or write? _____

What is your degree of fluency for each language listed? _____

What professional, trade, or business activities are you involved with, relevant to the job for which you are applying? _____

Employment Experience
List current or most recent employment first. Include military service, if any.

Employer _____ Phone Number _____
Address   Street _____
                   City, State, Zip Code _____
Manager's name and title _____
Employed from _____ to _____
Starting position _____ Final position _____
Starting salary _____ Final salary _____
Primary responsibilities _____
_____
_____

Reason for leaving _____
- -
Employer _____ Phone Number _____
Address   Street _____
                   City, State, Zip Code _____
Manager's name and title _____
Employed from _____ to _____
Starting position _____ Final position _____
Starting salary _____ Final salary _____
Primary responsibilities _____
_____
_____

Reason for leaving _____
- -
Employer _____ Phone Number _____
Address   Street _____
                   City, State, Zip Code _____
Manager's name and title _____
Employed from _____ to _____
Starting position _____ Final position _____
Starting salary _____ Final salary _____
Primary responsibilities _____
_____
_____

Reason for leaving _____
- -

Employer _____ Phone Number _____
Address   Street _____
                City, State, Zip Code _____
Manager's name and title _____
Employed from _____ to _____
Starting position _____ Final position _____
Starting salary _____ Final salary _____
Primary responsibilities _____
_____
_____

Reason for leaving _____
- -

List any professional licenses: _____
_____

List any work-related awards: _____
_____

List any professional publications: _____
_____

List all business machines you can operate and computer software with which you are
familiar: _____
_____

Education and Training
List all schools attended, including high school, college, graduate school, business
school, trade and technical institutions.

Name _____
Address Street _____
               City, State, Zip Code _____
Number of years completed _____ Degree/Diploma _____
- -
Name _____
Address   Street _____
                City, State, Zip Code _____
Number of years completed _____ Degree/Diploma _____
- -
Name _____
Address   Street _____
                City, State, Zip Code _____
Number of years completed _____ Degree/Diploma _____
- -
Name _____
Address   Street _____
                City, State, Zip Code _____
Number of years completed _____ Degree/Diploma _____
- -

List any academic achievements or extracurricular activities relative to the position applied for: _____

Identify any additional knowledge, skills, or qualifications that will be helpful to us in considering your application for employment: _____

Please provide the name, title, address, and telephone number of three business or academic references, other than current or former employers, who are not related to you.
Reference 1: _____
Reference 2: _____
Reference 3: _____

Conditions of Employment:
- *References and Background Checks.* I understand that my employment may be based on receipt of satisfactory information from former employers, schools, and other references, as well as satisfactory results of a background check, including criminal history, credit history, and Social Security number verification, if deemed appropriate. I authorize JavaCorp and its representatives to investigate, without liability, any information supplied by me. I also authorize listed employers, schools, and references, as well as other reference sources, to make full disclosure to any relevant inquiries by JavaCorp and its representatives without liability. In the event that JavaCorp is unable to verify any reference stated on this application, it is my responsibility to furnish the necessary documentation.

  ( ) You may contact my current employer at this time.
  ( ) You may not contact my current employer at this time. Should I receive a formal offer of employment, you may contact my current employer at that time.

- *Drug Testing.* Except as limited by law, I accept that JavaCorp may test applicants and employees prior to or during employment for the use of illegal drugs and controlled substances.

- *Employment-at-Will.* I understand that employees hired by JavaCorp may terminate their employment at any time, with or without notice or cause. Likewise, JavaCorp may terminate the employment of any of its employees at any time, with or without notice or cause. I further understand that if hired, my employment is for no definite period of time, and if terminated, JavaCorp is liable only for wages earned as of the date of termination. In addition, no representative of JavaCorp, other than the president or a designated official, has any authority to enter into any agreement, oral or written, for employment for any specified period of time or to make any agreement or assurances contrary to this policy. Nothing in this application shall be interpreted to be in conflict with or to eliminate or modify in any way the employment-at-will status of JavaCorp employees.

- *Minimum Age Compliance.* If I am under the minimum working age, I agree to furnish a work permit prior to hire.

- *Immigration Reform and Control Act of 1986 Compliance.* I understand that in compliance with the Immigration Reform and Control Act of 1986, I will be expected to produce the required documentation to establish my identity and eligibility to work. Employment by JavaCorp is contingent upon my producing the required documentation or evidence of having applied for it within three calendar days after hire.

- *JavaCorp Policies.* If hired, I agree to abide by the policies, procedures, and regulations of JavaCorp.

- *Confidentiality.* If hired, I agree to be discreet when discussing any financial, proprietary, trade, or other confidential information related to JavaCorp business activities. I understand that revealing such information is grounds for immediate termination.

- *Application Content Certification.* I certify that all of the information contained in this application is true and complete to the best of my knowledge.

Signed _____

Date _____

Appendix F: Interview Evaluation Form

Applicant   Date   Interviewed by

Position   Department

Summary of relevant experience _____

_____

_____

Summary of relevant educational degrees and achievements _____

_____

_____

Relationship between job requirements and applicant's qualifications:

    Job Requirements   Applicant's Qualifications

1. _____   _____

2. _____   _____

3. _____   _____

4. _____   _____

5. _____   _____

6. _____   _____

7. _____   _____

8. _____   _____

Additional relevant factors (e.g., test scores) _____

_____

Overall Evaluation: ( )   Meets Job Requirements

                    ( )   Fails to Meet Job Requirements

Supporting comments _____

_____

_____

Appendix G: Exempt Reference Form

This is a detailed employment reference form for exempt applicants. It may be submitted as a written request or conducted as a telephone reference. Although it is unlikely that all questions will result in answers, the form targets a sufficient number of categories relevant to exempt-level positions so that even if only half are answered, the prospective employer is likely to gain valuable insight into the applicant's qualifications.

Applicant   Position

Person Contacted   Title
Company   Telephone No.
Address

Reference conducted by   Date

The above-named person has applied to us for employment. He/She has listed you as a former employer, and has authorized us to conduct a reference check. We need your assistance in verifying and providing certain information regarding his/her work performance.

1. _____ worked in the _____ department as a(n) _____ from _____ to _____.

   ( ) Correct   ( ) Incorrect

   If incorrect, please explain.

2. His/Her primary responsibilities were:

3. He/She stated that his/her reason for terminating employment with your company was _____.

   ( ) Correct   ( ) Incorrect

   If incorrect, please explain.

4. How would you evaluate his/her overall work performance?

5. What were his/her greatest strengths?

6. What areas required improvement and/or additional training?

7. What made him/her an effective manager?

8. Describe a job-related situation involving pressure.

9. Describe how he/she handled a difficult job-related task.

10. Describe his/her management style.

11. Describe his/her decision-making style.

12. Describe his/her approach to time management.

13. Describe a situation involving delegation.

14. Describe a deadline he/she had to meet.

15. How did he/she handle repetitious tasks?

16. Describe how he/she responded to a new assignment.

17. Describe any work-related travel required, in terms of location, duration, and frequency.

18. This job calls for the ability to _____.
    What experience did he/she have in doing this job? (This question can be expanded to encompass several different factors. Use your job description as a guide.)

19. How effectively did he/she interact with peers? Senior management? Employees? Customers/Clients? Please be specific.

20. Would you rehire him/her? ( ) Yes ( ) No. If no, why not?

Appendix H: Nonexempt Reference Form

This is a detailed employment reference form for nonexempt applicants. It may be submitted as a written request or conducted as a telephone reference. Although it is unlikely that all questions will result in answers, the form targets a sufficient number of categories relevant to nonexempt-level positions so that even if only half are answered, the prospective employer is likely to gain valuable insight into the applicant's qualifications.

Applicant   Position

Person Contacted   Title
Company   Telephone No.
Address

Reference conducted by   Date

The above-named person has applied to us for employment. He/She has listed you as a former employer, and has authorized us to conduct a reference check. We need your assistance in verifying and providing certain information regarding his/her work performance.

1. _____worked in the _____ department as a(n) _____ from _____ to _____.

   ( ) Correct   ( ) Incorrect

   If incorrect, please explain.

2. His/Her primary responsibilities were:

3. He/She stated that his/her reason for terminating employment with your company was _____.

   ( ) Correct   ( ) Incorrect

   If incorrect, please explain.

341

4. How would you evaluate his/her overall work performance?

5. What were his/her greatest strengths?

6. Describe some tasks that he/she performed particularly well.

7. What areas required improvement and/or additional training?

8. How closely did you need to supervise his/her work?

9. Describe his/her ability to successfully perform multiple tasks. Please be specific.

10. How did he/she handle repetitious tasks?

11. Describe how he/she reacted to being given a new assignment.

12. Tell me about some of the questions he/she has asked when confronted with a new assignment.

13. Was there ever a time when he/she performed an assignment unsatisfactorily? Tell me about it.

14. How did he/she react to criticism? Give me a specific example.

15. How effectively did he/she interact with coworkers? With management?

16. How would you compare his/her work upon termination with his/her performance at the time of hire?

17. This job calls for the ability to _____.
    What experience did he/she have in doing this task? (This question can be expanded to encompass several different factors. Use your job description as a guide.)

18. Would you rehire him/her?   ( ) Yes   ( ) No. If no, why not?

Index